i No Ou

1

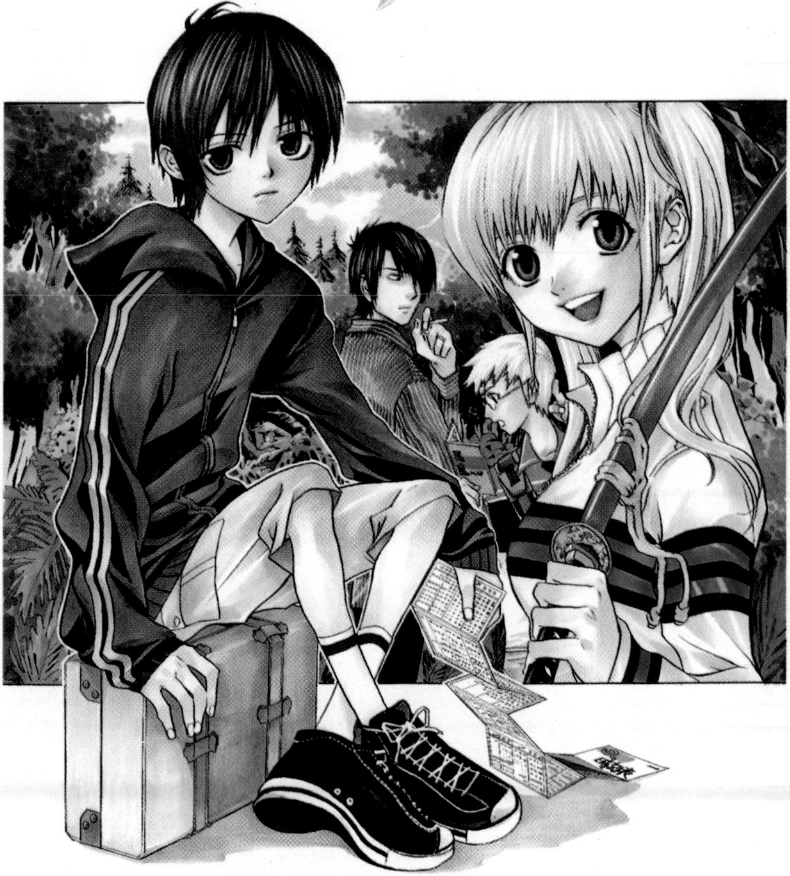

Yuhki Kamatani

Nabari No Ou 1

Yuhki Kamatani

Contents

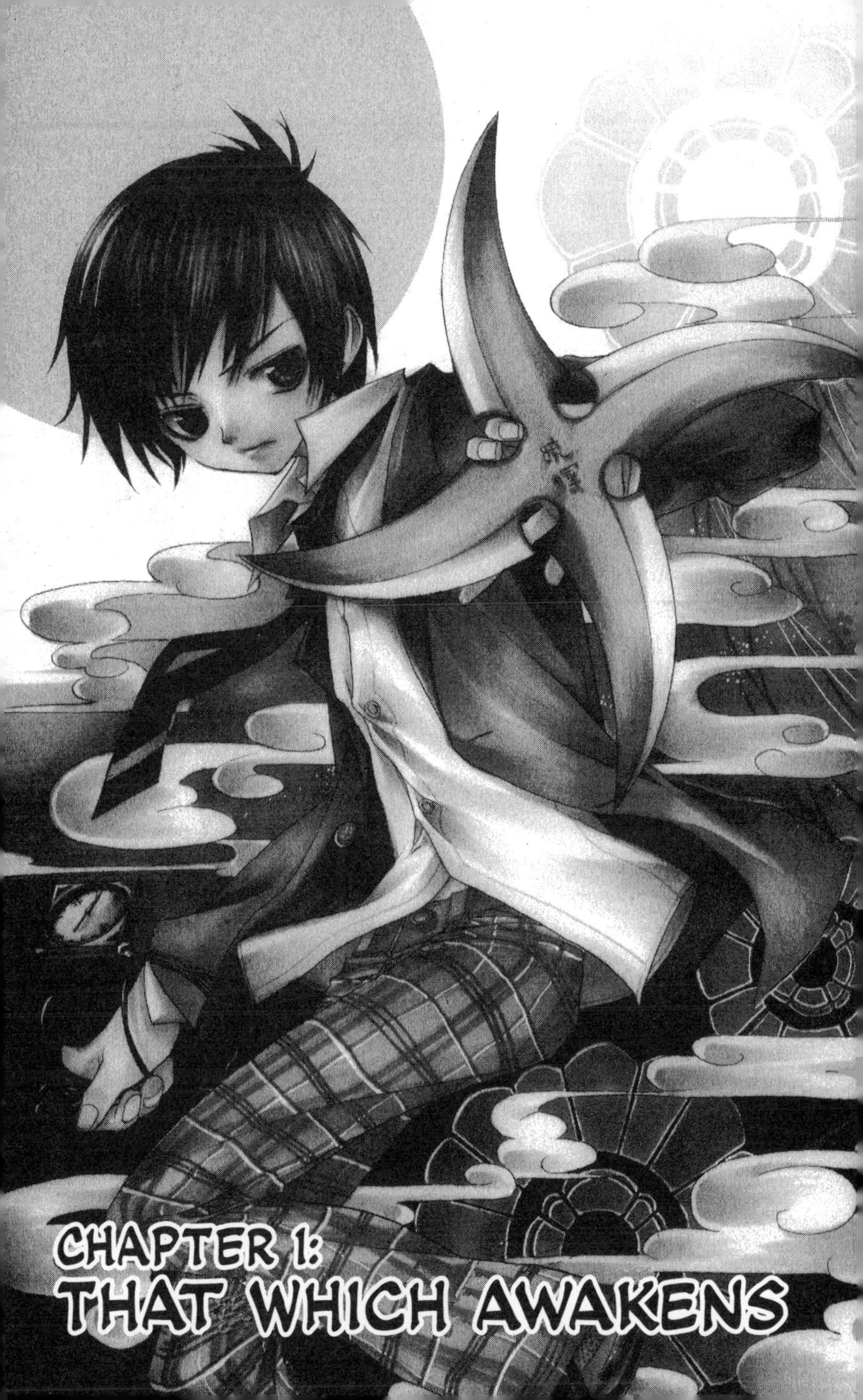
CHAPTER 1:
THAT WHICH AWAKENS

THE SECRET ART WITH WHICH IT IS SAID ONE CAN RULE NOT ONLY THE WORLD OF SHINOBI, BUT THE SURFACE WORLD AS WELL.

"SHINRA BANSHOU."

HE WHO WOULD STAND ABOVE ALL THINGS WOULD BEST DESIRE IT.

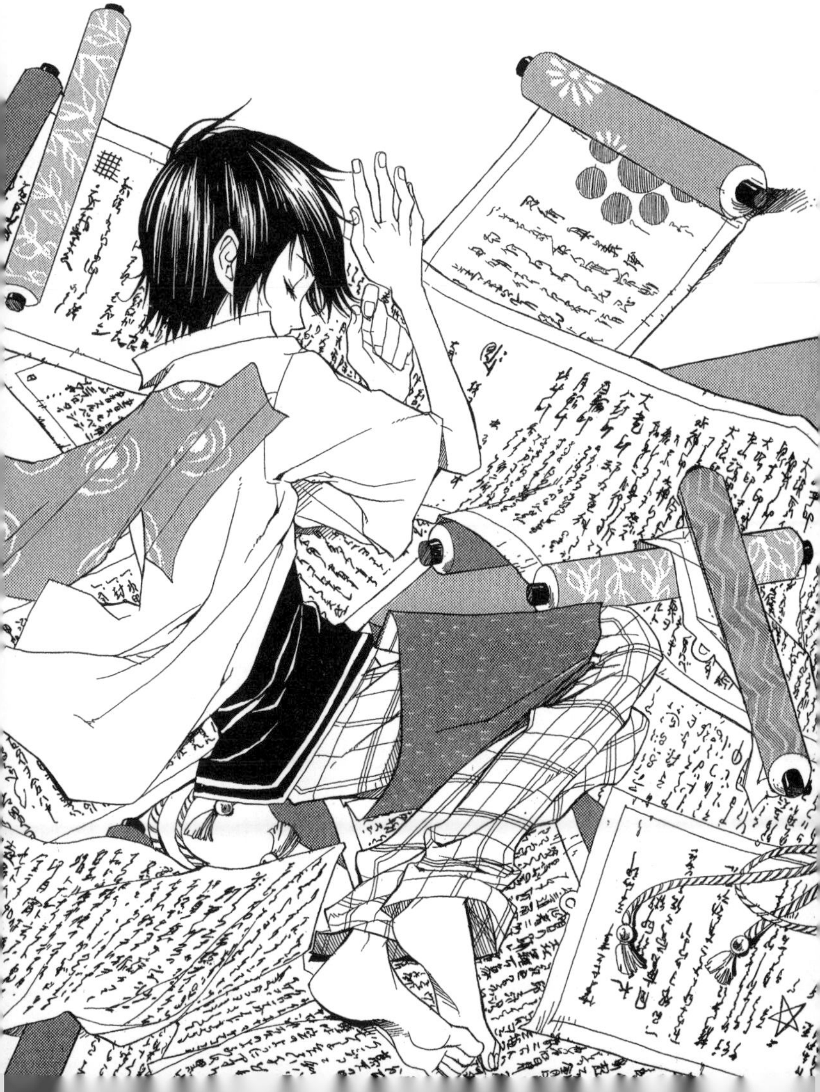

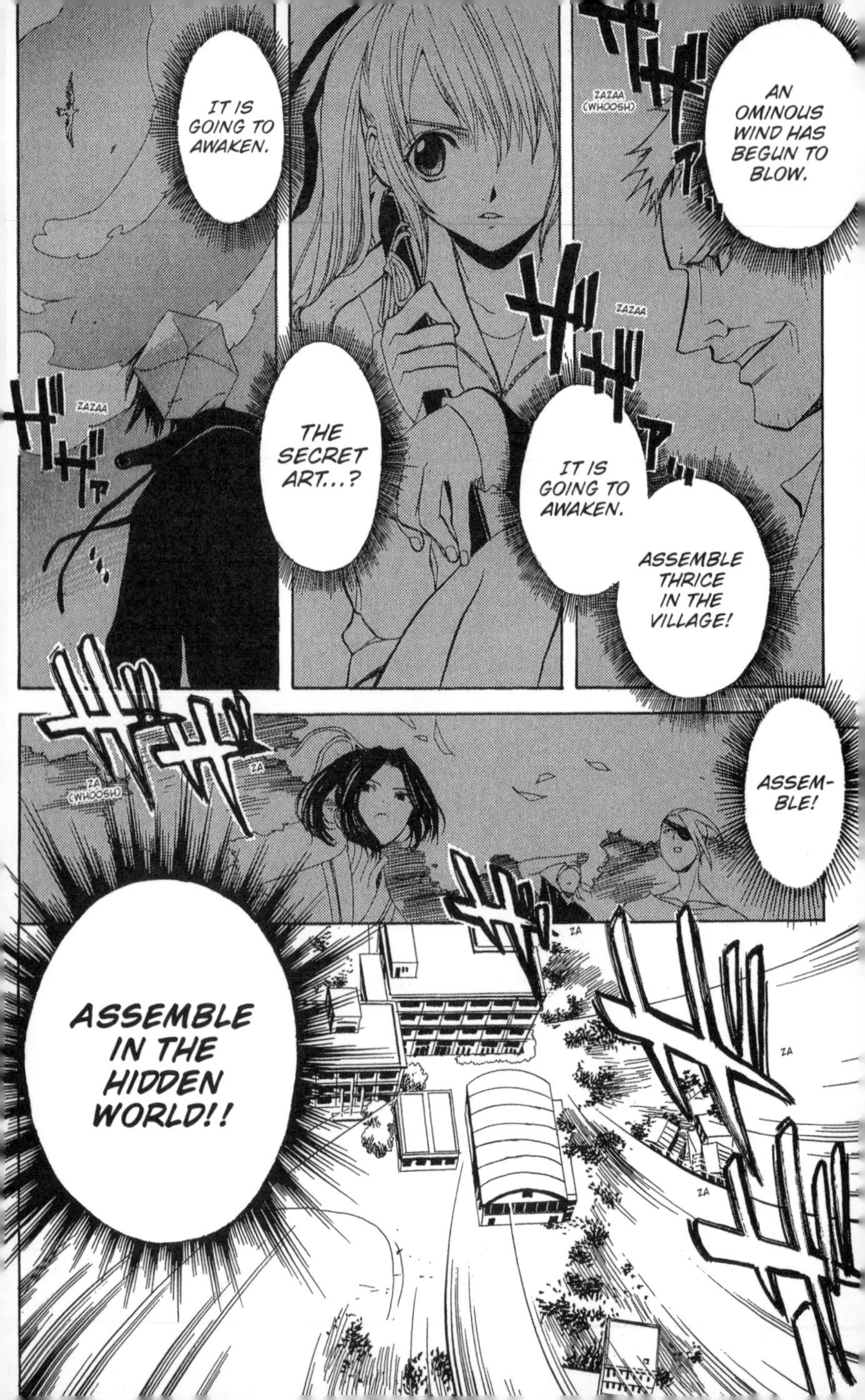

AN OMINOUS WIND HAS BEGUN TO BLOW.
ZAZAA (WHOOSH)
ZAZAA
IT IS GOING TO AWAKEN.
ASSEMBLE THRICE IN THE VILLAGE!
THE SECRET ART...?
IT IS GOING TO AWAKEN.
ZAZAA
...
ASSEM-BLE!
ZA
ZA (WHOOSH)
ZA
ZA
ZA
ASSEMBLE IN THE HIDDEN WORLD!!

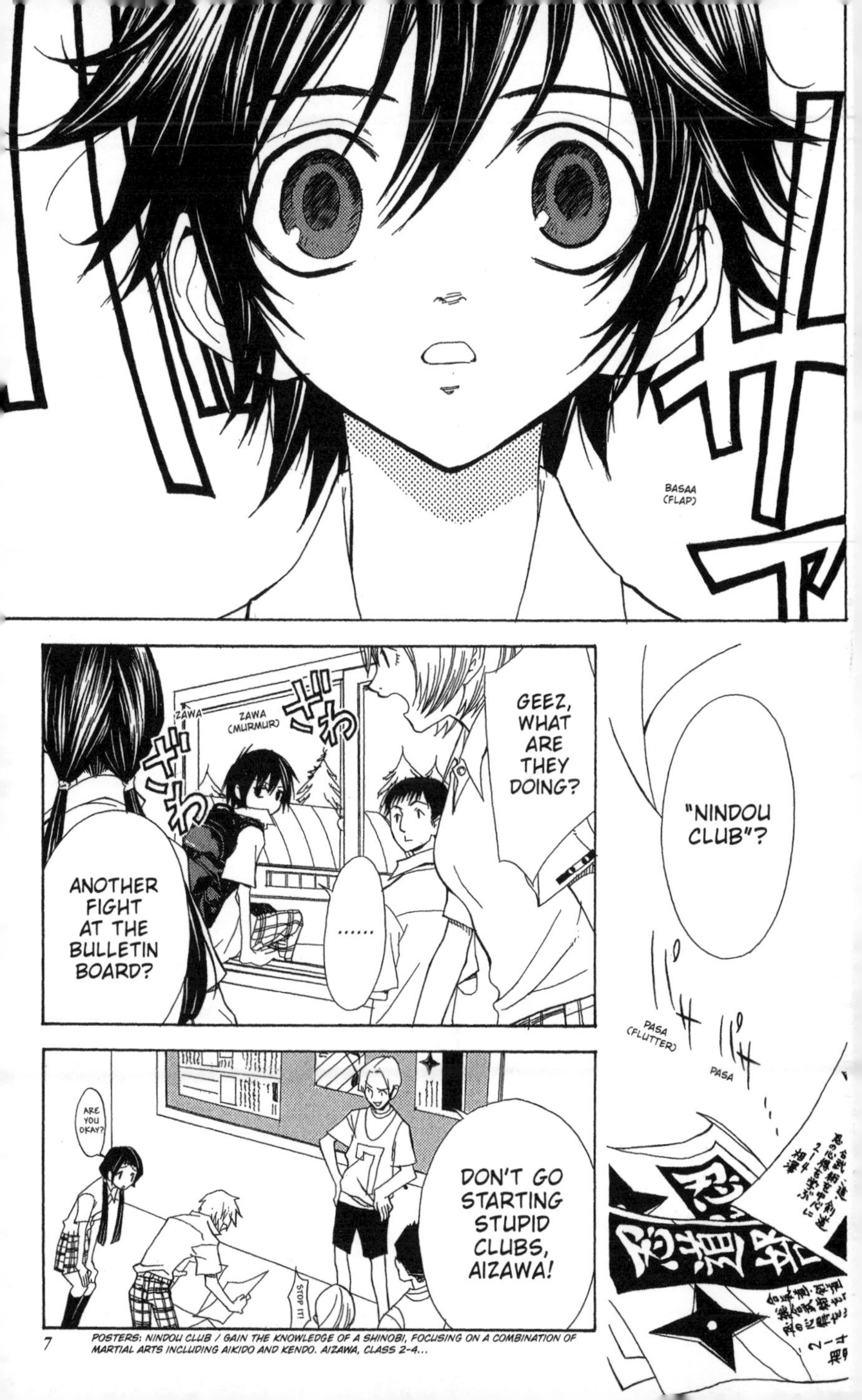
BASAA (FLAP)
"NINDOU CLUB"?
PASA (FLUTTER)
PASA
GEEZ, WHAT ARE THEY DOING?
ZAWA (MURMUR)
ZAWA
......
ANOTHER FIGHT AT THE BULLETIN BOARD?
DON'T GO STARTING STUPID CLUBS, AIZAWA!
STOP IT!
ARE YOU OKAY?

POSTERS: NINDOU CLUB / GAIN THE KNOWLEDGE OF A SHINOBI, FOCUSING ON A COMBINATION OF MARTIAL ARTS INCLUDING AIKIDO AND KENDO. AIZAWA, CLASS 2-4...

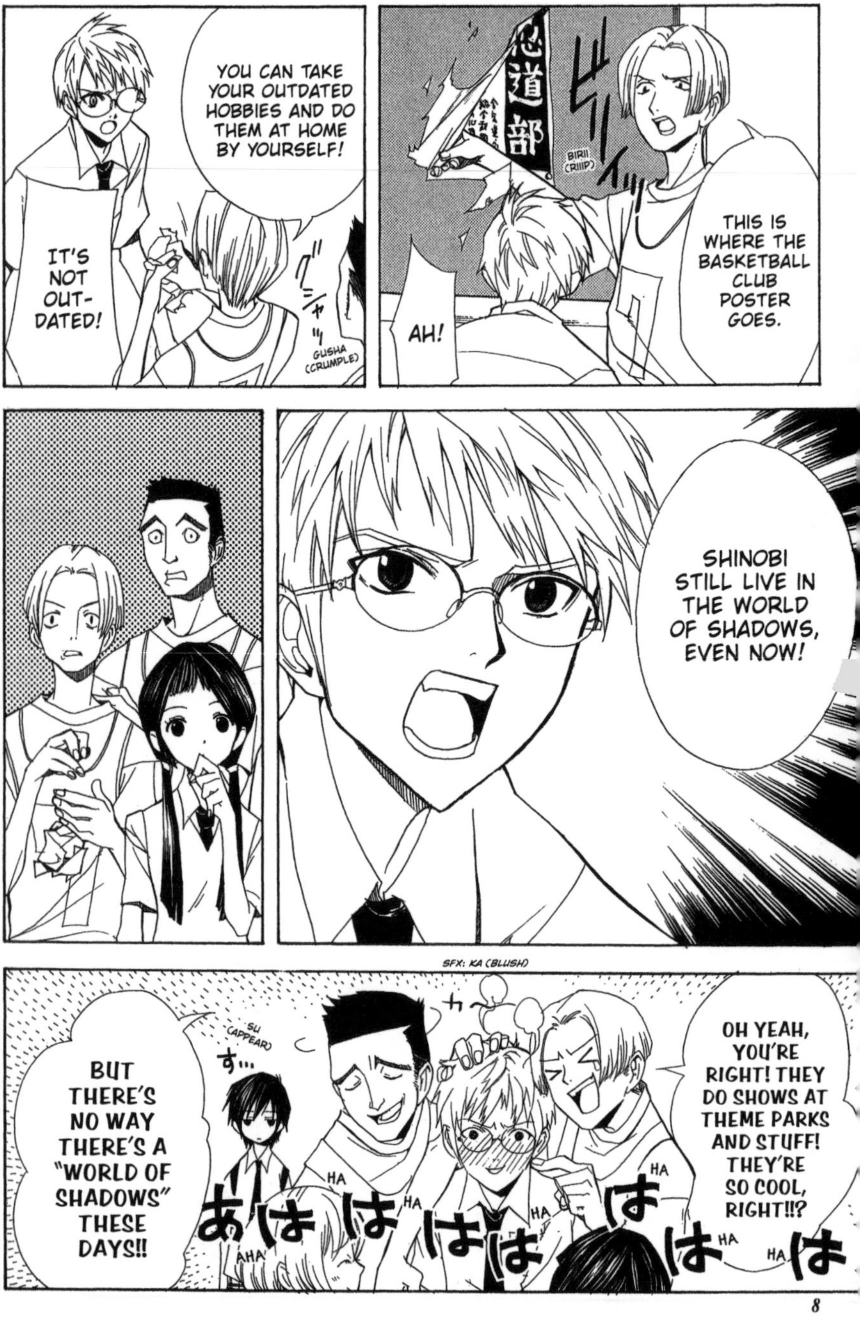

BIRII (RIIIP)
THIS IS WHERE THE BASKETBALL CLUB POSTER GOES.
AH!
YOU CAN TAKE YOUR OUTDATED HOBBIES AND DO THEM AT HOME BY YOURSELF!
GUSHA (CRUMPLE)
IT'S NOT OUT-DATED!
SHINOBI STILL LIVE IN THE WORLD OF SHADOWS, EVEN NOW!
SFX: KA (BLUSH)
OH YEAH, YOU'RE RIGHT! THEY DO SHOWS AT THEME PARKS AND STUFF! THEY'RE SO COOL, RIGHT!!?
HA HA HA HA HA HA AHA
あはははははは
SU (APPEAR)
BUT THERE'S NO WAY THERE'S A "WORLD OF SHADOWS" THESE DAYS!!

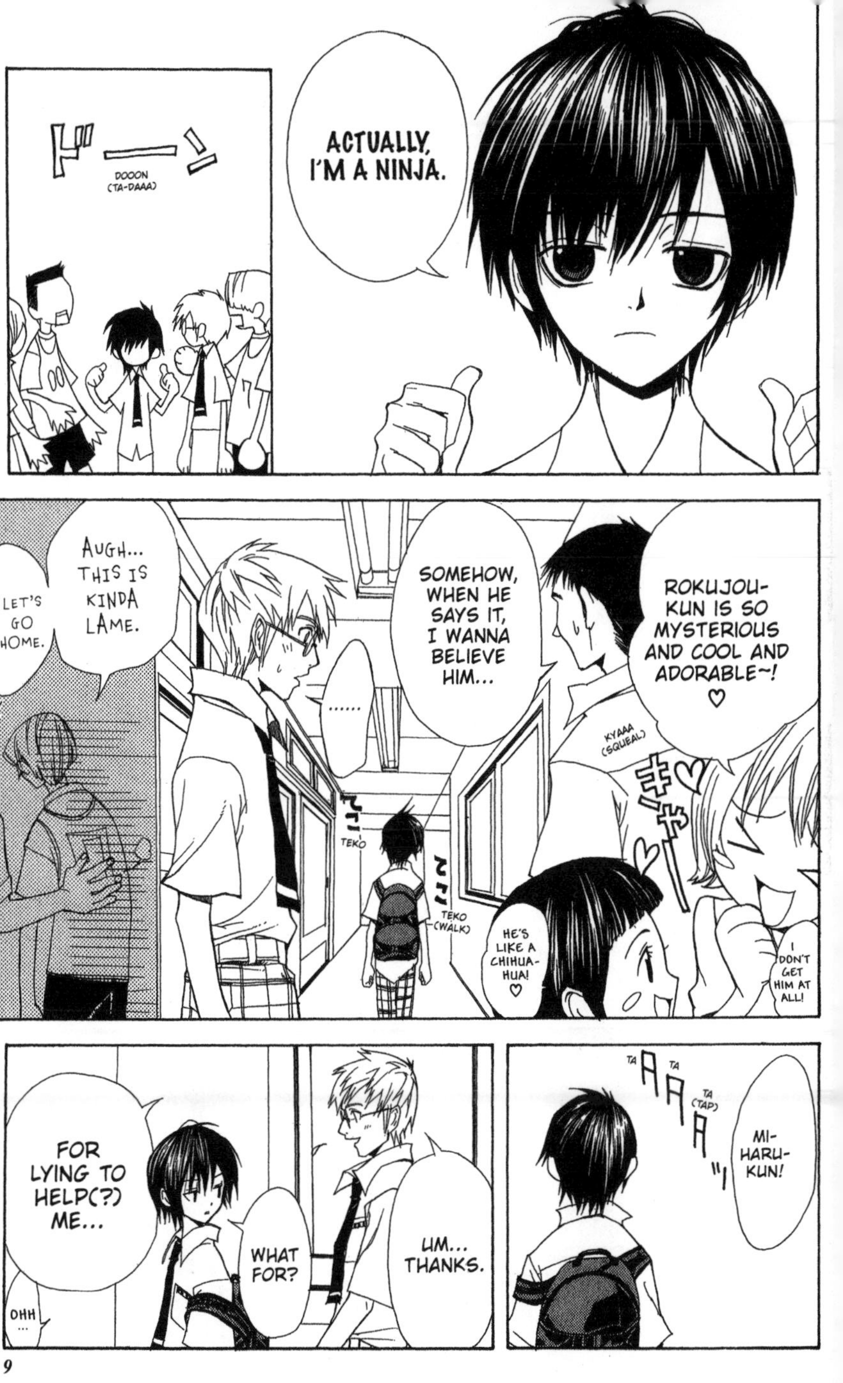
ACTUALLY, I'M A NINJA.
DOOON (TA-DAAA)
ROKUJOU-KUN IS SO MYSTERIOUS AND COOL AND ADORABLE~! ♡
KYAAA (SQUEAL)
I DON'T GET HIM AT ALL!
HE'S LIKE A CHIHUAHUA! ♡
SOMEHOW, WHEN HE SAYS IT, I WANNA BELIEVE HIM...
......
TEKO
TEKO (WALK)
AUGH... THIS IS KINDA LAME.
LET'S GO HOME.
YEAH...
TA TA TA (TAP)
MI-HARU-KUN!
UM... THANKS.
WHAT FOR?
FOR LYING TO HELP(?) ME...
OHH...

AH!!

LATER.

...WHAT?

GASA (RUSTLE)

I'D LOVE TO HAVE YOU JOIN THE NINDOU CLUB, MIHARU-KUN!

BASICALLY, WE'RE A CLUB THAT TRAINS OUR MINDS AND BODIES WITH A COMBINATION OF MARTIAL ARTS BASED ON KENDO, KARATE, AND AIKIDO.

IN ADDITION TO THAT, WE STUDY THE WISDOM OF OUR ANCESTORS, CALLED "NINJUTSU." AND SO WE CALL IT NINDOU...

THAT IS—

......

JI (STARE)

ATAFUTA (RUSH) あたふた

HE'S STILL AT IT.

WE CALL IT NINDOU, BUT IT'S NOT LIKE WE'LL BE WEARING BLACK CLOTHES AND WALKING ON WATER OR ANYTHING!

10

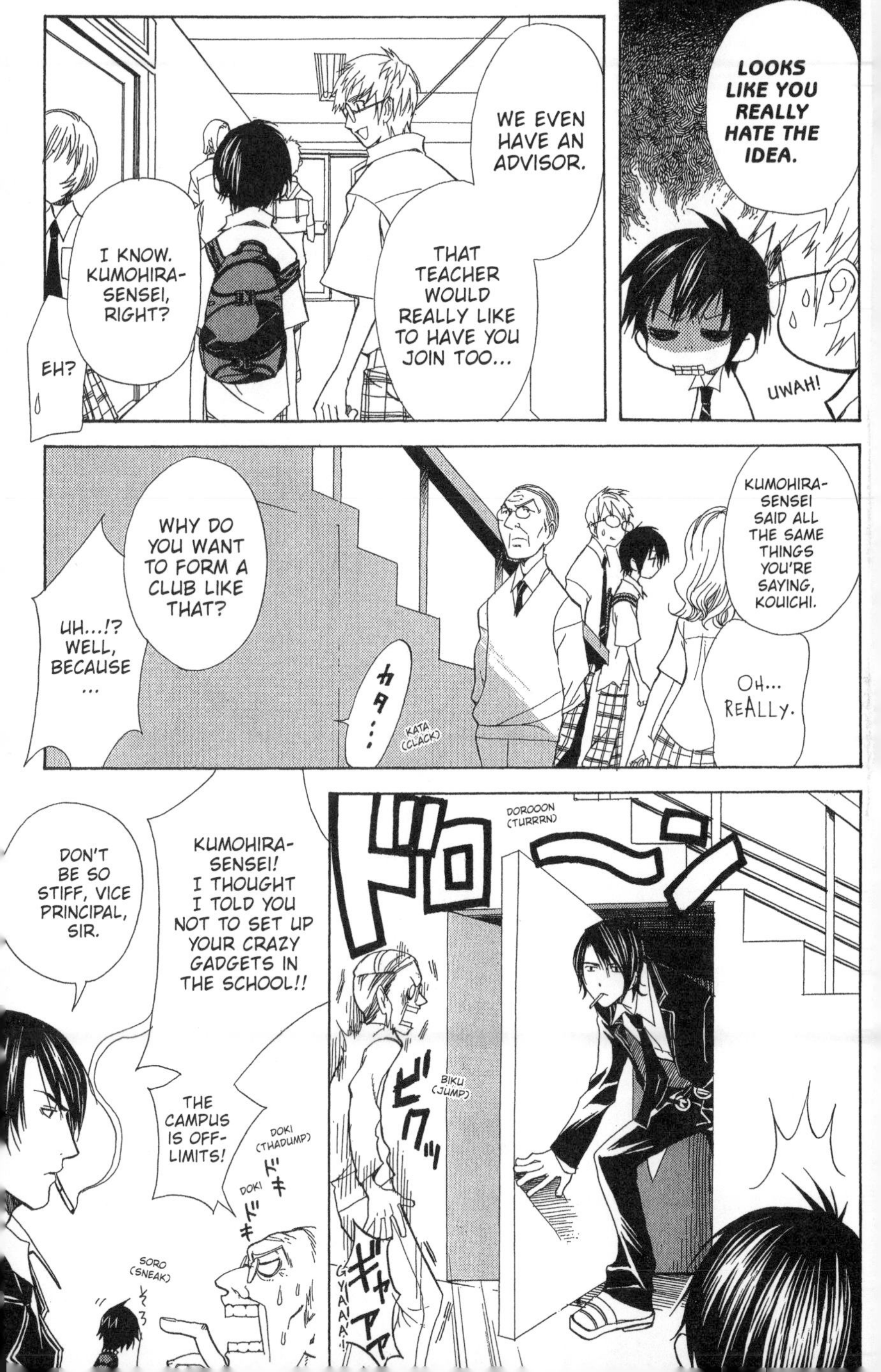
LOOKS LIKE YOU REALLY HATE THE IDEA.
UWAH!
WE EVEN HAVE AN ADVISOR.
THAT TEACHER WOULD REALLY LIKE TO HAVE YOU JOIN TOO...
I KNOW. KUMOHIRA-SENSEI, RIGHT?
EH?
KUMOHIRA-SENSEI SAID ALL THE SAME THINGS YOU'RE SAYING, KOUICHI.
OH... REALLY.
カタ…
KATA (CLACK)
WHY DO YOU WANT TO FORM A CLUB LIKE THAT?
UH...!? WELL, BECAUSE ...
ドローン
DOROOON (TURRRN)
ビクッ
BIKU (JUMP)
ギャアア
GYAAA!
KUMOHIRA-SENSEI! I THOUGHT I TOLD YOU NOT TO SET UP YOUR CRAZY GADGETS IN THE SCHOOL!!
DON'T BE SO STIFF, VICE PRINCIPAL, SIR.
THE CAMPUS IS OFF-LIMITS!
ドキ ドキ
DOKI (THADUMP) DOKI
そろ
SORO (SNEAK)

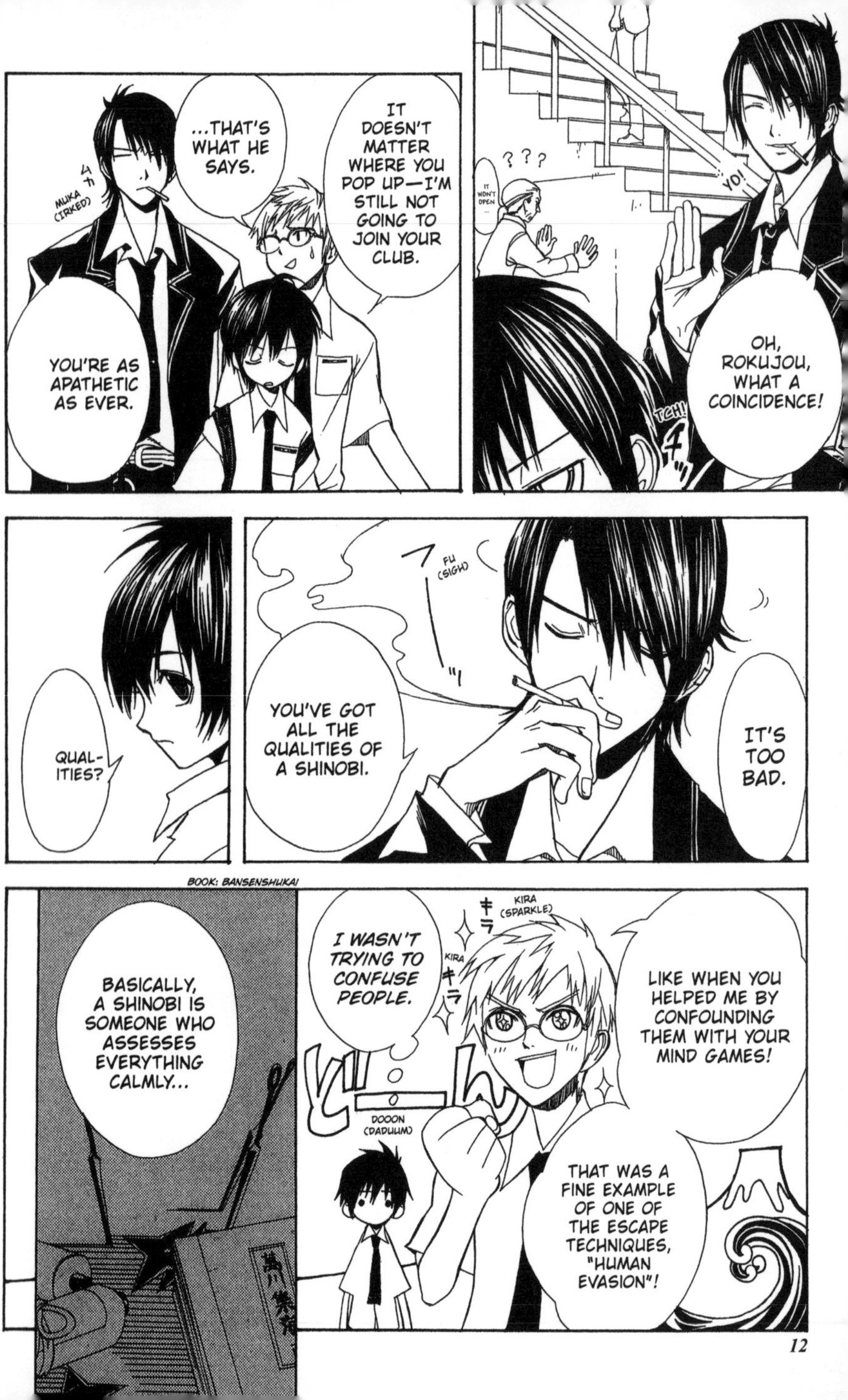
YO!
???
IT WON'T OPEN ...
OH, ROKUJOU, WHAT A COINCIDENCE!
TCH!
IT DOESN'T MATTER WHERE YOU POP UP—I'M STILL NOT GOING TO JOIN YOUR CLUB.
...THAT'S WHAT HE SAYS.
MUKA (IRKED)
YOU'RE AS APATHETIC AS EVER.
IT'S TOO BAD.
FU (SIGH)
YOU'VE GOT ALL THE QUALITIES OF A SHINOBI.
QUAL-ITIES?
BOOK: BANSENSHUKAI
LIKE WHEN YOU HELPED ME BY CONFOUNDING THEM WITH YOUR MIND GAMES!
THAT WAS A FINE EXAMPLE OF ONE OF THE ESCAPE TECHNIQUES, "HUMAN EVASION"!
KIRA (SPARKLE)
KIRA
I WASN'T TRYING TO CONFUSE PEOPLE.
DOOON (DADUUM)
BASICALLY, A SHINOBI IS SOMEONE WHO ASSESSES EVERYTHING CALMLY...

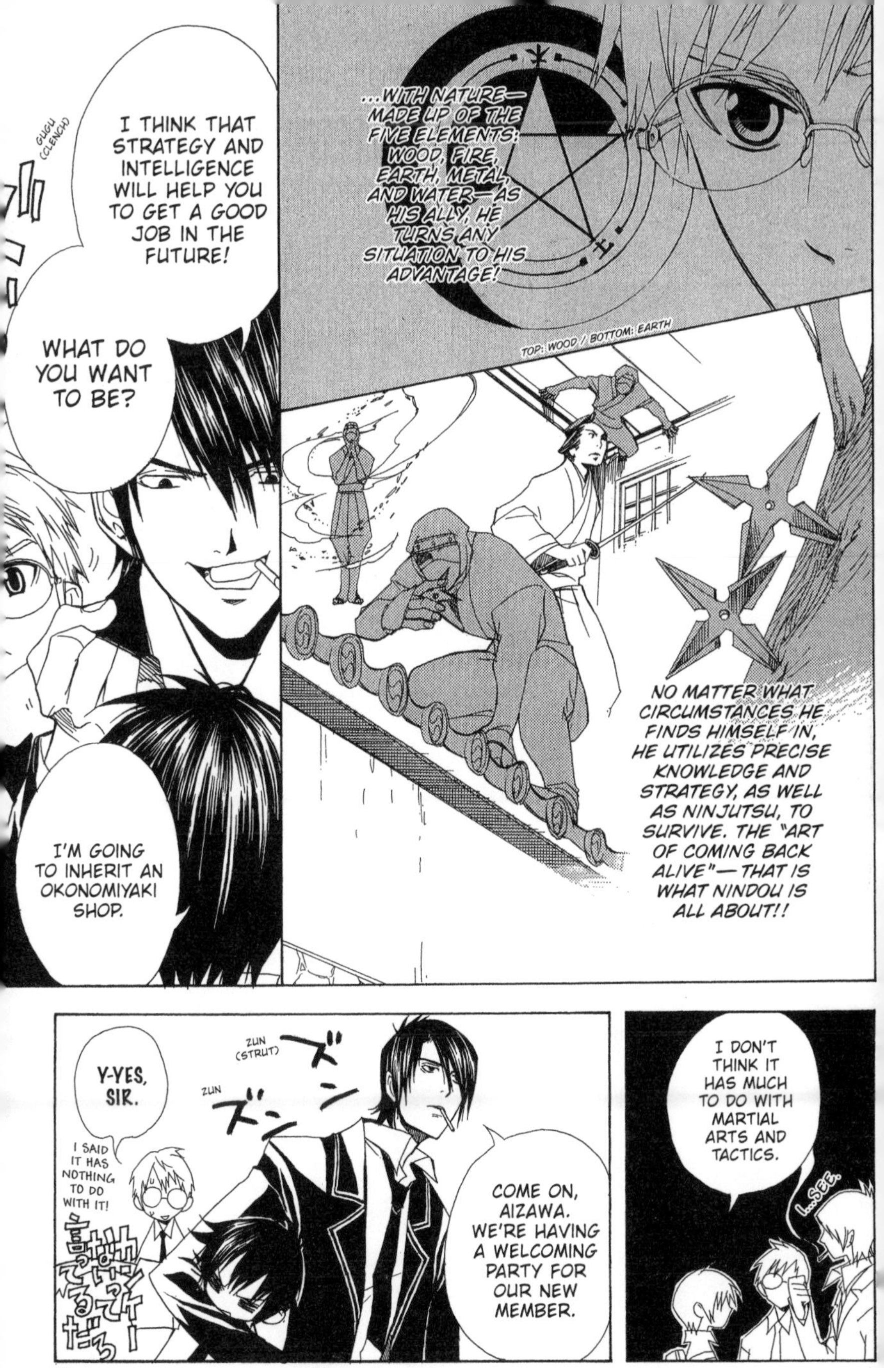
...WITH NATURE—MADE UP OF THE FIVE ELEMENTS: WOOD, FIRE, EARTH, METAL, AND WATER—AS HIS ALLY, HE TURNS ANY SITUATION TO HIS ADVANTAGE!
TOP: WOOD / BOTTOM: EARTH
NO MATTER WHAT CIRCUMSTANCES HE FINDS HIMSELF IN, HE UTILIZES PRECISE KNOWLEDGE AND STRATEGY, AS WELL AS NINJUTSU, TO SURVIVE. THE "ART OF COMING BACK ALIVE"—THAT IS WHAT NINDOU IS ALL ABOUT!!
I THINK THAT STRATEGY AND INTELLIGENCE WILL HELP YOU TO GET A GOOD JOB IN THE FUTURE!
GUGU (CLENCH)
WHAT DO YOU WANT TO BE?
I'M GOING TO INHERIT AN OKONOMIYAKI SHOP.
I DON'T THINK IT HAS MUCH TO DO WITH MARTIAL ARTS AND TACTICS.
I...SEE.
COME ON, AIZAWA. WE'RE HAVING A WELCOMING PARTY FOR OUR NEW MEMBER.
ZUN (STRUT)
ZUN
Y-YES, SIR.
I SAID IT HAS NOTHING TO DO WITH IT!

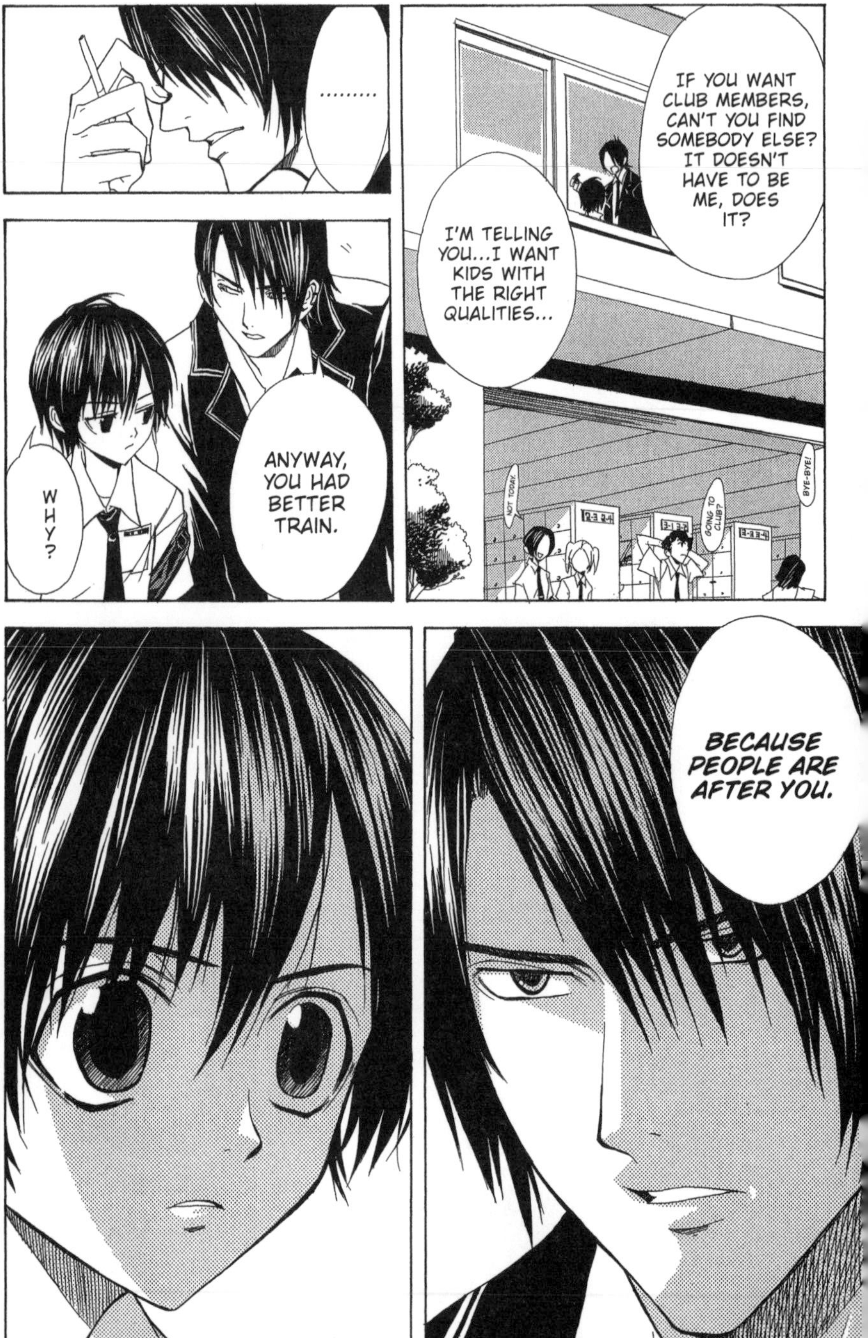
IF YOU WANT CLUB MEMBERS, CAN'T YOU FIND SOMEBODY ELSE? IT DOESN'T HAVE TO BE ME, DOES IT?
I'M TELLING YOU...I WANT KIDS WITH THE RIGHT QUALITIES...
BYE-BYE!
GOING TO CLUB?
NOT TODAY.
....
ANYWAY, YOU HAD BETTER TRAIN.
WHY?
BECAUSE PEOPLE ARE AFTER YOU.

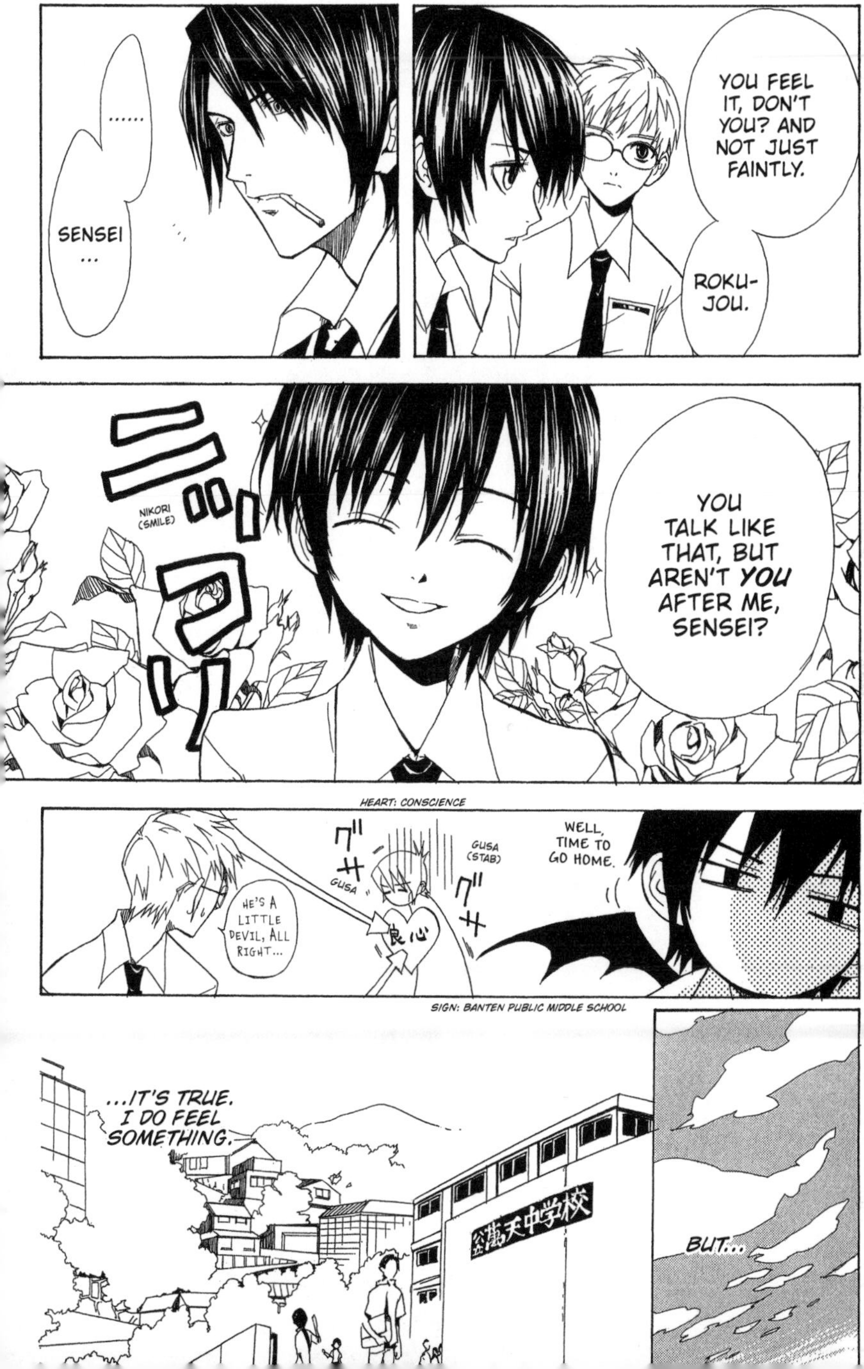
YOU FEEL IT, DON'T YOU? AND NOT JUST FAINTLY.
ROKU-JOU.
......
SENSEI ...
YOU TALK LIKE THAT, BUT AREN'T YOU AFTER ME, SENSEI?
NIKORI (SMILE)
HEART: CONSCIENCE
WELL, TIME TO GO HOME.
GUSA (STAB)
GUSA
良心
HE'S A LITTLE DEVIL, ALL RIGHT...
SIGN: BANTEN PUBLIC MIDDLE SCHOOL
BUT...
...IT'S TRUE. I DO FEEL SOMETHING.

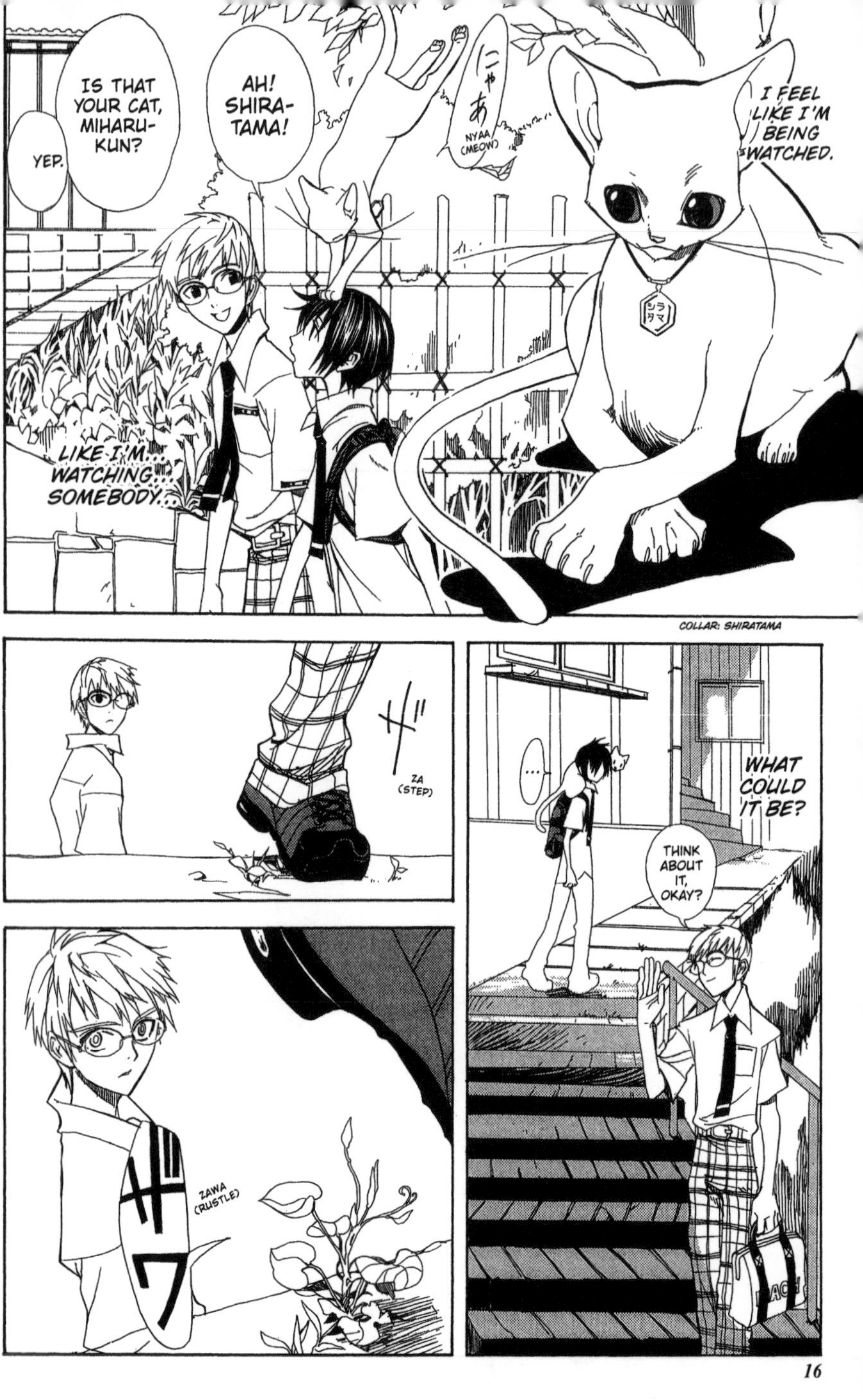
I FEEL LIKE I'M BEING WATCHED.
にゃあ
NYAA (MEOW)
シラタマ
AH! SHIRATAMA!
IS THAT YOUR CAT, MIHARU-KUN?
YEP.
LIKE I'M... WATCHING... SOMEBODY...
COLLAR: SHIRATAMA
WHAT COULD IT BE?
...
THINK ABOUT IT, OKAY?
ZA (STEP)
ZAWA (RUSTLE)

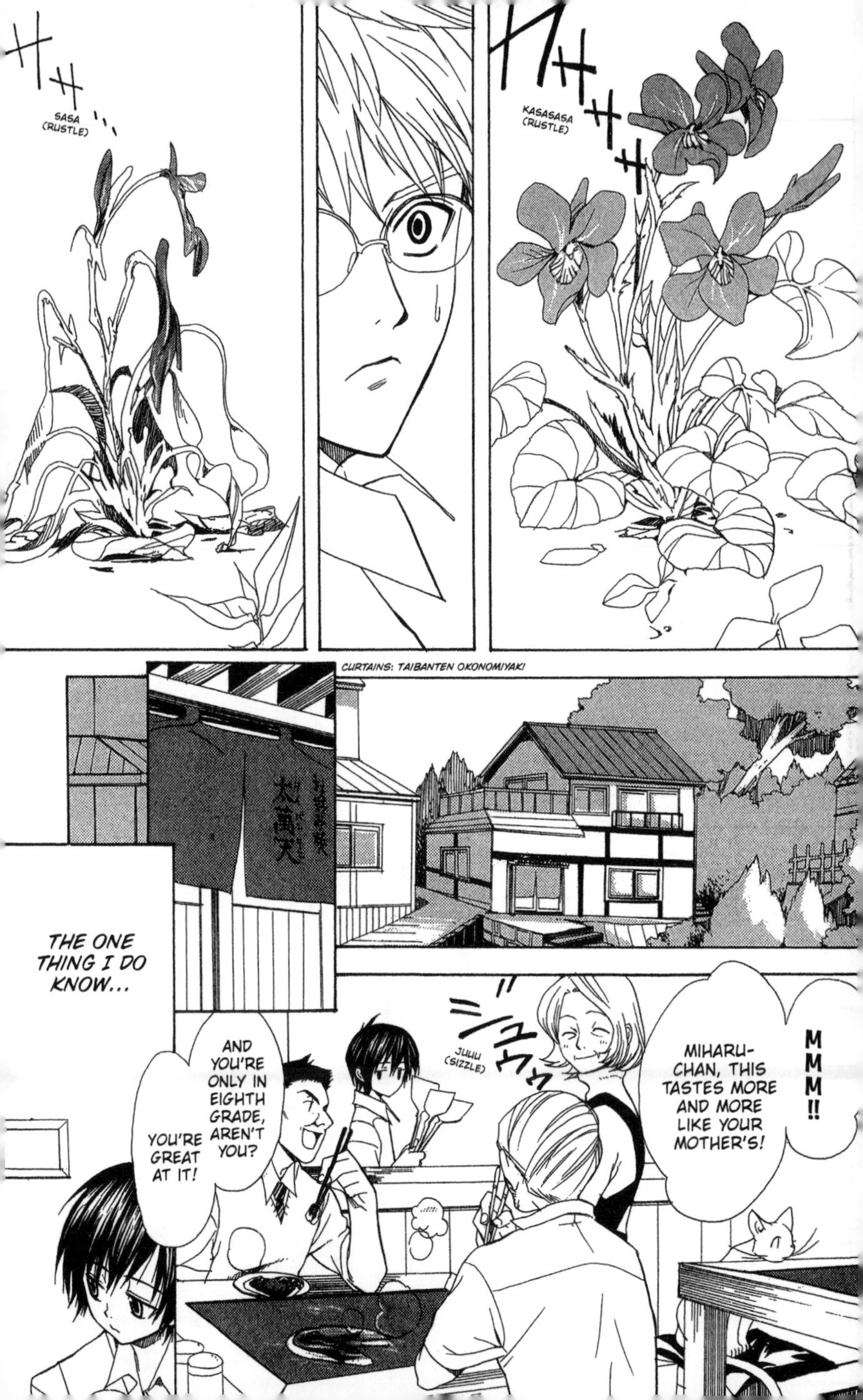
KASASASA (RUSTLE)
SASA (RUSTLE)
CURTAINS: TAIBANTEN OKONOMIYAKI
THE ONE THING I DO KNOW...
MMM!!
MIHARU-CHAN, THIS TASTES MORE AND MORE LIKE YOUR MOTHER'S!
JUUU (SIZZLE)
AND YOU'RE ONLY IN EIGHTH GRADE, AREN'T YOU?
YOU'RE GREAT AT IT!

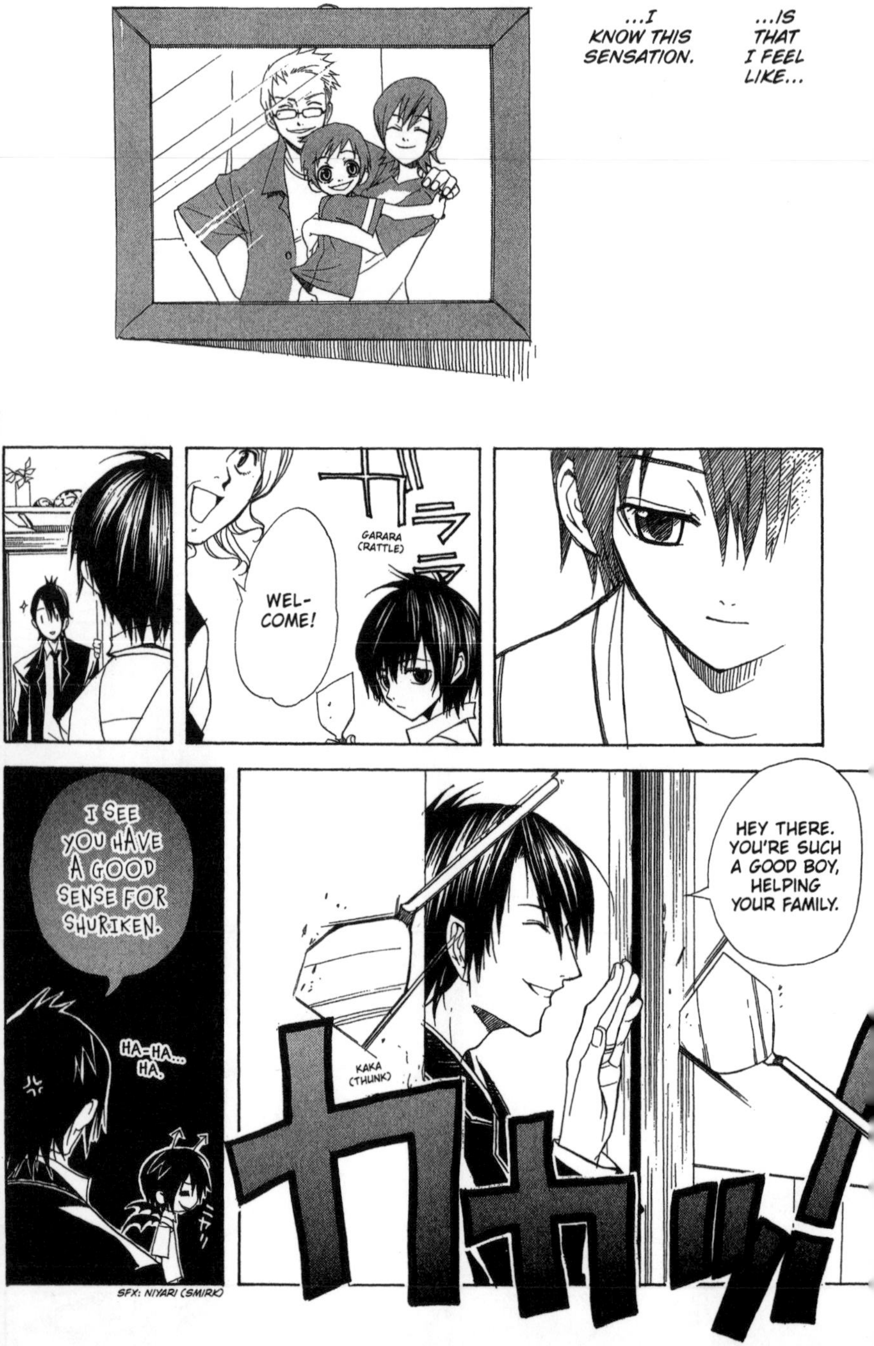
...IS THAT I FEEL LIKE...
...I KNOW THIS SENSATION.
GARARA (RATTLE)
WEL-COME!
HEY THERE. YOU'RE SUCH A GOOD BOY, HELPING YOUR FAMILY.
KAKA (THUNK)
I SEE YOU HAVE A GOOD SENSE FOR SHURIKEN.
HA-HA... HA.
SFX: NIYARI (SMIRK)

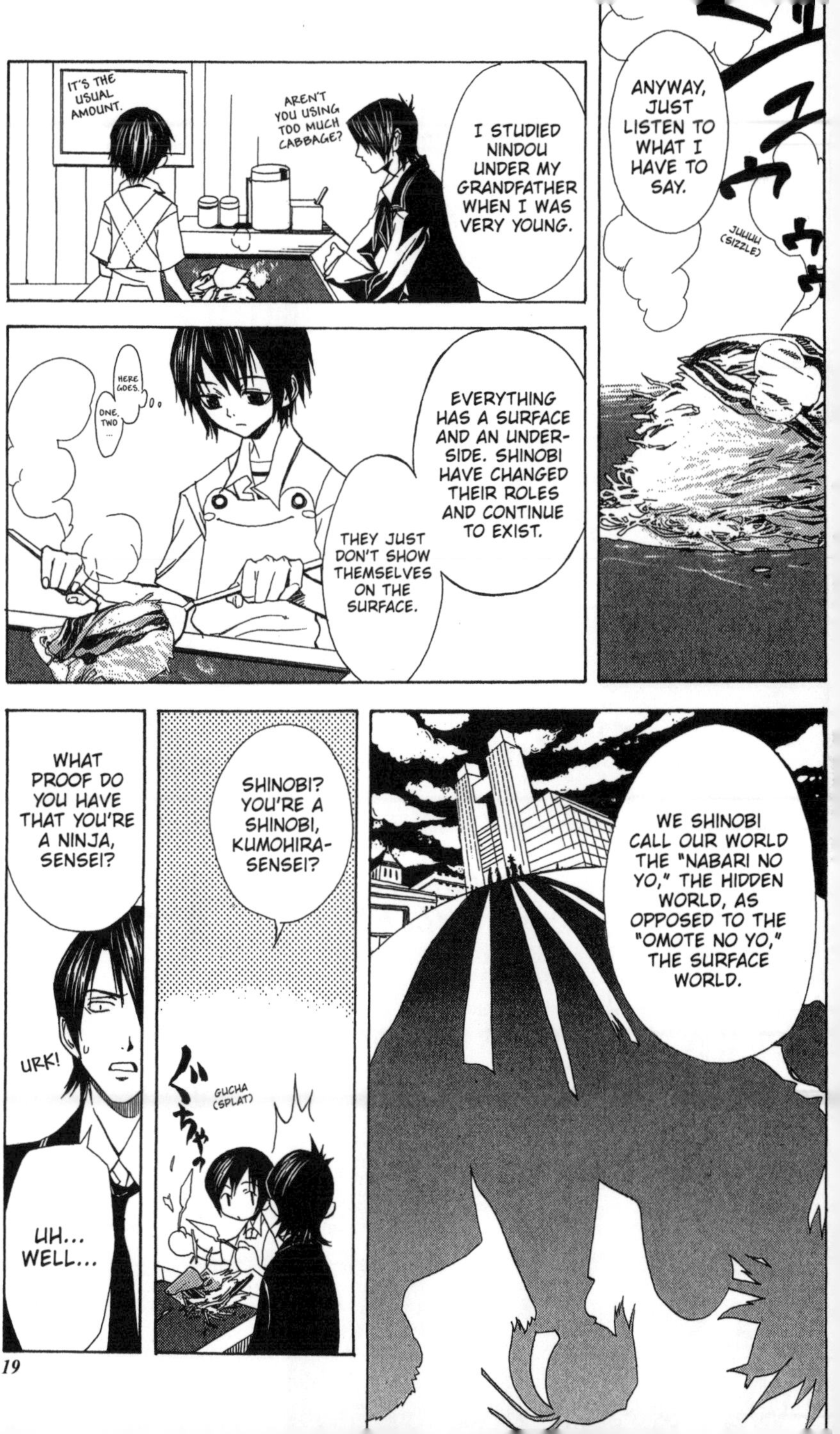
ANYWAY, JUST LISTEN TO WHAT I HAVE TO SAY.
JUUUU (SIZZLE)
I STUDIED NINDOU UNDER MY GRANDFATHER WHEN I WAS VERY YOUNG.
AREN'T YOU USING TOO MUCH CABBAGE?
IT'S THE USUAL AMOUNT.
EVERYTHING HAS A SURFACE AND AN UNDER-SIDE. SHINOBI HAVE CHANGED THEIR ROLES AND CONTINUE TO EXIST.
THEY JUST DON'T SHOW THEMSELVES ON THE SURFACE.
HERE GOES.
ONE, TWO ...
WE SHINOBI CALL OUR WORLD THE "NABARI NO YO," THE HIDDEN WORLD, AS OPPOSED TO THE "OMOTE NO YO," THE SURFACE WORLD.
SHINOBI? YOU'RE A SHINOBI, KUMOHIRA-SENSEI?
GUCHA (SPLAT)
WHAT PROOF DO YOU HAVE THAT YOU'RE A NINJA, SENSEI?
URK!
UH... WELL...

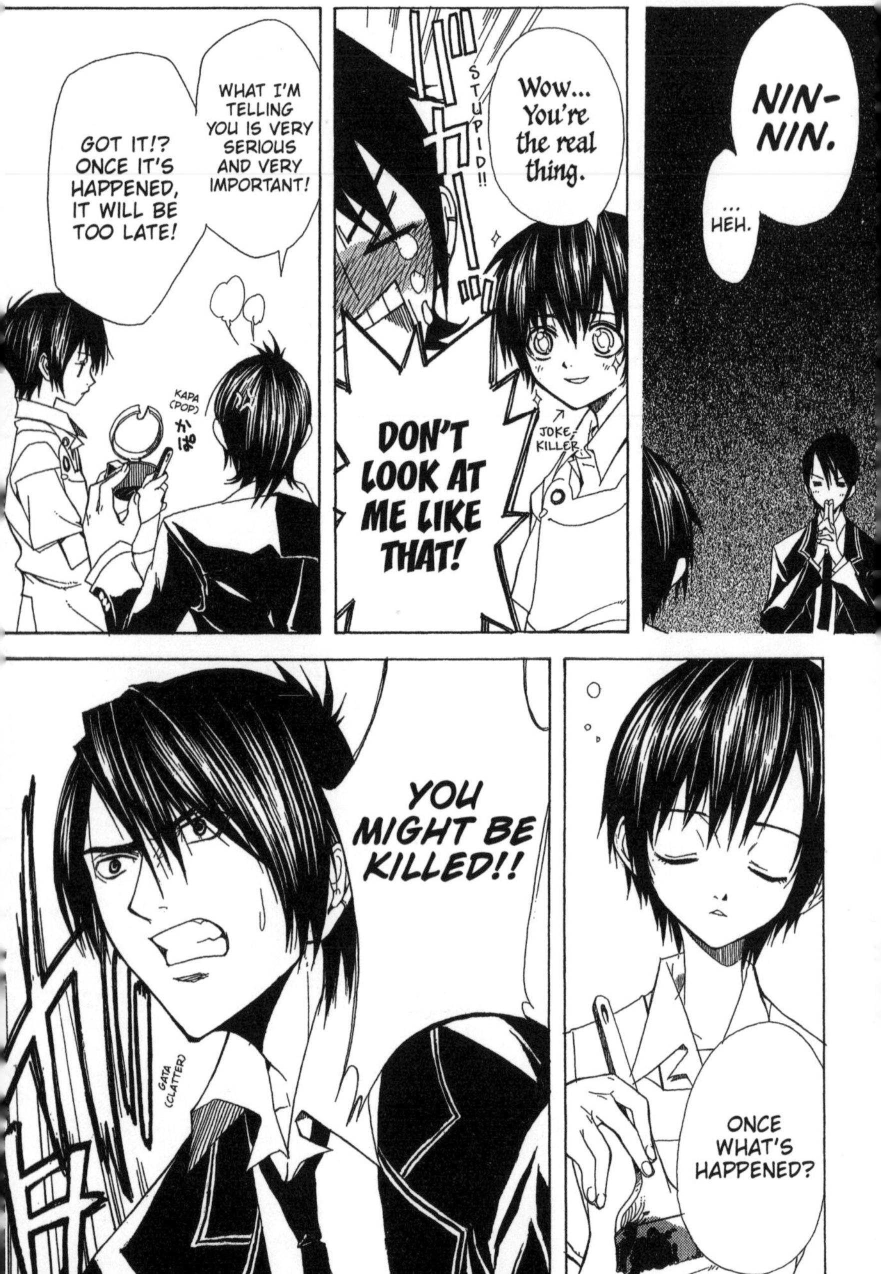
NIN-NIN.
...HEH.
STUPID!!
Wow... You're the real thing.
DON'T LOOK AT ME LIKE THAT!
JOKE-KILLER
WHAT I'M TELLING YOU IS VERY SERIOUS AND VERY IMPORTANT!
GOT IT!? ONCE IT'S HAPPENED, IT WILL BE TOO LATE!
KAPA (POP)
かぽ
ONCE WHAT'S HAPPENED?
YOU MIGHT BE KILLED!!
GATA (CLATTER)

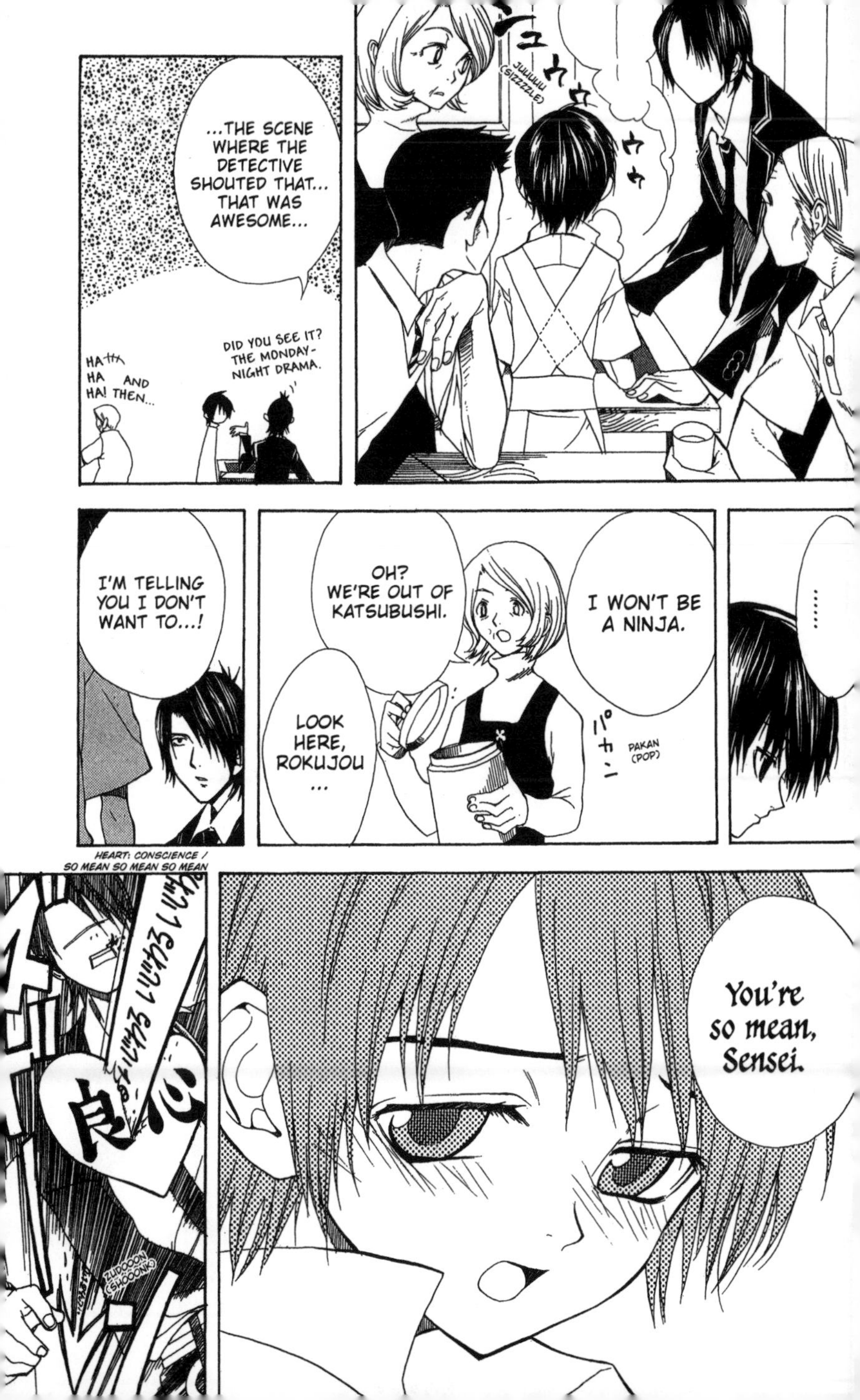
JUUUUU (SIZZZZLE)
...THE SCENE WHERE THE DETECTIVE SHOUTED THAT... THAT WAS AWESOME...
DID YOU SEE IT? THE MONDAY-NIGHT DRAMA.
HA HA HA! AND THEN...
......
I WON'T BE A NINJA.
PAKAN (POP)
OH? WE'RE OUT OF KATSUBUSHI.
LOOK HERE, ROKUJOU...
I'M TELLING YOU I DON'T WANT TO...!
You're so mean, Sensei.
HEART: CONSCIENCE / SO MEAN SO MEAN SO MEAN
ZUDOOON (SHOOONK)

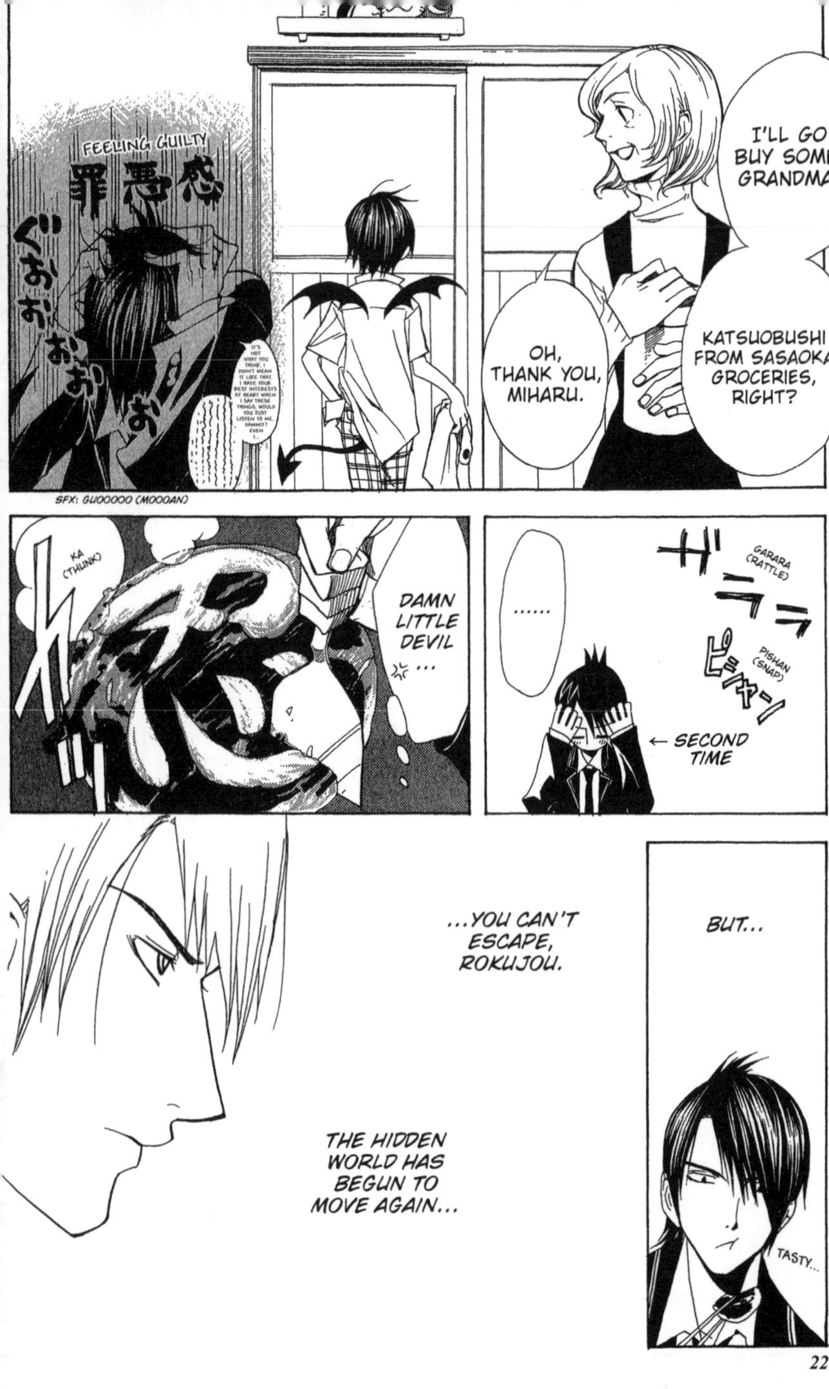
I'LL GO BUY SOME, GRANDMA.
KATSUOBUSHI FROM SASAOKA GROCERIES, RIGHT?
OH, THANK YOU, MIHARU.
IT'S NOT WHAT YOU THINK. I DIDN'T MEAN IT LIKE THAT. I HAVE YOUR BEST INTERESTS AT HEART WHEN I SAY THESE THINGS, WOULD YOU JUST LISTEN TO ME, DAMMIT? EVEN I...
FEELING GUILTY
罪悪感
ぐおおおおおお
SFX: GUOOOOO (MOOOAN)
......
GARARA (RATTLE)
ガラララ
PISHAN (SNAP)
ピシャン
← SECOND TIME
DAMN LITTLE DEVIL ...
KA (THUNK)
BUT...
TASTY...
...YOU CAN'T ESCAPE, ROKUJOU.
THE HIDDEN WORLD HAS BEGUN TO MOVE AGAIN...

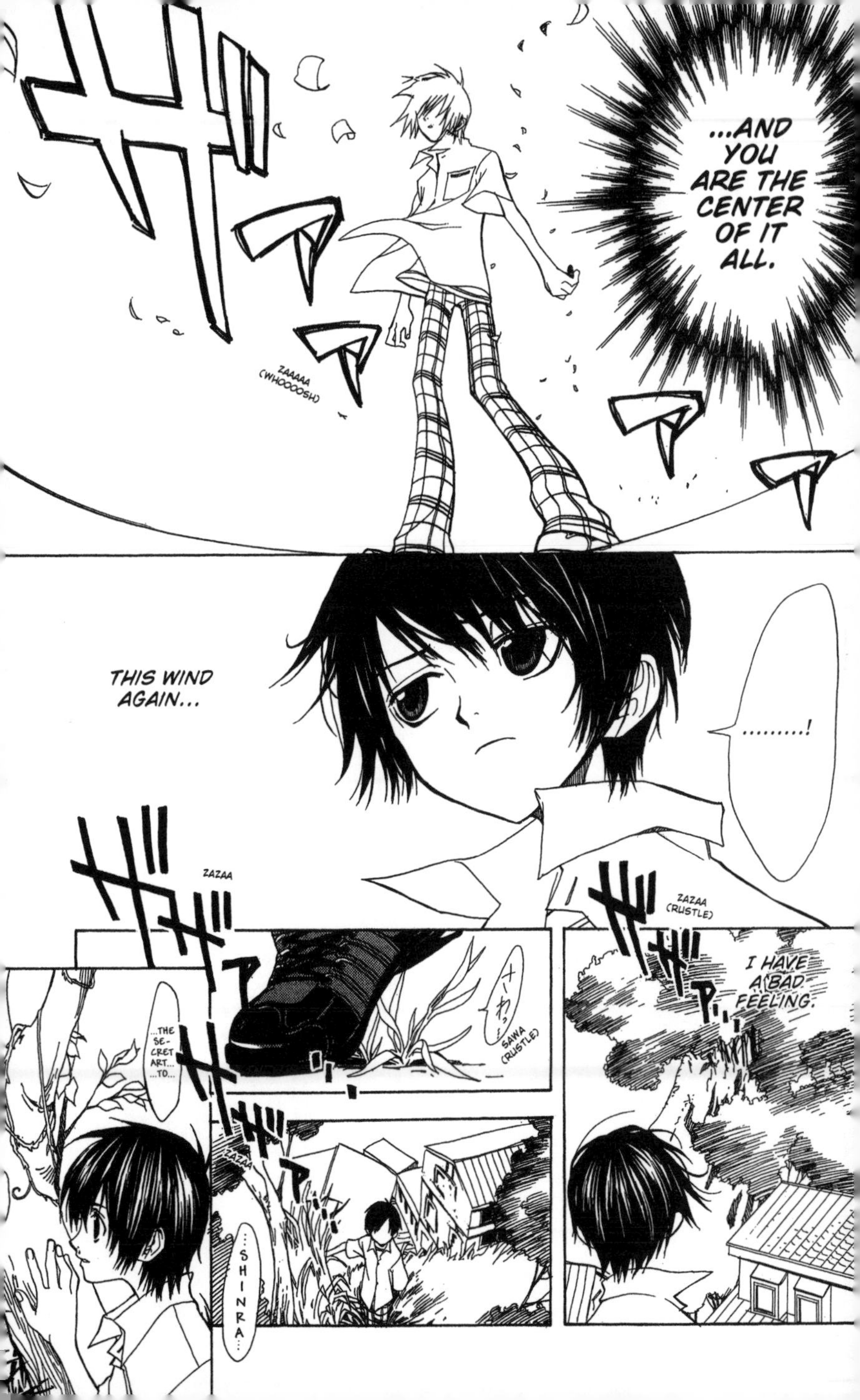

...AND YOU ARE THE CENTER OF IT ALL.
ZAAAAA (WHOOOOSH)
..........!
THIS WIND AGAIN...
ZAZAA
ZAZAA (RUSTLE)
I HAVE A BAD FEELING.
SAWA (RUSTLE)
ZAZAA
...SHINRA...
...THE SE-CRET ART... ...TO...

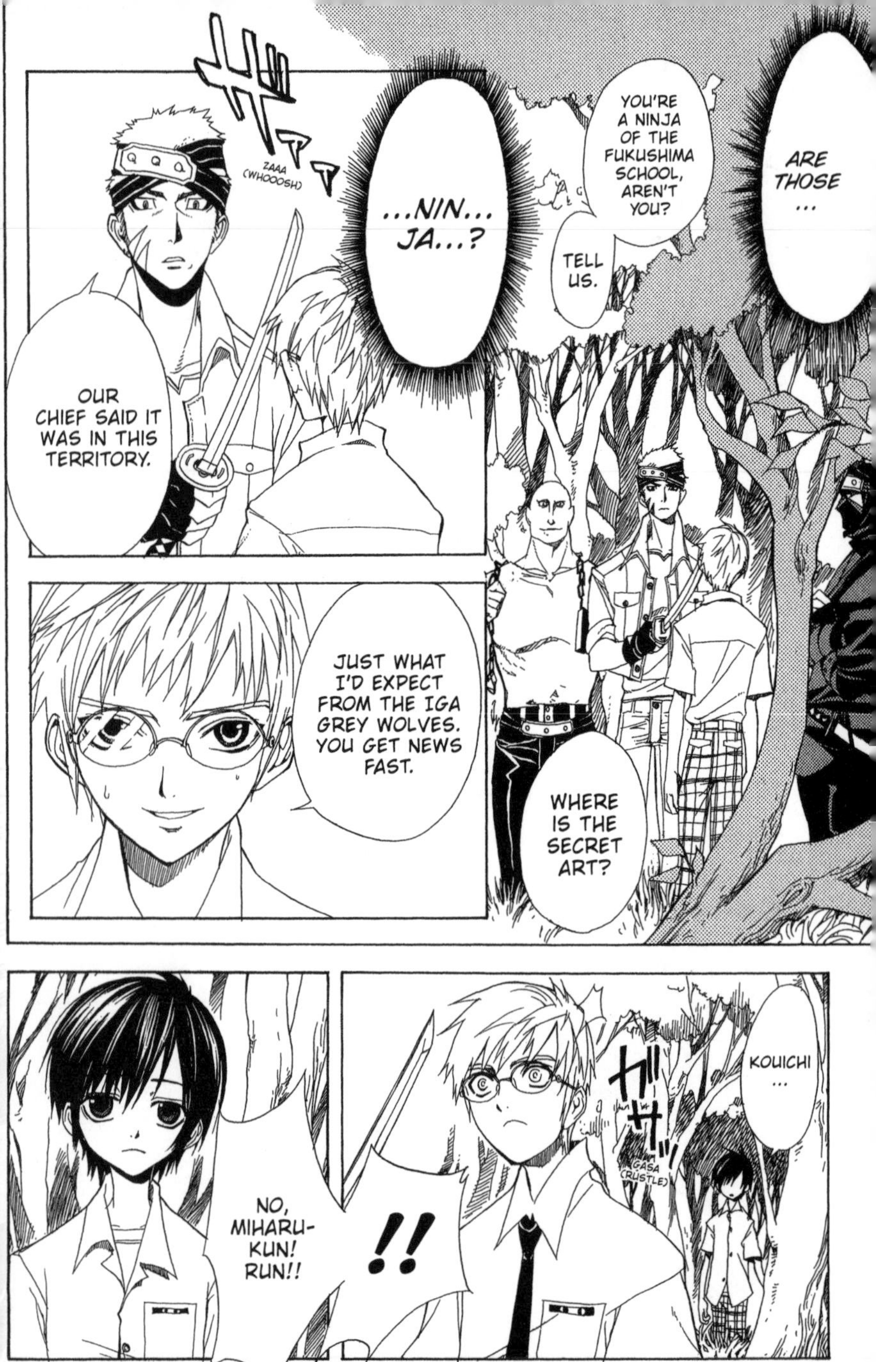
ARE THOSE ...
YOU'RE A NINJA OF THE FUKUSHIMA SCHOOL, AREN'T YOU?
TELL US.
WHERE IS THE SECRET ART?
...NIN... JA...?
ZAAA (WHOOOSH)
OUR CHIEF SAID IT WAS IN THIS TERRITORY.
JUST WHAT I'D EXPECT FROM THE IGA GREY WOLVES. YOU GET NEWS FAST.
KOUICHI ...
GASA (RUSTLE)
!!
NO, MIHARU-KUN! RUN!!

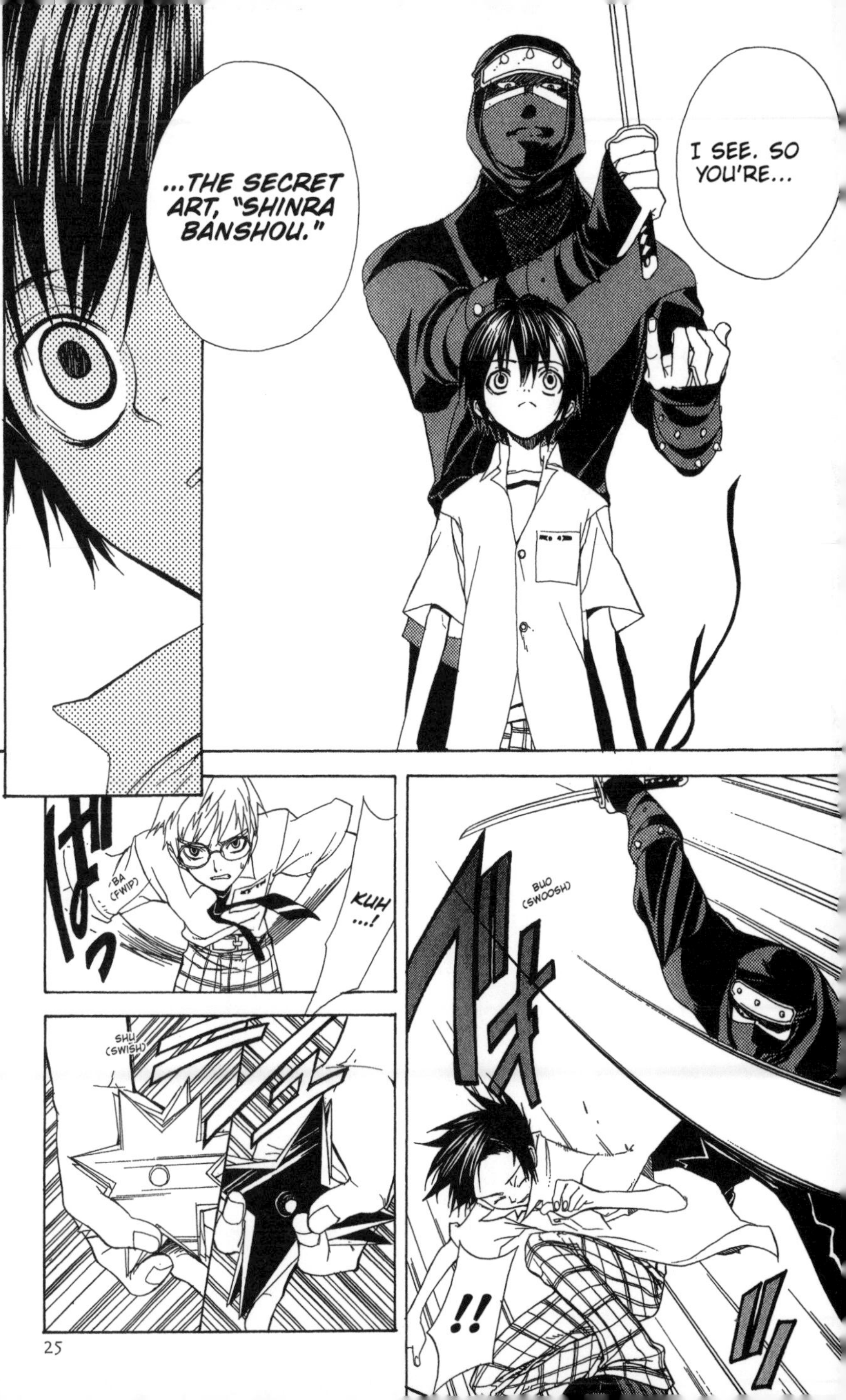
I SEE. SO YOU'RE...
...THE SECRET ART, "SHINRA BANSHOU."
BUO (SWOOSH)
!!
BA (FWIP)
KUH ...!
SHU (SWISH)

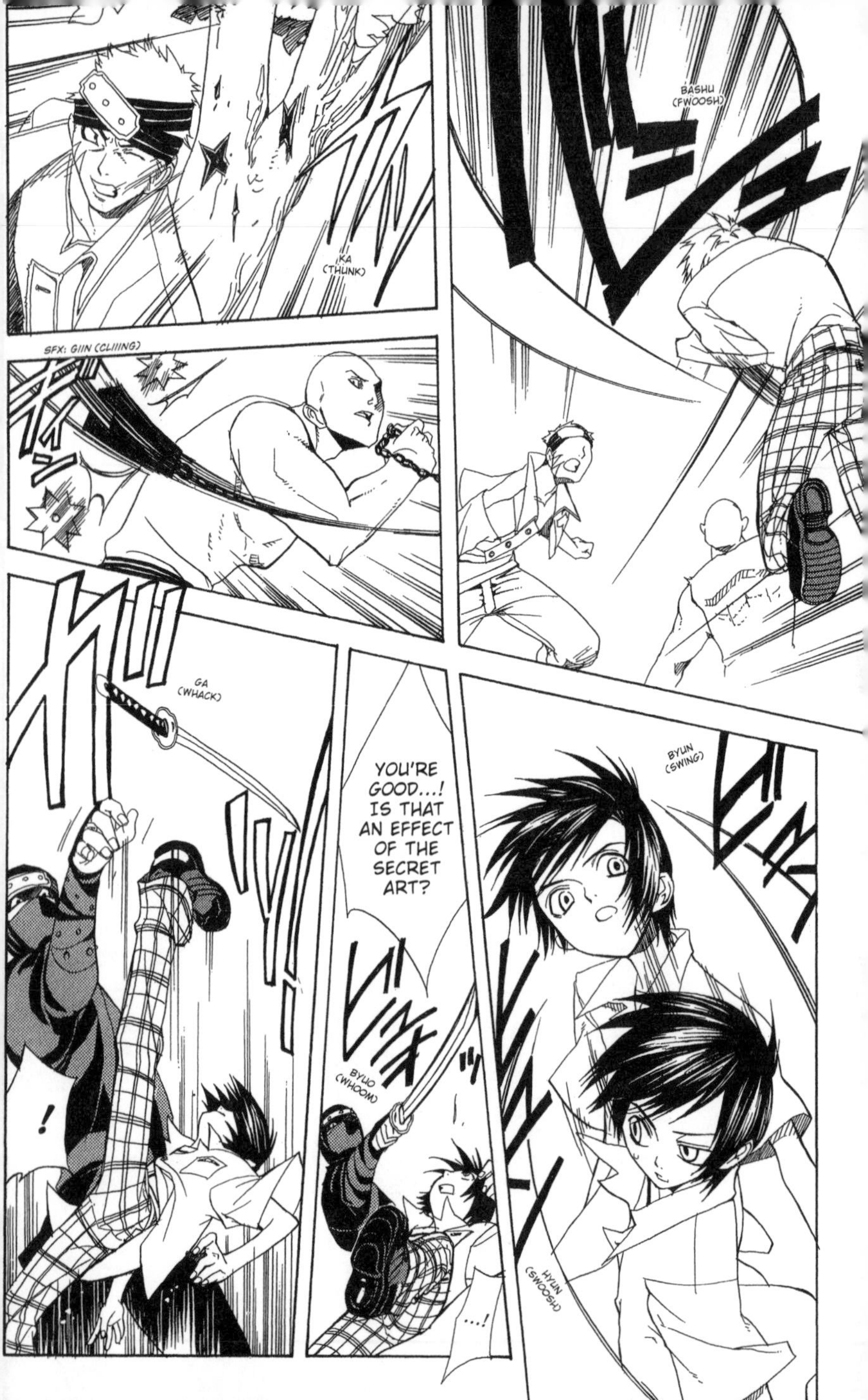
BASHU (FWOOSH)
KA (THUNK)
SFX: GIIN (CLIIING)
BYUN (SWING)
HYUN (SWOOSH)
YOU'RE GOOD...! IS THAT AN EFFECT OF THE SECRET ART?
BYUO (WHOOM)
...!
GA (WHACK)
!

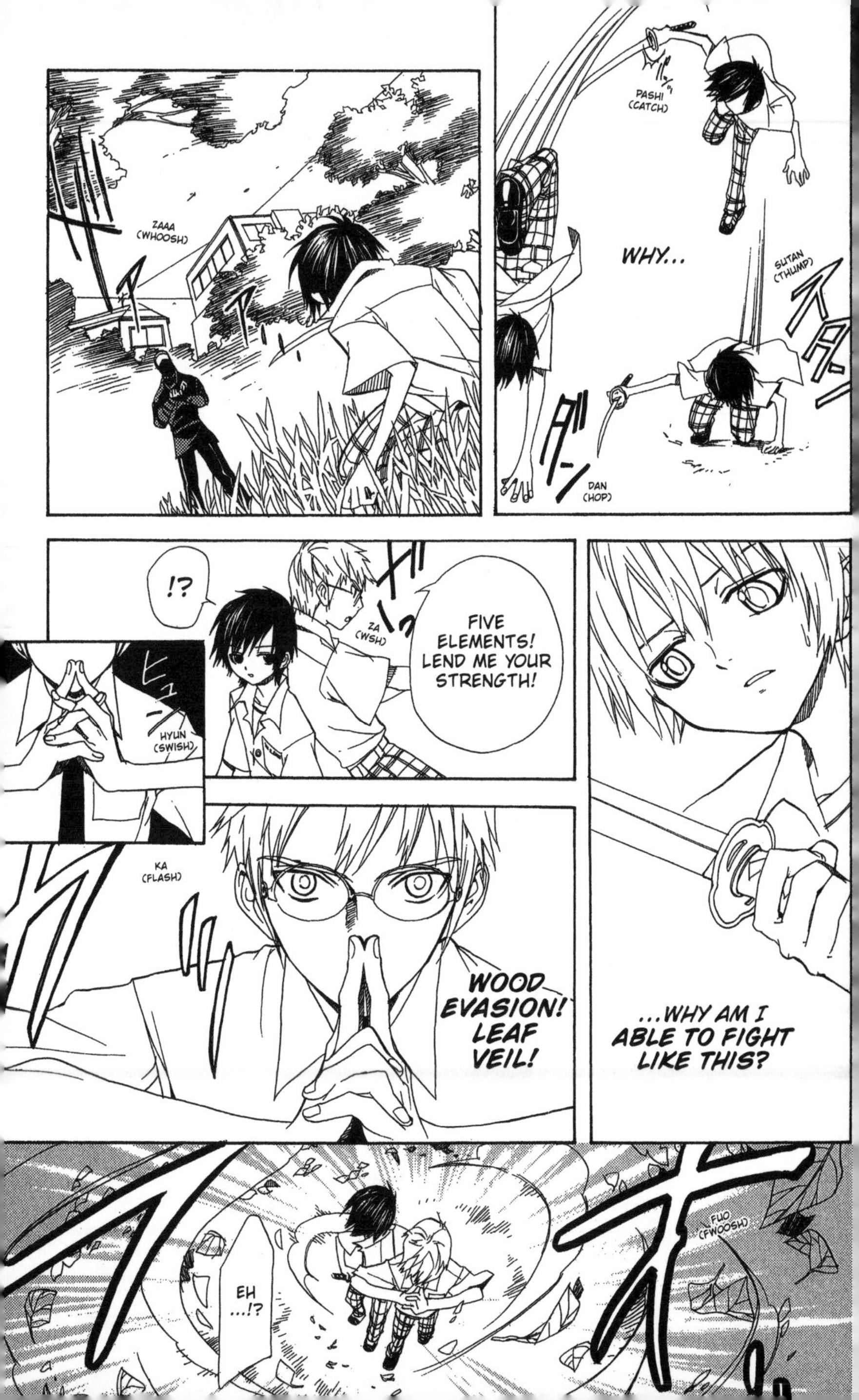
PASHI (CATCH)
WHY...
SUTAN (THUMP)
DAN (HOP)
ZAAA (WHOOSH)
...WHY AM I ABLE TO FIGHT LIKE THIS?
!?
ZA (WSH)
FIVE ELEMENTS! LEND ME YOUR STRENGTH!
HYUN (SWISH)
KA (FLASH)
WOOD EVASION! LEAF VEIL!
FUO (FWOOSH)
EH ...!?

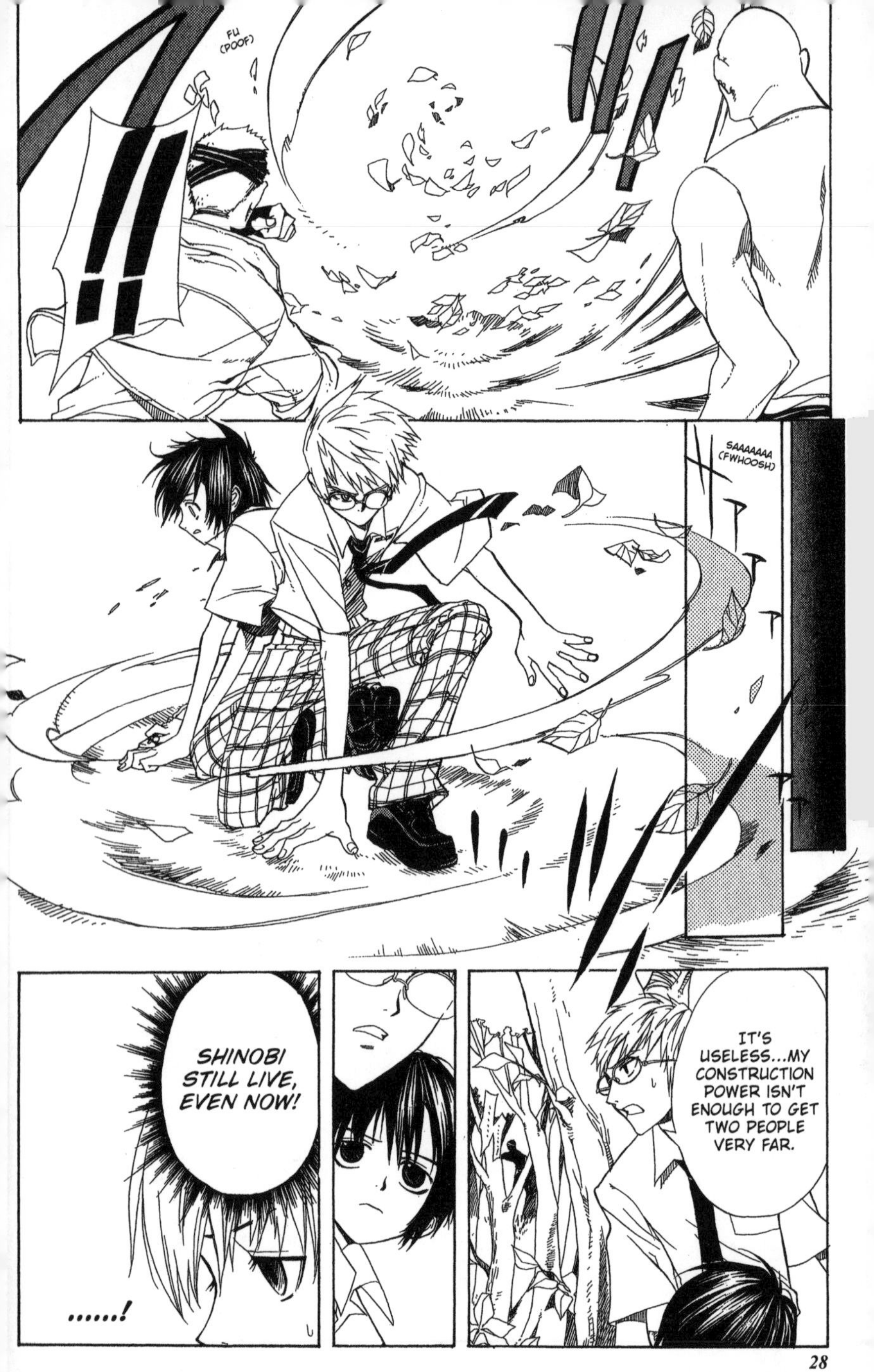
FU (POOF)
SAAAAAAA (FWHOOSH)
IT'S USELESS...MY CONSTRUCTION POWER ISN'T ENOUGH TO GET TWO PEOPLE VERY FAR.
SHINOBI STILL LIVE, EVEN NOW!
......!

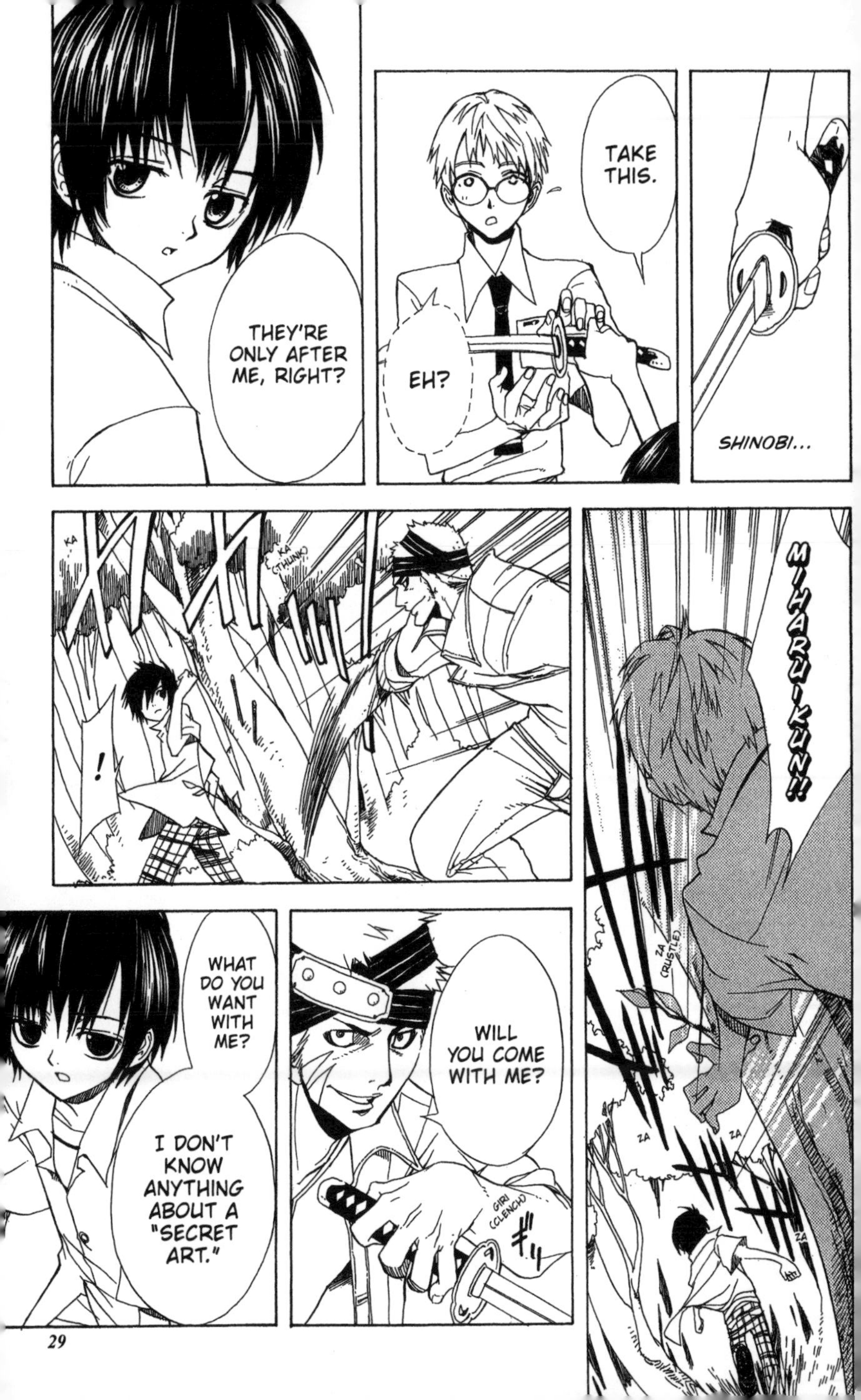
SHINOBI...
TAKE THIS.
EH?
THEY'RE ONLY AFTER ME, RIGHT?
MIHARU-KUN!!
ZA (RUSTLE)
ZA
ZA
ZA
KA (THUNK)
KA
!
WILL YOU COME WITH ME?
GIRI (CLENCH)
WHAT DO YOU WANT WITH ME?
I DON'T KNOW ANYTHING ABOUT A "SECRET ART."

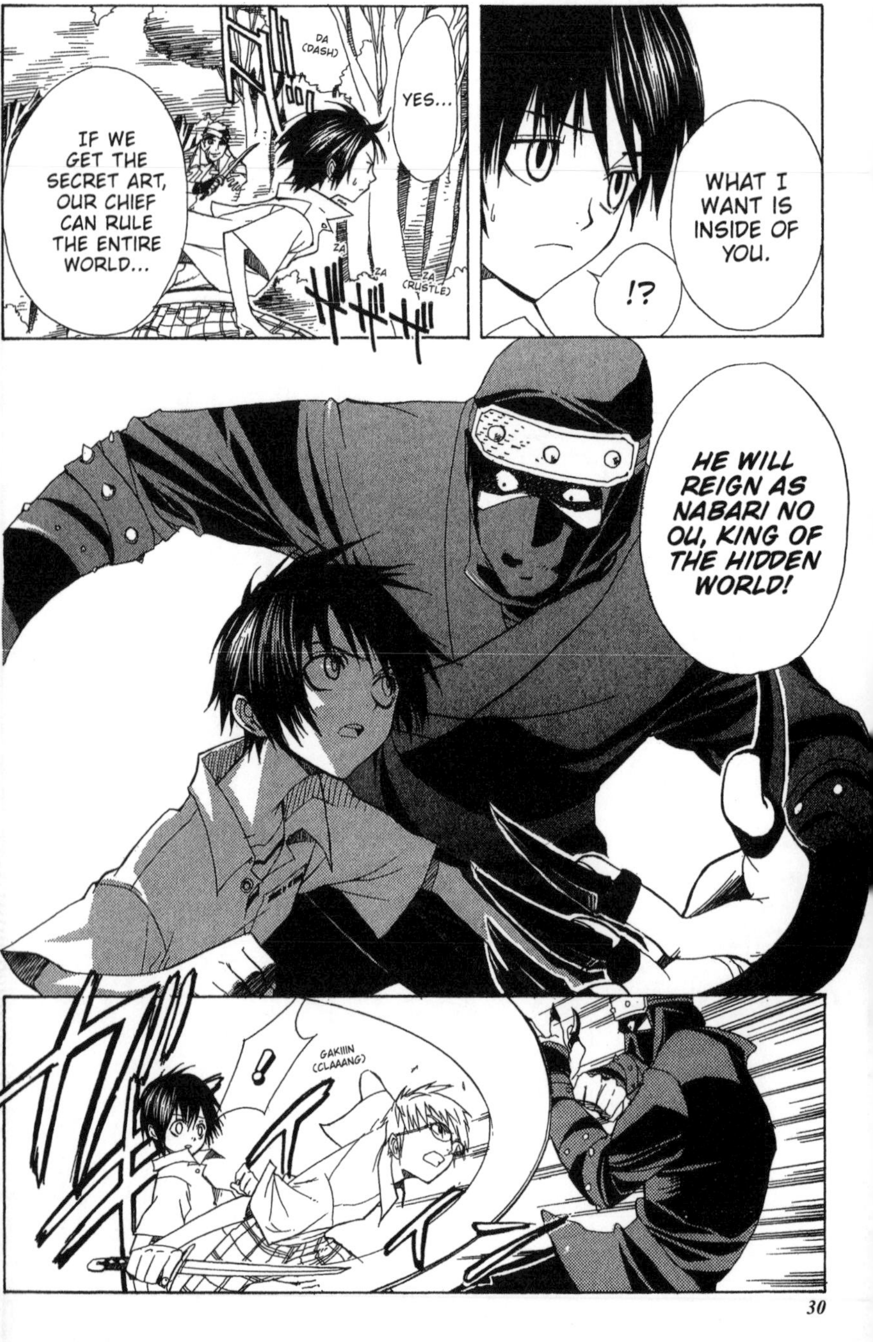
WHAT I WANT IS INSIDE OF YOU.
!?
YES...
DA (DASH)
IF WE GET THE SECRET ART, OUR CHIEF CAN RULE THE ENTIRE WORLD...
ZA
ZA
ZA (RUSTLE)
HE WILL REIGN AS NABARI NO OU, KING OF THE HIDDEN WORLD!
GAKIIN (CLAAANG)
!

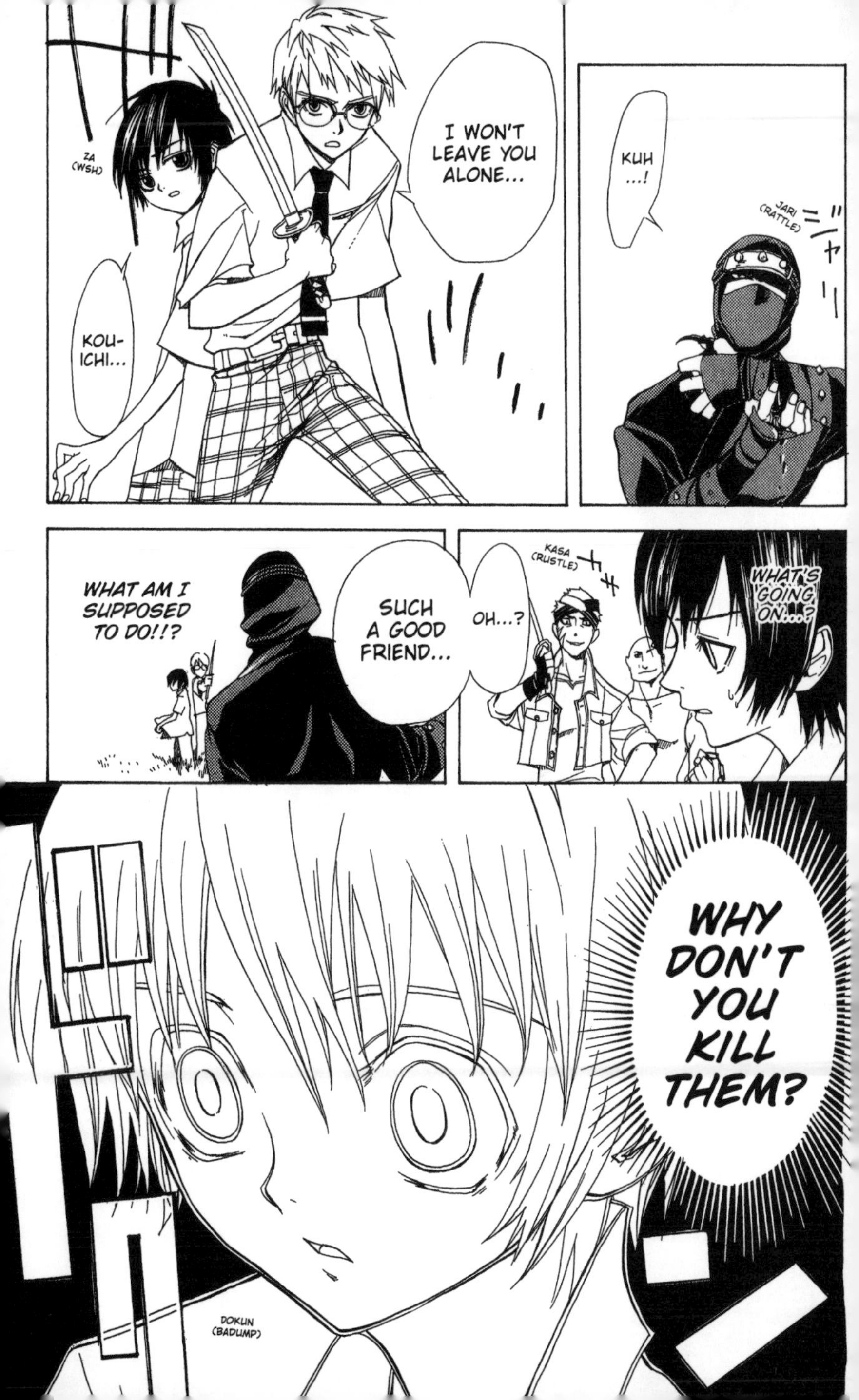
KUH ...!
JARI (RATTLE)
I WON'T LEAVE YOU ALONE...
ZA (WSH)
KOU-ICHI...
WHAT'S GOING ON...?
KASA (RUSTLE)
OH...?
SUCH A GOOD FRIEND...
WHAT AM I SUPPOSED TO DO!!?
WHY DON'T YOU KILL THEM?
DOKUN (BADUMP)

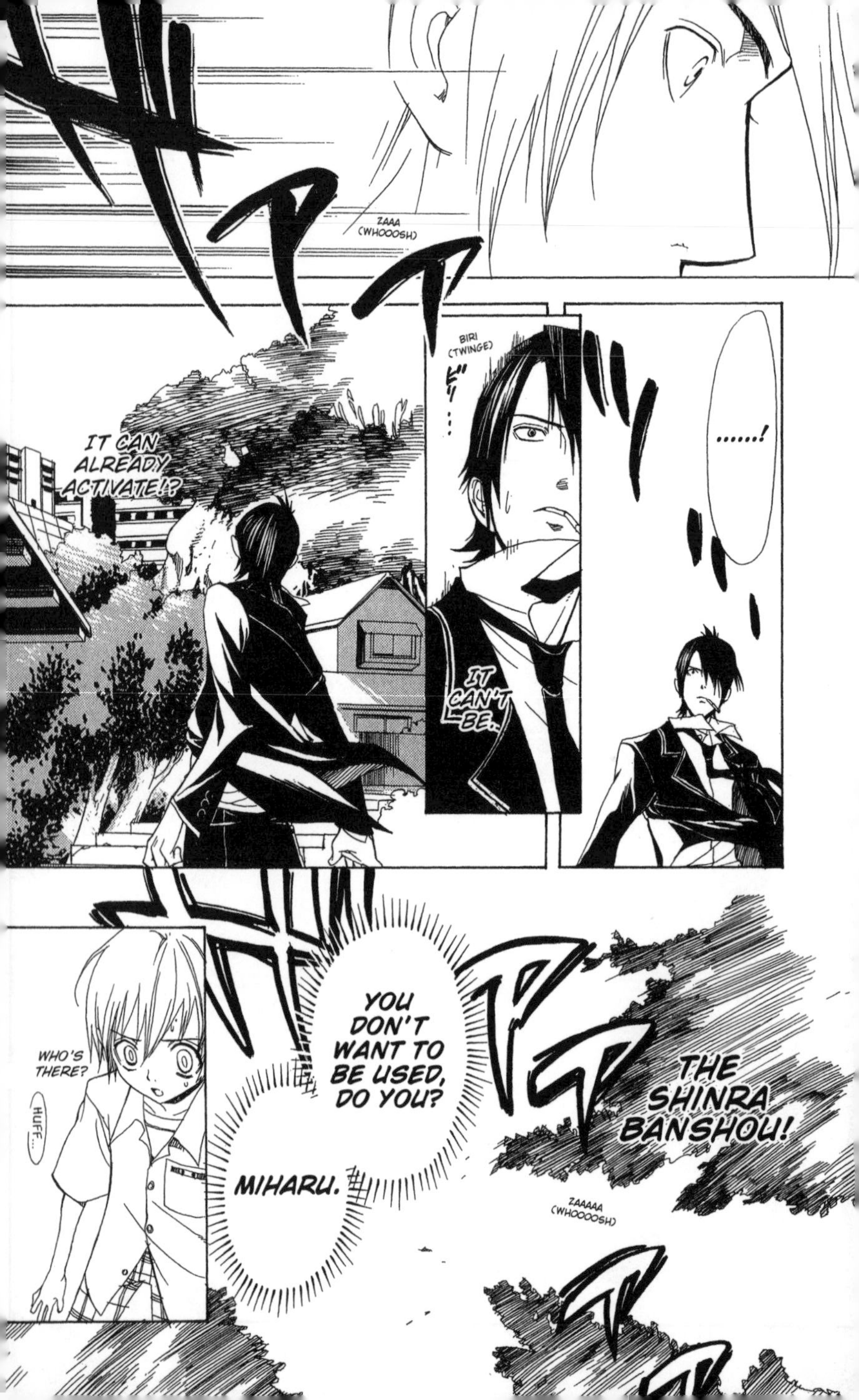
ZAAA
(WHOOOSH)
......!
BIRI
(TWINGE)
IT CAN'T BE..
IT CAN ALREADY ACTIVATE!?
THE SHINRA BANSHOU!
YOU DON'T WANT TO BE USED, DO YOU?
MIHARU.
ZAAAAA
(WHOOOOSH)
WHO'S THERE?
HUFF...

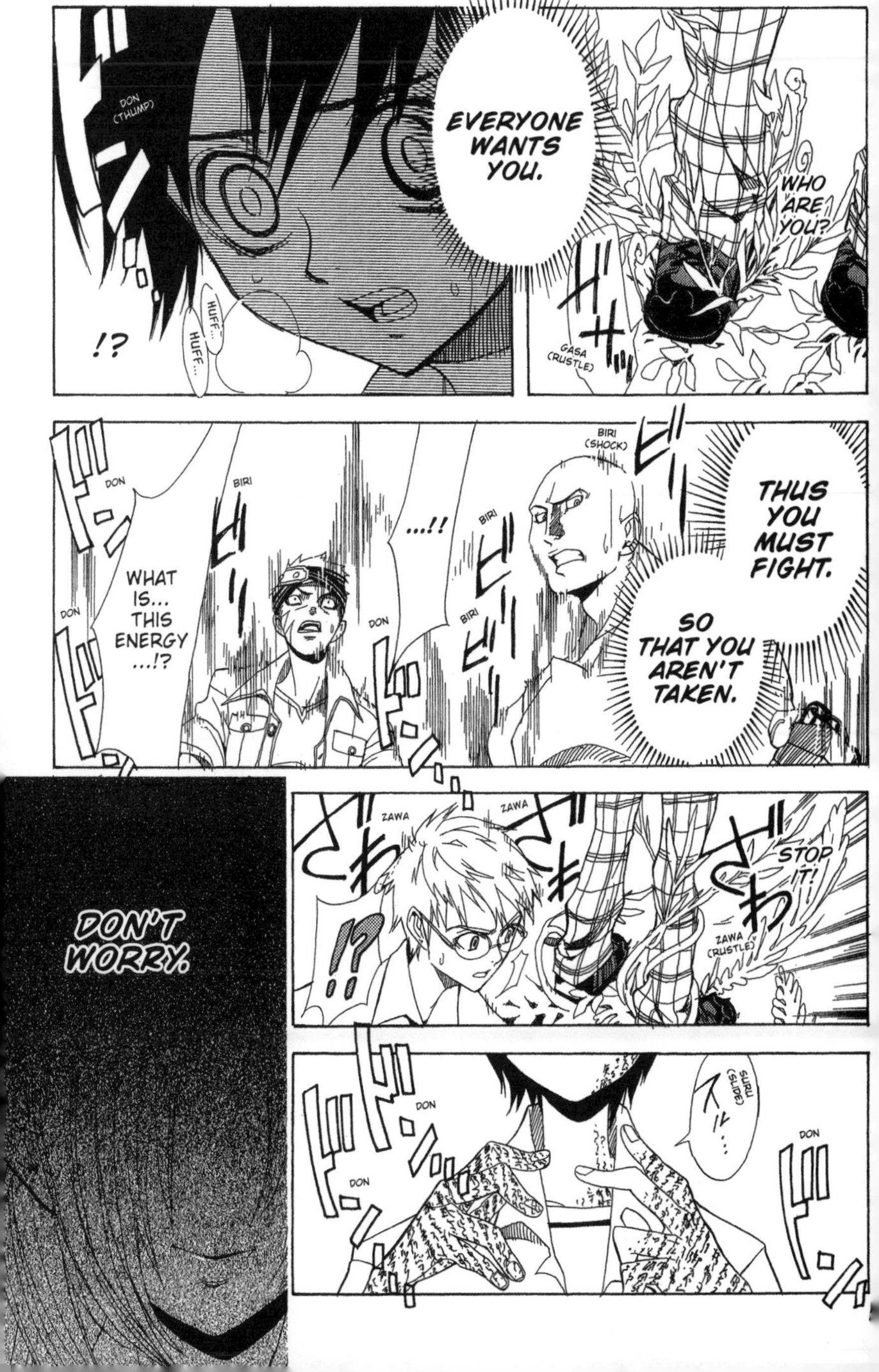
WHO ARE YOU?
GASA (RUSTLE)
EVERYONE WANTS YOU.
DON (THUMP)
HUFF... HUFF...
!?
BIRI (SHOCK)
THUS YOU MUST FIGHT.
SO THAT YOU AREN'T TAKEN.
BIRI
BIRI
...!!
DON
BIRI
WHAT IS... THIS ENERGY ...!?
DON
DON
STOP IT!
ZAWA (RUSTLE)
ZAWA
ZAWA
!?
DON
SURU (SLIDE)
DON
DON
DON'T WORRY.

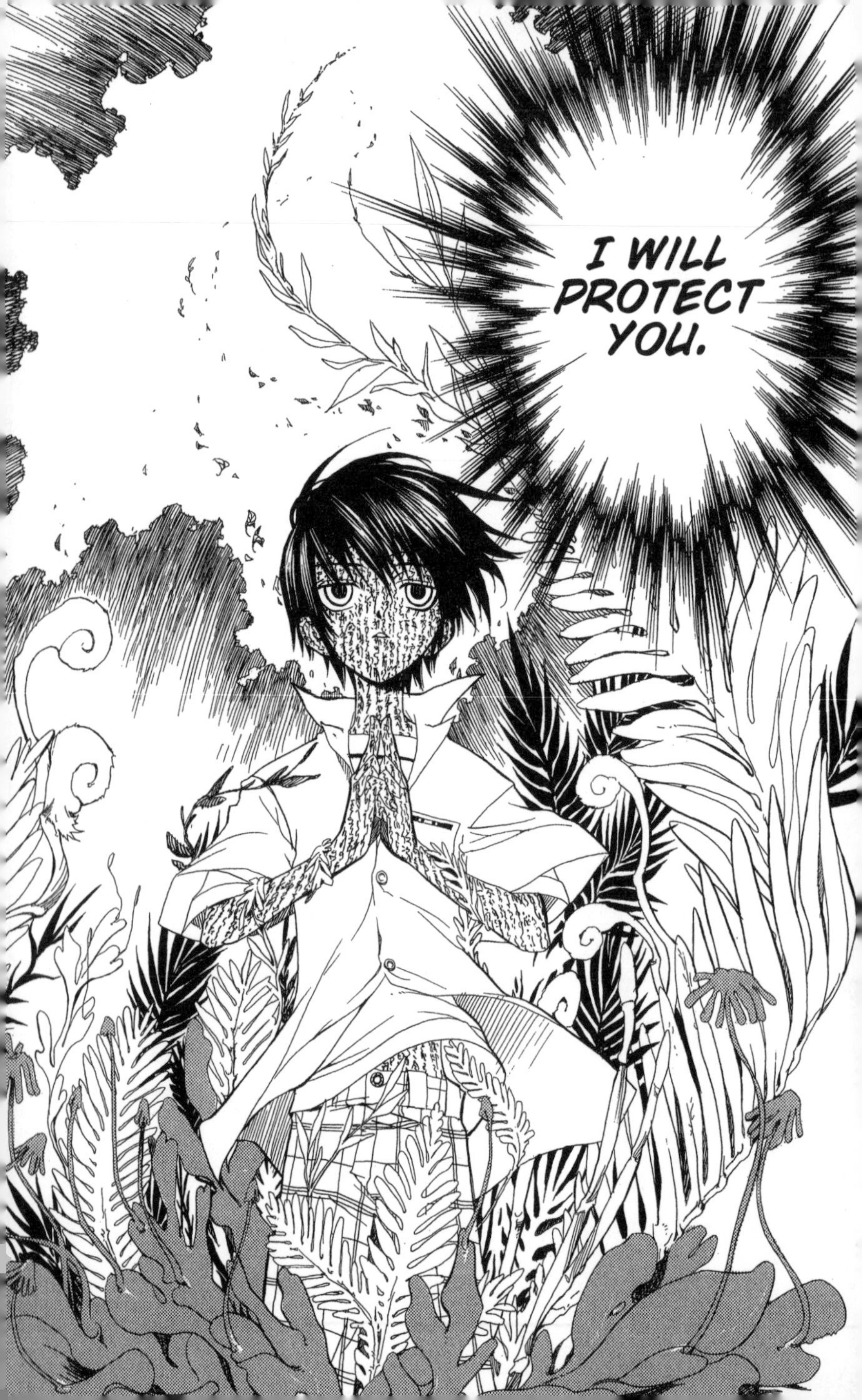
I WILL PROTECT YOU.

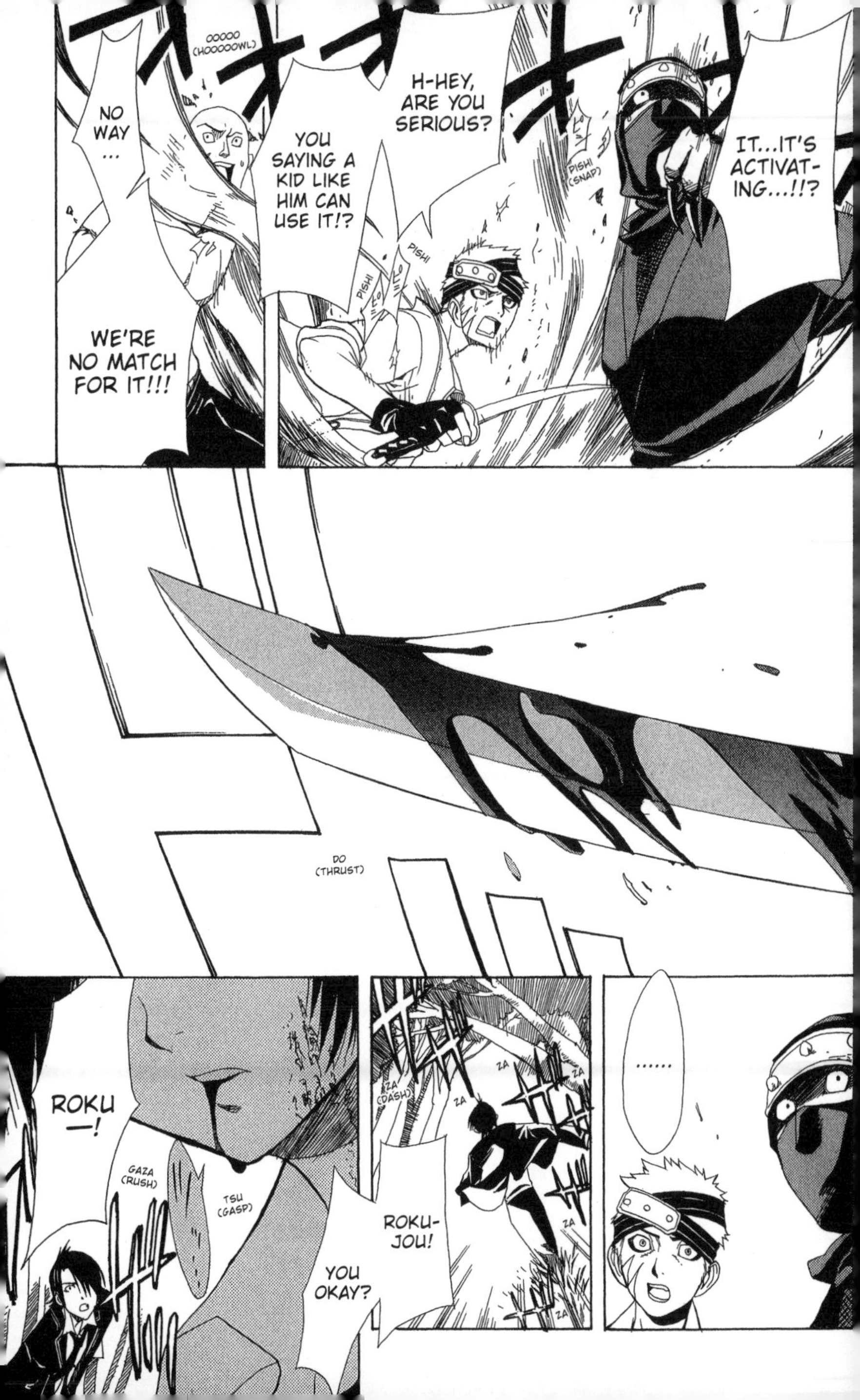
IT...IT'S ACTIVAT-ING...!!?
PISHI (SNAP)
H-HEY, ARE YOU SERIOUS?
YOU SAYING A KID LIKE HIM CAN USE IT!?
PISHI
PISHI
OOOOO (HOOOOOWL)
NO WAY ...
WE'RE NO MATCH FOR IT!!!
DO (THRUST)
......
ZA
ZA
ZA
ZA (DASH)
ZA
ZA
ROKU-JOU!
YOU OKAY?
TSU (GASP)
GAZA (RUSH)
ROKU—!

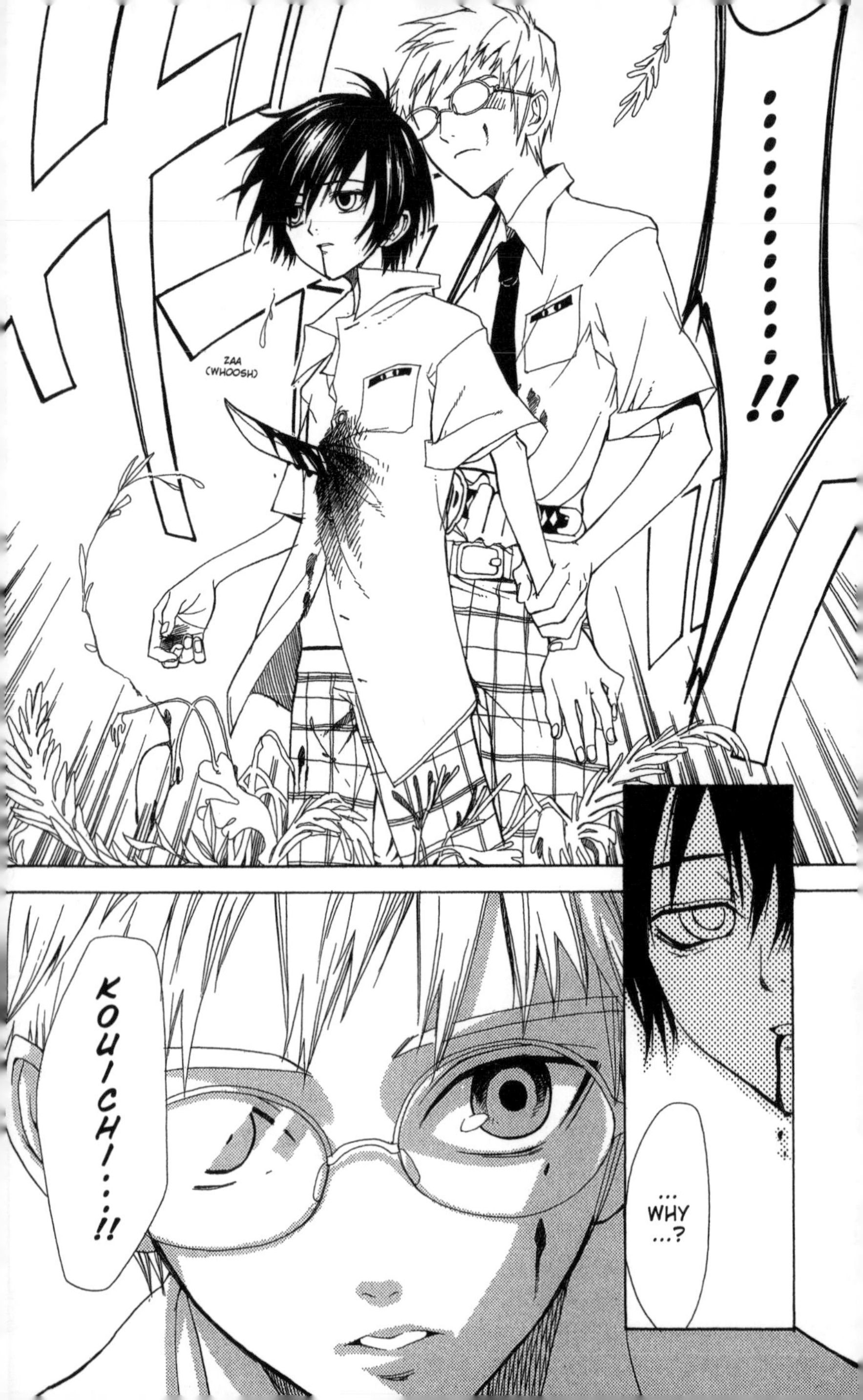
..........!!
ZAA (WHOOSH)
... WHY ...?
KOUICHI...!!

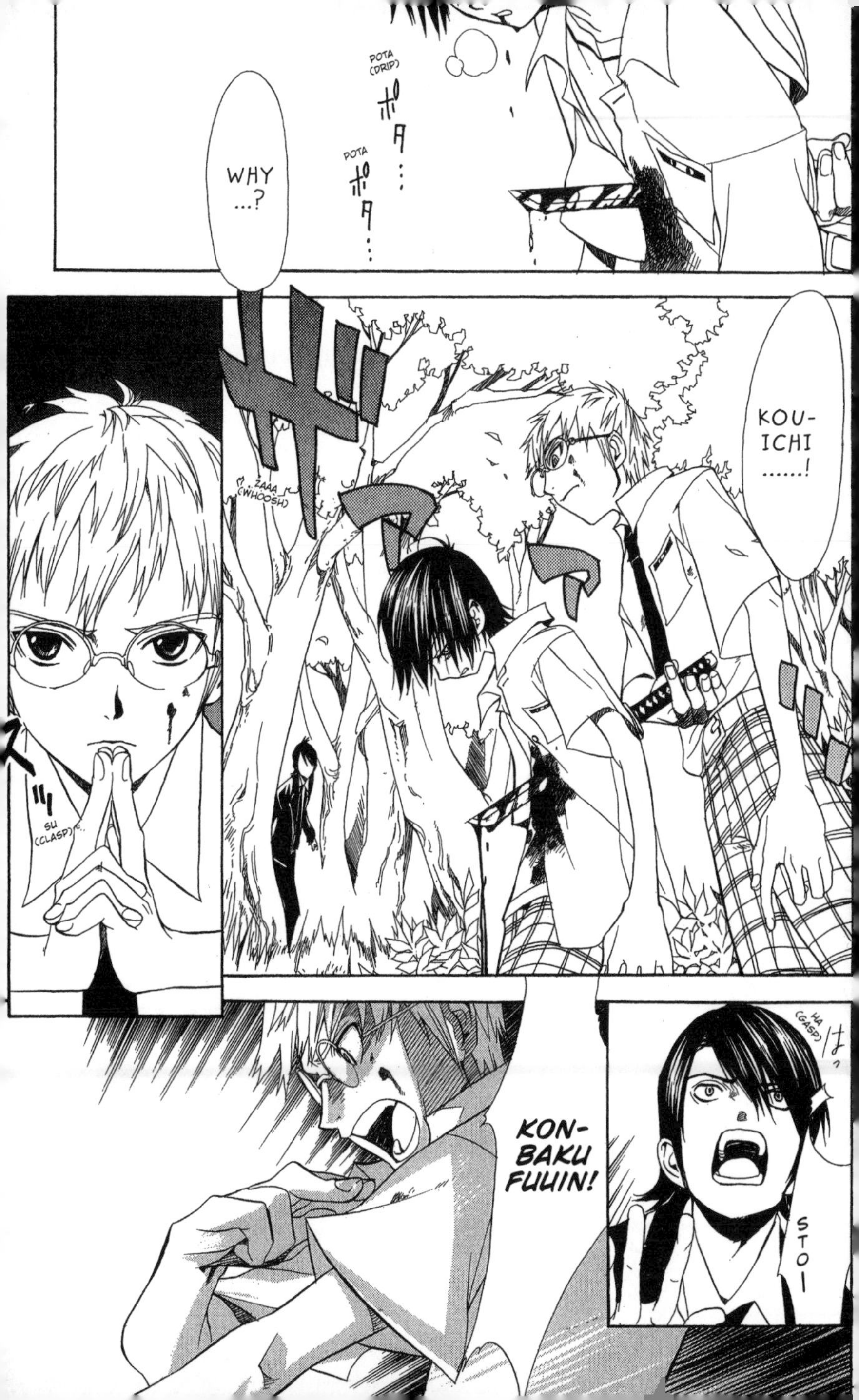
POTA (DRIP)
POTA
WHY ...?
KOU-ICHI ......!
ZAAA (WHOOSH)
SU (CLASP)
HA (GASP)
KON-BAKU FUUIN!
STOI

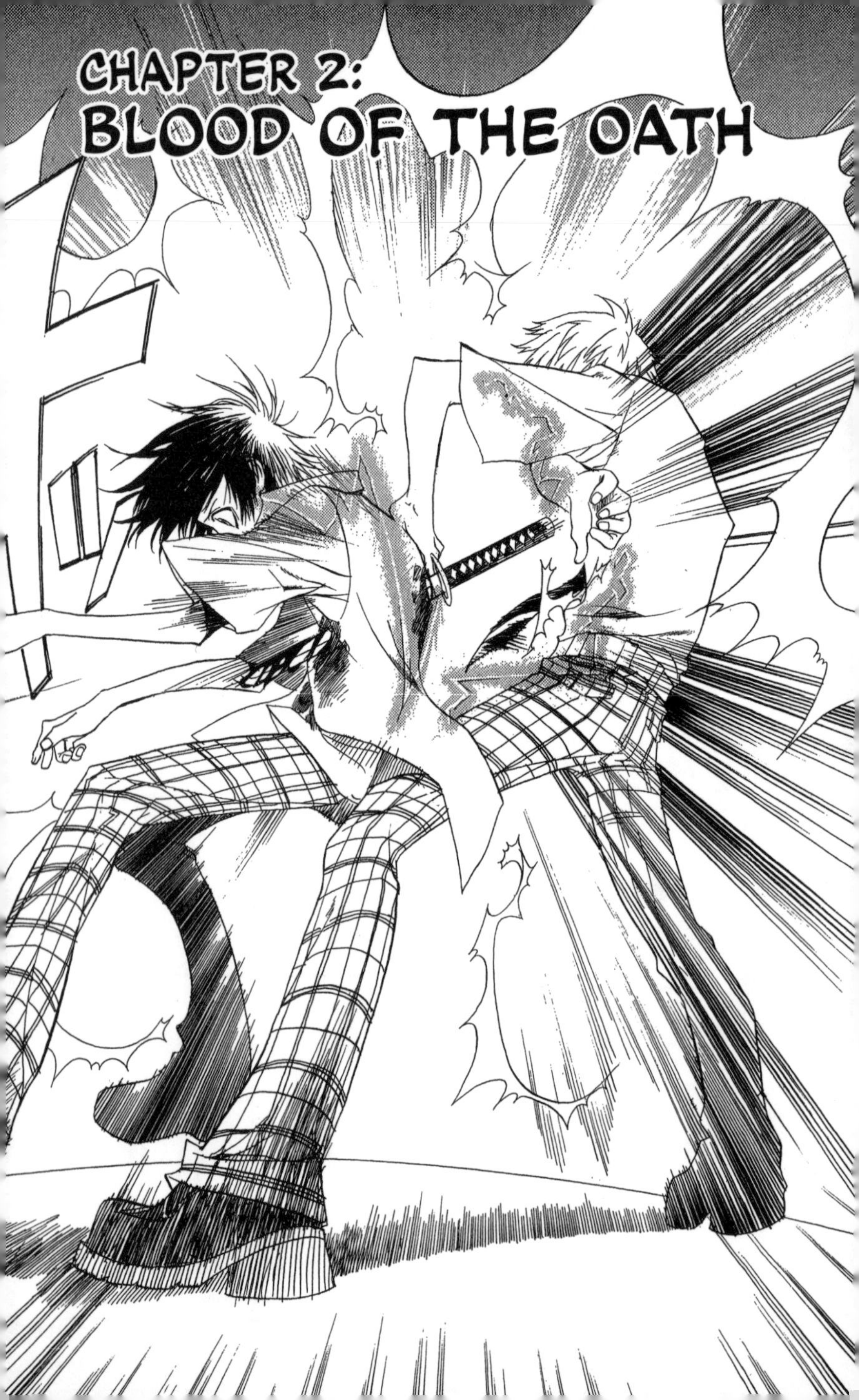
CHAPTER 2:
BLOOD OF THE OATH

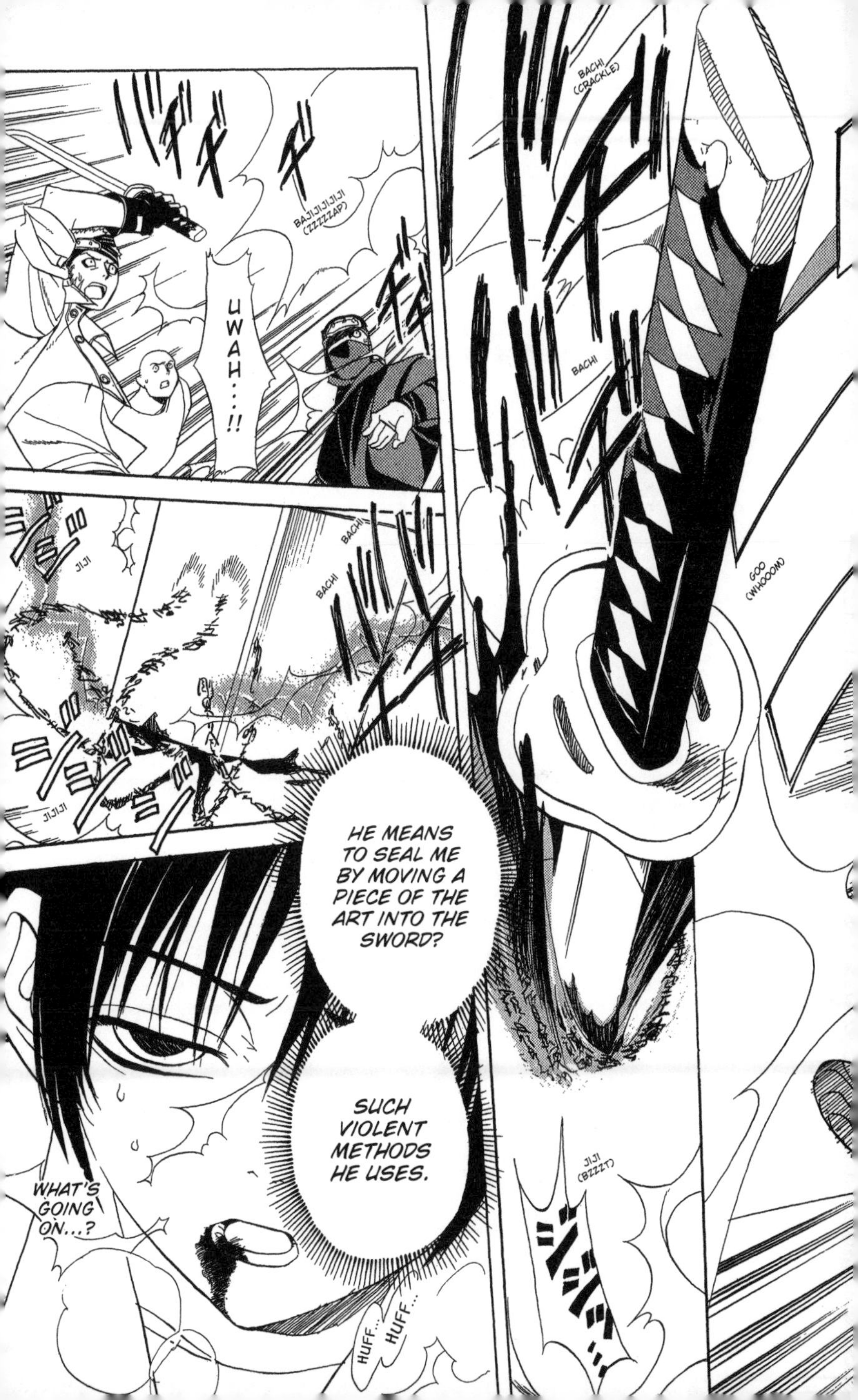
BACHI (CRACKLE)
BACHI
GOO (WHOOOM)
JIJI (BZZZT)
BAJIJIJIJI (ZZZZZAP)
UWAH...!!
BACHI
BACHI
JIJI
JIJIJI
HE MEANS TO SEAL ME BY MOVING A PIECE OF THE ART INTO THE SWORD?
SUCH VIOLENT METHODS HE USES.
WHAT'S GOING ON...?
HUFF... HUFF...

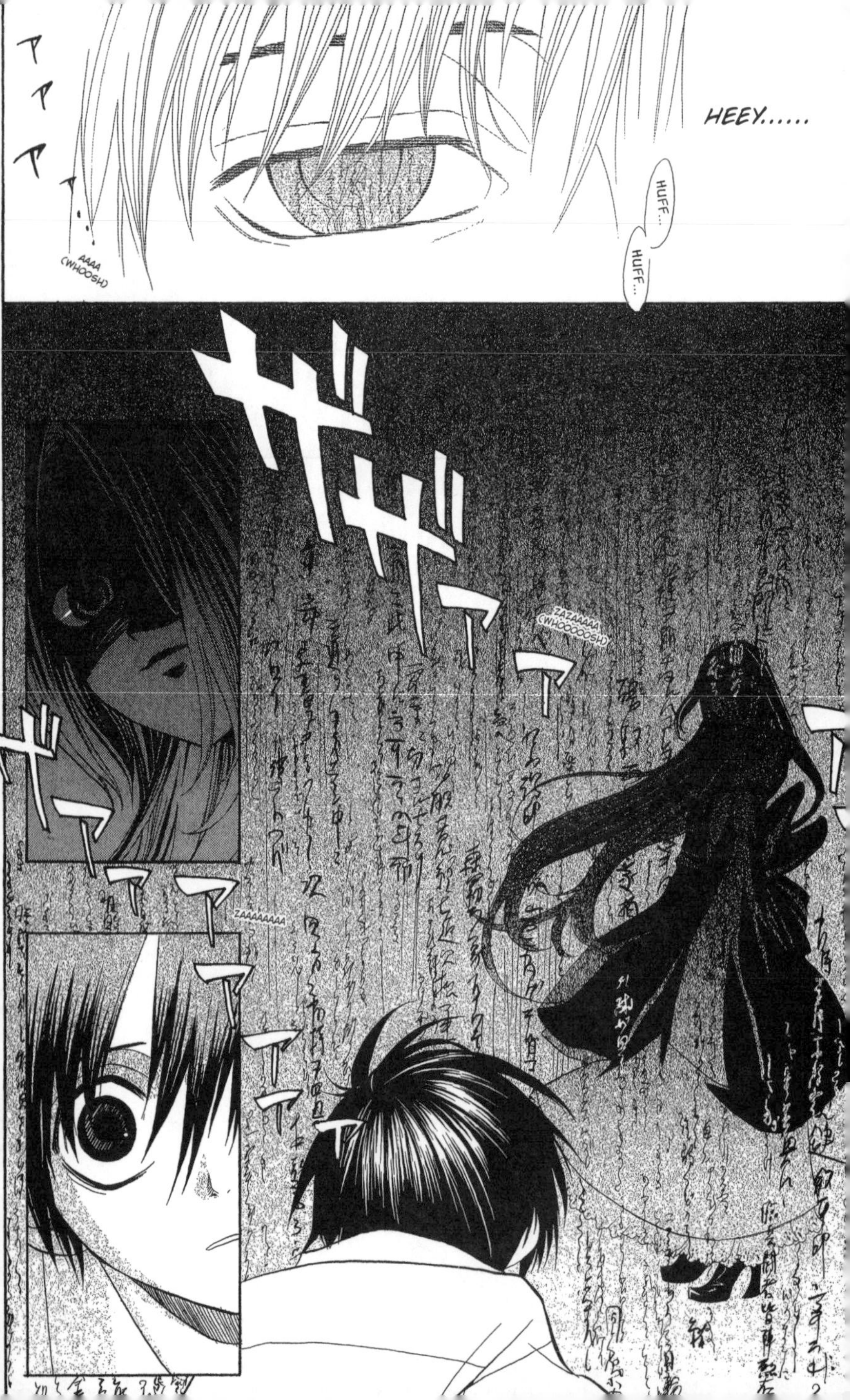
HEEY......
HUFF...
HUFF...
AAAA (WHOOSH)
ZAZAAAAA (WHOOOOOSH)
ZAAAAAAAA

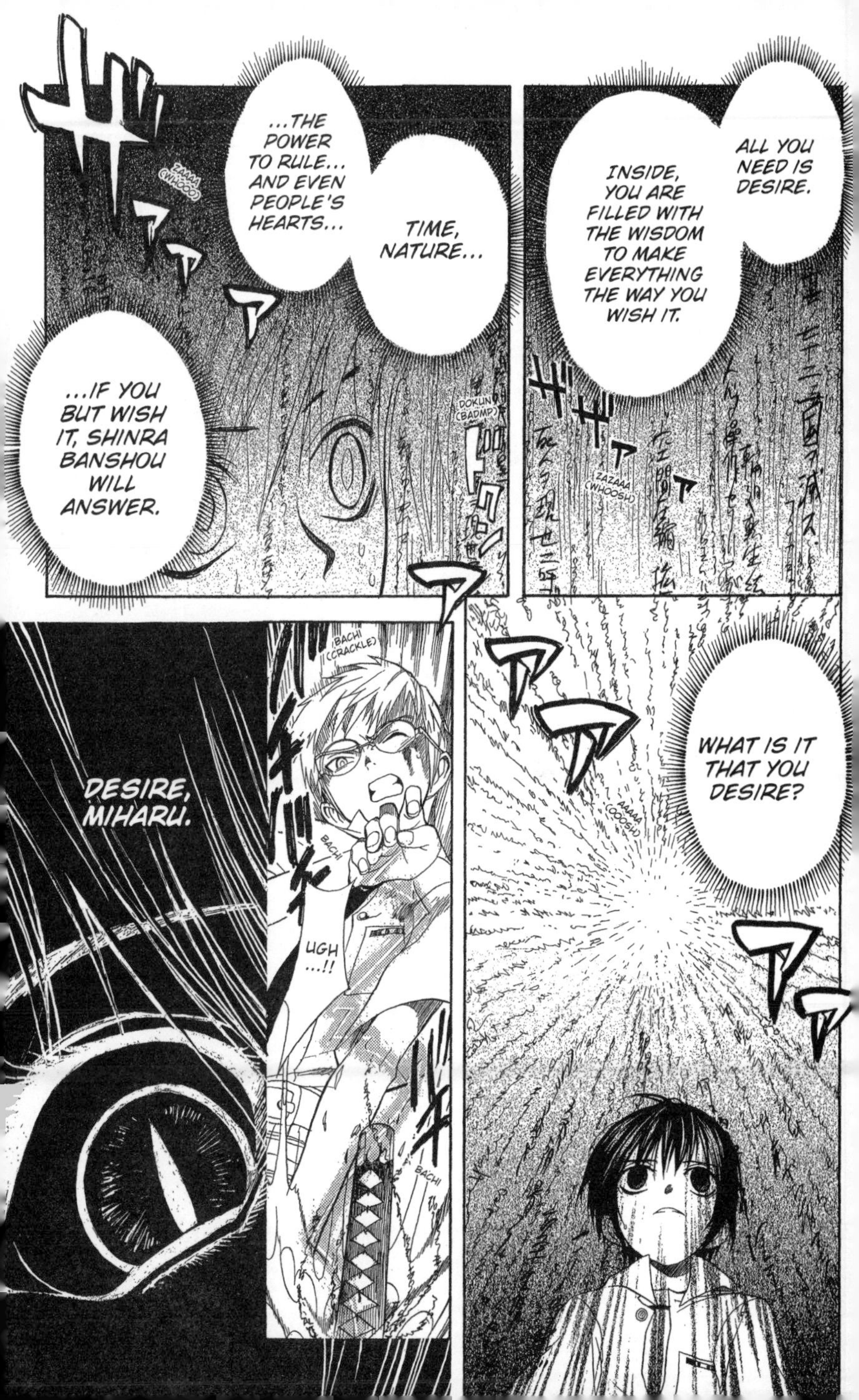
ALL YOU NEED IS DESIRE.
INSIDE, YOU ARE FILLED WITH THE WISDOM TO MAKE EVERYTHING THE WAY YOU WISH IT.
ZAZAAA (WHOOSH)
TIME, NATURE...
...THE POWER TO RULE... AND EVEN PEOPLE'S HEARTS...
DOKUN (BADMP)
...IF YOU BUT WISH IT, SHINRA BANSHOU WILL ANSWER.
WHAT IS IT THAT YOU DESIRE?
AAAAA (OOOSH)
BACHI (CRACKLE)
BACHI
UGH ...!!
BACHI
DESIRE, MIHARU.

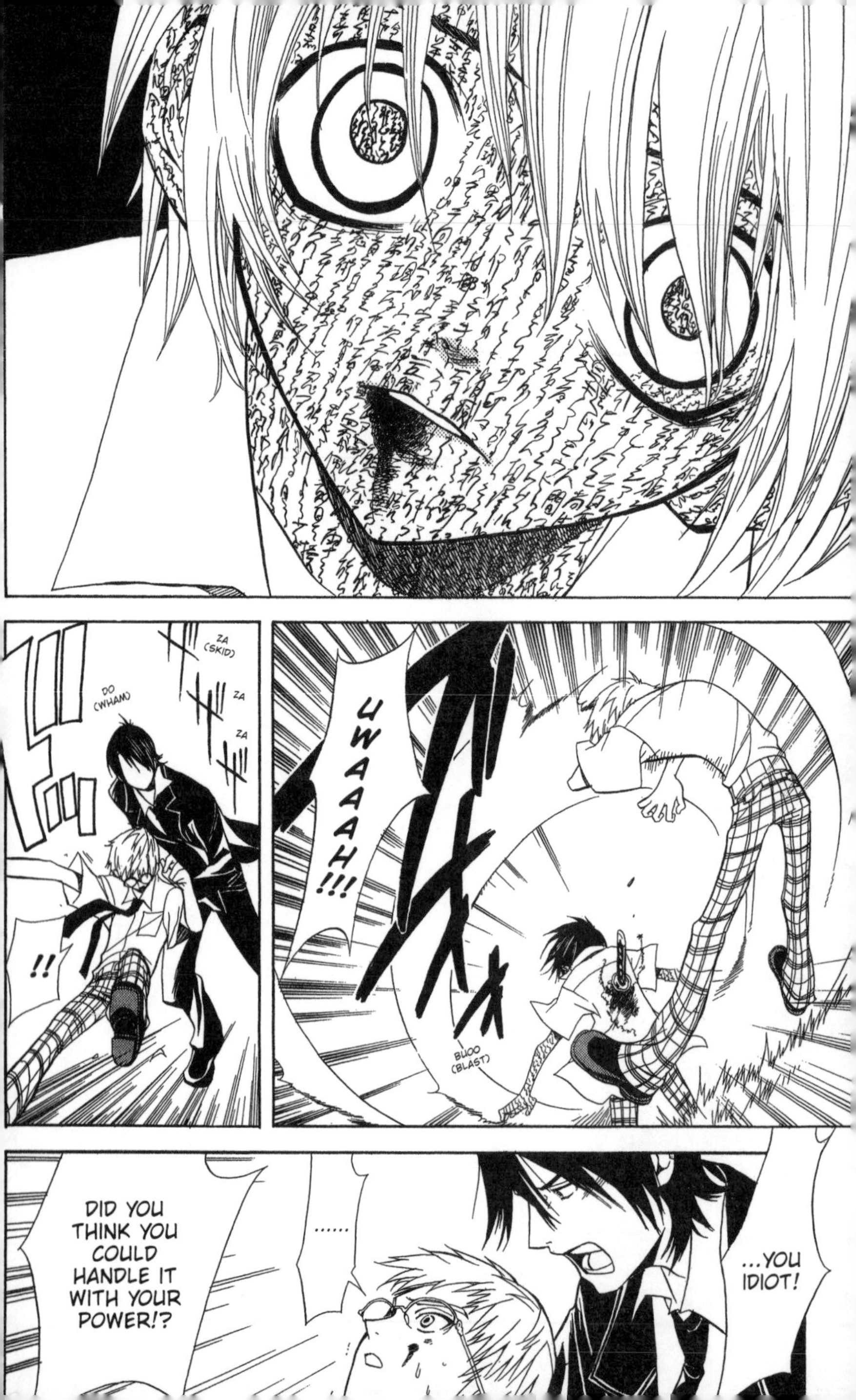
UWAAAAH!!!
BUOO (BLAST)
ZA (SKID)
ZA
ZA
DO (WHAM)
!!
...YOU IDIOT!
......
DID YOU THINK YOU COULD HANDLE IT WITH YOUR POWER!?

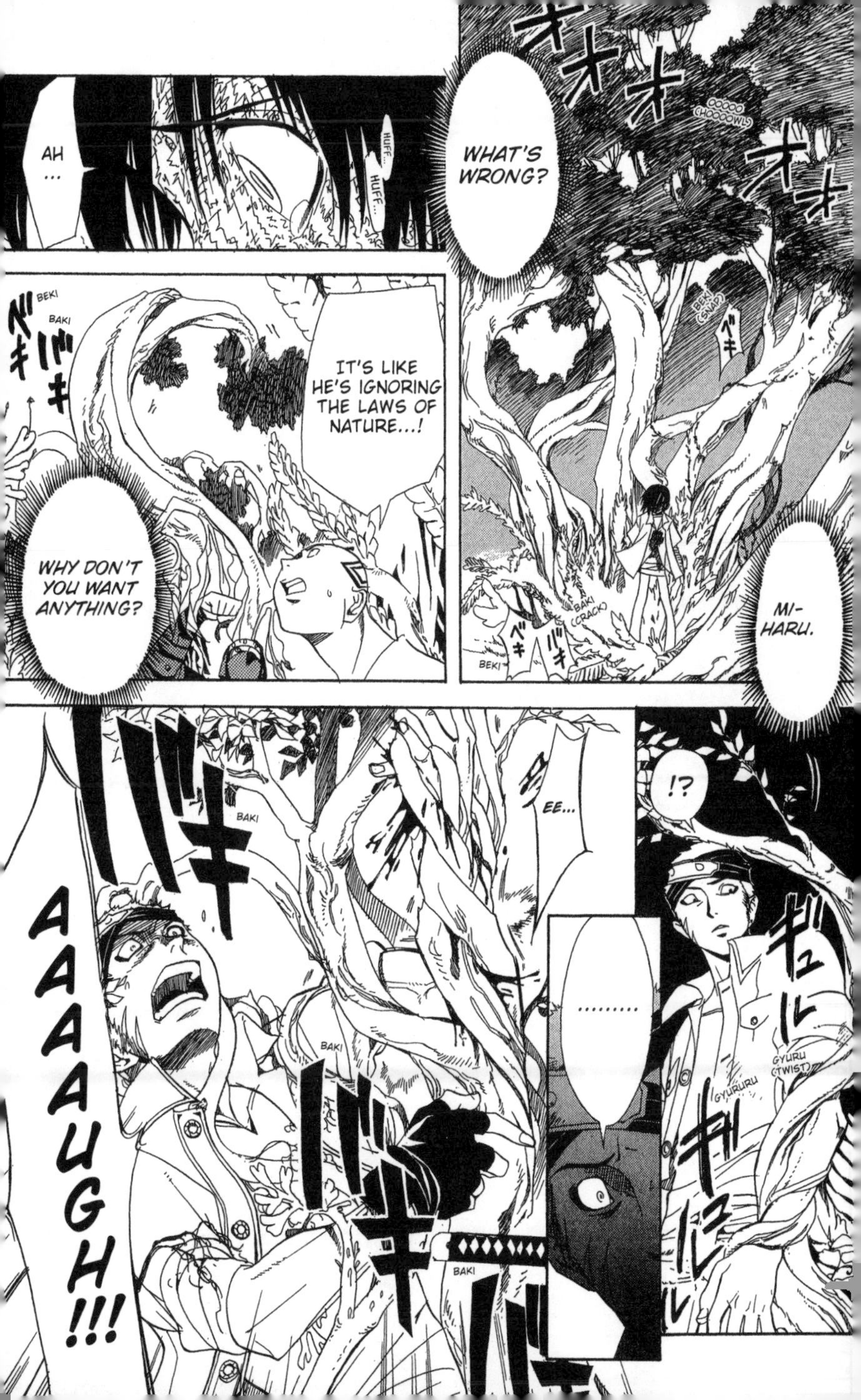
WHAT'S WRONG?
OOOOO (HOOOOWL)
BEKI (SNAP)
BAKI (CRACK)
BEKI
MI-HARU.
AH ...
HUFF... HUFF...
BEKI
BAKI
IT'S LIKE HE'S IGNORING THE LAWS OF NATURE...!
WHY DON'T YOU WANT ANYTHING?
!?
GYURU (TWIST)
GYURURU
....
EE...
BAKI
BAKI
BAKI
AAAAUGH!!!

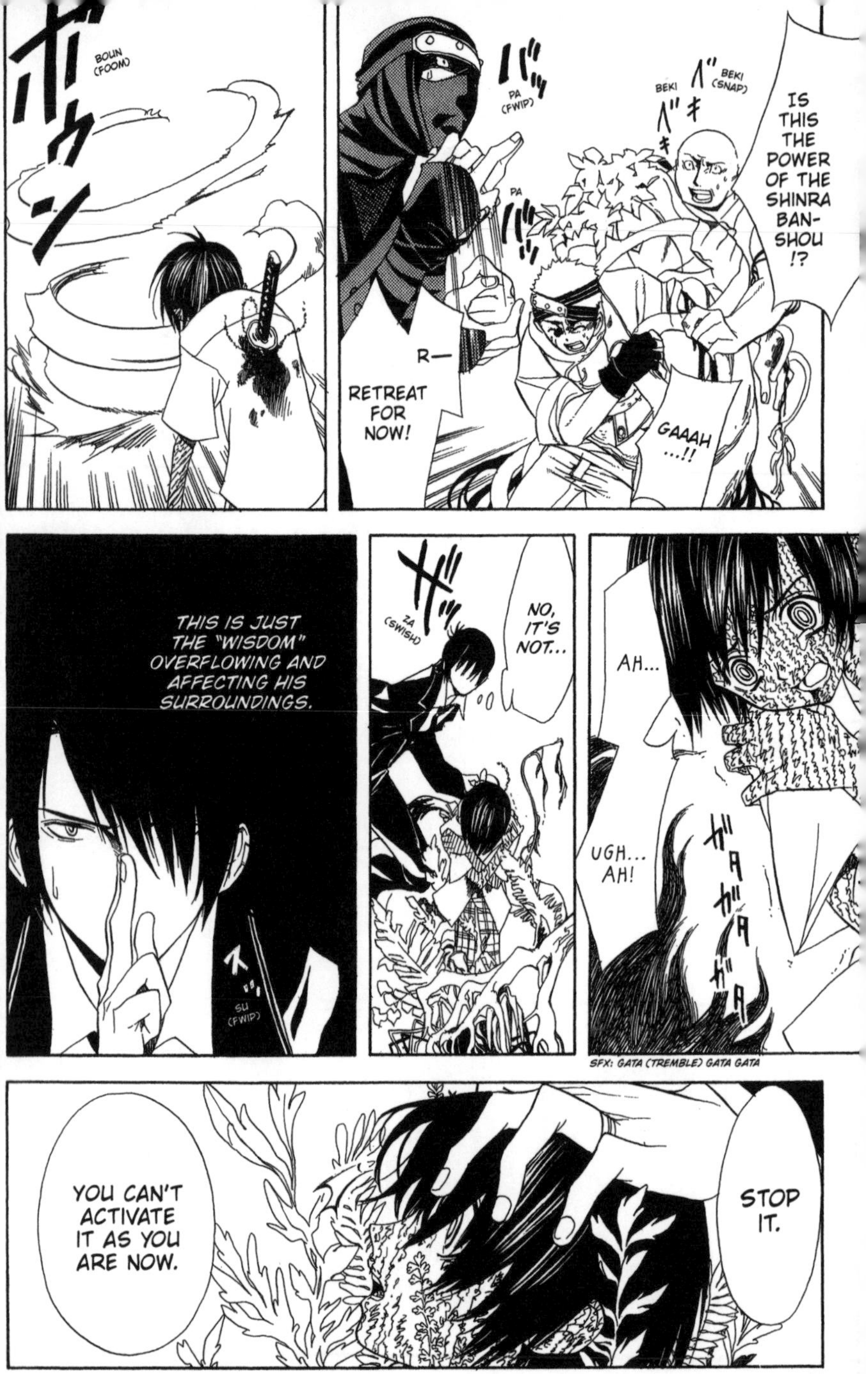
BEKI (SNAP)
BEKI
IS THIS THE POWER OF THE SHINRA BAN-SHOU!?
PA (FWIP)
PA
R—
RETREAT FOR NOW!
GAAAH...!!
BOUN (FOOM)
AH...
UGH... AH!
SFX: GATA (TREMBLE) GATA GATA
NO, IT'S NOT...
ZA (SWISH)
THIS IS JUST THE "WISDOM" OVERFLOWING AND AFFECTING HIS SURROUNDINGS.
SU (FWIP)
STOP IT.
YOU CAN'T ACTIVATE IT AS YOU ARE NOW.

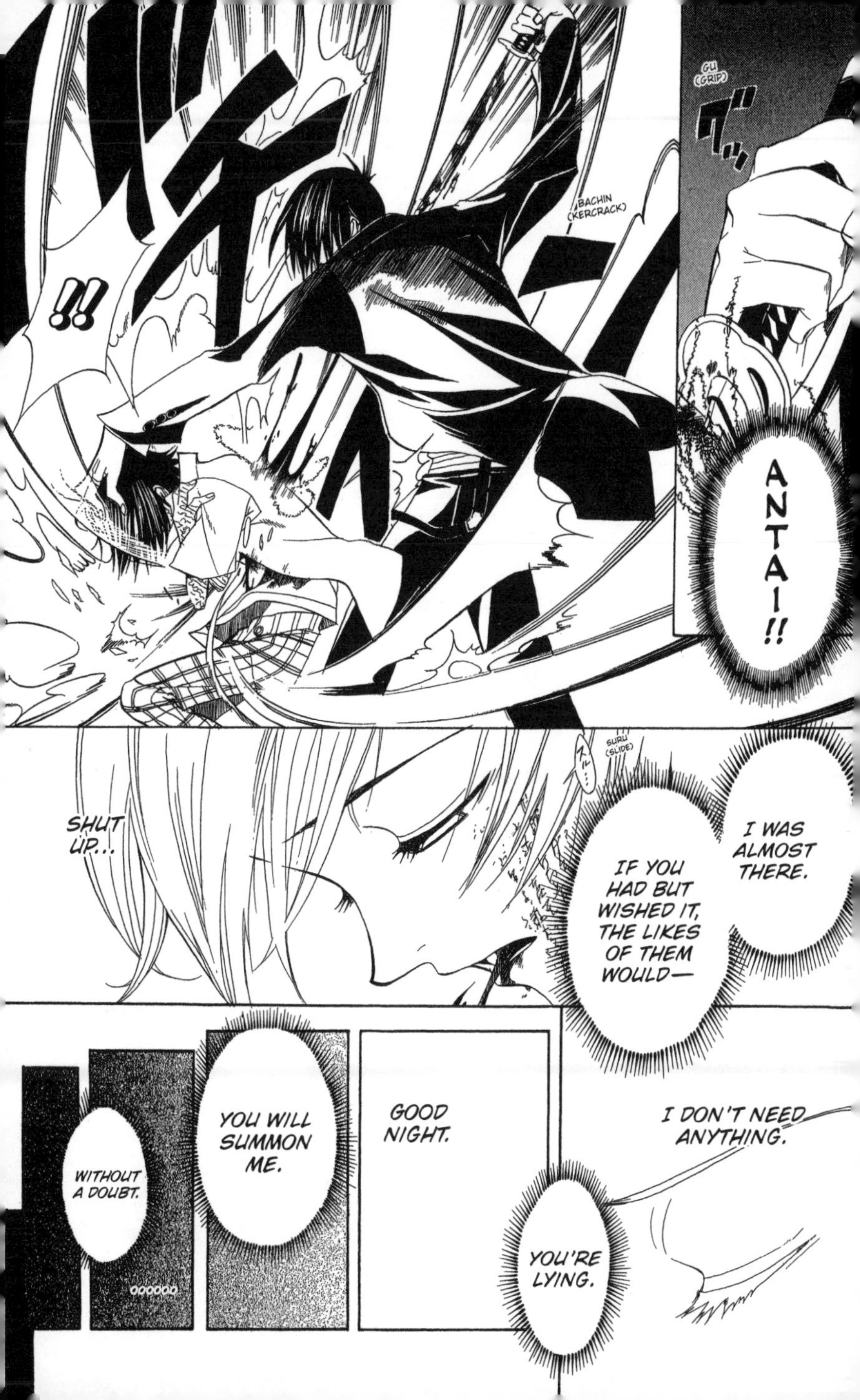
GU (GRIP)
BACHIN (KERCRACK)
ANTAI!!
!!
SURU (SLIDE)
I WAS ALMOST THERE.
IF YOU HAD BUT WISHED IT, THE LIKES OF THEM WOULD—
SHUT UP...
I DON'T NEED ANYTHING.
YOU'RE LYING.
GOOD NIGHT.
YOU WILL SUMMON ME.
WITHOUT A DOUBT.

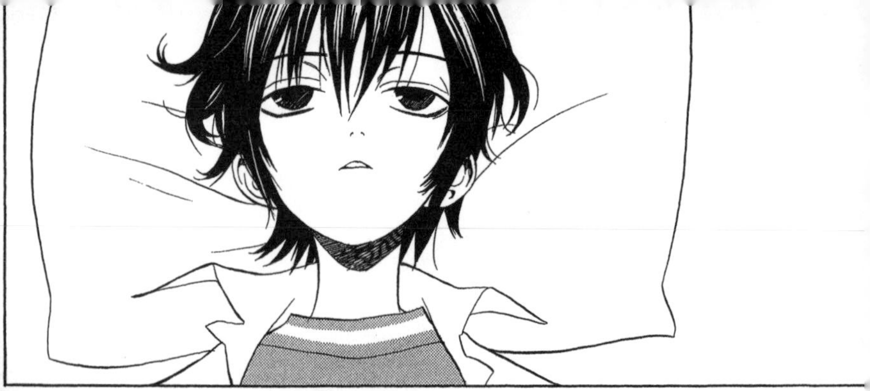

POSTER: BE CAREFUL OF FOOD POISONING

SFX: GAN (SHOCK)

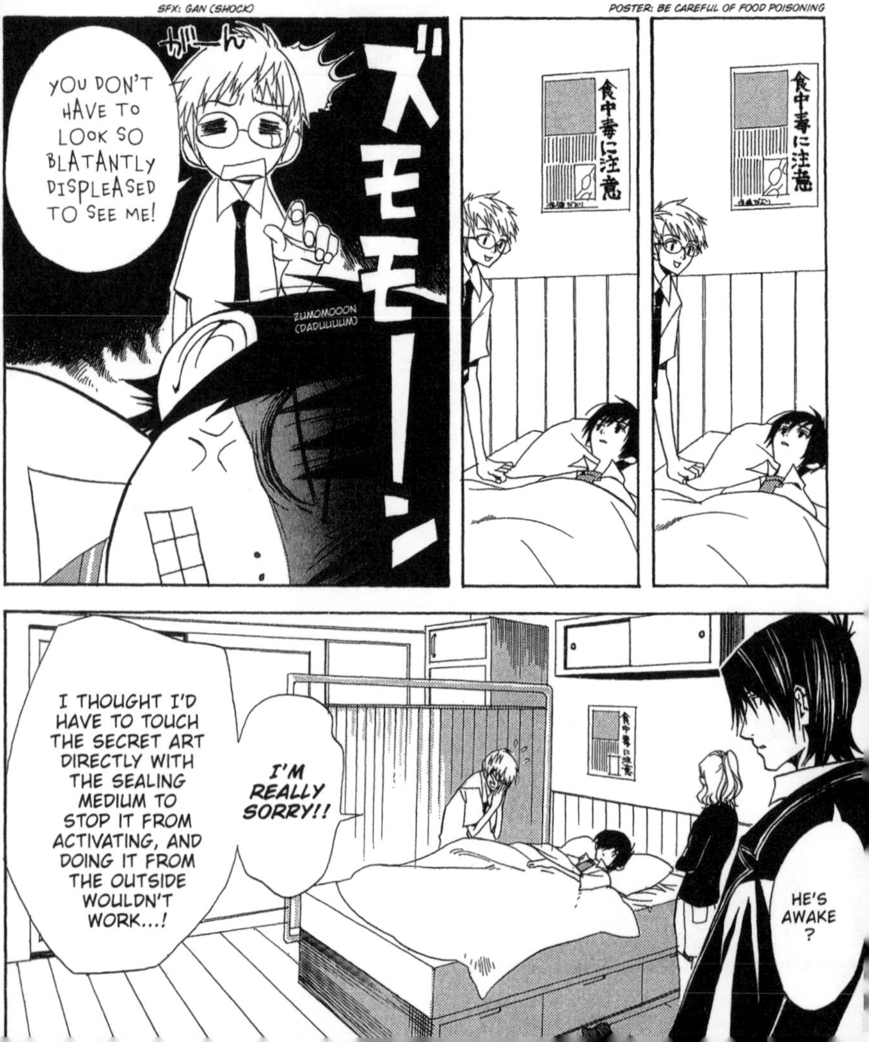
食中毒に注意
食中毒に注意
がーん
YOU DON'T HAVE TO LOOK SO BLATANTLY DISPLEASED TO SEE ME!
ズモモーン
ZUMOMOOON (DADUUUUM)
HE'S AWAKE?
I'M REALLY SORRY!!
I THOUGHT I'D HAVE TO TOUCH THE SECRET ART DIRECTLY WITH THE SEALING MEDIUM TO STOP IT FROM ACTIVATING, AND DOING IT FROM THE OUTSIDE WOULDN'T WORK...!

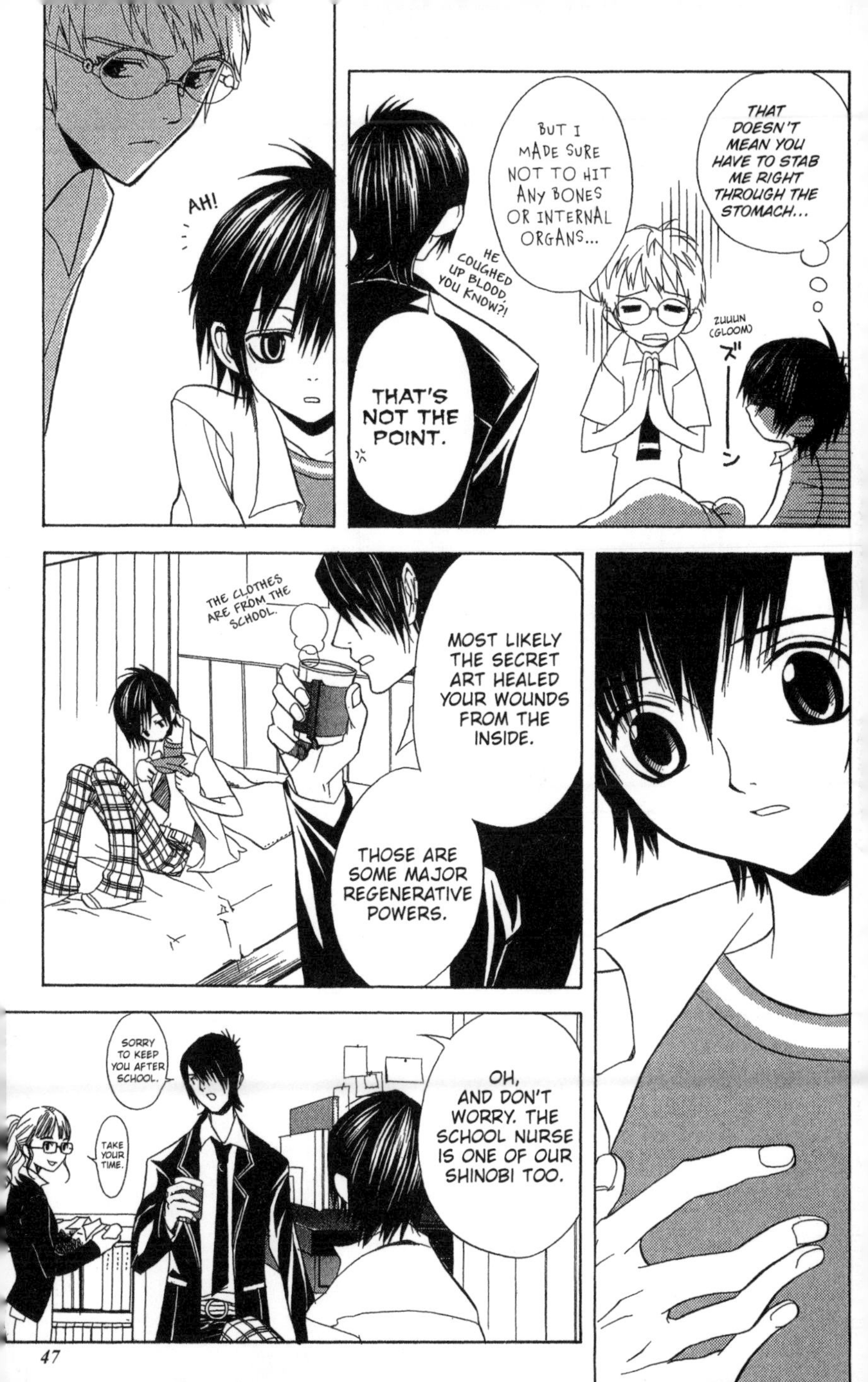
THAT DOESN'T MEAN YOU HAVE TO STAB ME RIGHT THROUGH THE STOMACH...
ZUUUN (GLOOM)
ズーーン
BUT I MADE SURE NOT TO HIT ANY BONES OR INTERNAL ORGANS...
HE COUGHED UP BLOOD, YOU KNOW?!
THAT'S NOT THE POINT.
AH!
MOST LIKELY THE SECRET ART HEALED YOUR WOUNDS FROM THE INSIDE.
THOSE ARE SOME MAJOR REGENERATIVE POWERS.
THE CLOTHES ARE FROM THE SCHOOL.
OH, AND DON'T WORRY. THE SCHOOL NURSE IS ONE OF OUR SHINOBI TOO.
SORRY TO KEEP YOU AFTER SCHOOL.
TAKE YOUR TIME.

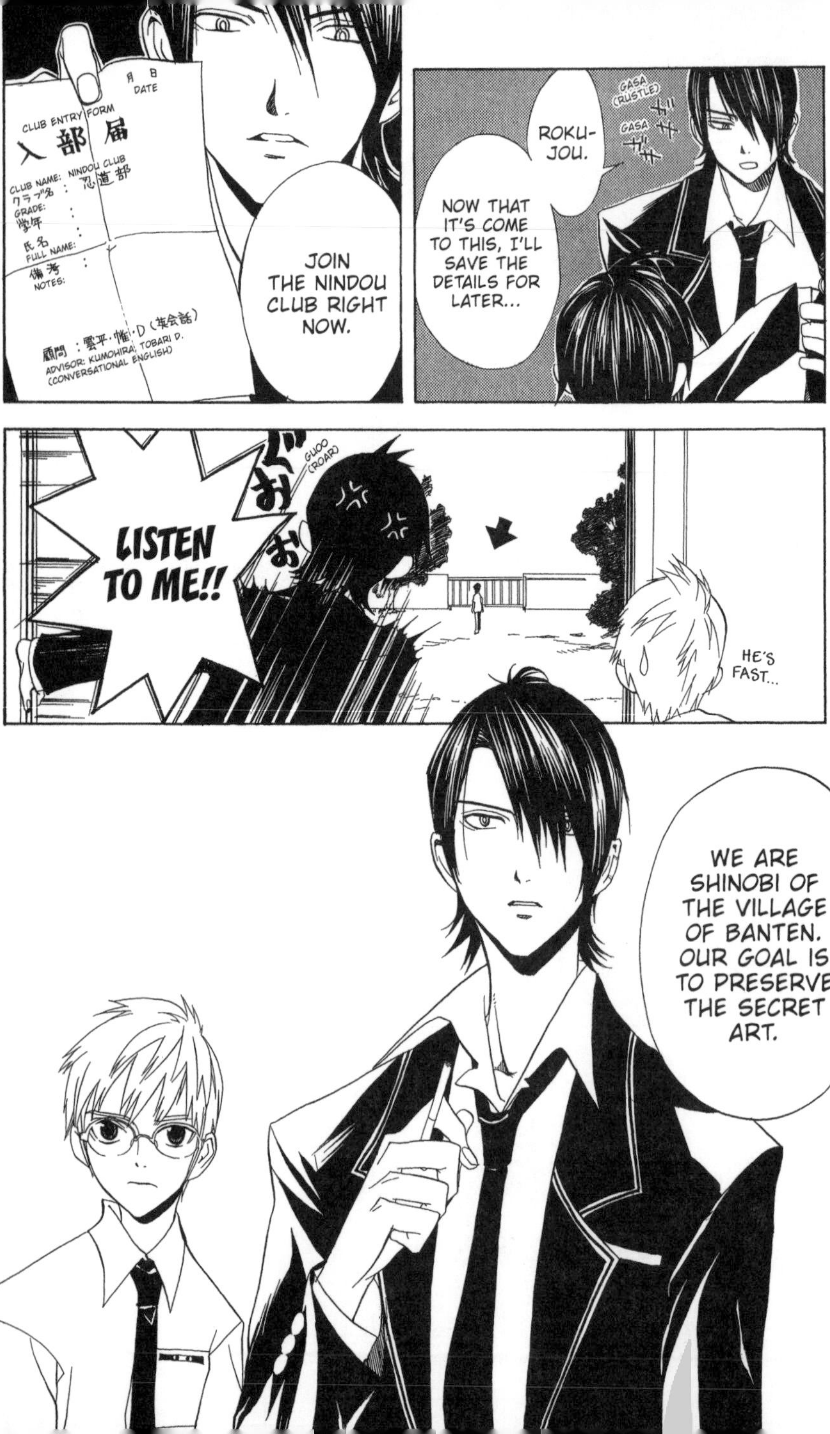
ROKU-JOU.
GASA (RUSTLE)
GASA
NOW THAT IT'S COME TO THIS, I'LL SAVE THE DETAILS FOR LATER...
月 日 DATE
CLUB ENTRY FORM
入部届
CLUB NAME: NINDOU CLUB
クラブ名：忍道部
GRADE:
学年：
氏名
FULL NAME:
備考
NOTES:
顧問：雲平・帷・D（英会話）
ADVISOR: KUMOHIRA, TOBARI D. (CONVERSATIONAL ENGLISH)
JOIN THE NINDOU CLUB RIGHT NOW.
HE'S FAST...
GUOO (ROAR)
LISTEN TO ME!!
WE ARE SHINOBI OF THE VILLAGE OF BANTEN. OUR GOAL IS TO PRESERVE THE SECRET ART.

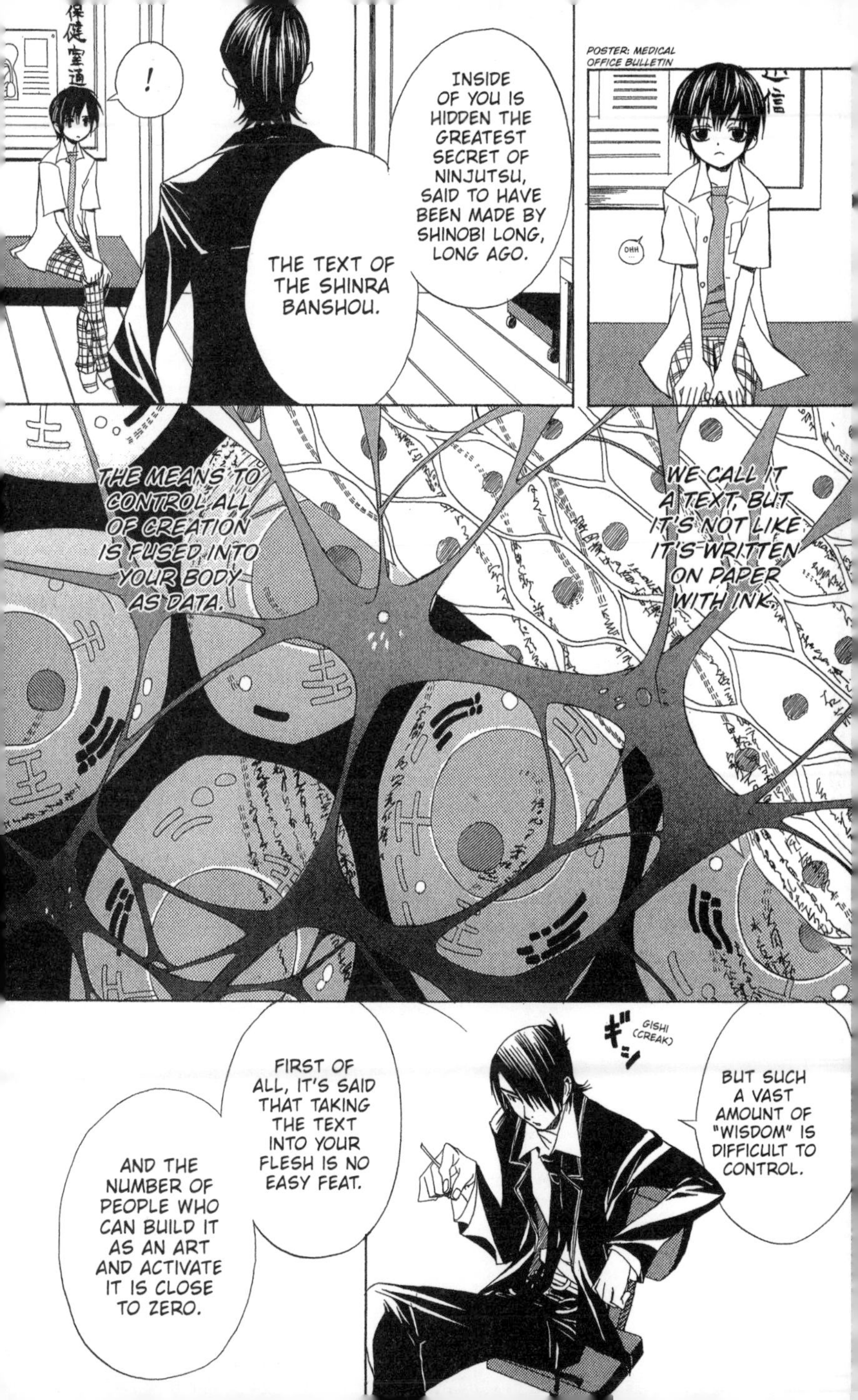

POSTER: MEDICAL OFFICE BULLETIN
OHH...
INSIDE OF YOU IS HIDDEN THE GREATEST SECRET OF NINJUTSU, SAID TO HAVE BEEN MADE BY SHINOBI LONG, LONG AGO.
THE TEXT OF THE SHINRA BANSHOU.
!
WE CALL IT A TEXT, BUT IT'S NOT LIKE IT'S WRITTEN ON PAPER WITH INK.
THE MEANS TO CONTROL ALL OF CREATION IS FUSED INTO YOUR BODY AS DATA.
GISHI (CREAK)
BUT SUCH A VAST AMOUNT OF "WISDOM" IS DIFFICULT TO CONTROL.
FIRST OF ALL, IT'S SAID THAT TAKING THE TEXT INTO YOUR FLESH IS NO EASY FEAT.
AND THE NUMBER OF PEOPLE WHO CAN BUILD IT AS AN ART AND ACTIVATE IT IS CLOSE TO ZERO.

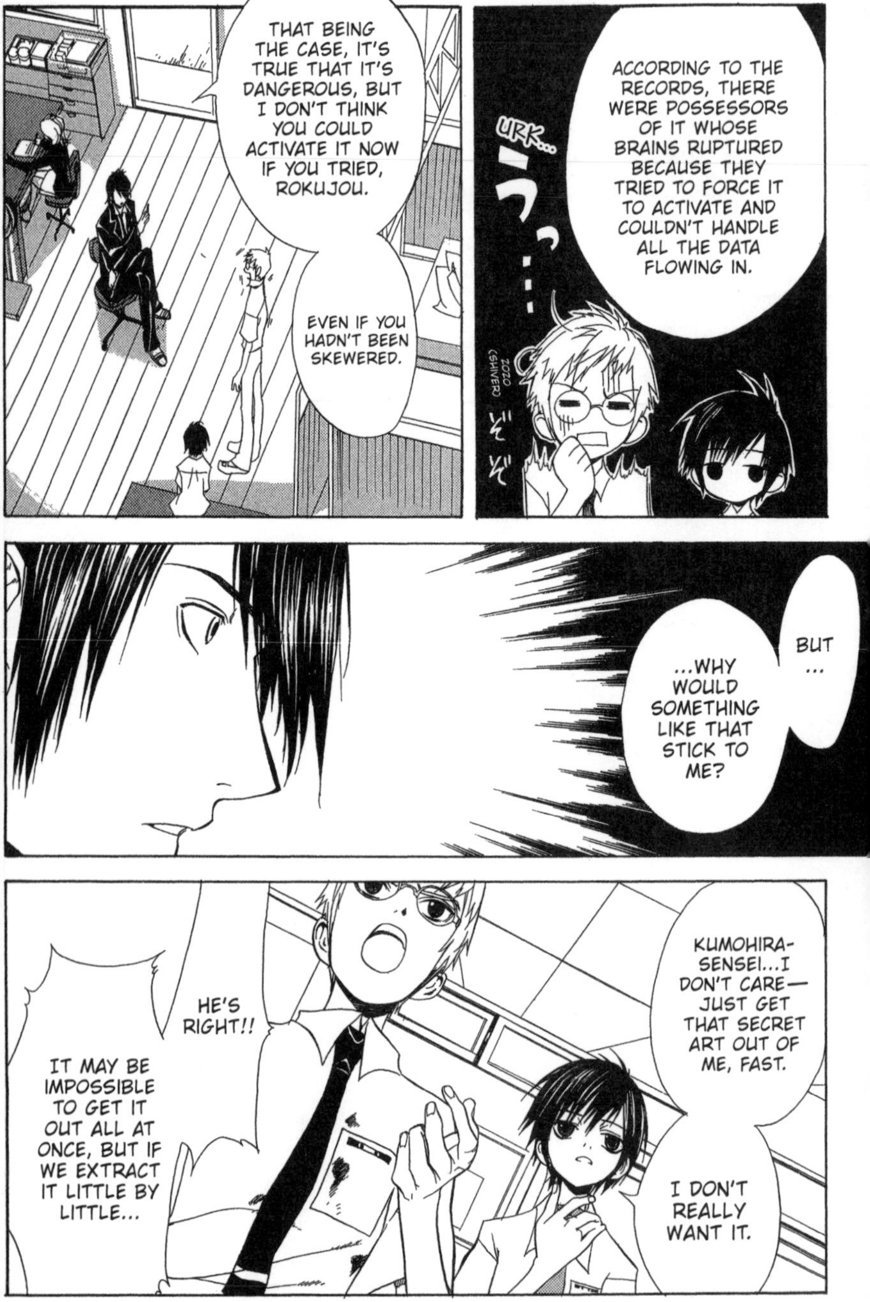
ACCORDING TO THE RECORDS, THERE WERE POSSESSORS OF IT WHOSE BRAINS RUPTURED BECAUSE THEY TRIED TO FORCE IT TO ACTIVATE AND COULDN'T HANDLE ALL THE DATA FLOWING IN.
URK...
うっ…
ZOZO (SHIVER)
ぞぞ
THAT BEING THE CASE, IT'S TRUE THAT IT'S DANGEROUS, BUT I DON'T THINK YOU COULD ACTIVATE IT NOW IF YOU TRIED, ROKUJOU.
EVEN IF YOU HADN'T BEEN SKEWERED.
BUT ...
...WHY WOULD SOMETHING LIKE THAT STICK TO ME?
KUMOHIRA-SENSEI...I DON'T CARE—JUST GET THAT SECRET ART OUT OF ME, FAST.
I DON'T REALLY WANT IT.
HE'S RIGHT!!
IT MAY BE IMPOSSIBLE TO GET IT OUT ALL AT ONCE, BUT IF WE EXTRACT IT LITTLE BY LITTLE...

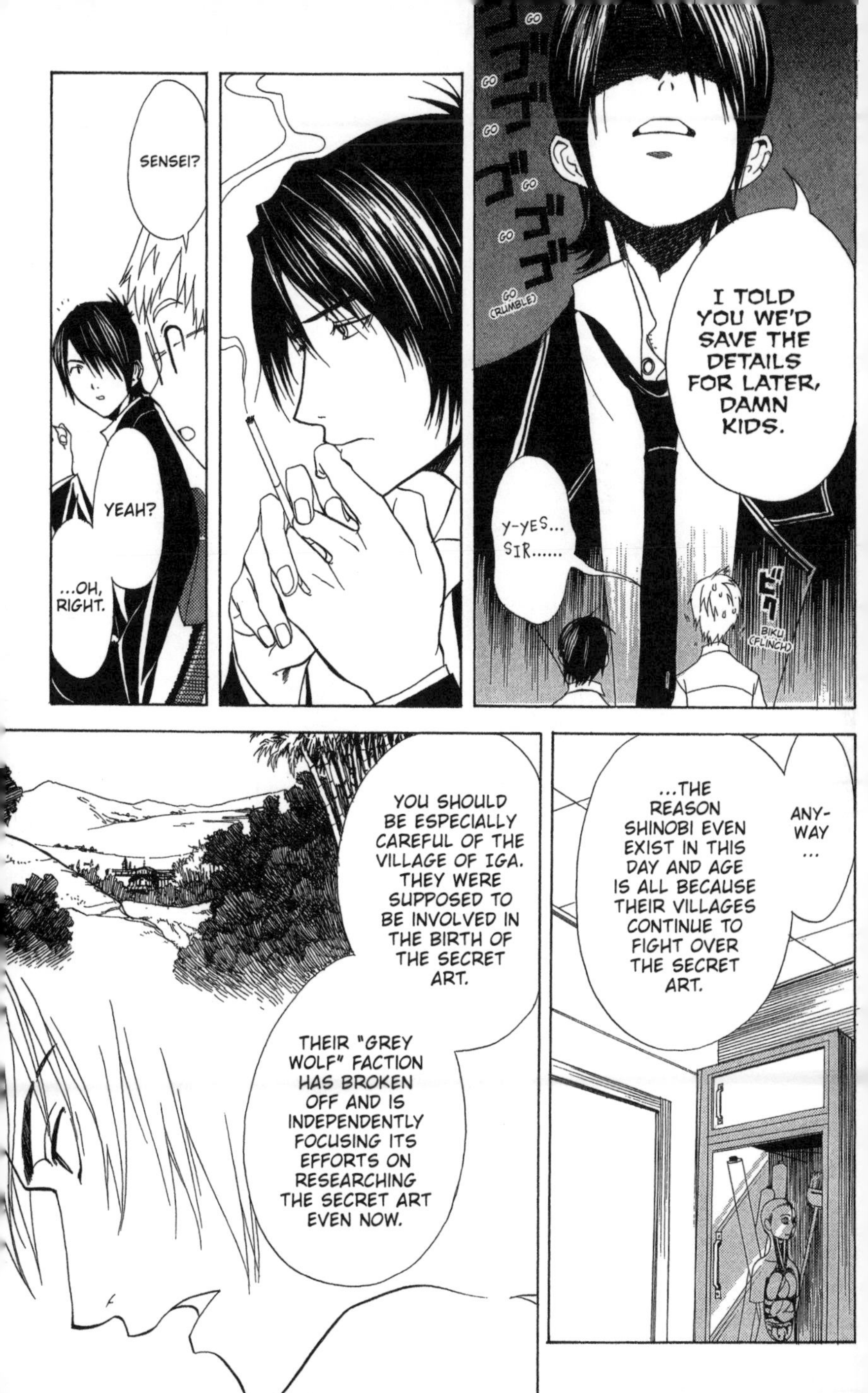
I TOLD YOU WE'D SAVE THE DETAILS FOR LATER, DAMN KIDS.
GO GO GO GO GO GO (RUMBLE)
BIKU (FLINCH)
Y-YES... SIR......
SENSEI?
YEAH?
...OH, RIGHT.
ANY-WAY ...
...THE REASON SHINOBI EVEN EXIST IN THIS DAY AND AGE IS ALL BECAUSE THEIR VILLAGES CONTINUE TO FIGHT OVER THE SECRET ART.
YOU SHOULD BE ESPECIALLY CAREFUL OF THE VILLAGE OF IGA. THEY WERE SUPPOSED TO BE INVOLVED IN THE BIRTH OF THE SECRET ART.
THEIR "GREY WOLF" FACTION HAS BROKEN OFF AND IS INDEPENDENTLY FOCUSING ITS EFFORTS ON RESEARCHING THE SECRET ART EVEN NOW.

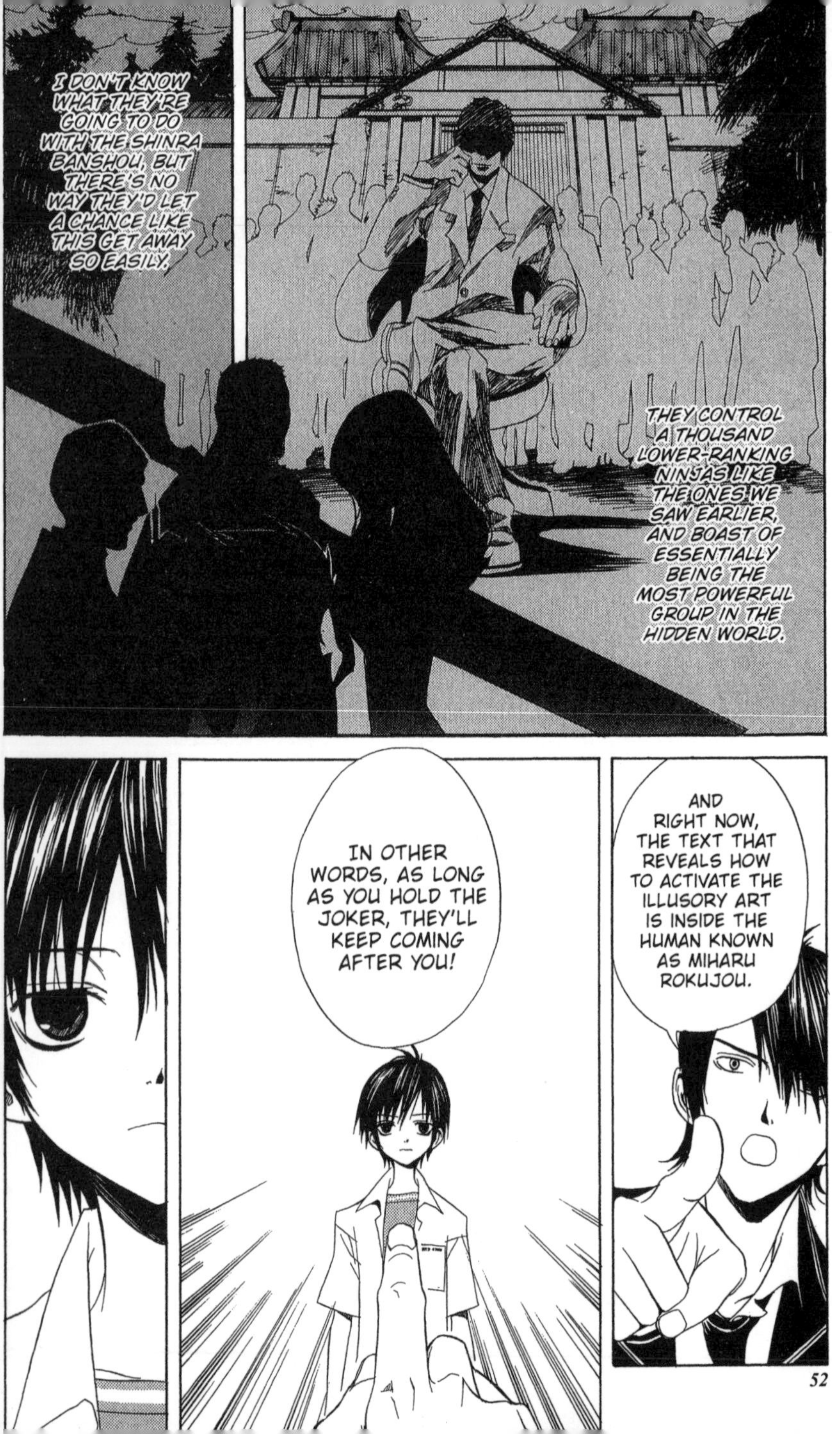
THEY CONTROL A THOUSAND LOWER-RANKING NINJAS LIKE THE ONES WE SAW EARLIER, AND BOAST OF ESSENTIALLY BEING THE MOST POWERFUL GROUP IN THE HIDDEN WORLD.
I DON'T KNOW WHAT THEY'RE GOING TO DO WITH THE SHINRA BANSHOU, BUT THERE'S NO WAY THEY'D LET A CHANCE LIKE THIS GET AWAY SO EASILY.
AND RIGHT NOW, THE TEXT THAT REVEALS HOW TO ACTIVATE THE ILLUSORY ART IS INSIDE THE HUMAN KNOWN AS MIHARU ROKUJOU.
IN OTHER WORDS, AS LONG AS YOU HOLD THE JOKER, THEY'LL KEEP COMING AFTER YOU!

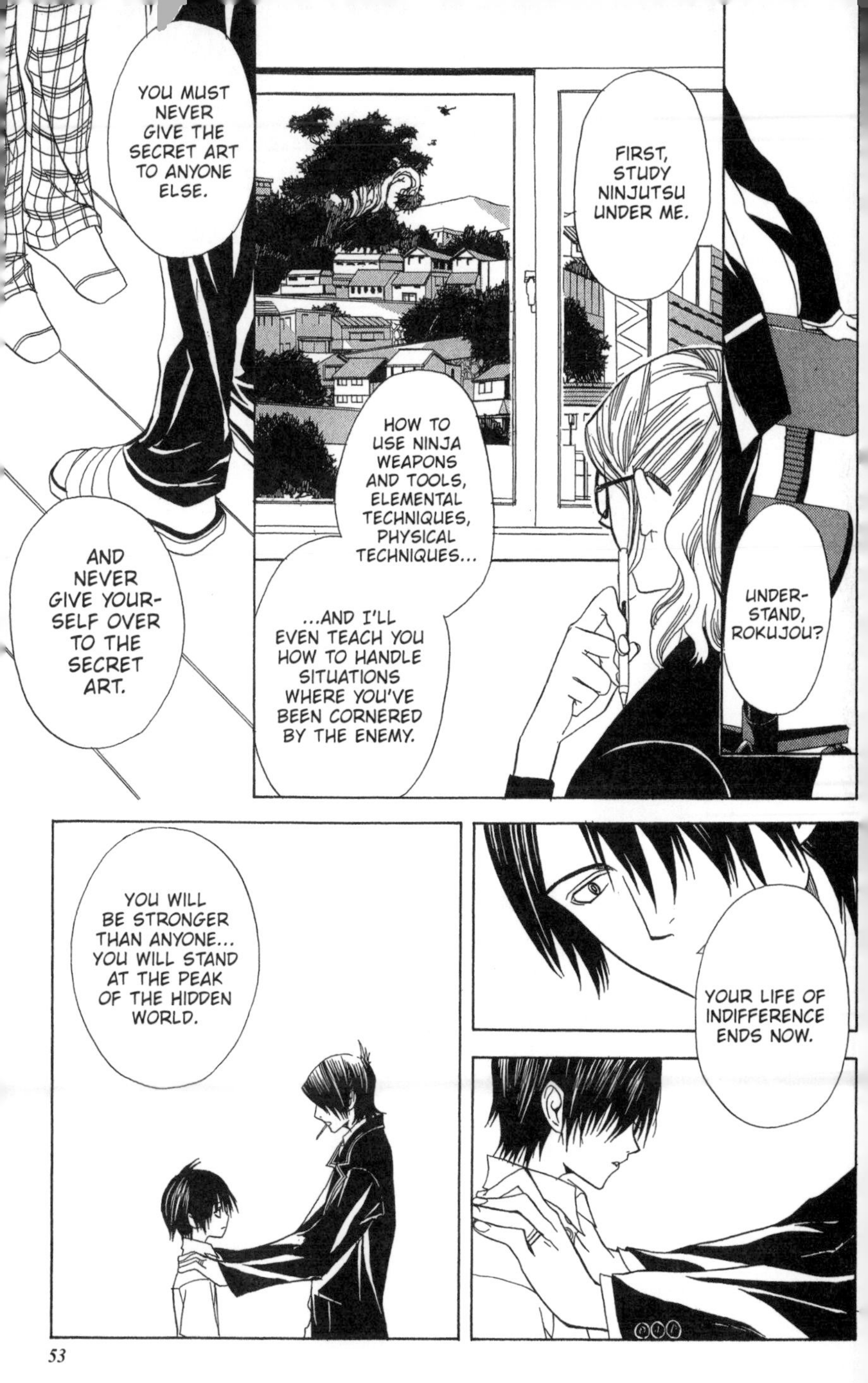
FIRST, STUDY NINJUTSU UNDER ME.
HOW TO USE NINJA WEAPONS AND TOOLS, ELEMENTAL TECHNIQUES, PHYSICAL TECHNIQUES...
...AND I'LL EVEN TEACH YOU HOW TO HANDLE SITUATIONS WHERE YOU'VE BEEN CORNERED BY THE ENEMY.
UNDER-STAND, ROKUJOU?
YOU MUST NEVER GIVE THE SECRET ART TO ANYONE ELSE.
AND NEVER GIVE YOUR-SELF OVER TO THE SECRET ART.
YOUR LIFE OF INDIFFERENCE ENDS NOW.
YOU WILL BE STRONGER THAN ANYONE... YOU WILL STAND AT THE PEAK OF THE HIDDEN WORLD.

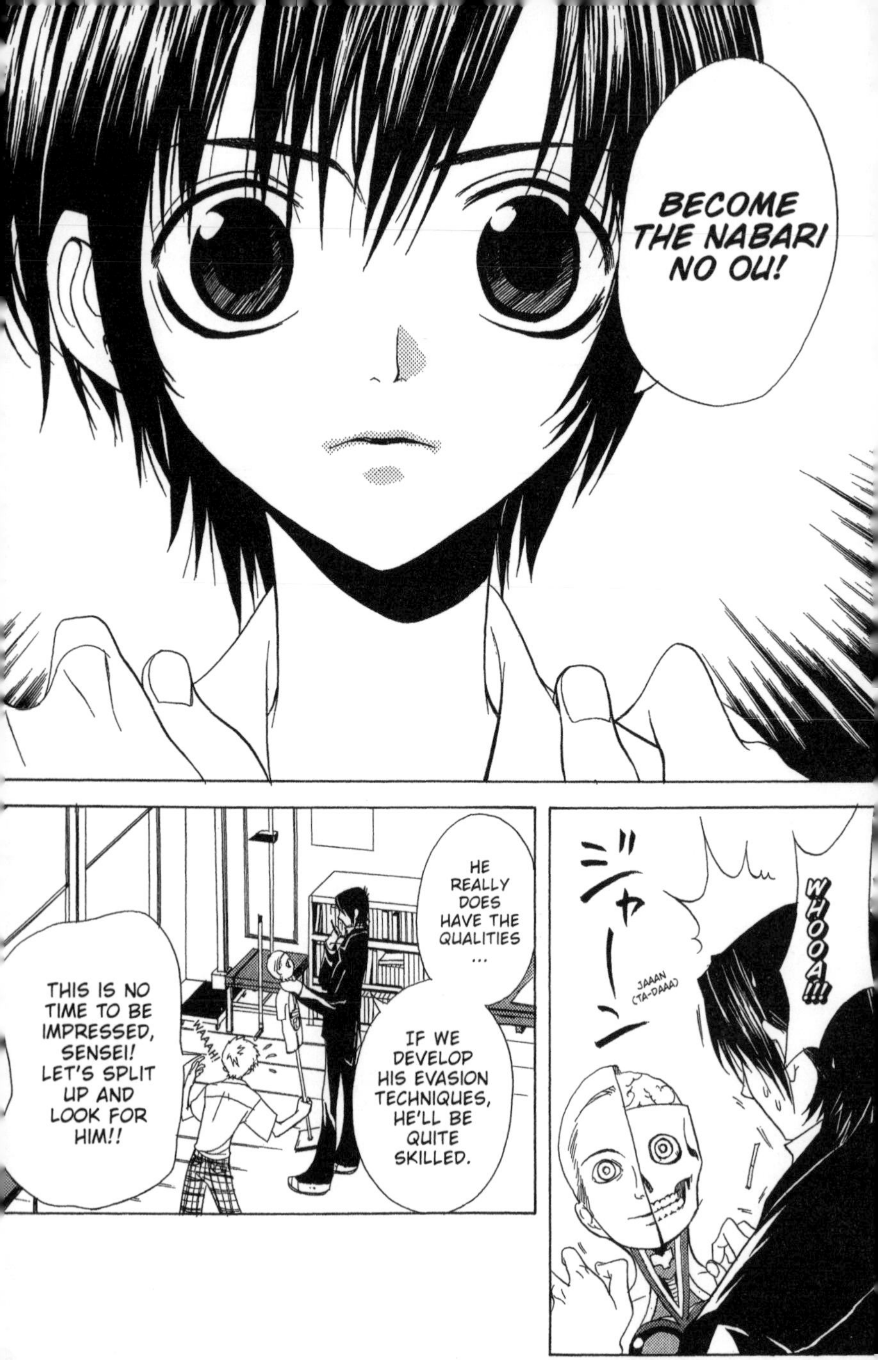
BECOME THE NABARI NO OU!
WHOOA!!!
ジャーン
JAAAN (TA-DAAA)
HE REALLY DOES HAVE THE QUALITIES ...
IF WE DEVELOP HIS EVASION TECHNIQUES, HE'LL BE QUITE SKILLED.
WAAAH!
THIS IS NO TIME TO BE IMPRESSED, SENSEI! LET'S SPLIT UP AND LOOK FOR HIM!!

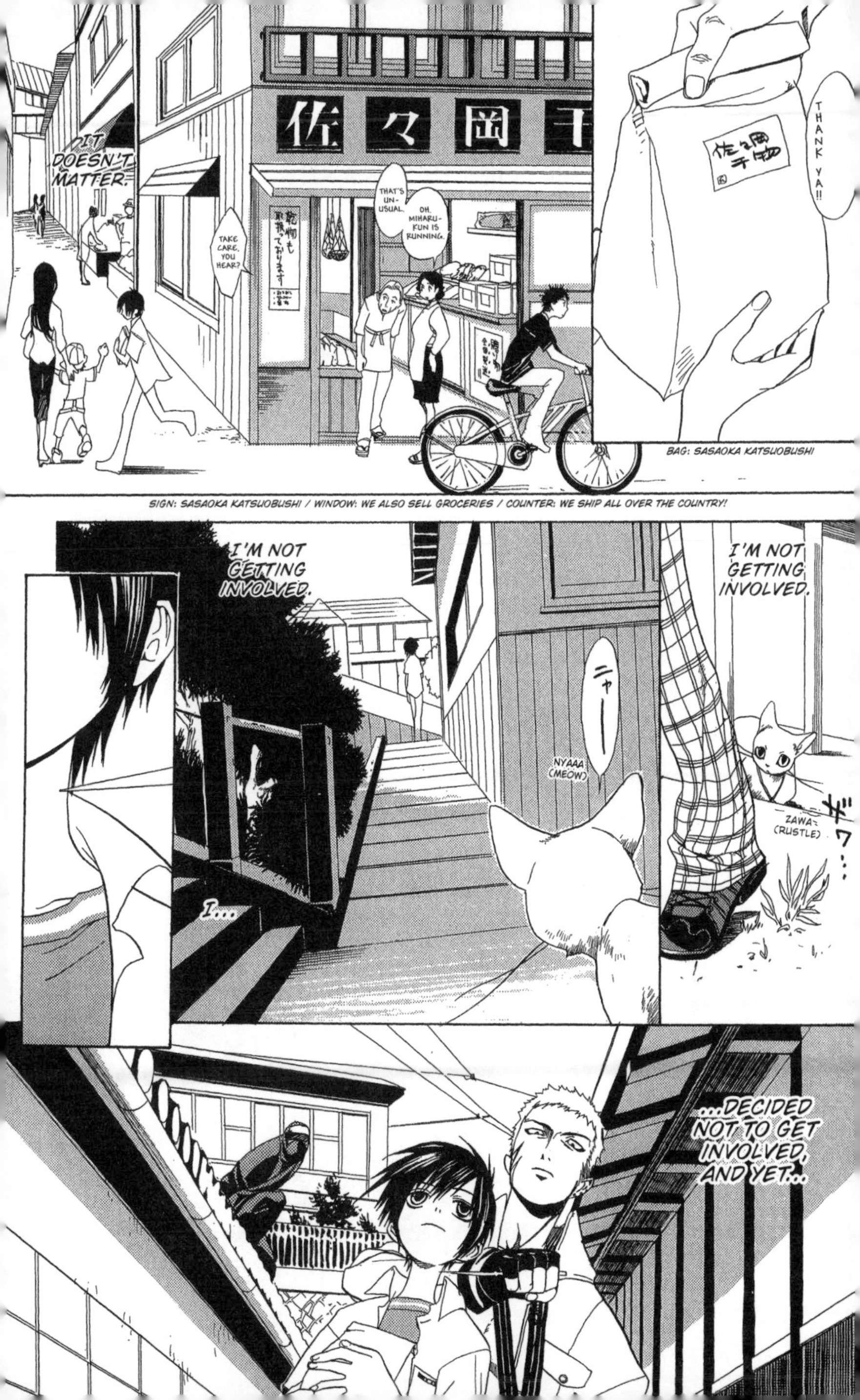
THANK YA!!
佐々岡干物
BAG: SASAOKA KATSUOBUSHI
佐々岡干
OH. MIHARU-KUN IS RUNNING.
THAT'S UN-USUAL.
TAKE CARE, YOU HEAR?
IT DOESN'T MATTER.
SIGN: SASAOKA KATSUOBUSHI / WINDOW: WE ALSO SELL GROCERIES / COUNTER: WE SHIP ALL OVER THE COUNTRY!
I'M NOT GETTING INVOLVED.
ザワ…
ZAWA (RUSTLE)
I'M NOT GETTING INVOLVED.
ニャー
NYAAA (MEOW)
I...
...DECIDED NOT TO GET INVOLVED, AND YET...

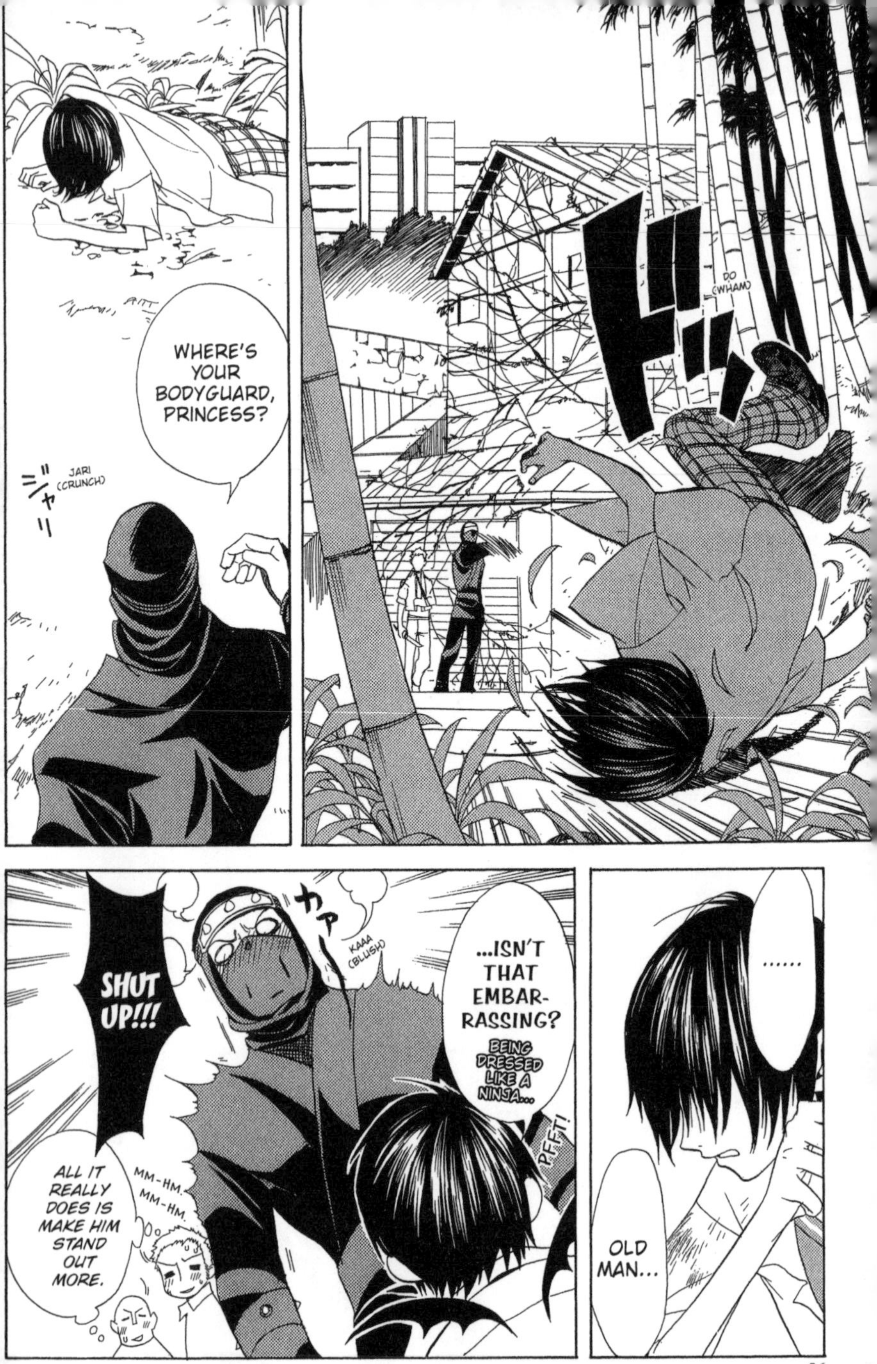
ドッ
DO (WHAM)
WHERE'S YOUR BODYGUARD, PRINCESS?
ジャリ
JARI (CRUNCH)
......
OLD MAN...
カァー
KAAA (BLUSH)
...ISN'T THAT EMBARRASSING?
BEING DRESSED LIKE A NINJA...
PFFT!
SHUT UP!!!
MM-HM. MM-HM.
ALL IT REALLY DOES IS MAKE HIM STAND OUT MORE.

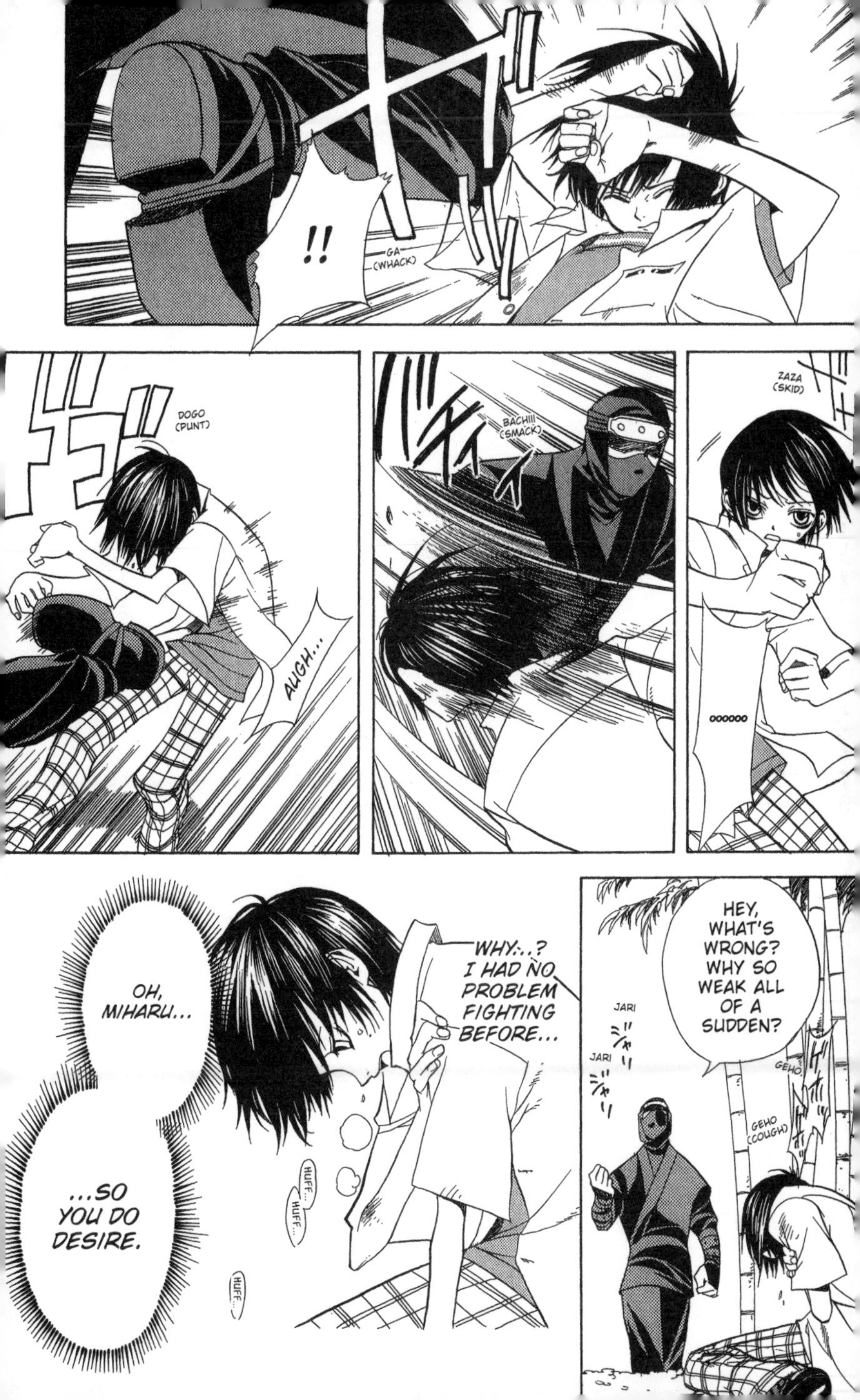
!!
GA (WHACK)
ZAZA (SKID)
......
BACHIII (SMACK)
DOGO (PUNT)
AUGH...
HEY, WHAT'S WRONG? WHY SO WEAK ALL OF A SUDDEN?
JARI
JARI
GEHO
GEHO (COUGH)
WHY...? I HAD NO PROBLEM FIGHTING BEFORE...
HUFF...
HUFF...
HUFF...
OH, MIHARU...
...SO YOU DO DESIRE.

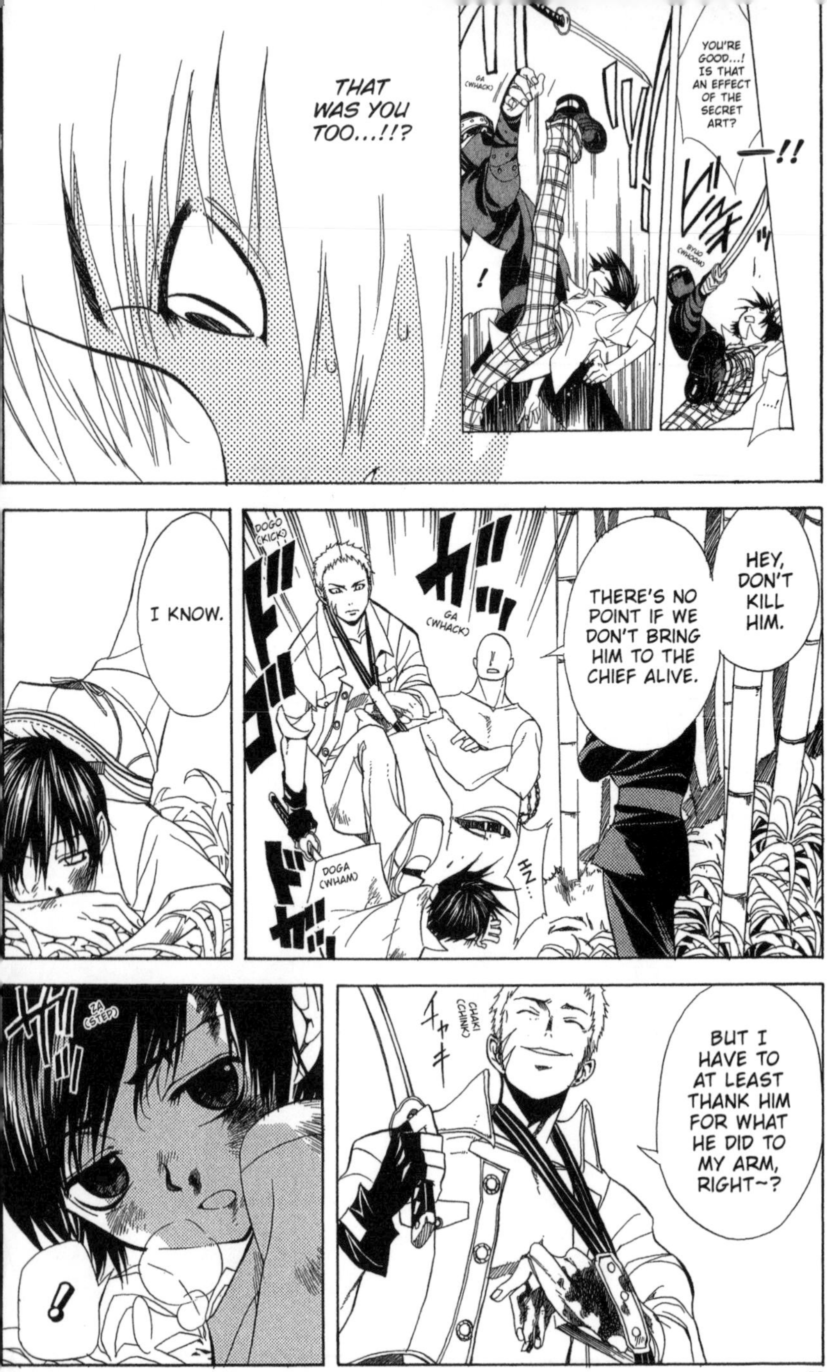
YOU'RE GOOD...! IS THAT AN EFFECT OF THE SECRET ART?
—!!
BYUO (WHOOM)
...!
GA (WHACK)
!
THAT WAS YOU TOO...!!?
HEY, DON'T KILL HIM.
THERE'S NO POINT IF WE DON'T BRING HIM TO THE CHIEF ALIVE.
DOGO (KICK)
GA (WHACK)
DOGA (WHAM)
HN...
I KNOW.
CHAKI (CHINK)
BUT I HAVE TO AT LEAST THANK HIM FOR WHAT HE DID TO MY ARM, RIGHT~?
ZA (STEP)
!

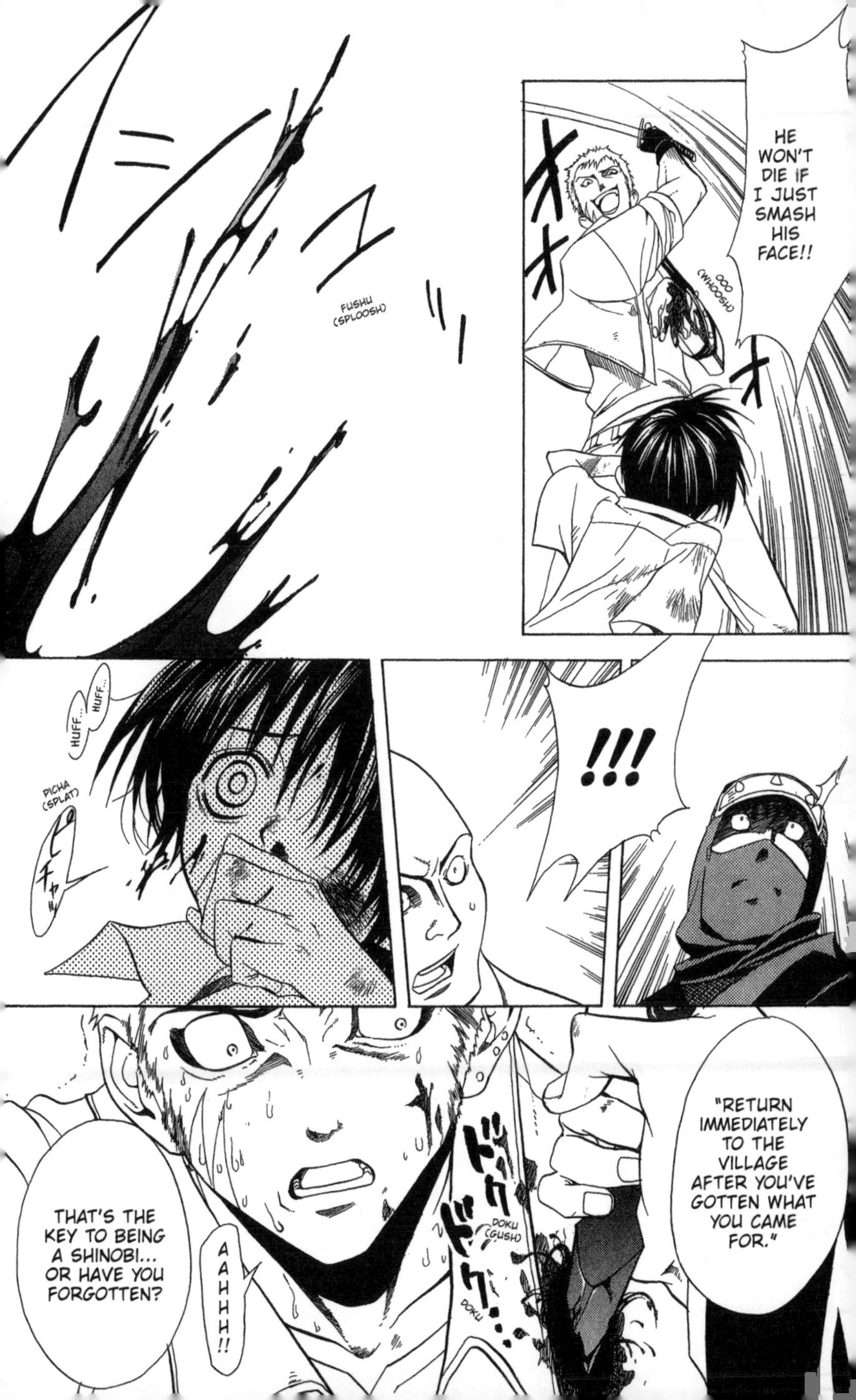
HE WON'T DIE IF I JUST SMASH HIS FACE!!
OOO (WHOOSH)
FUSHU (SPLOOSH)
!!!
HUFF... HUFF...
PICHA (SPLAT)
"RETURN IMMEDIATELY TO THE VILLAGE AFTER YOU'VE GOTTEN WHAT YOU CAME FOR."
DOKU (GUSH)
DOKU
AAHHH!!
THAT'S THE KEY TO BEING A SHINOBI... OR HAVE YOU FORGOTTEN?

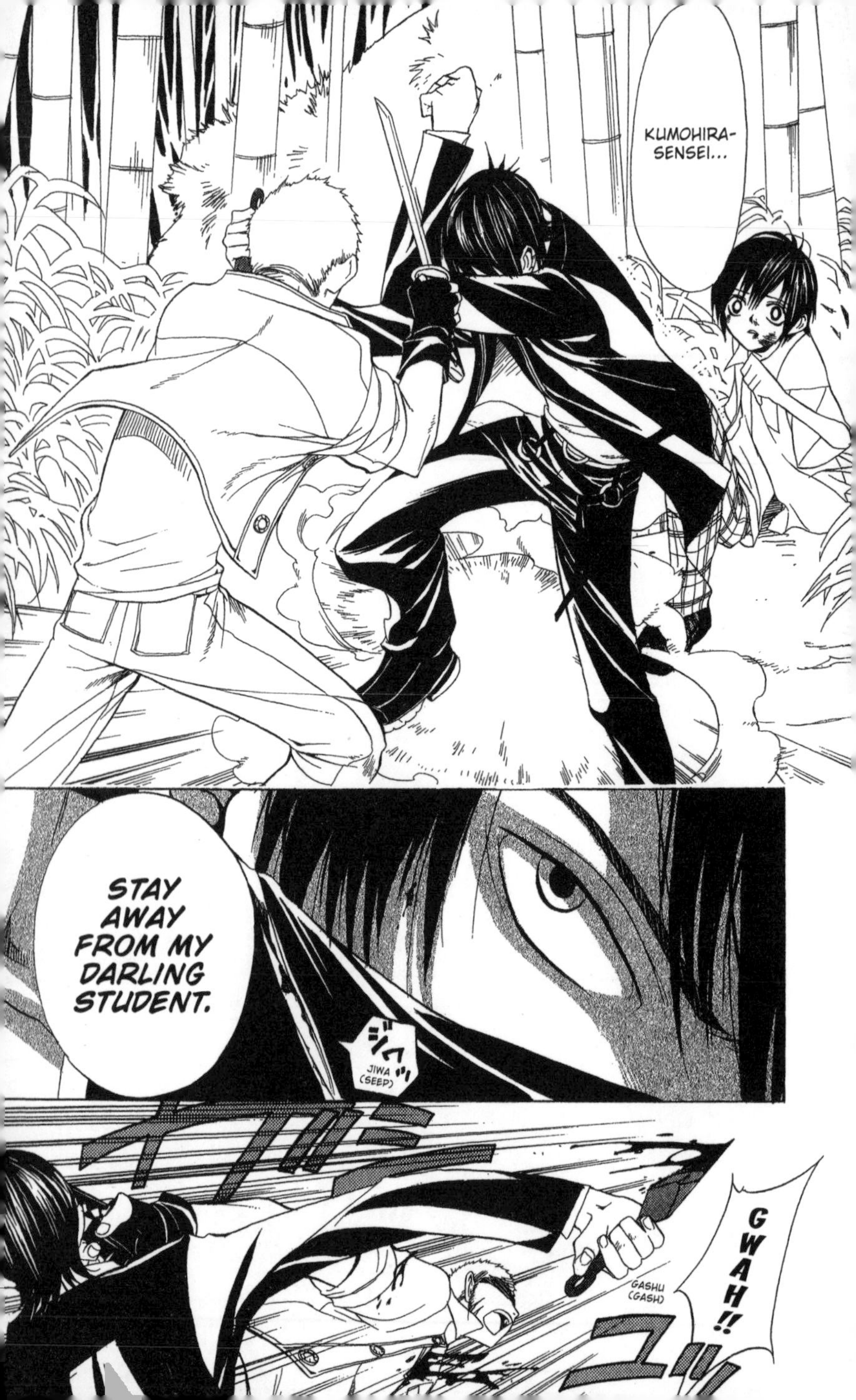
KUMOHIRA-SENSEI...
STAY AWAY FROM MY DARLING STUDENT.
JIWA (SEEP)
GWAH!!
GASHU (GASH)

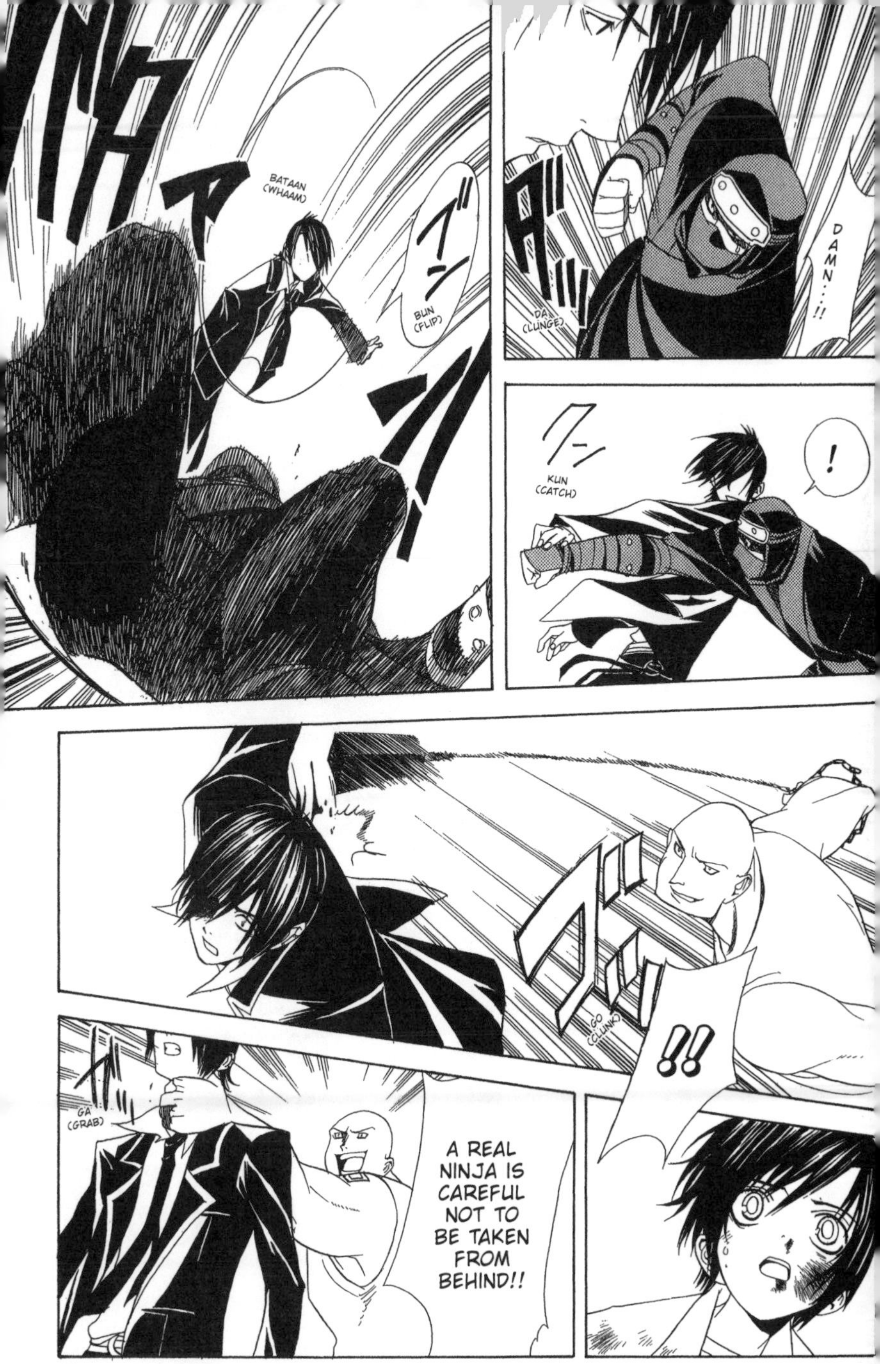
DA (LUNGE)
DAMN...!!
KUN (CATCH)
!
BATAAN (WHAAM)
BUN (FLIP)
GO (CLUNK)
!!
GA (GRAB)
A REAL NINJA IS CAREFUL NOT TO BE TAKEN FROM BEHIND!!

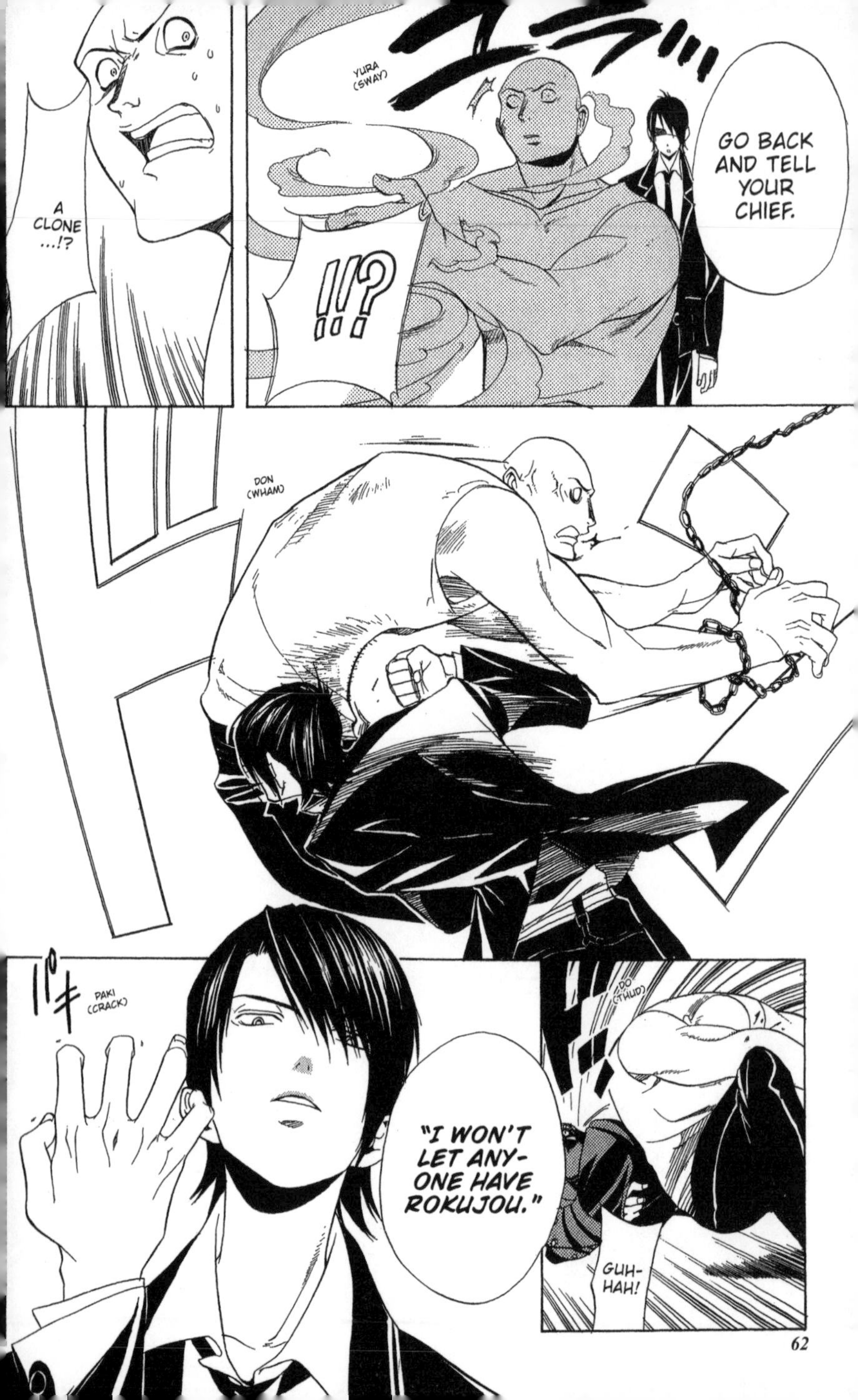
YURA (SWAY)
GO BACK AND TELL YOUR CHIEF.
!!?
A CLONE ...!?
DON (WHAM)
DO (THUD)
GUH-HAH!
PAKI (CRACK)
"I WON'T LET ANY-ONE HAVE ROKUJOU."

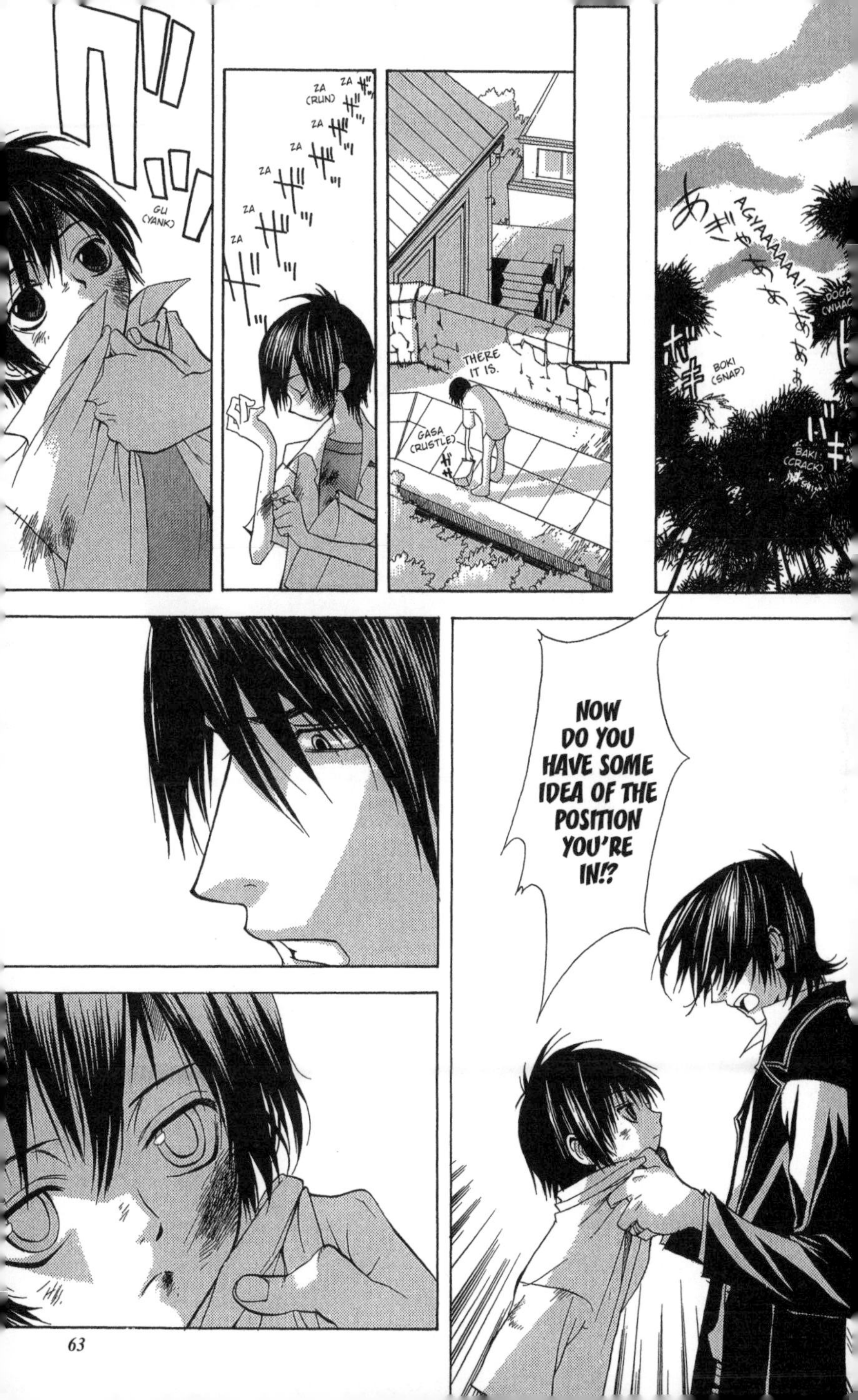
AGYAAAAAA!
DOGA
BOKI (SNAP)
BAKI (CRACK)
THERE IT IS.
GASA (RUSTLE)
ZA (RUN)
GU (YANK)
NOW DO YOU HAVE SOME IDEA OF THE POSITION YOU'RE IN!?

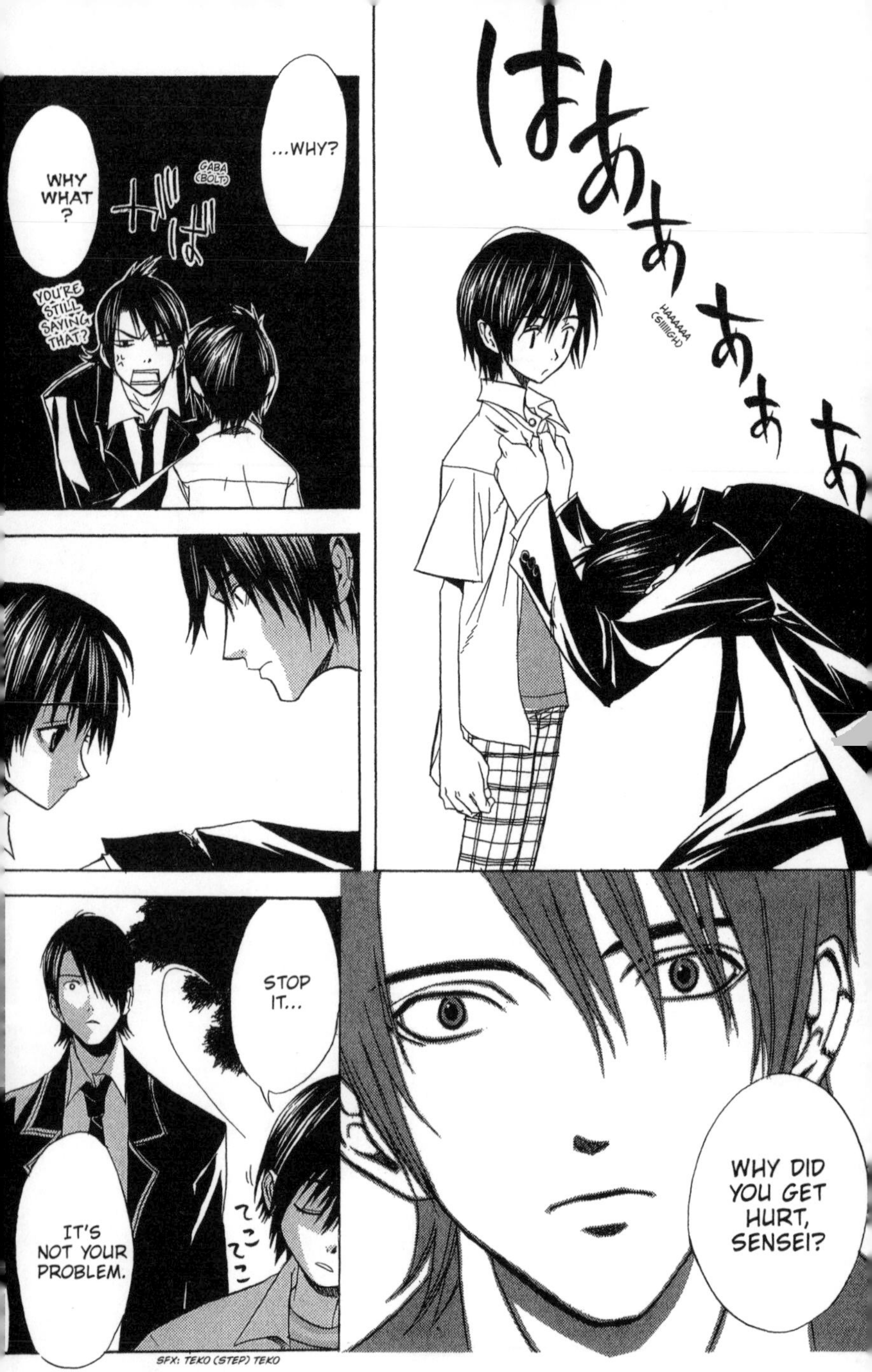
はあああぁぁあ
HAAAAAA (SIIIIGH)
...WHY?
GABA (BOLT)
がば
WHY WHAT?
YOU'RE STILL SAYING THAT?
WHY DID YOU GET HURT, SENSEI?
STOP IT...
てこてこ
IT'S NOT YOUR PROBLEM.
SFX: TEKO (STEP) TEKO

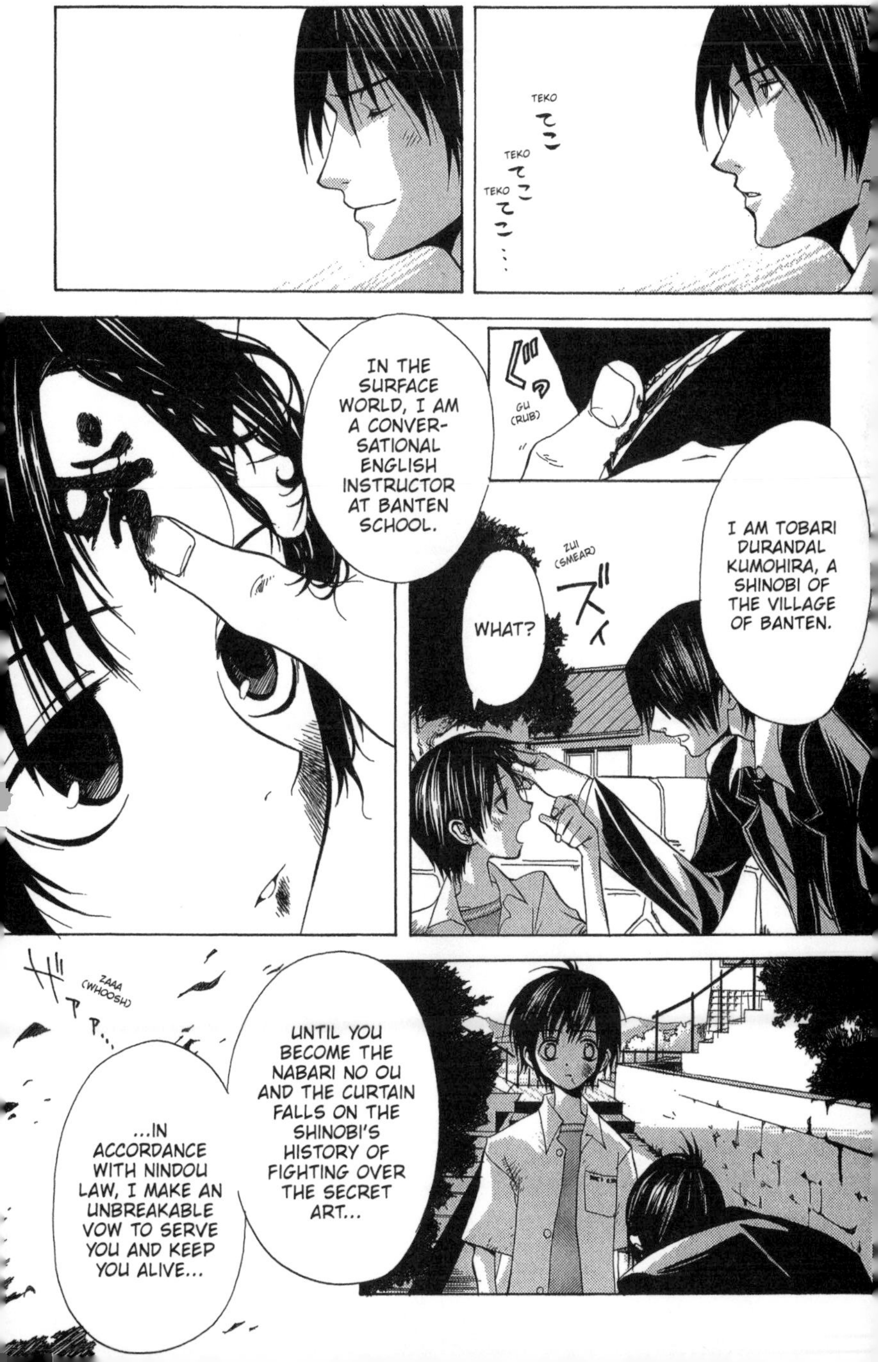
TEKO
てこ
TEKO
てこ
TEKO
てこ…
GU (RUB)
I AM TOBARI DURANDAL KUMOHIRA, A SHINOBI OF THE VILLAGE OF BANTEN.
ZUI (SMEAR)
ズイ
WHAT?
IN THE SURFACE WORLD, I AM A CONVER-SATIONAL ENGLISH INSTRUCTOR AT BANTEN SCHOOL.
UNTIL YOU BECOME THE NABARI NO OU AND THE CURTAIN FALLS ON THE SHINOBI'S HISTORY OF FIGHTING OVER THE SECRET ART…
…IN ACCORDANCE WITH NINDOU LAW, I MAKE AN UNBREAKABLE VOW TO SERVE YOU AND KEEP YOU ALIVE…
ZAAA (WHOOSH)
ザァァ…

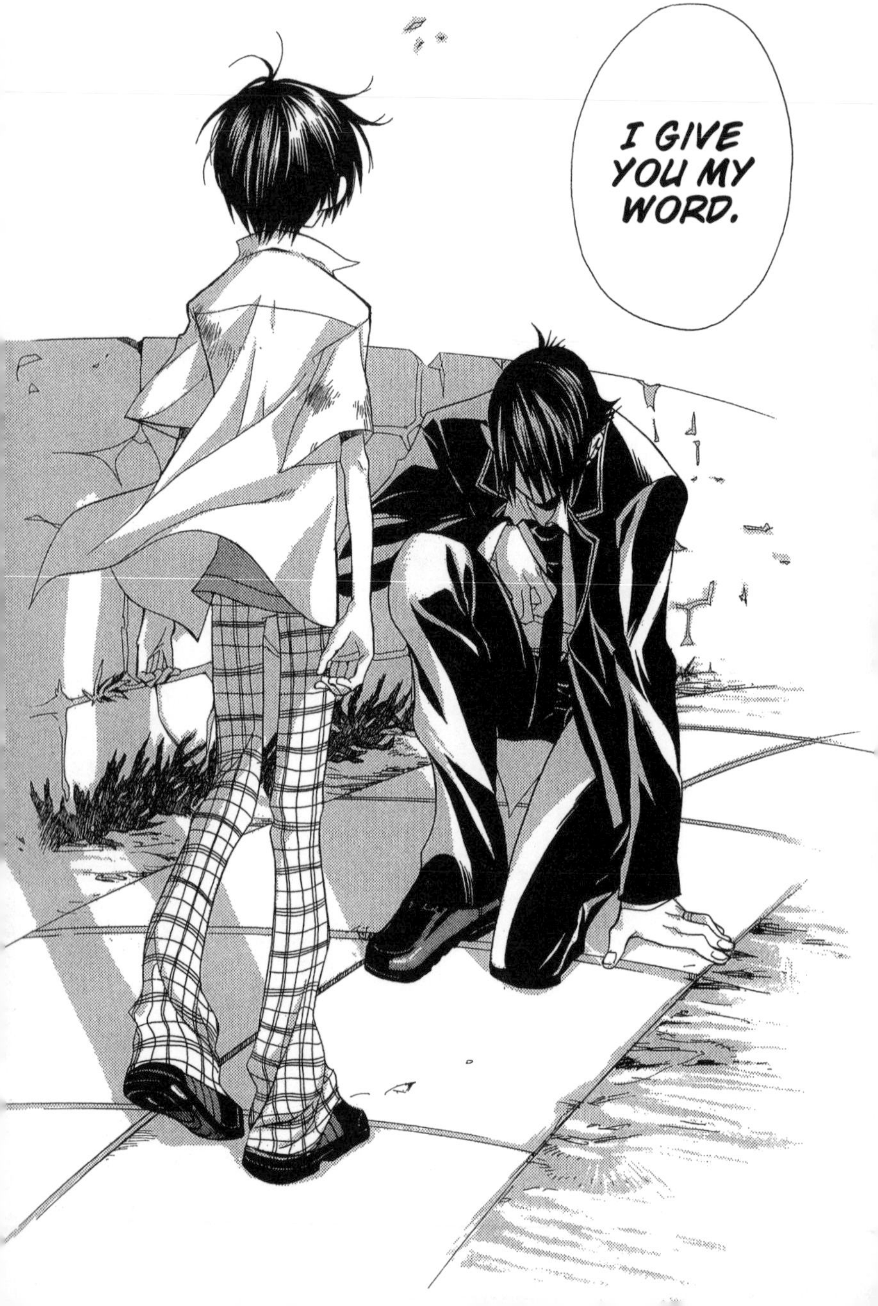
I GIVE YOU MY WORD.

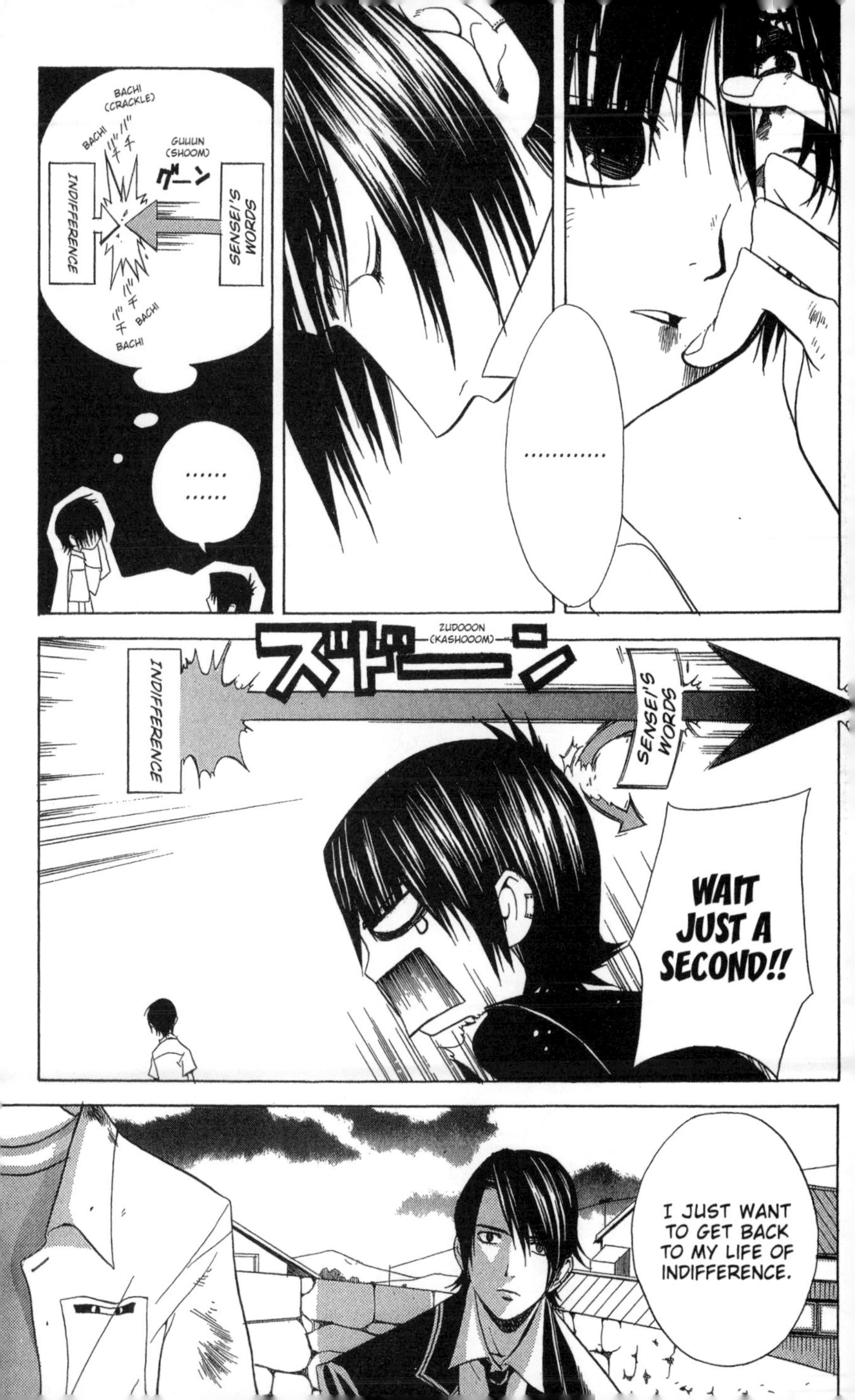
....
BACHI (CRACKLE)
BACHI
GUUUN (SHOOM)
SENSEI'S WORDS
INDIFFERENCE
BACHI
BACHI
....
ZUDOOON (KASHOOOM)
SENSEI'S WORDS
INDIFFERENCE
WAIT JUST A SECOND!!
I JUST WANT TO GET BACK TO MY LIFE OF INDIFFERENCE.

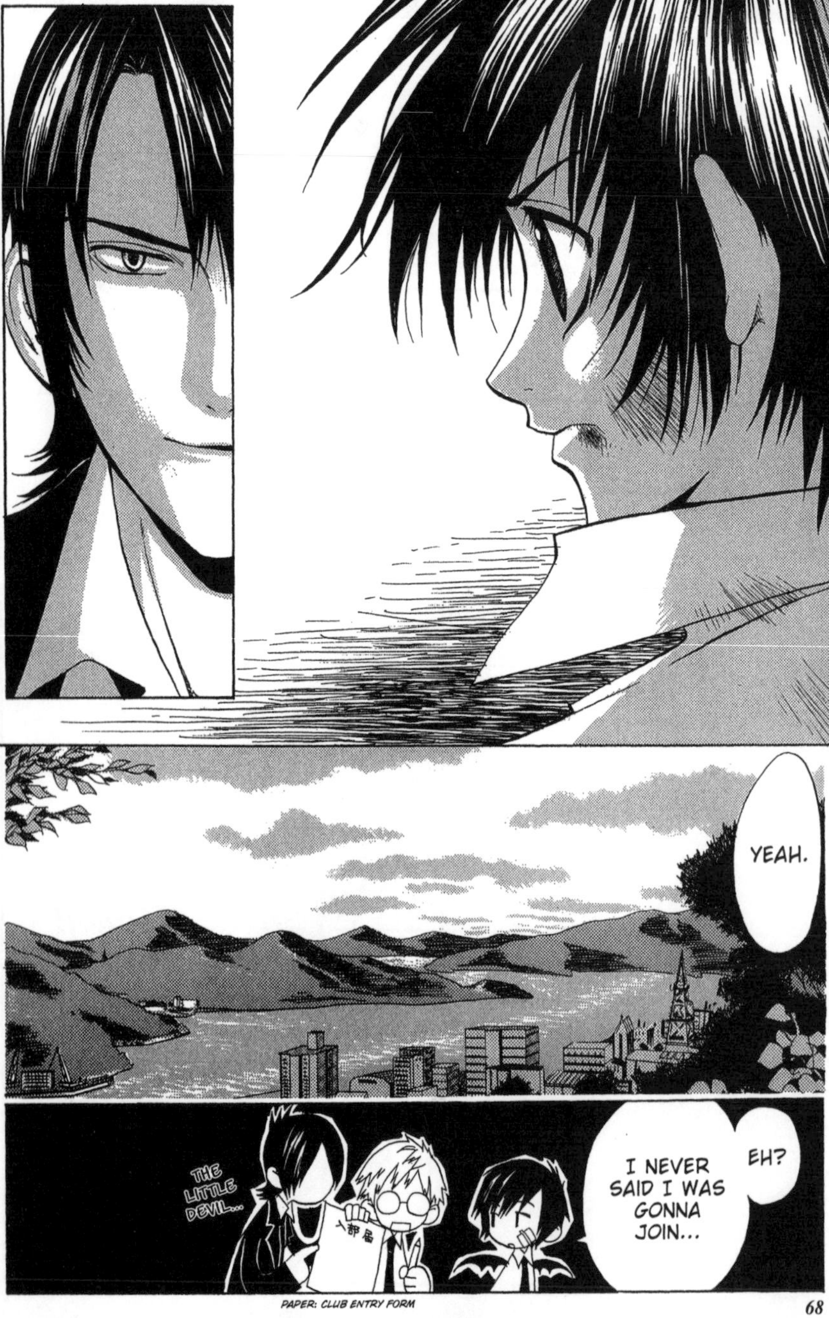
YEAH.
EH?
I NEVER SAID I WAS GONNA JOIN...
THE LITTLE DEVIL...
入部届

PAPER: CLUB ENTRY FORM

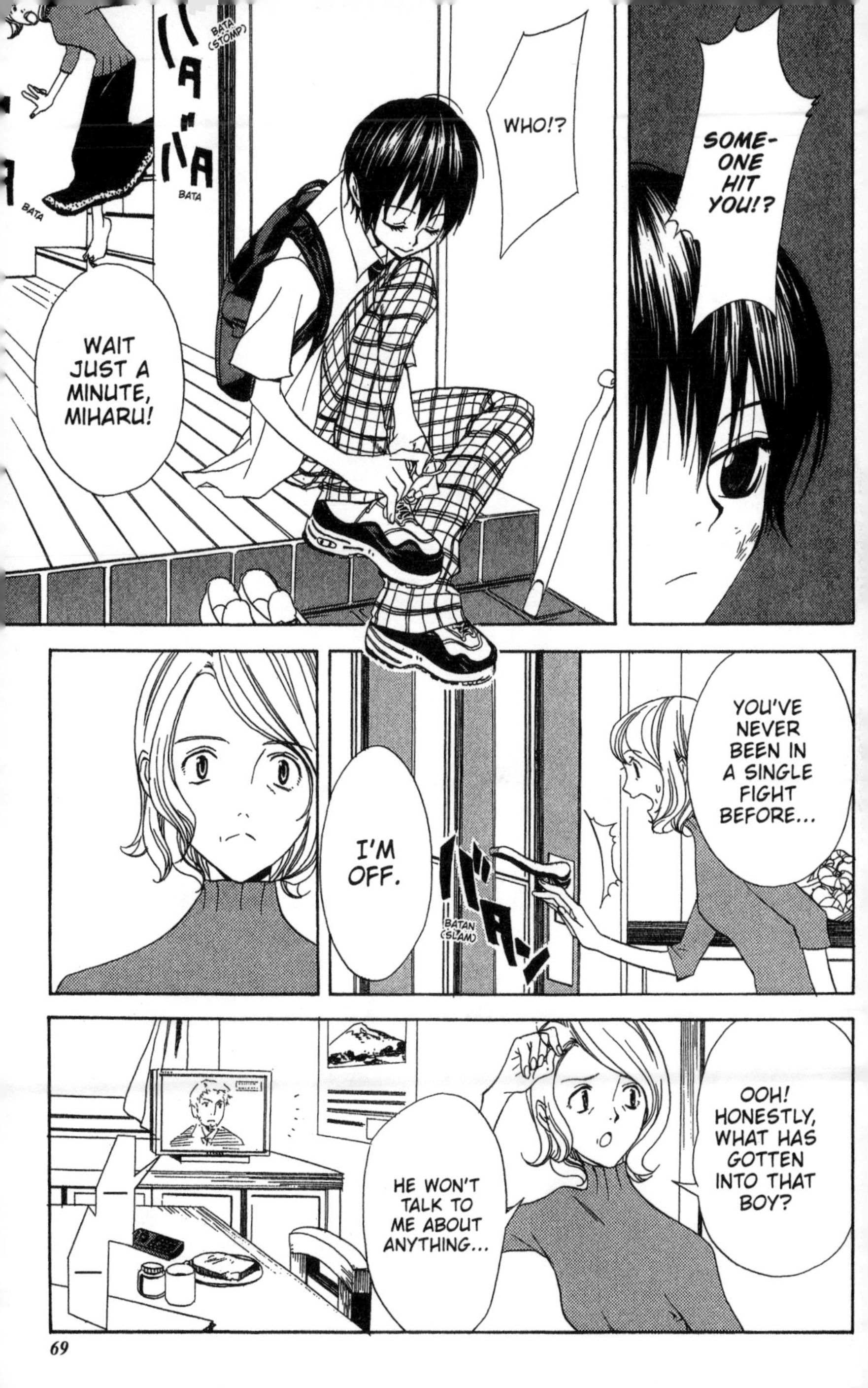
SOME-ONE HIT YOU!?
WHO!?
BATA (STOMP)
BATA
BATA
WAIT JUST A MINUTE, MIHARU!
YOU'VE NEVER BEEN IN A SINGLE FIGHT BEFORE...
I'M OFF.
BATAN (SLAM)
OOH! HONESTLY, WHAT HAS GOTTEN INTO THAT BOY?
HE WON'T TALK TO ME ABOUT ANYTHING...

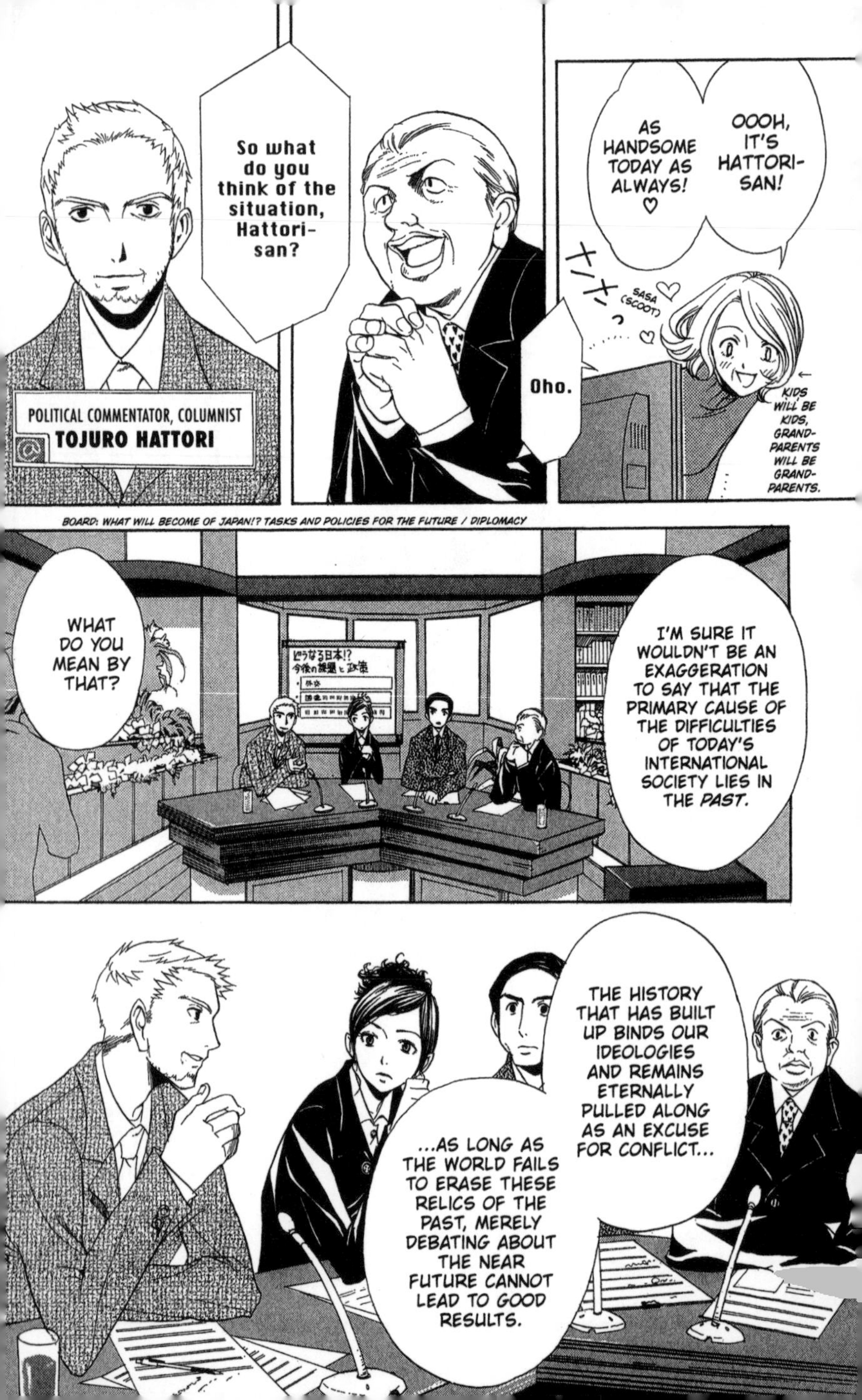
OOOH, IT'S HATTORI-SAN!
AS HANDSOME TODAY AS ALWAYS! ♡
SASA (SCOOT)
KIDS WILL BE KIDS, GRAND-PARENTS WILL BE GRAND-PARENTS.
Oho.
So what do you think of the situation, Hattori-san?
POLITICAL COMMENTATOR, COLUMNIST
TOJURO HATTORI
BOARD: WHAT WILL BECOME OF JAPAN!? TASKS AND POLICIES FOR THE FUTURE / DIPLOMACY
I'M SURE IT WOULDN'T BE AN EXAGGERATION TO SAY THAT THE PRIMARY CAUSE OF THE DIFFICULTIES OF TODAY'S INTERNATIONAL SOCIETY LIES IN THE *PAST*.
WHAT DO YOU MEAN BY THAT?
THE HISTORY THAT HAS BUILT UP BINDS OUR IDEOLOGIES AND REMAINS ETERNALLY PULLED ALONG AS AN EXCUSE FOR CONFLICT...
...AS LONG AS THE WORLD FAILS TO ERASE THESE RELICS OF THE PAST, MERELY DEBATING ABOUT THE NEAR FUTURE CANNOT LEAD TO GOOD RESULTS.

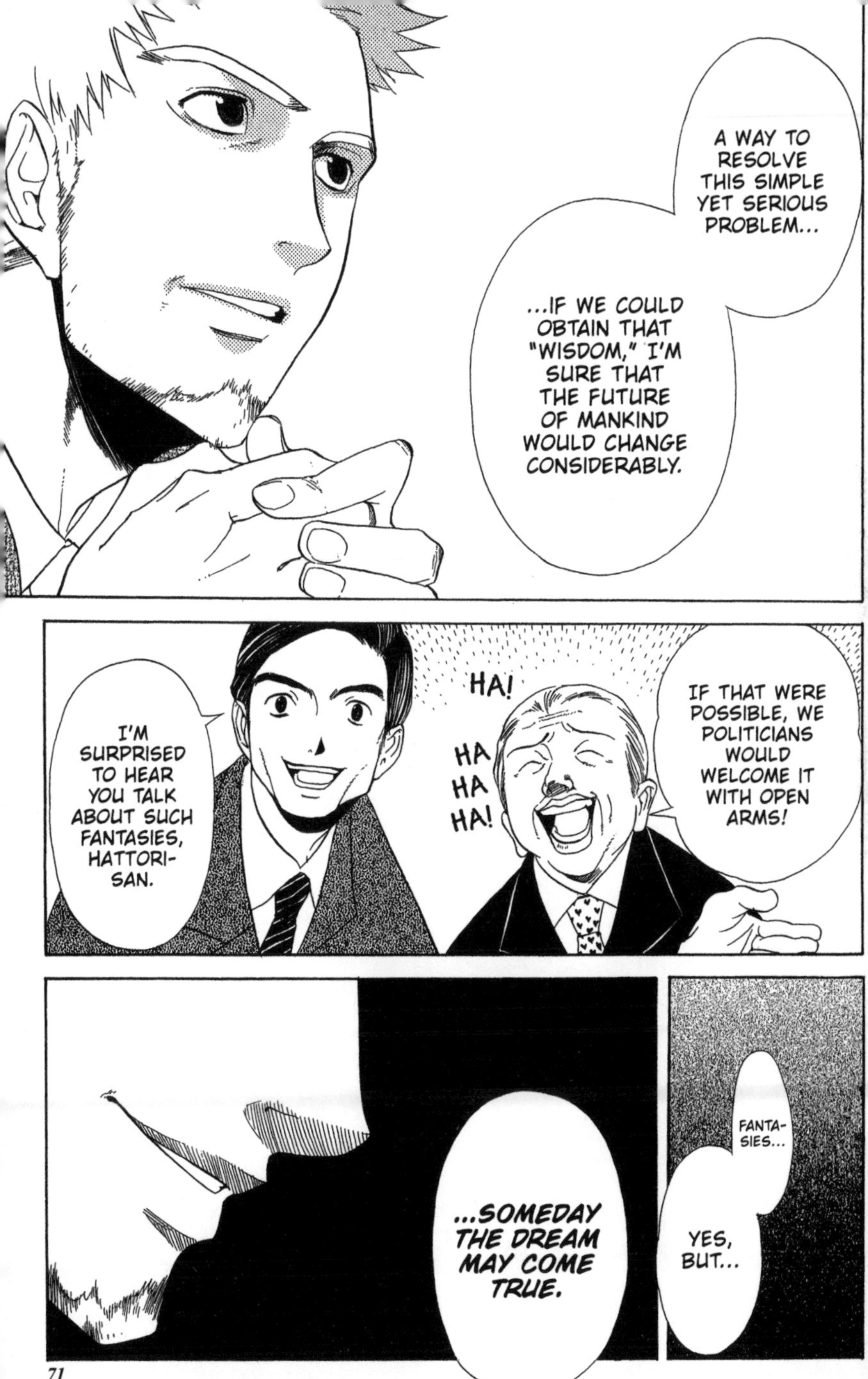
A WAY TO RESOLVE THIS SIMPLE YET SERIOUS PROBLEM...
...IF WE COULD OBTAIN THAT "WISDOM," I'M SURE THAT THE FUTURE OF MANKIND WOULD CHANGE CONSIDERABLY.
IF THAT WERE POSSIBLE, WE POLITICIANS WOULD WELCOME IT WITH OPEN ARMS!
HA!
HA HA HA!
I'M SURPRISED TO HEAR YOU TALK ABOUT SUCH FANTASIES, HATTORI-SAN.
FANTA-SIES...
YES, BUT...
...SOMEDAY THE DREAM MAY COME TRUE.

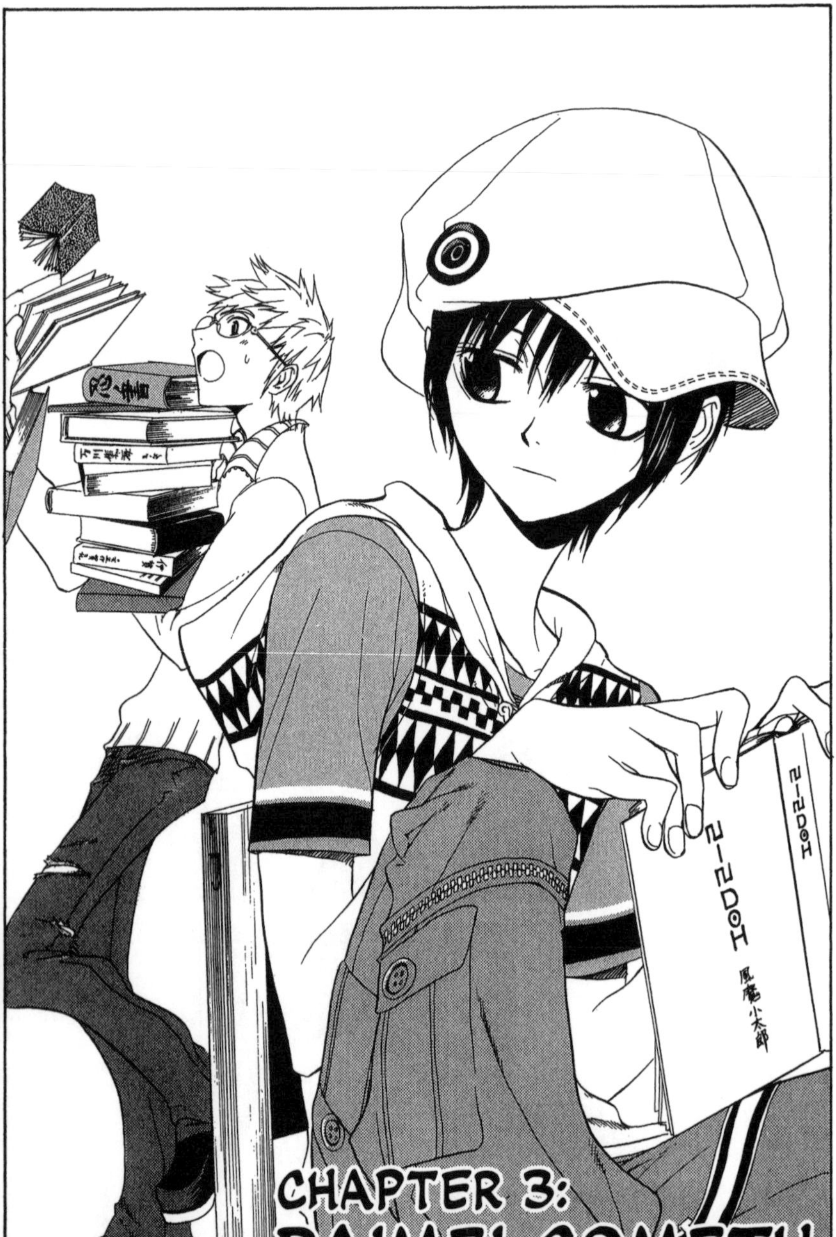
CHAPTER 3:
RAIMEI COMETH

BOOKS: NINJA TEXT / BANSENSHUKAI / IGA

BOOK: NINDOU BY KOTAROU FUUMA

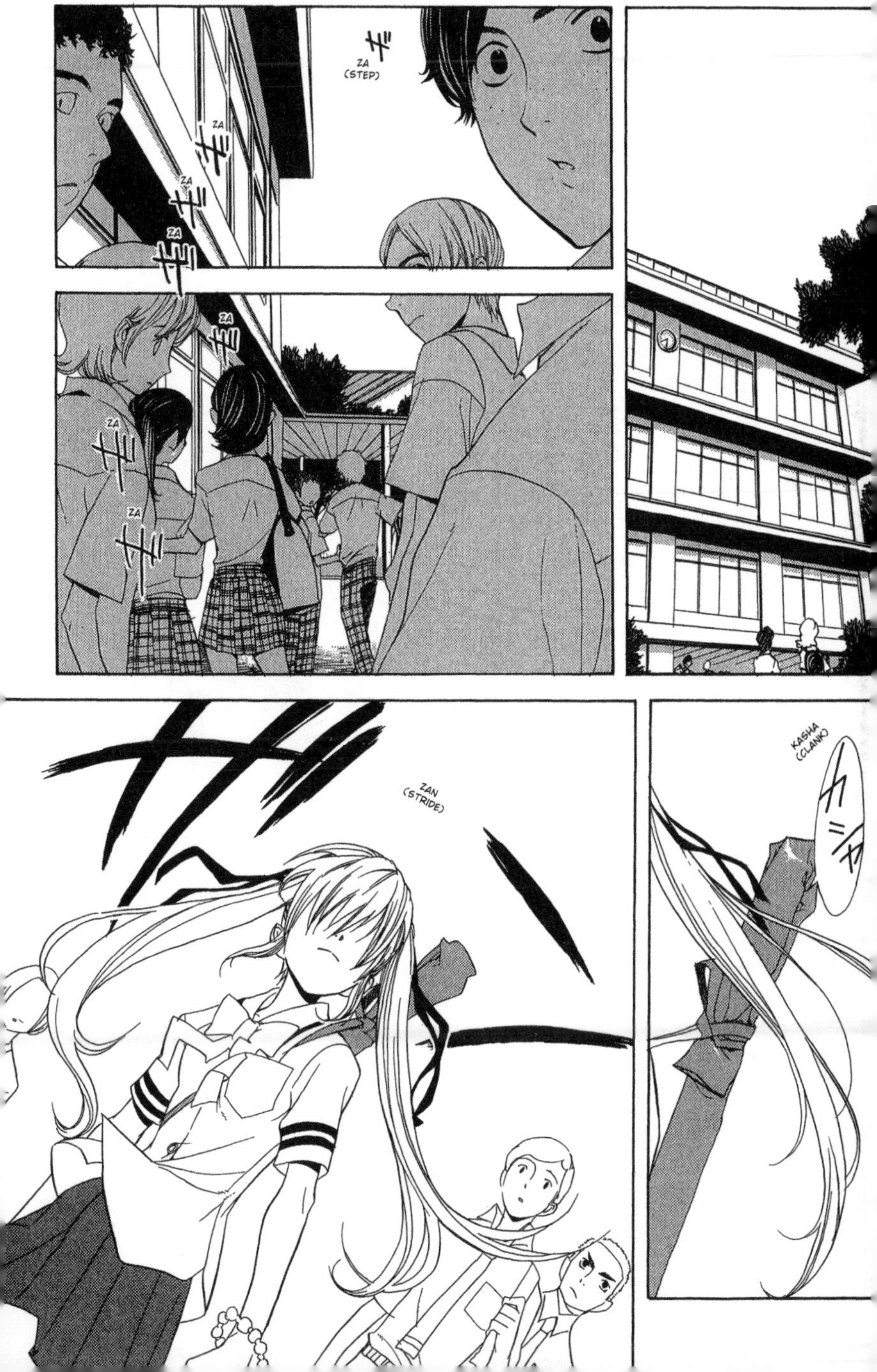
ZA
(STEP)
ZA
ZA
ZA
ZA
ZA
ZA
KASHA
(CLANK)
ZAN
(STRIDE)

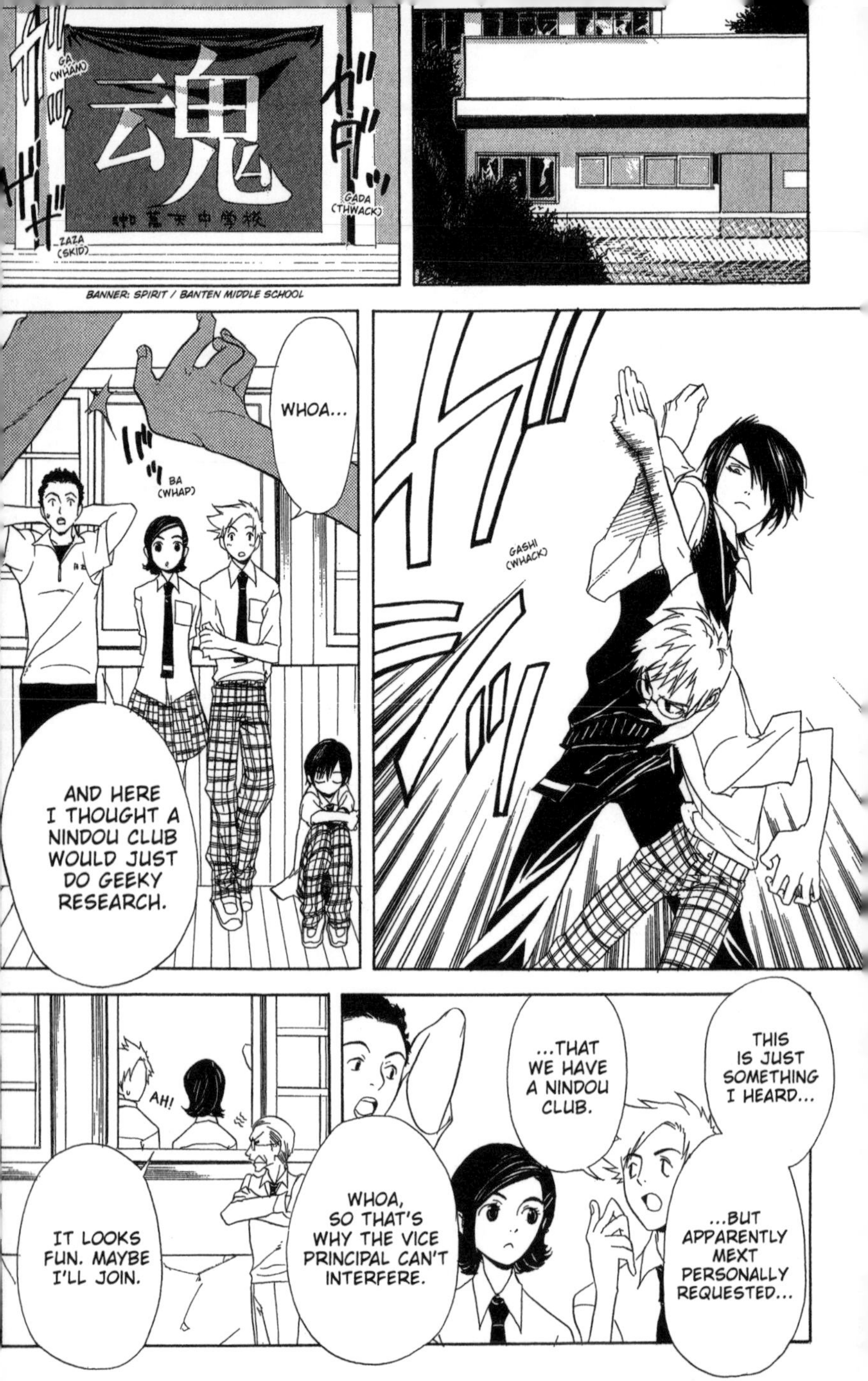
GA (WHAM)
GADA (THWACK)
ZAZA (SKID)
BANNER: SPIRIT / BANTEN MIDDLE SCHOOL
GASHI (WHACK)
WHOA...
BA (WHAP)
AND HERE I THOUGHT A NINDOU CLUB WOULD JUST DO GEEKY RESEARCH.
THIS IS JUST SOMETHING I HEARD...
...THAT WE HAVE A NINDOU CLUB.
...BUT APPARENTLY MEXT PERSONALLY REQUESTED...
WHOA, SO THAT'S WHY THE VICE PRINCIPAL CAN'T INTERFERE.
AH!
IT LOOKS FUN. MAYBE I'LL JOIN.

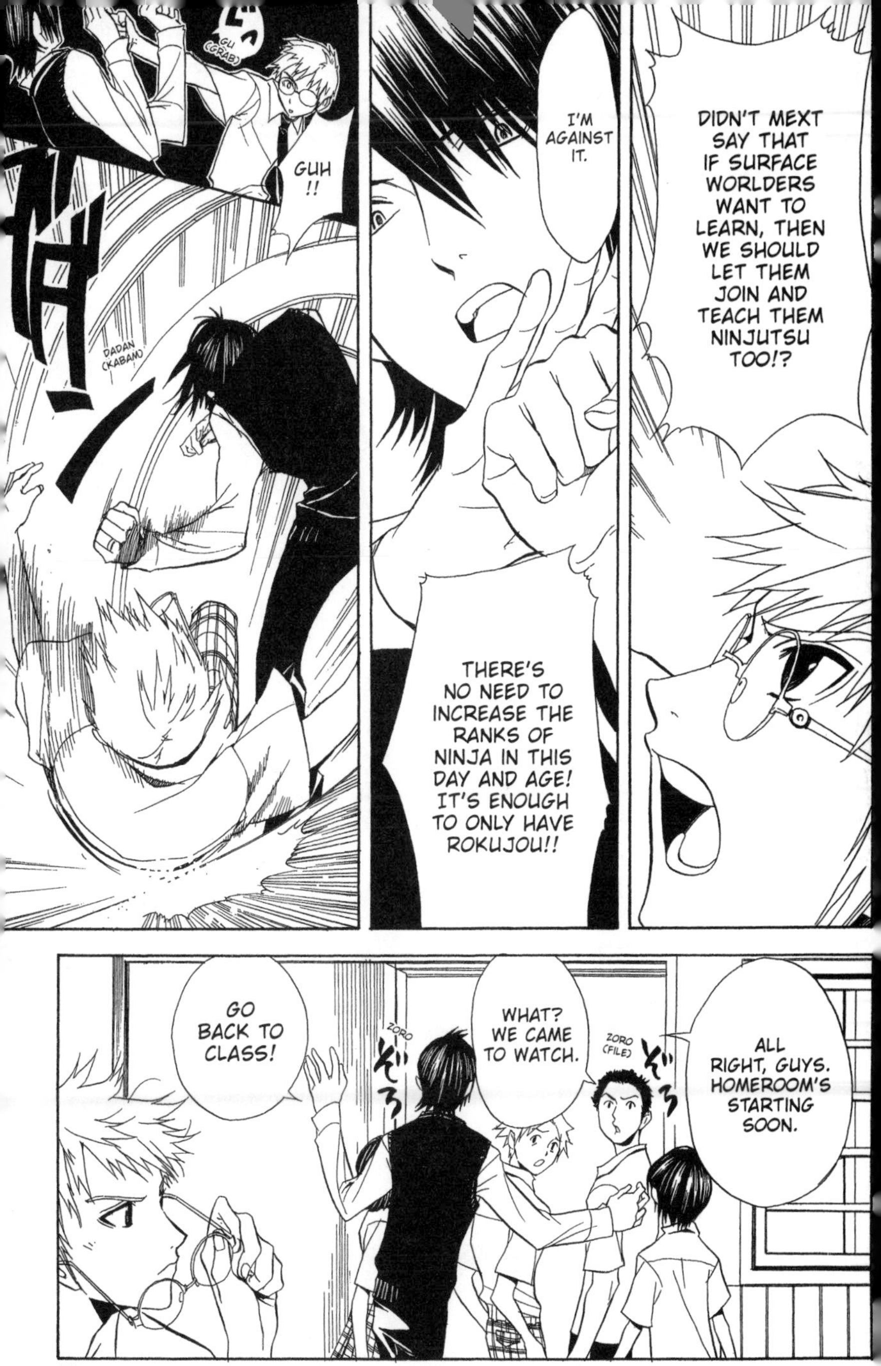
DIDN'T MEXT SAY THAT IF SURFACE WORLDERS WANT TO LEARN, THEN WE SHOULD LET THEM JOIN AND TEACH THEM NINJUTSU TOO!?
I'M AGAINST IT.
THERE'S NO NEED TO INCREASE THE RANKS OF NINJA IN THIS DAY AND AGE! IT'S ENOUGH TO ONLY HAVE ROKUJOU!!
GU (GRAB)
GUH !!
DADAN (KABAM)
ALL RIGHT, GUYS. HOMEROOM'S STARTING SOON.
ZORO (FILE)
WHAT? WE CAME TO WATCH.
ZORO
GO BACK TO CLASS!

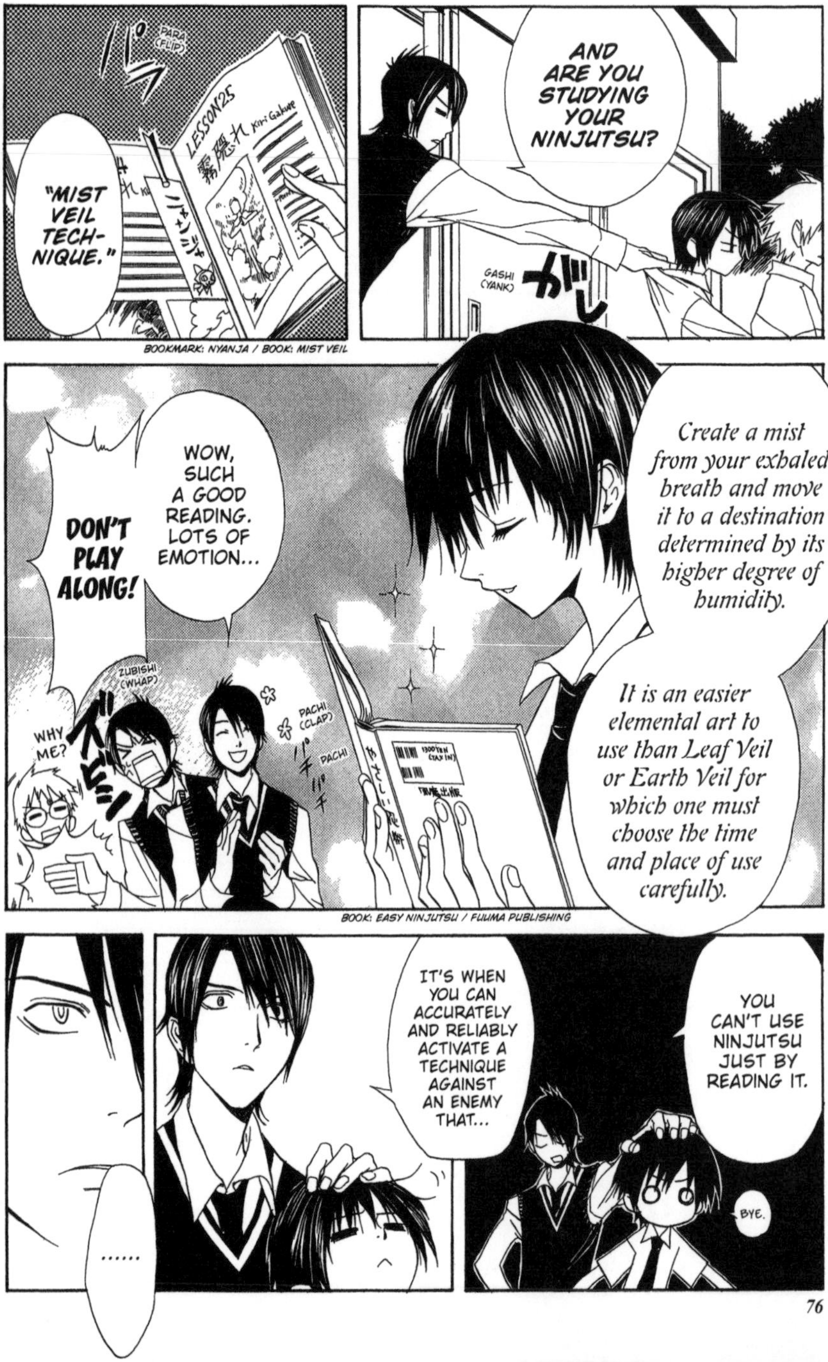
AND ARE YOU STUDYING YOUR NINJUTSU?
GASHI (YANK)
PARA (FLIP)
"MIST VEIL TECHNIQUE."
LESSON25
霧隠れ Kiri Gakure
BOOKMARK: NYANJA / BOOK: MIST VEIL
Create a mist from your exhaled breath and move it to a destination determined by its higher degree of humidity.
It is an easier elemental art to use than Leaf Veil or Earth Veil for which one must choose the time and place of use carefully.
WOW, SUCH A GOOD READING. LOTS OF EMOTION...
DON'T PLAY ALONG!
PACHI (CLAP)
PACHI
ZUBISHI (WHAP)
WHY ME?
1300YEN (TAX IN)
BOOK: EASY NINJUTSU / FUUMA PUBLISHING
YOU CAN'T USE NINJUTSU JUST BY READING IT.
BYE.
IT'S WHEN YOU CAN ACCURATELY AND RELIABLY ACTIVATE A TECHNIQUE AGAINST AN ENEMY THAT...
......

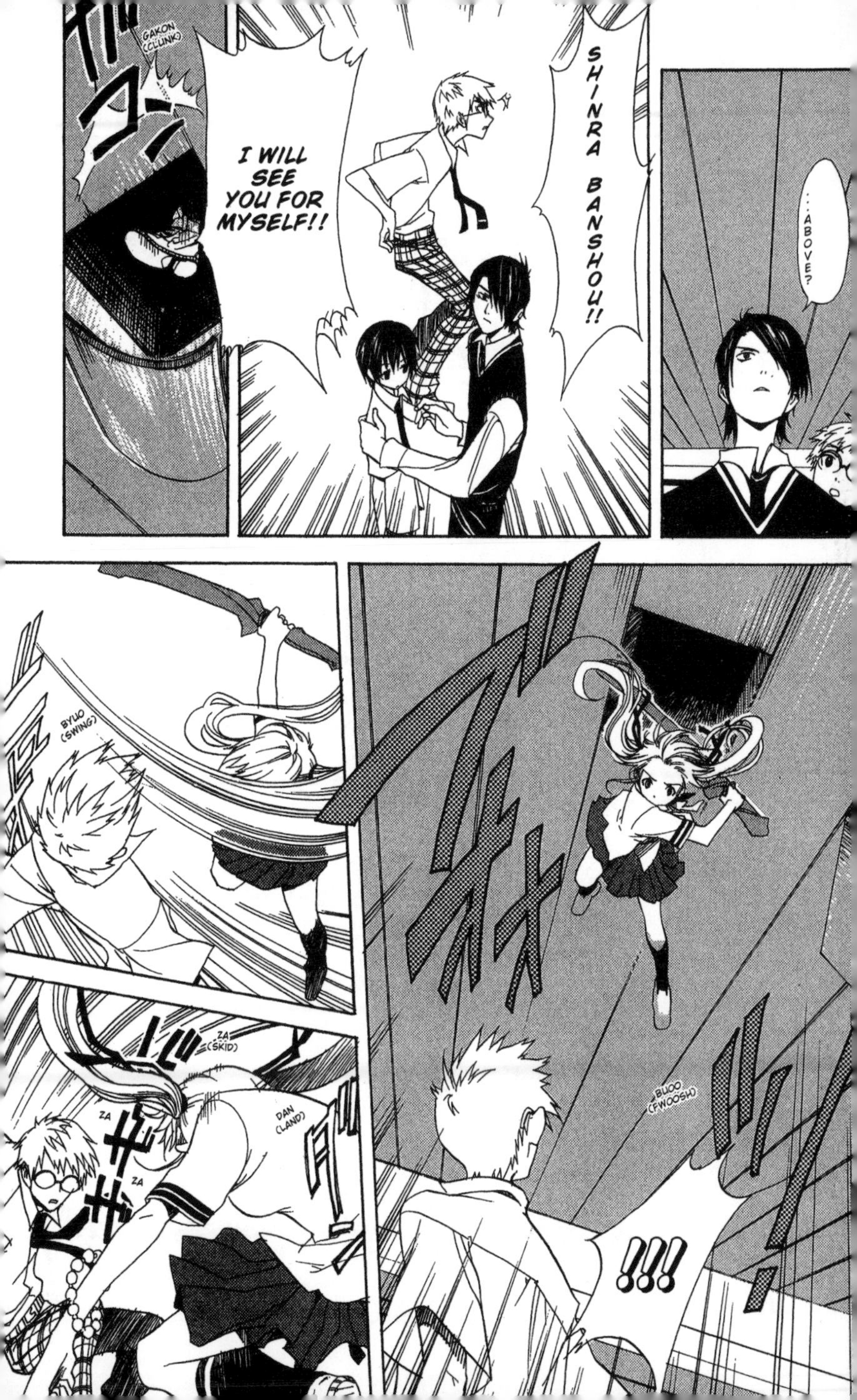
...ABOVE?
SHINRA BANSHOU!!
I WILL SEE YOU FOR MYSELF!!
GAKON (CLUNK)
BUOO (FWOOSH)
!!!
BYUO (SWING)
ZA (SKID)
DAN (LAND)
ZA
ZA

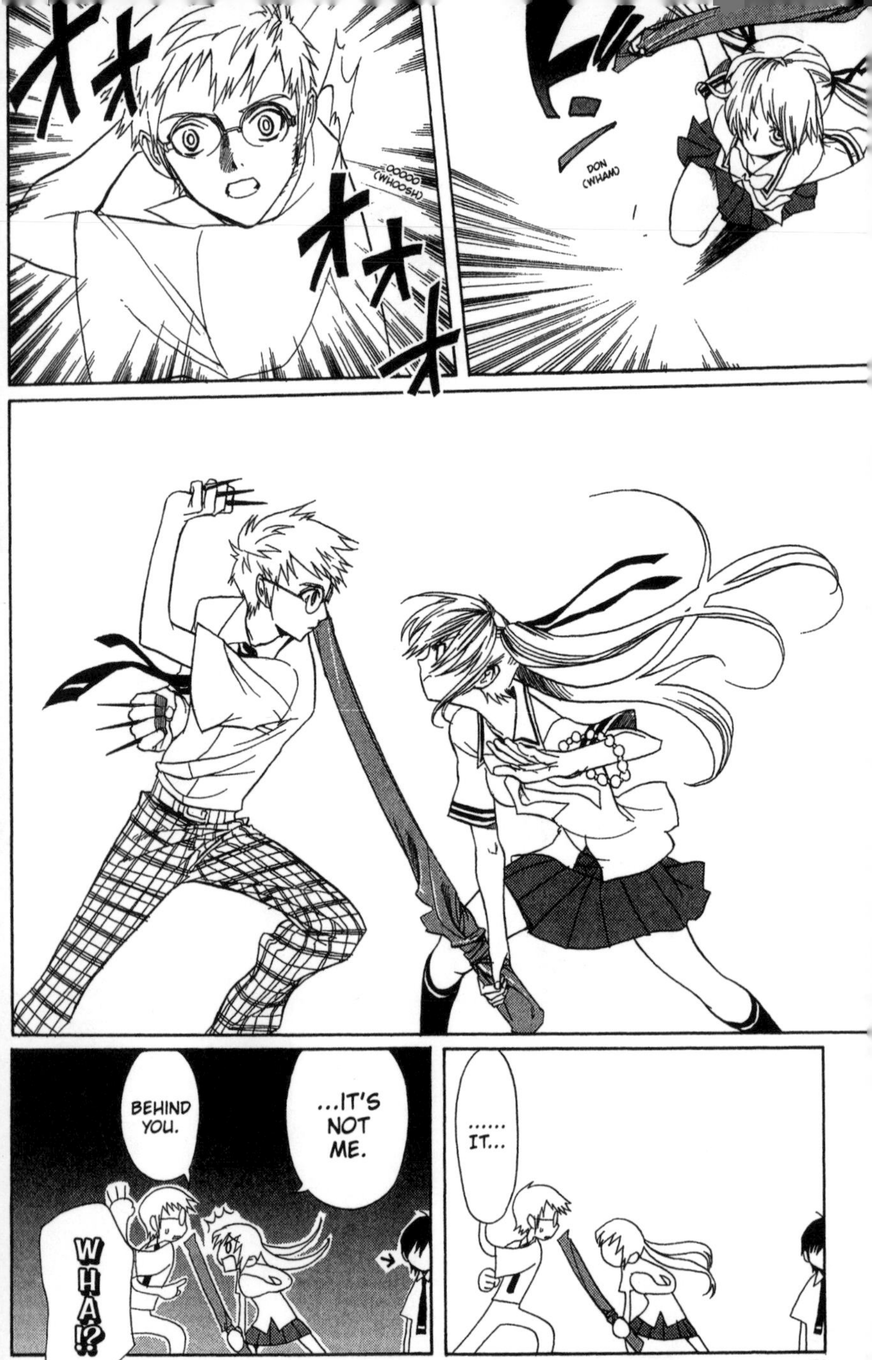
DON (WHAM)
OOOOO (WHOOSH)
...... IT...
...IT'S NOT ME.
BEHIND YOU.
WHA!?

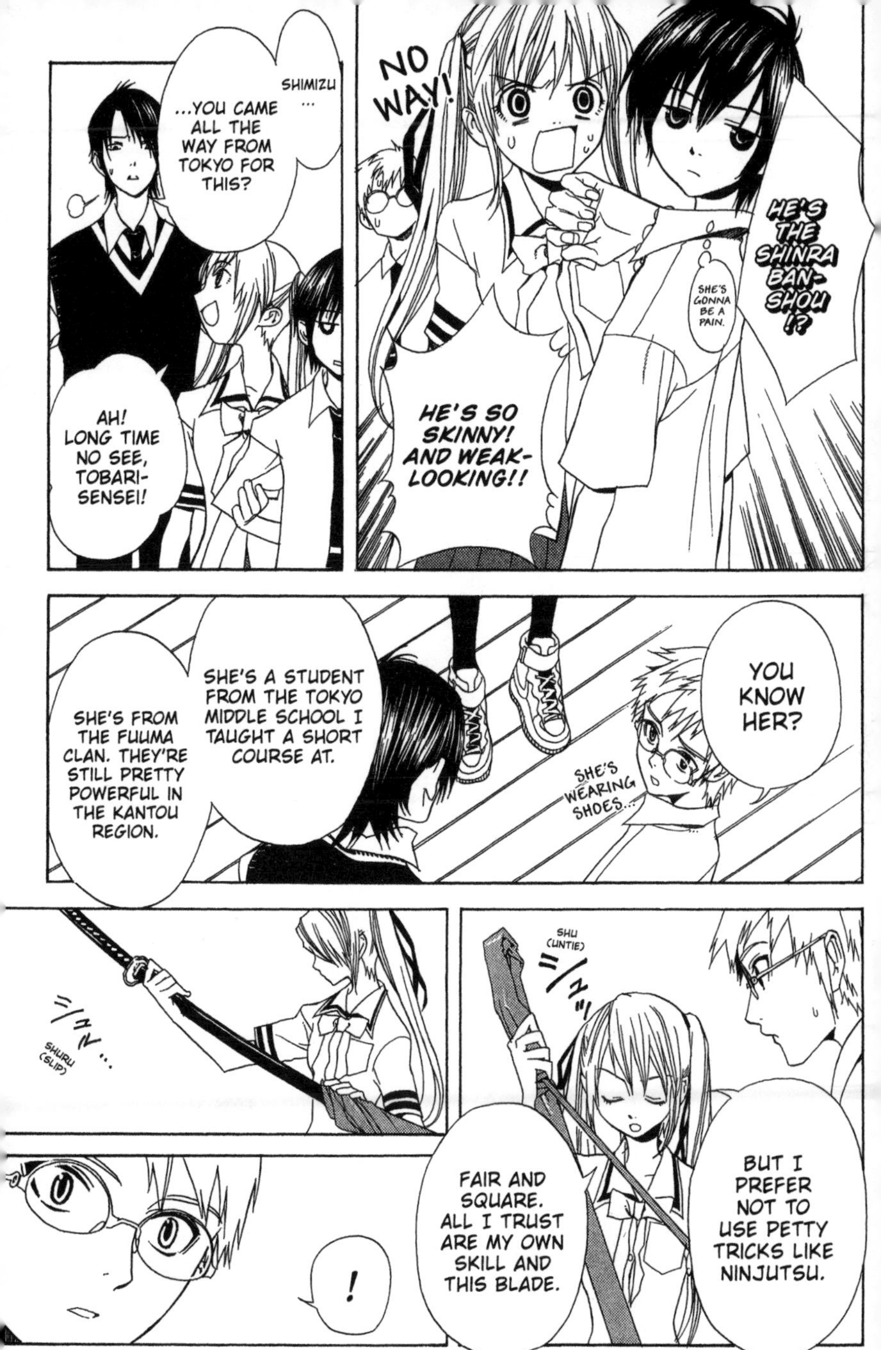
NO WAY!
HE'S THE SHINRA BAN-SHOU!?
SHE'S GONNA BE A PAIN.
HE'S SO SKINNY! AND WEAK-LOOKING!!
SHIMIZU ...
...YOU CAME ALL THE WAY FROM TOKYO FOR THIS?
AH! LONG TIME NO SEE, TOBARI-SENSEI!
YOU KNOW HER?
SHE'S WEARING SHOES...
SHE'S A STUDENT FROM THE TOKYO MIDDLE SCHOOL I TAUGHT A SHORT COURSE AT.
SHE'S FROM THE FUUMA CLAN. THEY'RE STILL PRETTY POWERFUL IN THE KANTOU REGION.
SHU (UNTIE)
BUT I PREFER NOT TO USE PETTY TRICKS LIKE NINJUTSU.
FAIR AND SQUARE. ALL I TRUST ARE MY OWN SKILL AND THIS BLADE.
SHURU (SLIP)
!

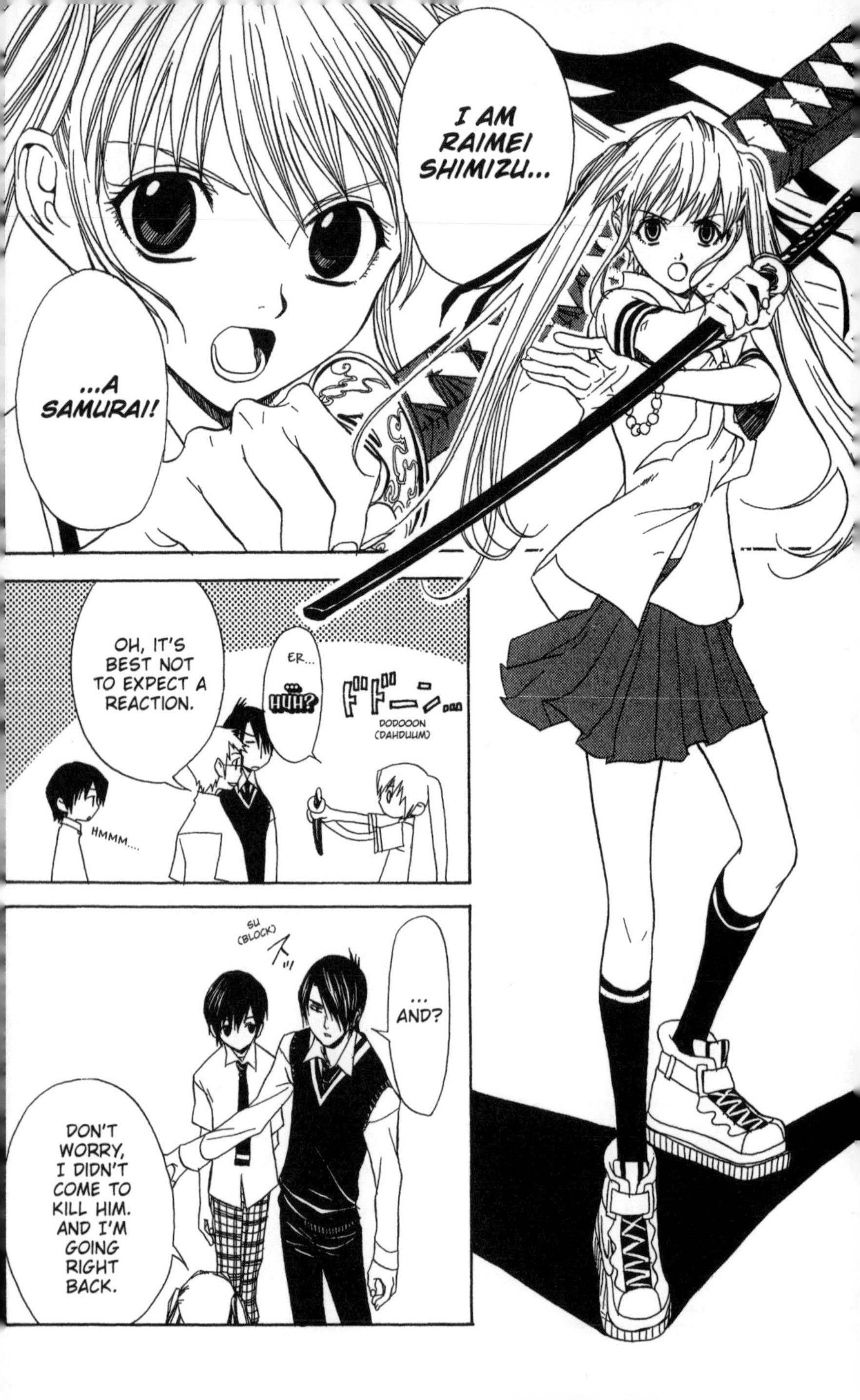
I AM RAIMEI SHIMIZU...
...A SAMURAI!
ER... ...HUH?
DODOOON (DAHDUUM)
OH, IT'S BEST NOT TO EXPECT A REACTION.
HMMM....
SU (BLOCK)
...AND?
DON'T WORRY, I DIDN'T COME TO KILL HIM. AND I'M GOING RIGHT BACK.

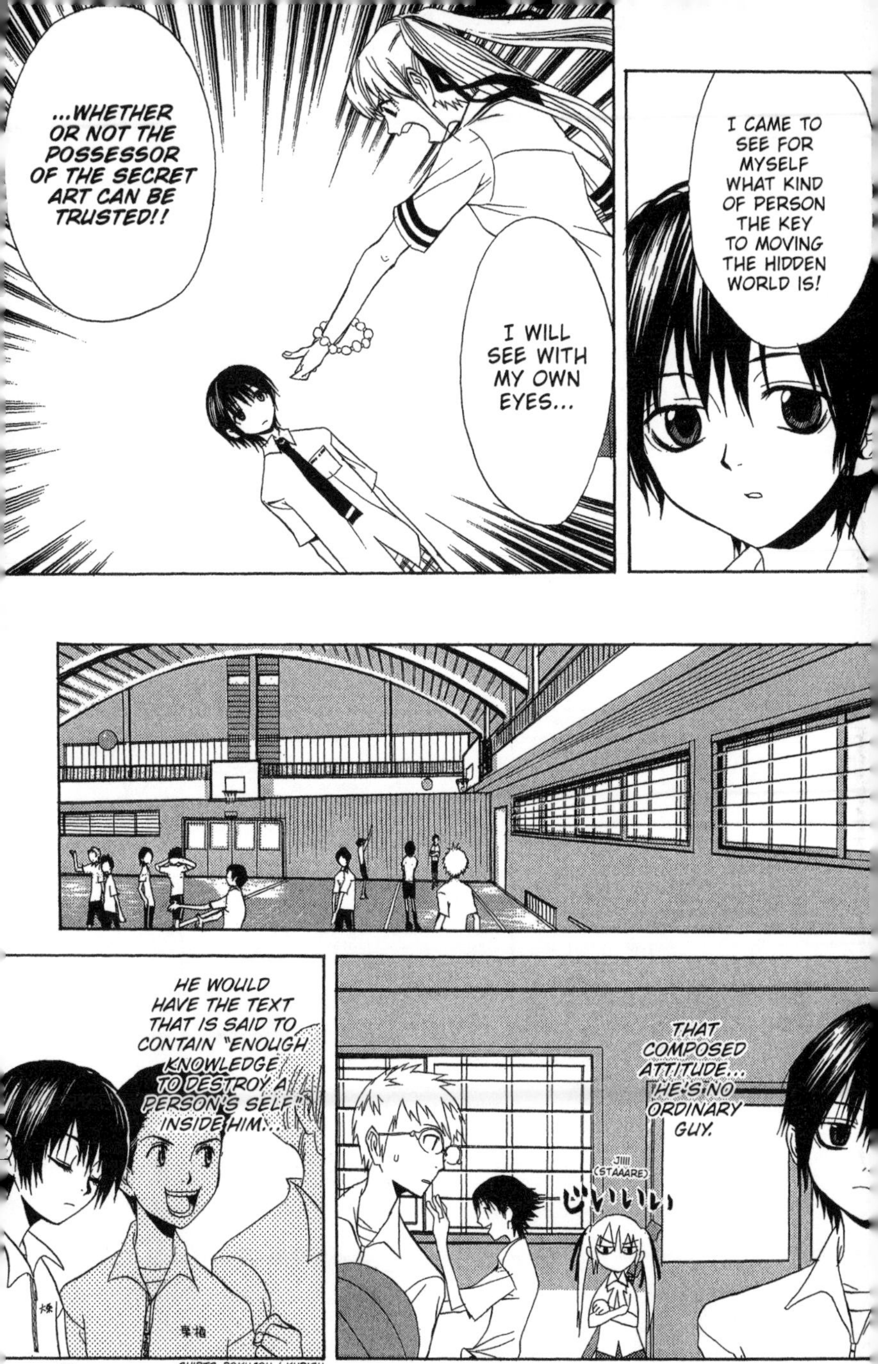
I CAME TO SEE FOR MYSELF WHAT KIND OF PERSON THE KEY TO MOVING THE HIDDEN WORLD IS!
I WILL SEE WITH MY OWN EYES...
...WHETHER OR NOT THE POSSESSOR OF THE SECRET ART CAN BE TRUSTED!!
THAT COMPOSED ATTITUDE... HE'S NO ORDINARY GUY.
じいいいい
JIIII (STAAARE)
HE WOULD HAVE THE TEXT THAT IS SAID TO CONTAIN "ENOUGH KNOWLEDGE TO DESTROY A PERSON'S SELF" INSIDE HIM...
SHIRTS: ROKUJOU / KURISU

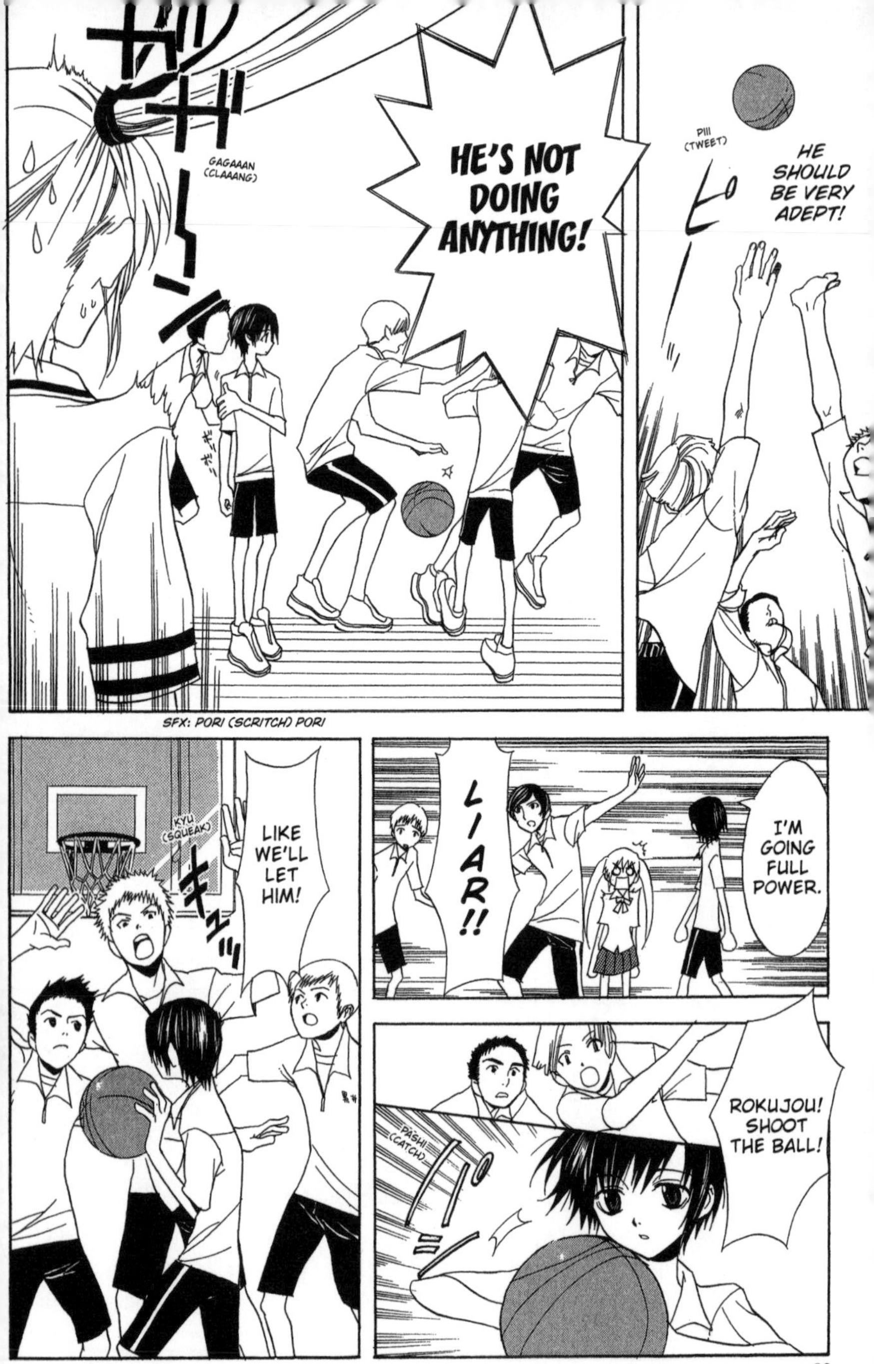
PIII (TWEET)
HE SHOULD BE VERY ADEPT!
HE'S NOT DOING ANYTHING!
GAGAAAN (CLAAANG)
SFX: PORI (SCRITCH) PORI
I'M GOING FULL POWER.
LIAR!!
ROKUJOU! SHOOT THE BALL!
PASHI (CATCH)
LIKE WE'LL LET HIM!
KYU (SQUEAK)

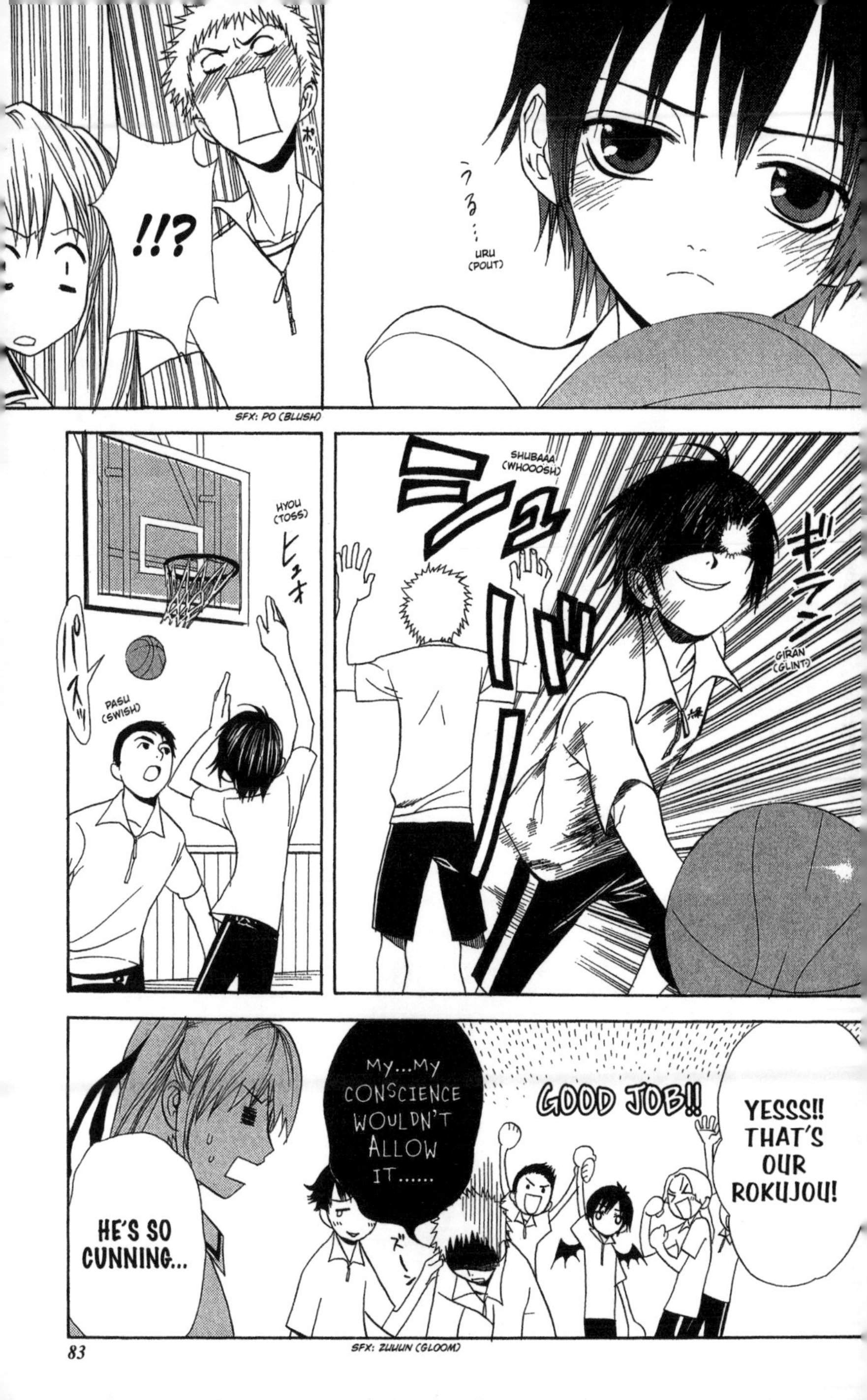
URU (POUT)
!!?
SFX: PO (BLUSH)
SHUBAAA (WHOOOSH)
GIRAN (GLINT)
HYOU (TOSS)
PASU (SWISH)
YESSS!! THAT'S OUR ROKUJOU!
GOOD JOB!!
My...My CONSCIENCE WOULDN'T ALLOW IT......
HE'S SO CUNNING...
SFX: ZUUUN (GLOOM)

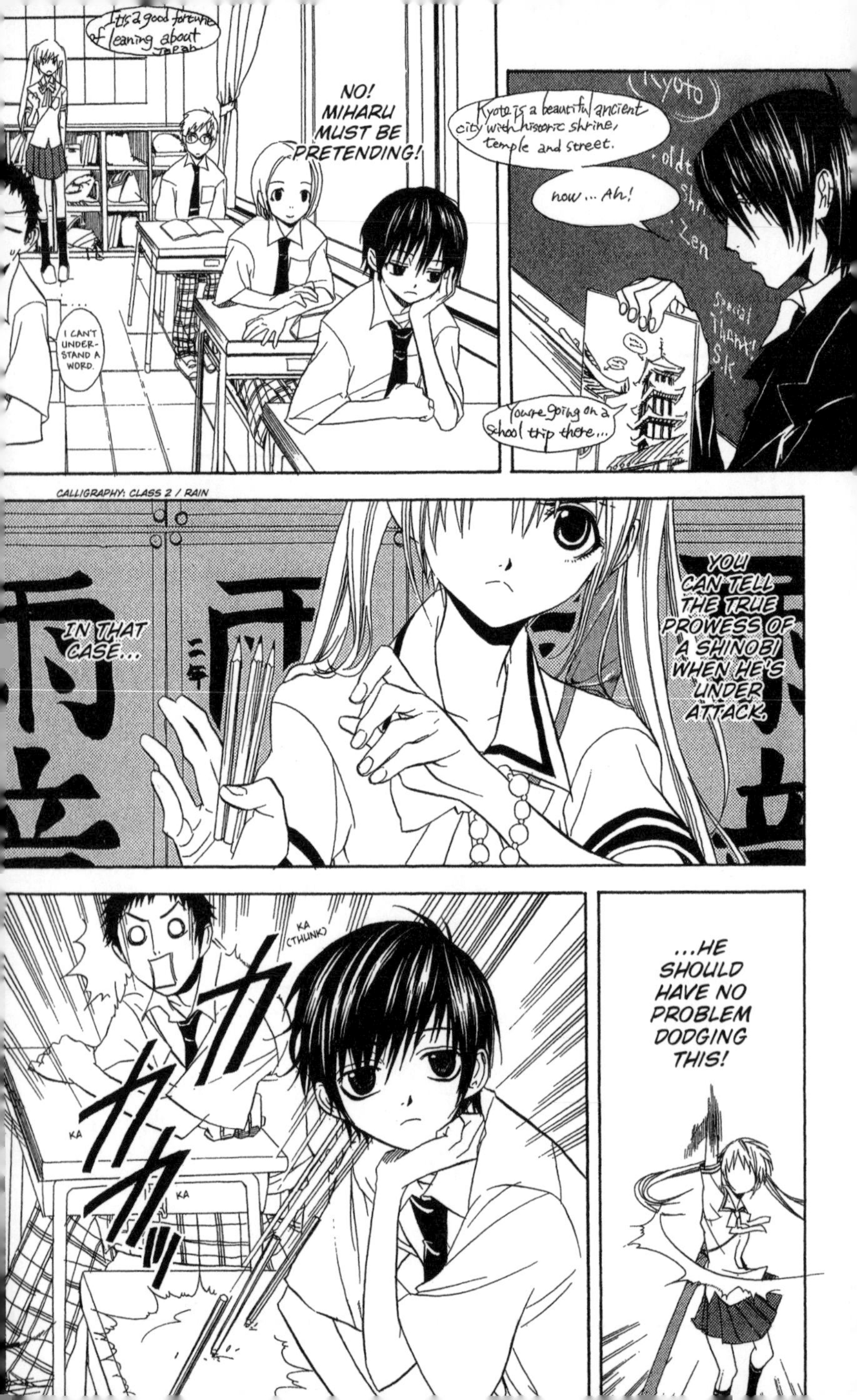
Kyoto is a beautiful ancient city with historic shrine, temple and street.
now... Ah!
You're going on a school trip there...
NO! MIHARU MUST BE PRETENDING!
It's a good fortune of leaning about Japan.
...
I CAN'T UNDERSTAND A WORD.
CALLIGRAPHY: CLASS 2 / RAIN
YOU CAN TELL THE TRUE PROWESS OF A SHINOBI WHEN HE'S UNDER ATTACK.
IN THAT CASE...
...HE SHOULD HAVE NO PROBLEM DODGING THIS!
KA (THUNK)
KA
KA

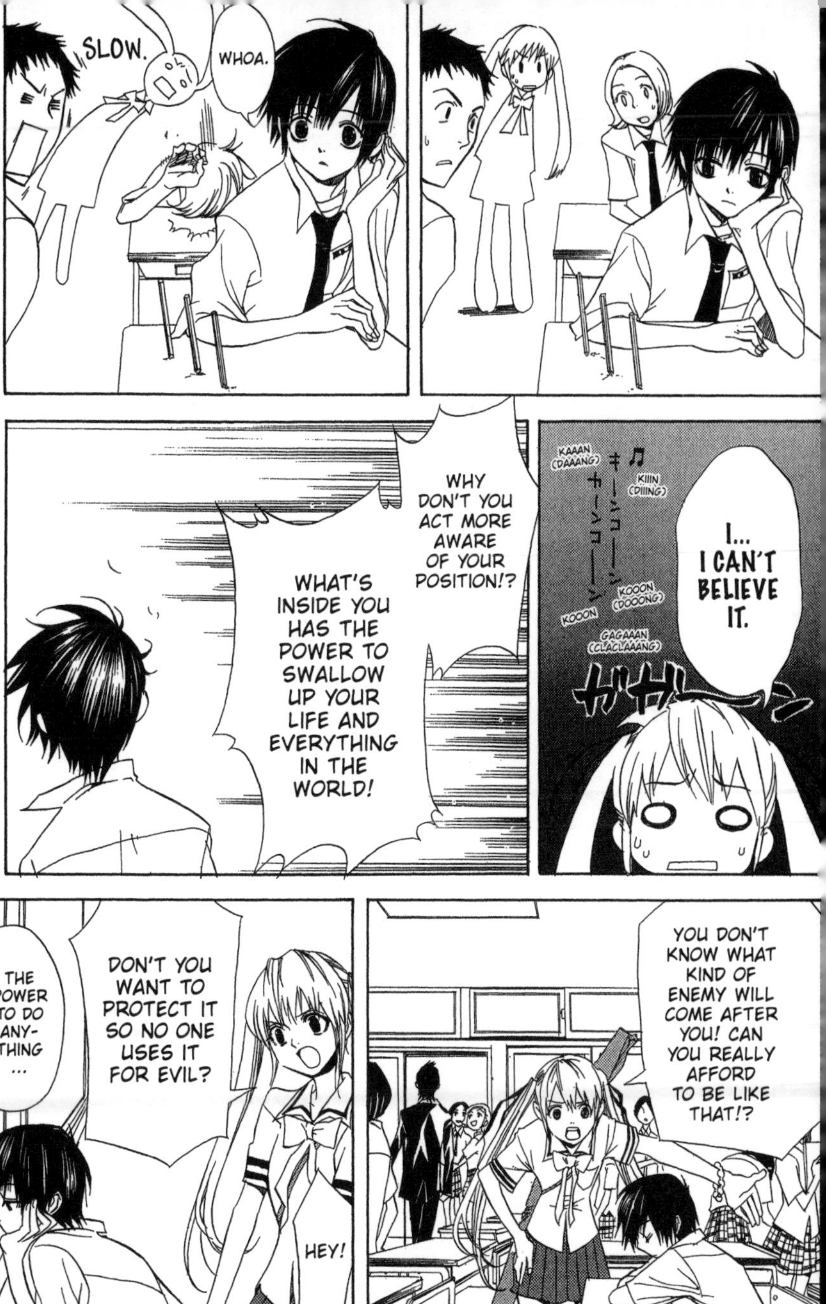
WHOA.
SLOW.
I... I CAN'T BELIEVE IT.
KAAAN (DAAANG)
KIIN (DIIING)
KOOON (DOOONG)
KOOON
GAGAAAN (CLACLAAANG)
WHY DON'T YOU ACT MORE AWARE OF YOUR POSITION!?
WHAT'S INSIDE YOU HAS THE POWER TO SWALLOW UP YOUR LIFE AND EVERYTHING IN THE WORLD!
YOU DON'T KNOW WHAT KIND OF ENEMY WILL COME AFTER YOU! CAN YOU REALLY AFFORD TO BE LIKE THAT!?
DON'T YOU WANT TO PROTECT IT SO NO ONE USES IT FOR EVIL?
THE POWER TO DO ANYTHING...
HEY!

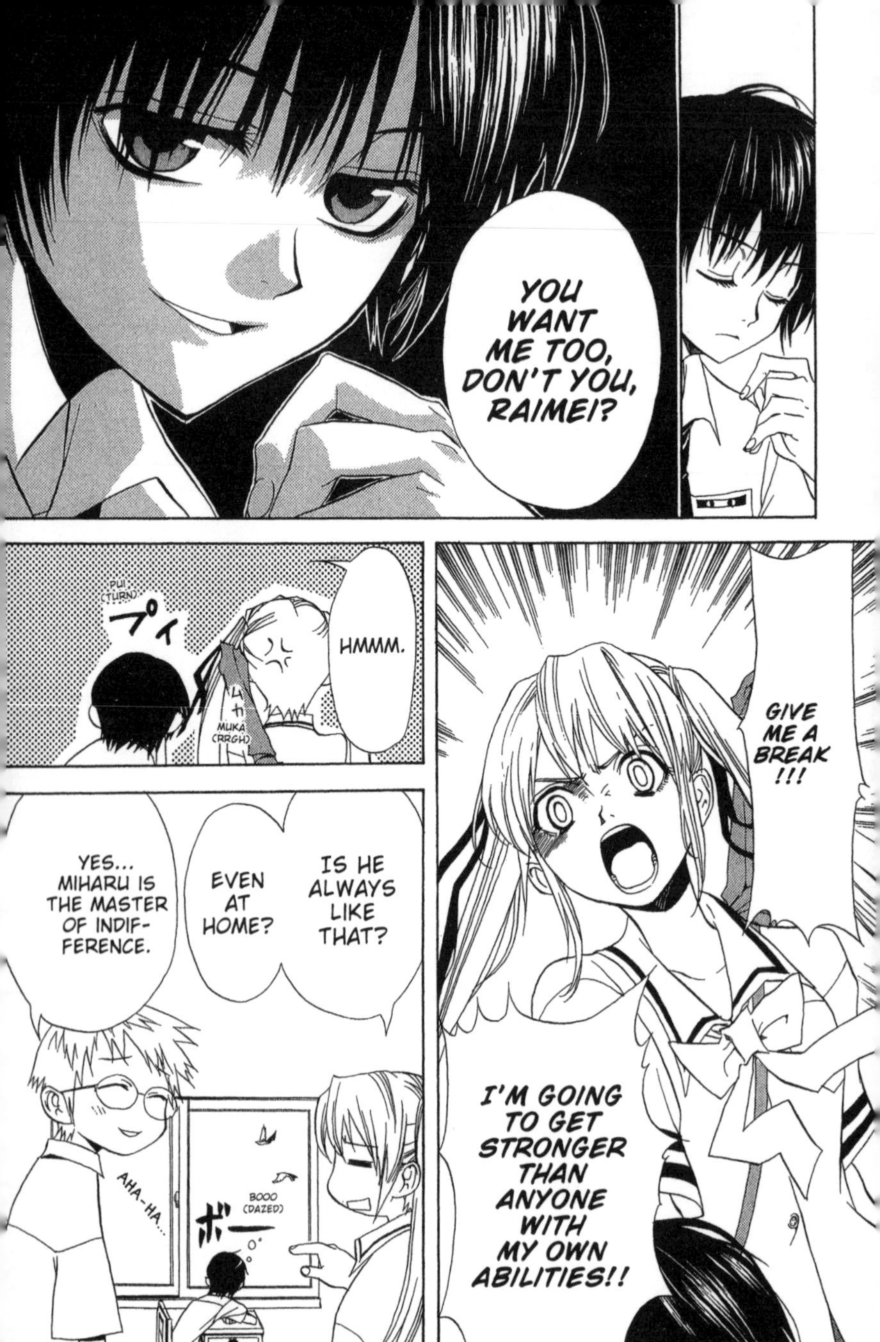
YOU WANT ME TOO, DON'T YOU, RAIMEI?
GIVE ME A BREAK !!!
I'M GOING TO GET STRONGER THAN ANYONE WITH MY OWN ABILITIES!!
HMMM.
プイ
PUI (TURN)
ムカ
MUKA (RRGH)
IS HE ALWAYS LIKE THAT?
EVEN AT HOME?
YES... MIHARU IS THE MASTER OF INDIF-FERENCE.
AHA-HA...
ボー
BOOO (DAZED)

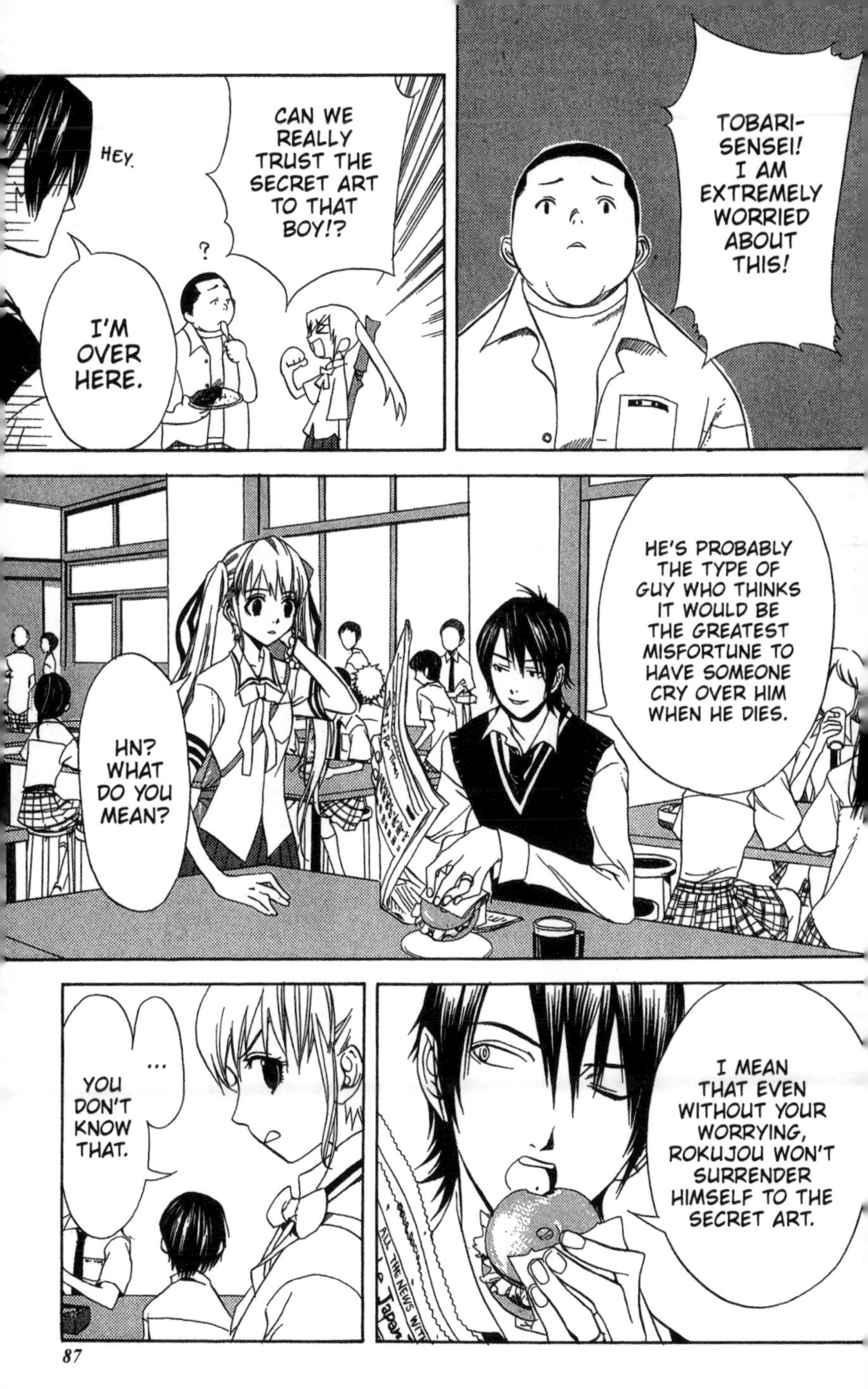
TOBARI-SENSEI! I AM EXTREMELY WORRIED ABOUT THIS!
CAN WE REALLY TRUST THE SECRET ART TO THAT BOY!?
HEY.
?
I'M OVER HERE.
HE'S PROBABLY THE TYPE OF GUY WHO THINKS IT WOULD BE THE GREATEST MISFORTUNE TO HAVE SOMEONE CRY OVER HIM WHEN HE DIES.
HN? WHAT DO YOU MEAN?
I MEAN THAT EVEN WITHOUT YOUR WORRYING, ROKUJOU WON'T SURRENDER HIMSELF TO THE SECRET ART.
...
YOU DON'T KNOW THAT.

CARTON: RAKKUMI

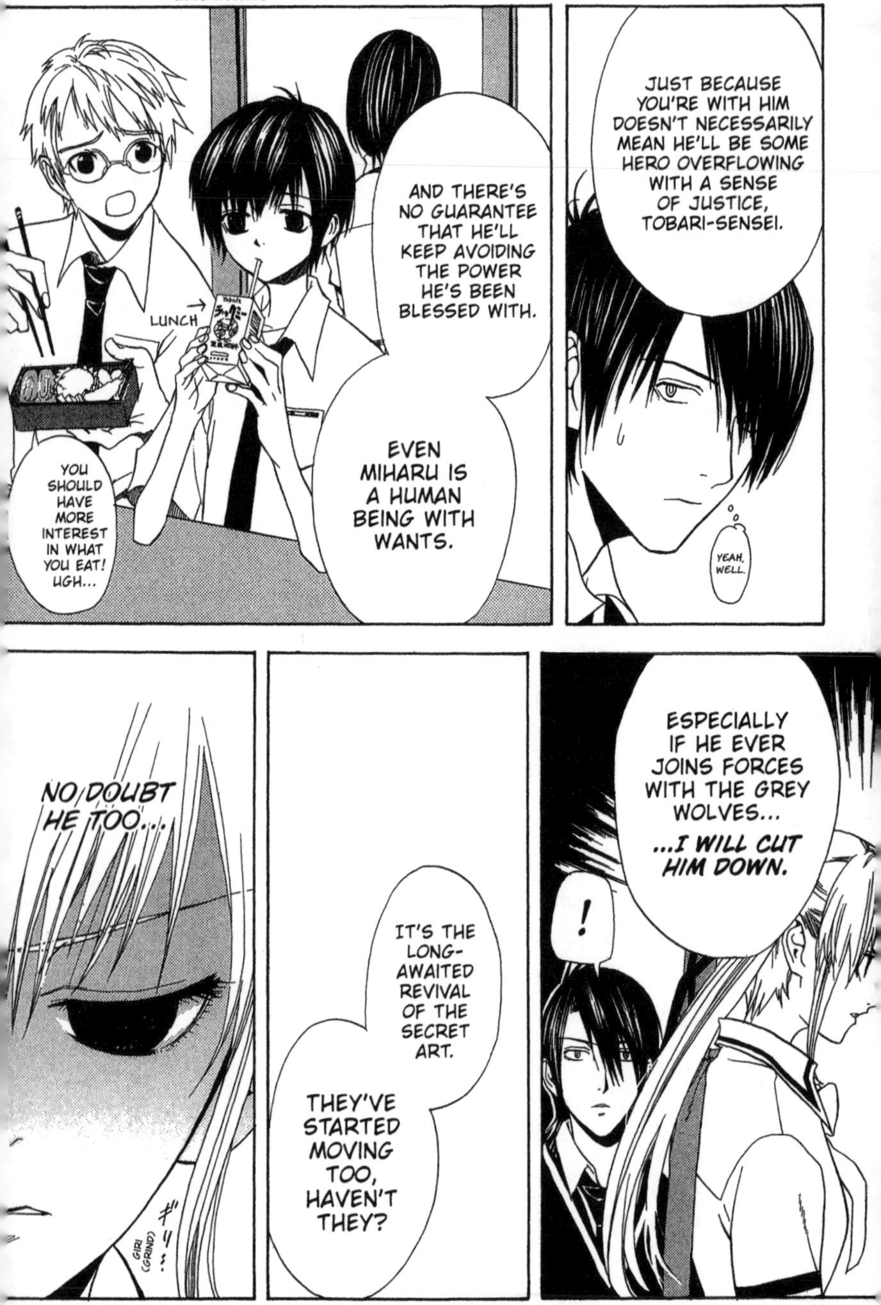
JUST BECAUSE YOU'RE WITH HIM DOESN'T NECESSARILY MEAN HE'LL BE SOME HERO OVERFLOWING WITH A SENSE OF JUSTICE, TOBARI-SENSEI.
YEAH, WELL.
AND THERE'S NO GUARANTEE THAT HE'LL KEEP AVOIDING THE POWER HE'S BEEN BLESSED WITH.
EVEN MIHARU IS A HUMAN BEING WITH WANTS.
LUNCH
YOU SHOULD HAVE MORE INTEREST IN WHAT YOU EAT! UGH...
ESPECIALLY IF HE EVER JOINS FORCES WITH THE GREY WOLVES...
...I WILL CUT HIM DOWN.
!
IT'S THE LONG-AWAITED REVIVAL OF THE SECRET ART.
THEY'VE STARTED MOVING TOO, HAVEN'T THEY?
NO DOUBT HE TOO...
GIRI (GRIND)

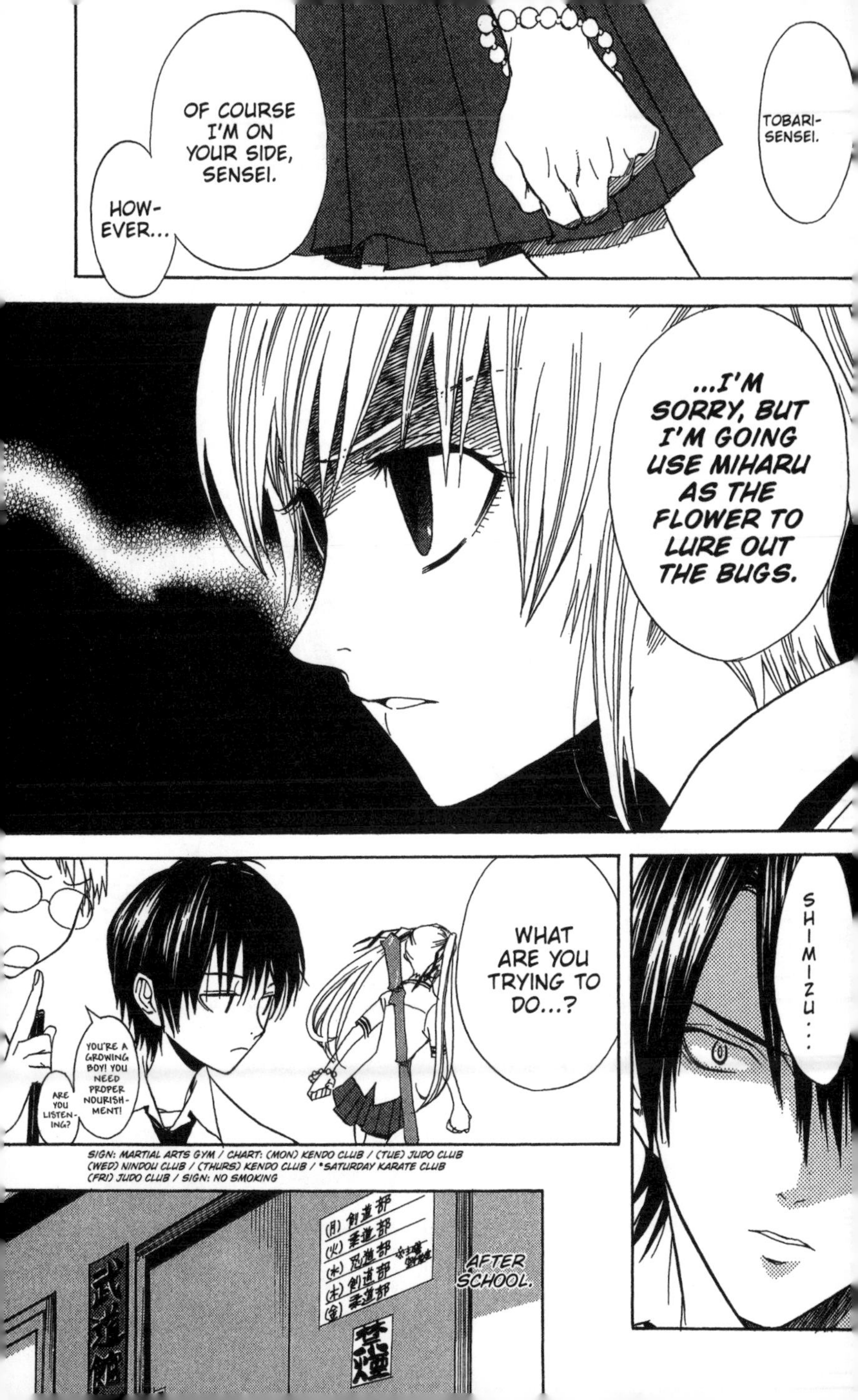
TOBARI-SENSEI.
OF COURSE I'M ON YOUR SIDE, SENSEI.
HOW-EVER...
...I'M SORRY, BUT I'M GOING USE MIHARU AS THE FLOWER TO LURE OUT THE BUGS.
SHIMIZU...
WHAT ARE YOU TRYING TO DO...?
YOU'RE A GROWING BOY! YOU NEED PROPER NOURISH-MENT!
ARE YOU LISTEN-ING?
SIGN: MARTIAL ARTS GYM / CHART: (MON) KENDO CLUB / (TUE) JUDO CLUB (WED) NINDOU CLUB / (THURS) KENDO CLUB / *SATURDAY KARATE CLUB (FRI) JUDO CLUB / SIGN: NO SMOKING
AFTER SCHOOL.
武道館
(月) 剣道部
(火) 柔道部
(水) 忍道部
(木) 剣道部
(金) 柔道部
禁煙

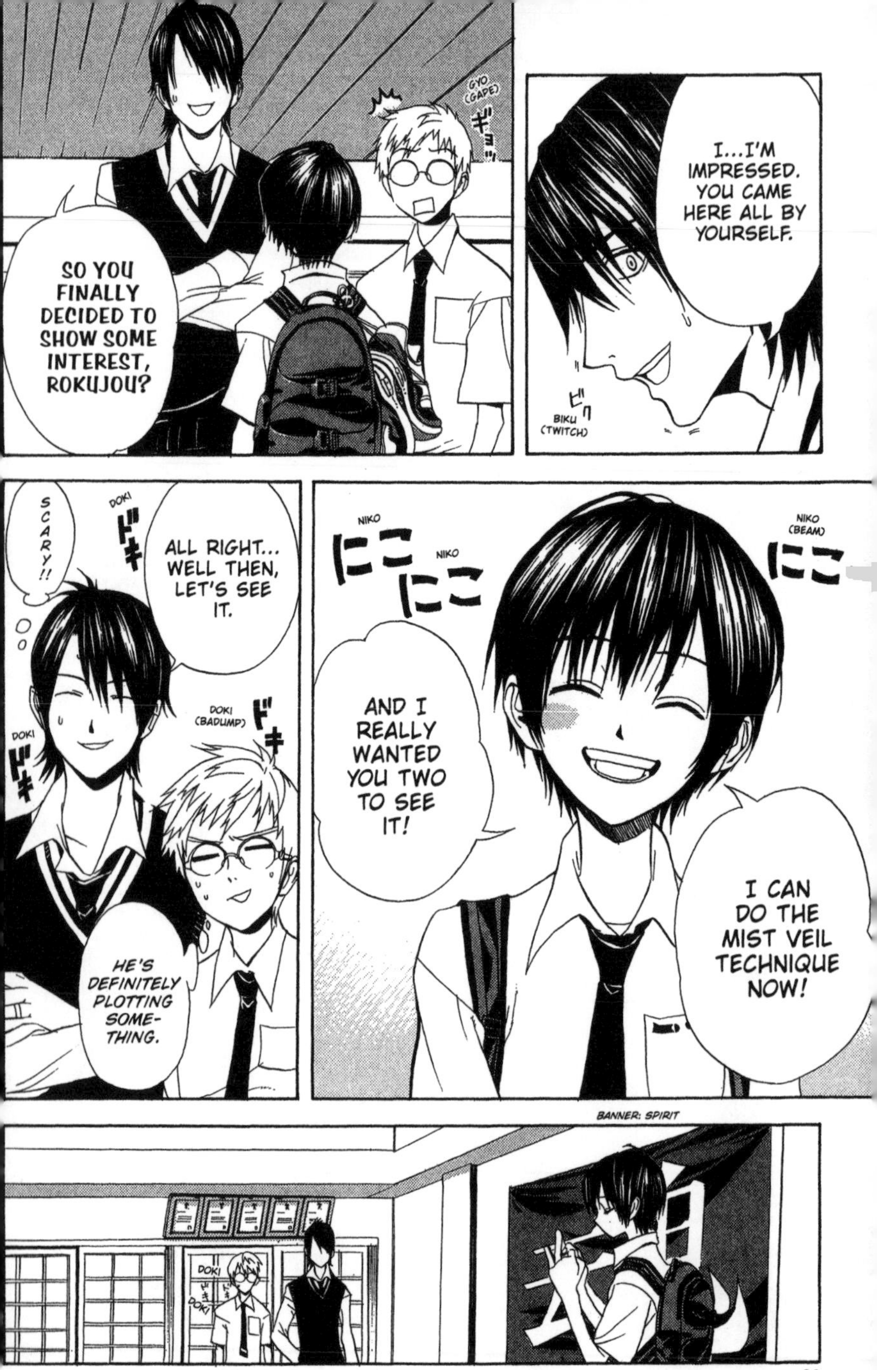
I...I'M IMPRESSED. YOU CAME HERE ALL BY YOURSELF.
BIKU (TWITCH)
GYO (GAPE)
SO YOU FINALLY DECIDED TO SHOW SOME INTEREST, ROKUJOU?
NIKO (BEAM)
NIKO
NIKO
AND I REALLY WANTED YOU TWO TO SEE IT!
I CAN DO THE MIST VEIL TECHNIQUE NOW!
DOKI
ALL RIGHT... WELL THEN, LET'S SEE IT.
SCARY!!
DOKI (BADUMP)
DOKI
HE'S DEFINITELY PLOTTING SOME-THING.
BANNER: SPIRIT
DOKI
DOKI

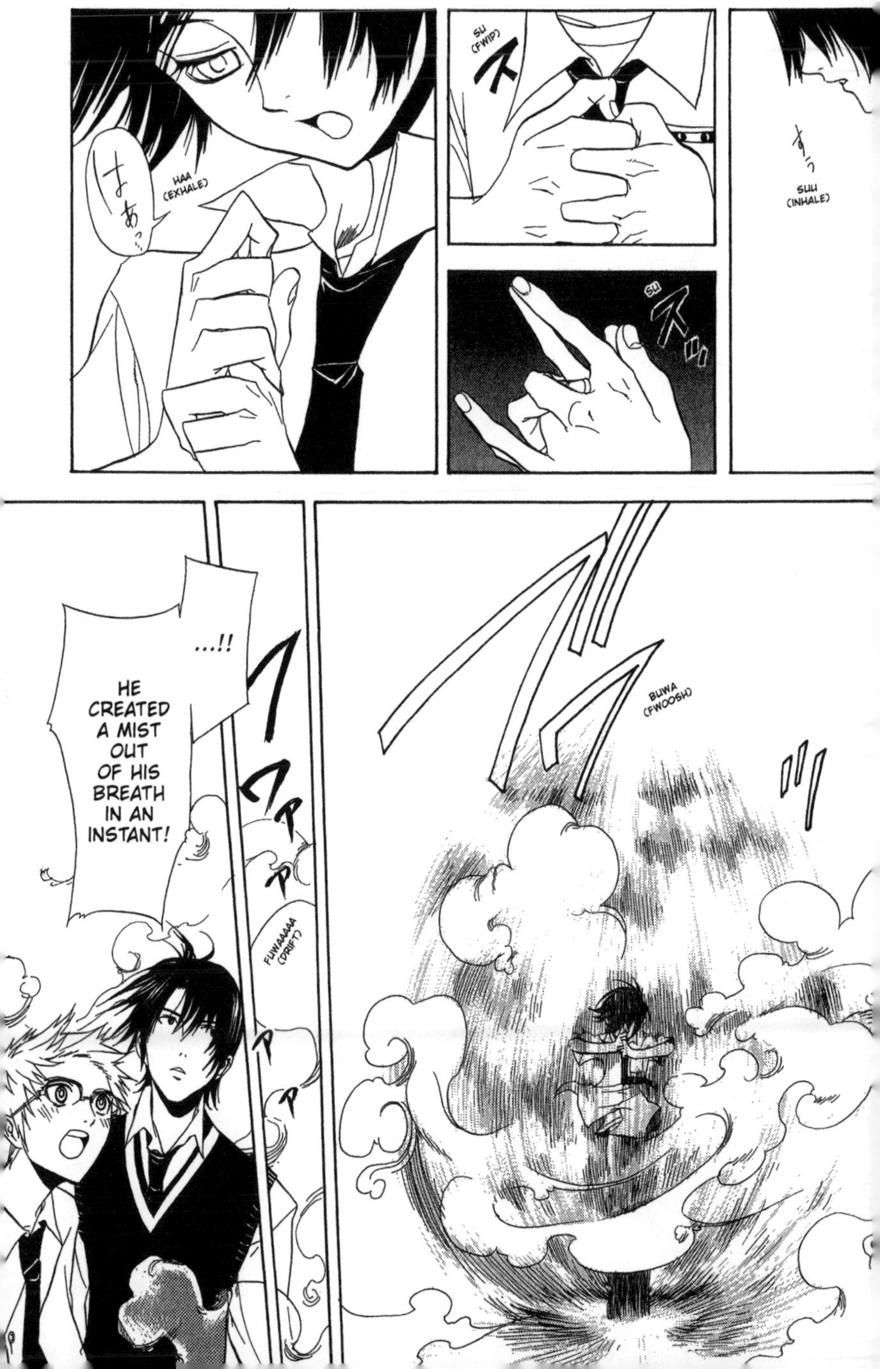
すぅ
SUU (INHALE)
ス
SU (FWIP)
ス
SU
はあっ
HAA (EXHALE)
BUWA (FWOOSH)
FUWAAAAA (DRIFT)
...!!
HE CREATED A MIST OUT OF HIS BREATH IN AN INSTANT!

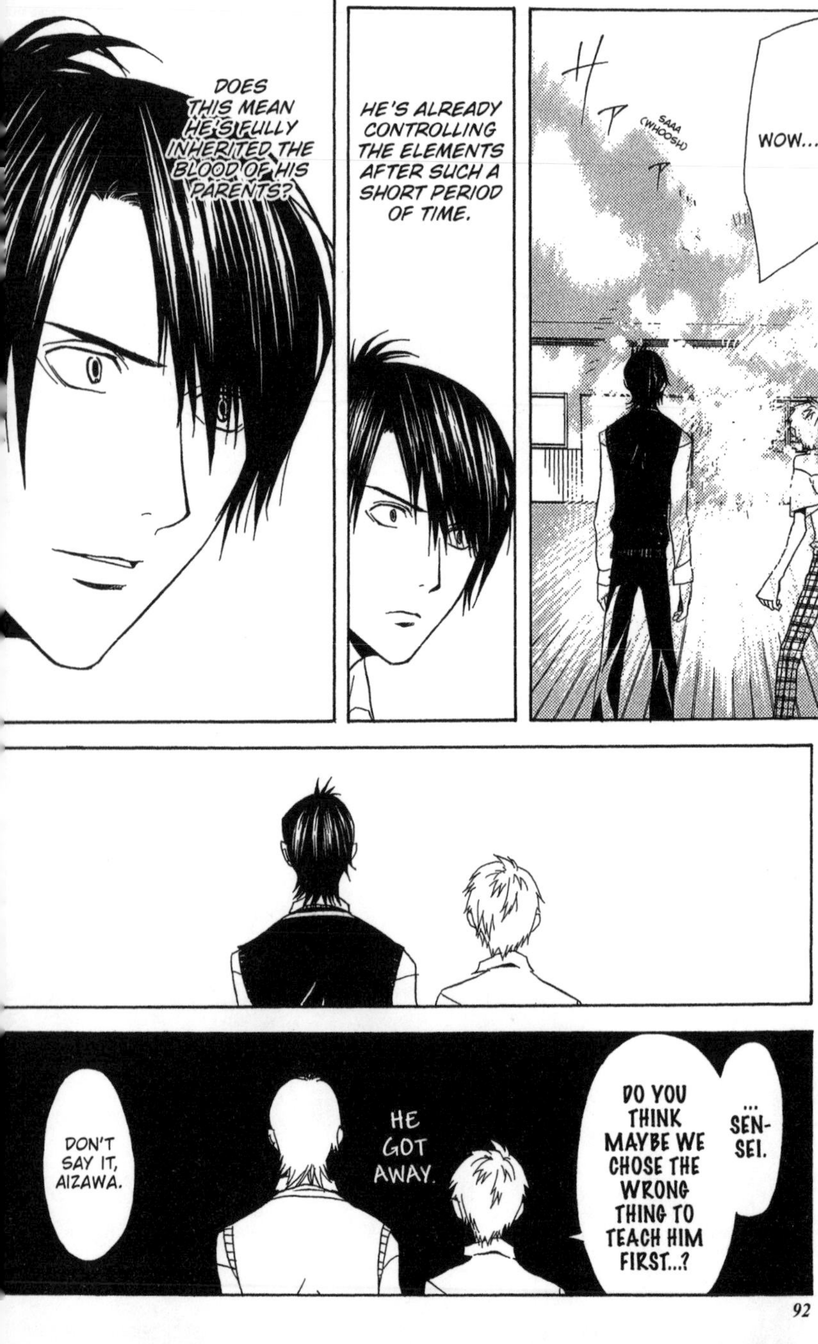

WOW...!
SAAA (WHOOSH)
HE'S ALREADY CONTROLLING THE ELEMENTS AFTER SUCH A SHORT PERIOD OF TIME.
DOES THIS MEAN HE'S FULLY INHERITED THE BLOOD OF HIS PARENTS?
... SEN-SEI.
DO YOU THINK MAYBE WE CHOSE THE WRONG THING TO TEACH HIM FIRST...?
HE GOT AWAY.
DON'T SAY IT, AIZAWA.

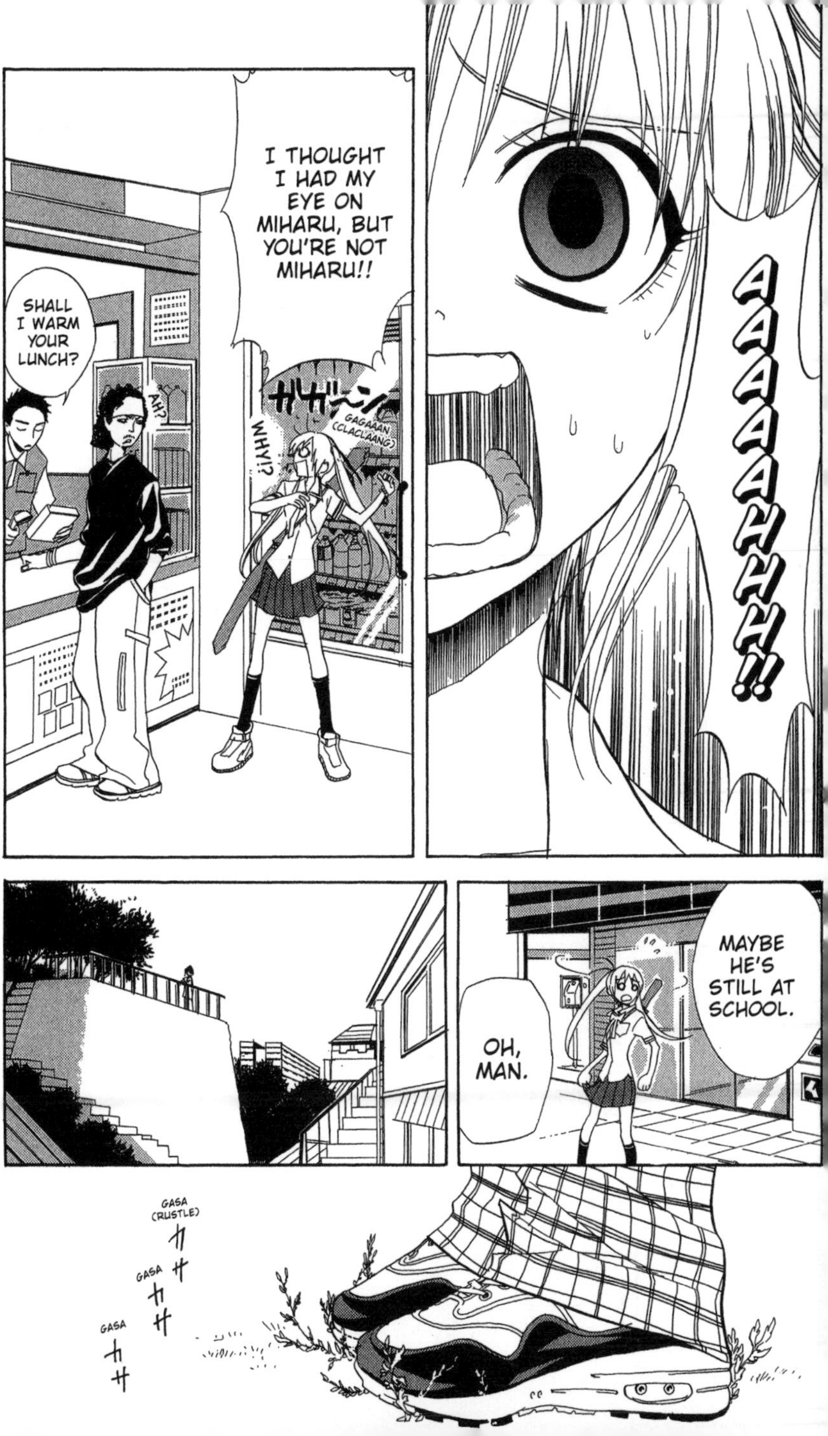
AAAAAAHHH!!
I THOUGHT I HAD MY EYE ON MIHARU, BUT YOU'RE NOT MIHARU!!
GAGAAAN (CLACLAANG)
WHY!?
AH?
SHALL I WARM YOUR LUNCH?
MAYBE HE'S STILL AT SCHOOL.
OH, MAN.
GASA (RUSTLE)
GASA
GASA

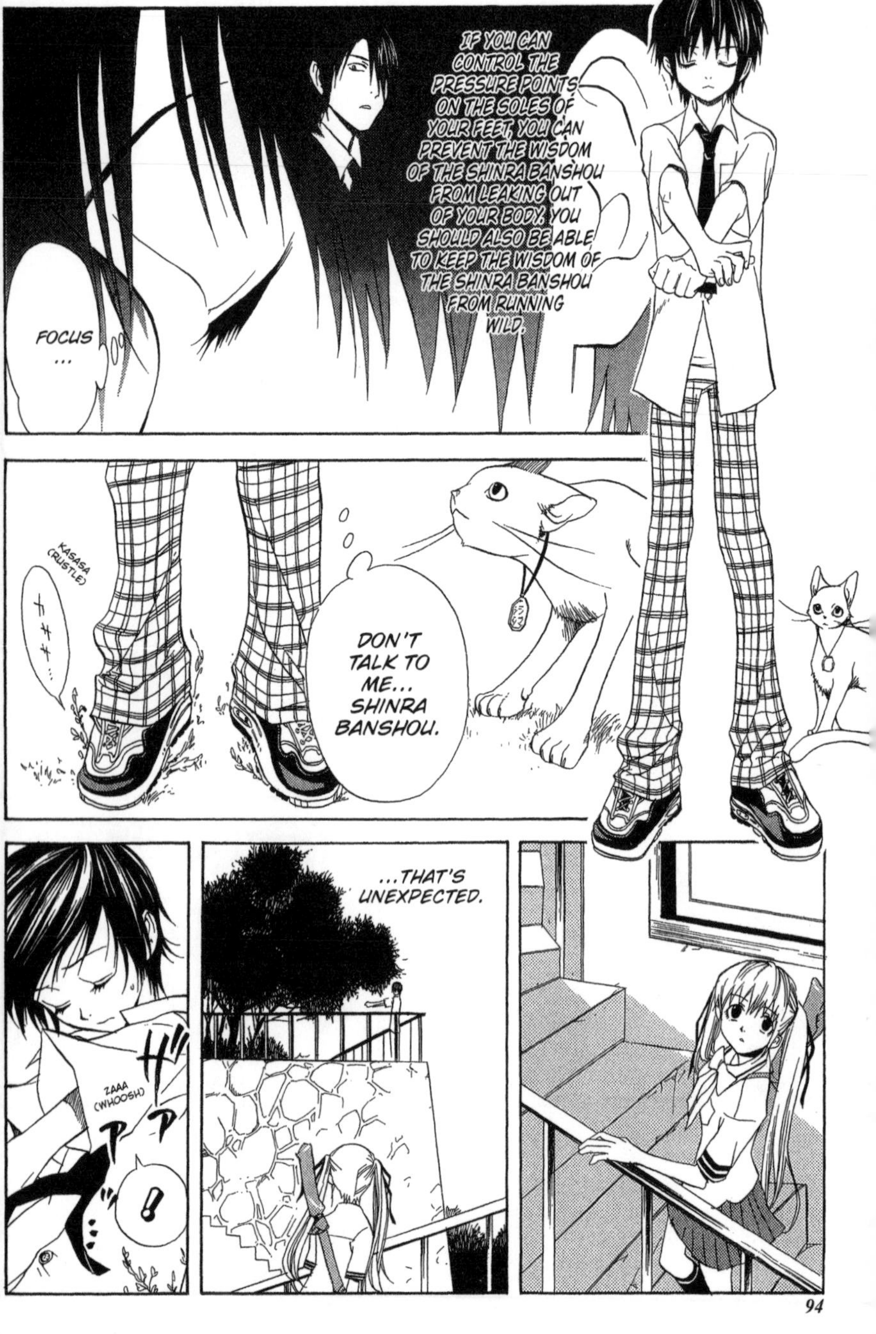

IF YOU CAN CONTROL THE PRESSURE POINTS ON THE SOLES OF YOUR FEET, YOU CAN PREVENT THE WISDOM OF THE SHINRA BANSHOU FROM LEAKING OUT OF YOUR BODY. YOU SHOULD ALSO BE ABLE TO KEEP THE WISDOM OF THE SHINRA BANSHOU FROM RUNNING WILD.
FOCUS ...
DON'T TALK TO ME... SHINRA BANSHOU.
KASASA (RUSTLE)
...THAT'S UNEXPECTED.
ZAAA (WHOOSH)
!

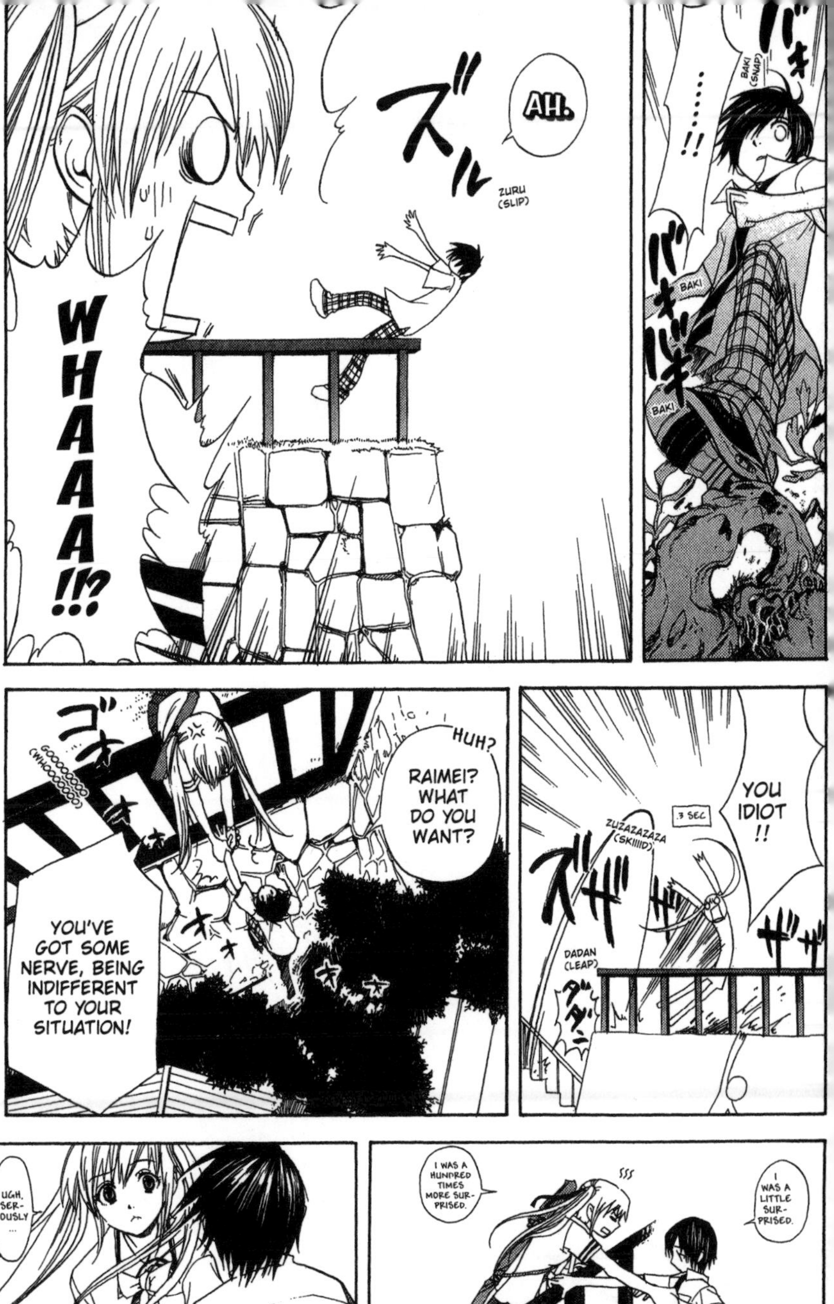
......!!
BAKI (SNAP)
BAKI
BAKI
AH.
ZURU (SLIP)
WHAAAA!!?
YOU IDIOT!!
.3 SEC
ZUZAZAZAZA (SKIIIID)
DADAN (LEAP)
HUH?
RAIMEI? WHAT DO YOU WANT?
GOOOOOOOOO (WHOOOOOOOO)
YOU'VE GOT SOME NERVE, BEING INDIFFERENT TO YOUR SITUATION!
I WAS A LITTLE SURPRISED.
I WAS A HUNDRED TIMES MORE SURPRISED.
UGH, SERIOUSLY ...

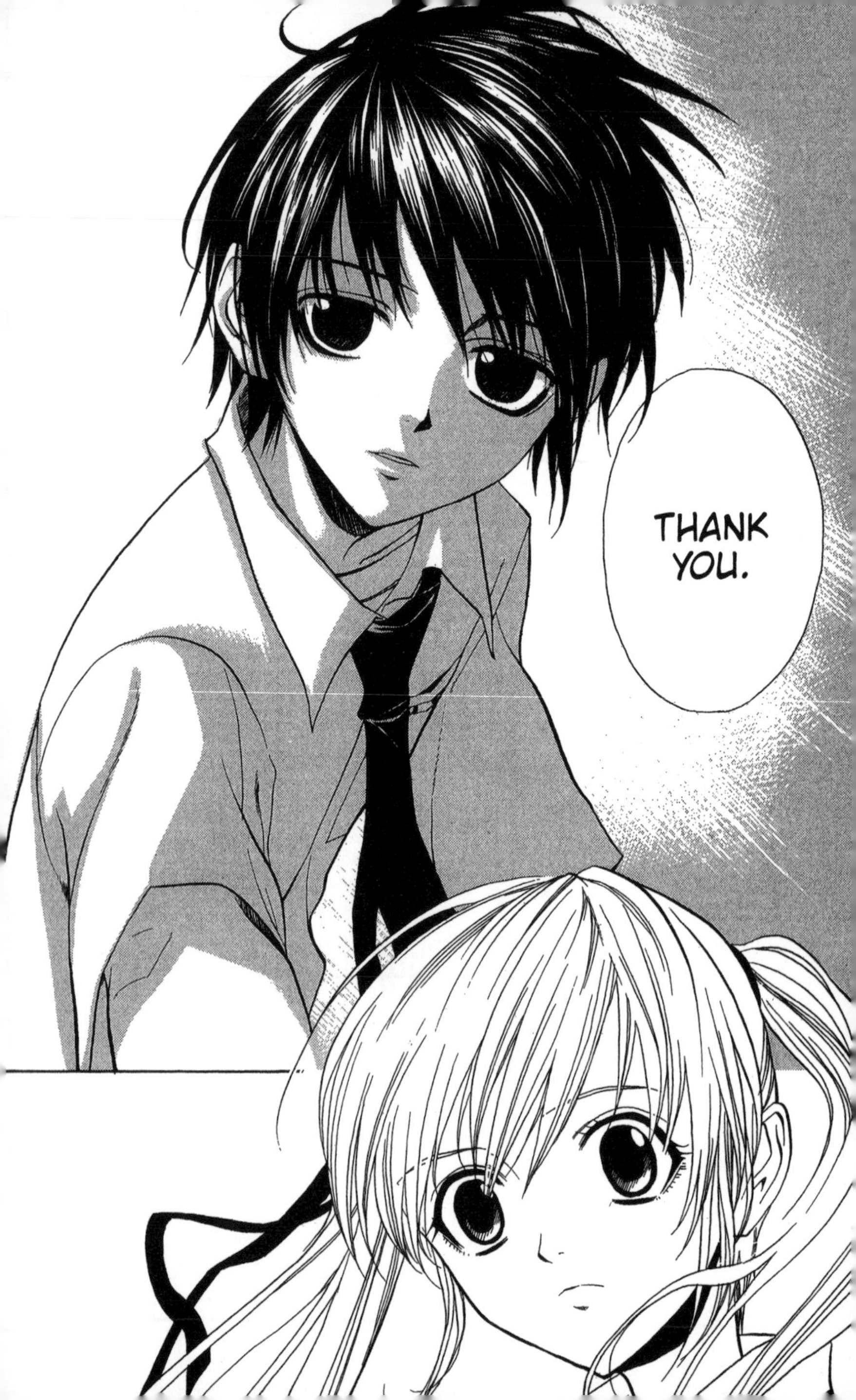
THANK YOU.

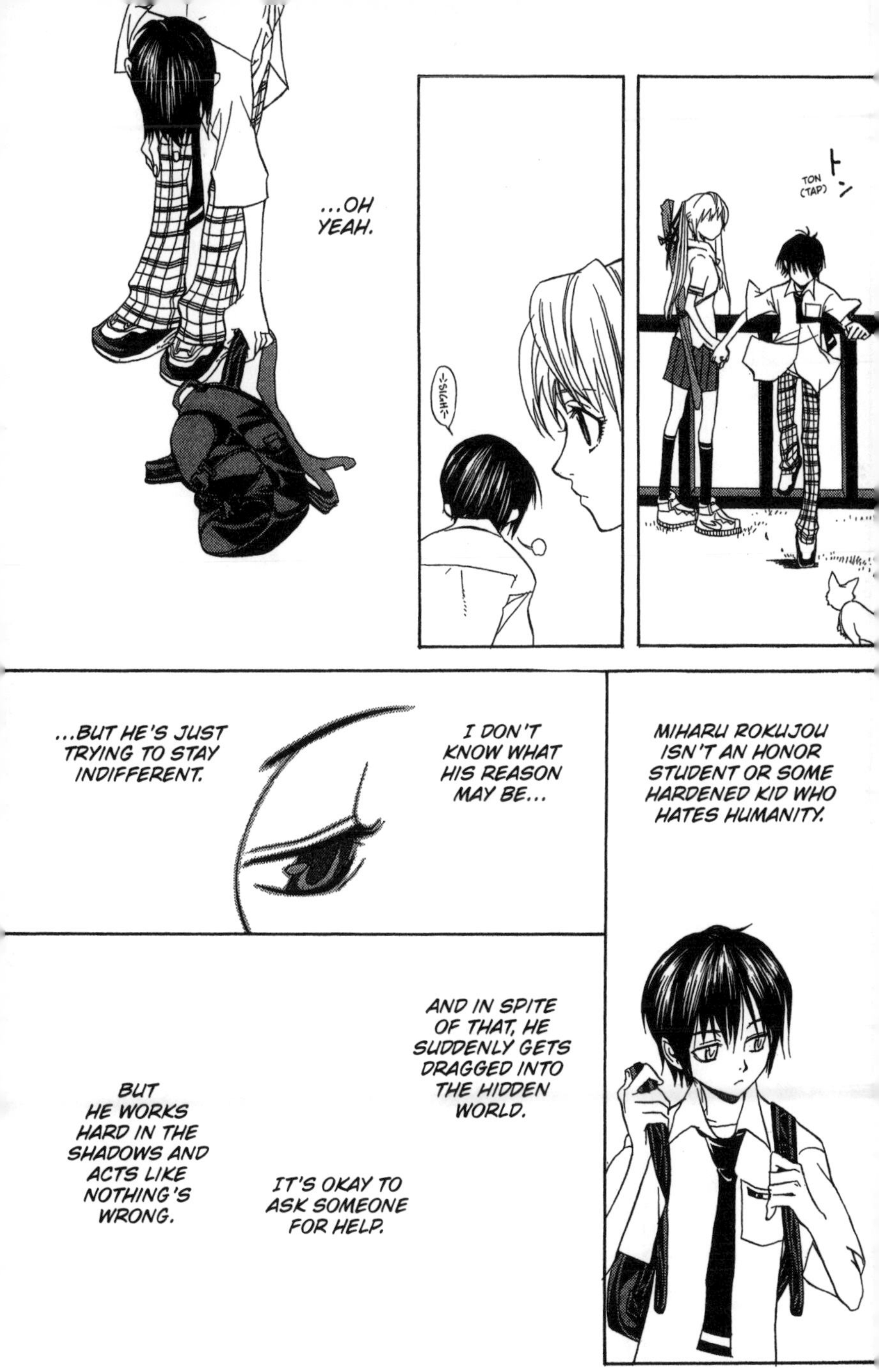

TON (TAP)
-SIGH-
...OH YEAH.
MIHARU ROKUJOU ISN'T AN HONOR STUDENT OR SOME HARDENED KID WHO HATES HUMANITY.
I DON'T KNOW WHAT HIS REASON MAY BE...
...BUT HE'S JUST TRYING TO STAY INDIFFERENT.
AND IN SPITE OF THAT, HE SUDDENLY GETS DRAGGED INTO THE HIDDEN WORLD.
BUT HE WORKS HARD IN THE SHADOWS AND ACTS LIKE NOTHING'S WRONG.
IT'S OKAY TO ASK SOMEONE FOR HELP.

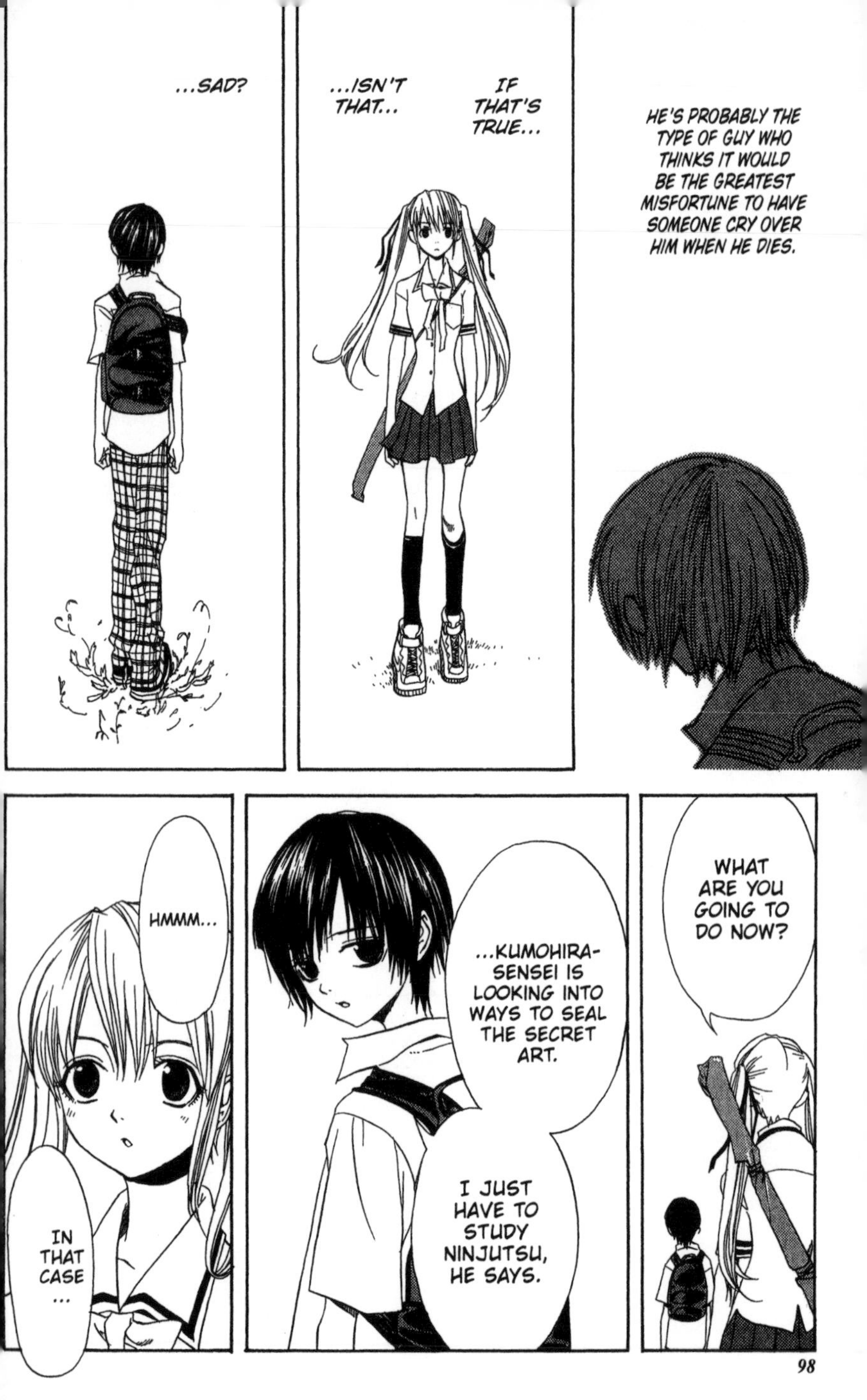
HE'S PROBABLY THE TYPE OF GUY WHO THINKS IT WOULD BE THE GREATEST MISFORTUNE TO HAVE SOMEONE CRY OVER HIM WHEN HE DIES.
IF THAT'S TRUE...
...ISN'T THAT...
...SAD?
WHAT ARE YOU GOING TO DO NOW?
...KUMOHIRA-SENSEI IS LOOKING INTO WAYS TO SEAL THE SECRET ART.
I JUST HAVE TO STUDY NINJUTSU, HE SAYS.
HMMM...
IN THAT CASE...

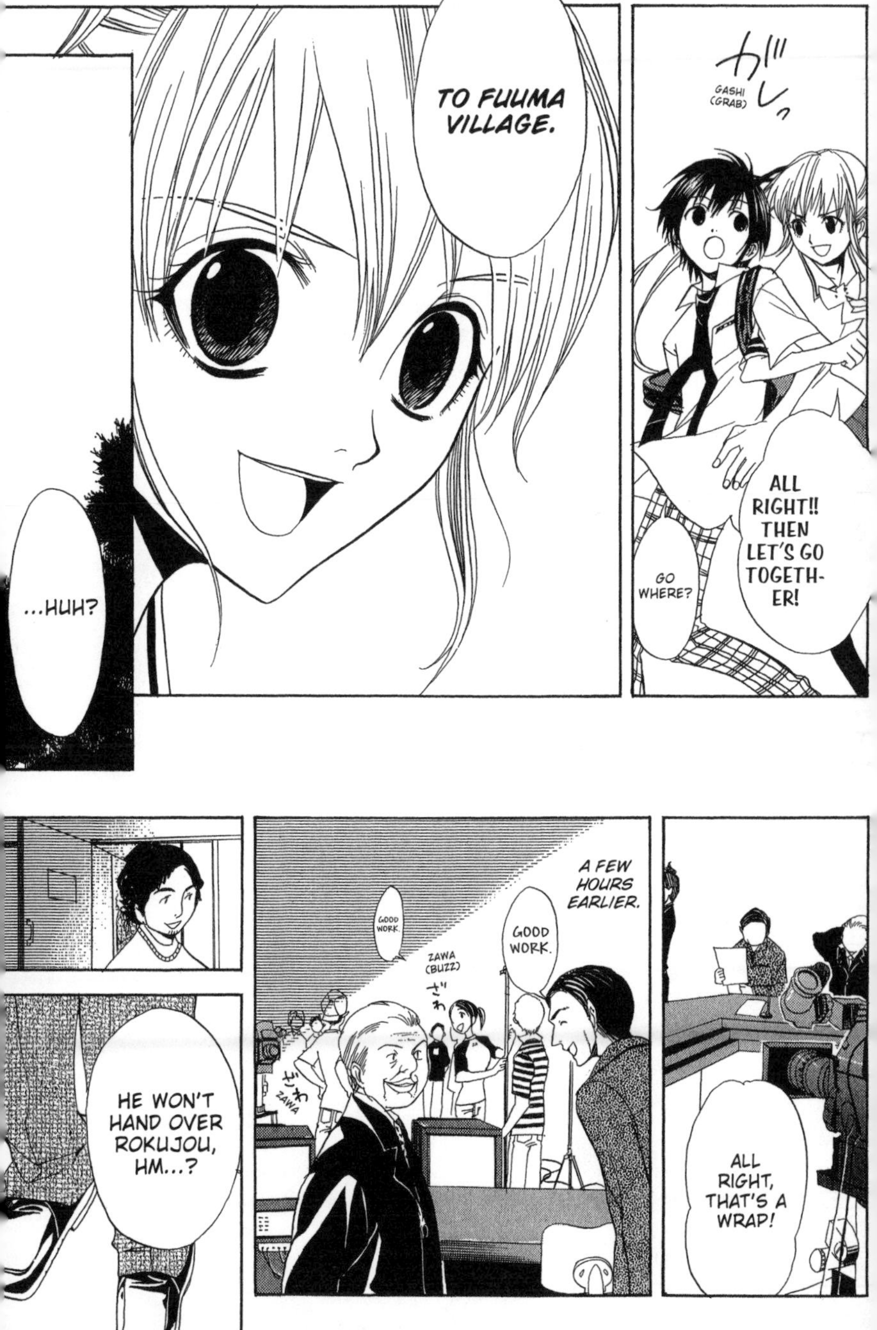
GASHI (GRAB)
ALL RIGHT!! THEN LET'S GO TOGETHER!
GO WHERE?
TO FUUMA VILLAGE.
...HUH?
ALL RIGHT, THAT'S A WRAP!
A FEW HOURS EARLIER.
GOOD WORK.
ZAWA (BUZZ)
GOOD WORK.
ZAWA
HE WON'T HAND OVER ROKUJOU, HM...?

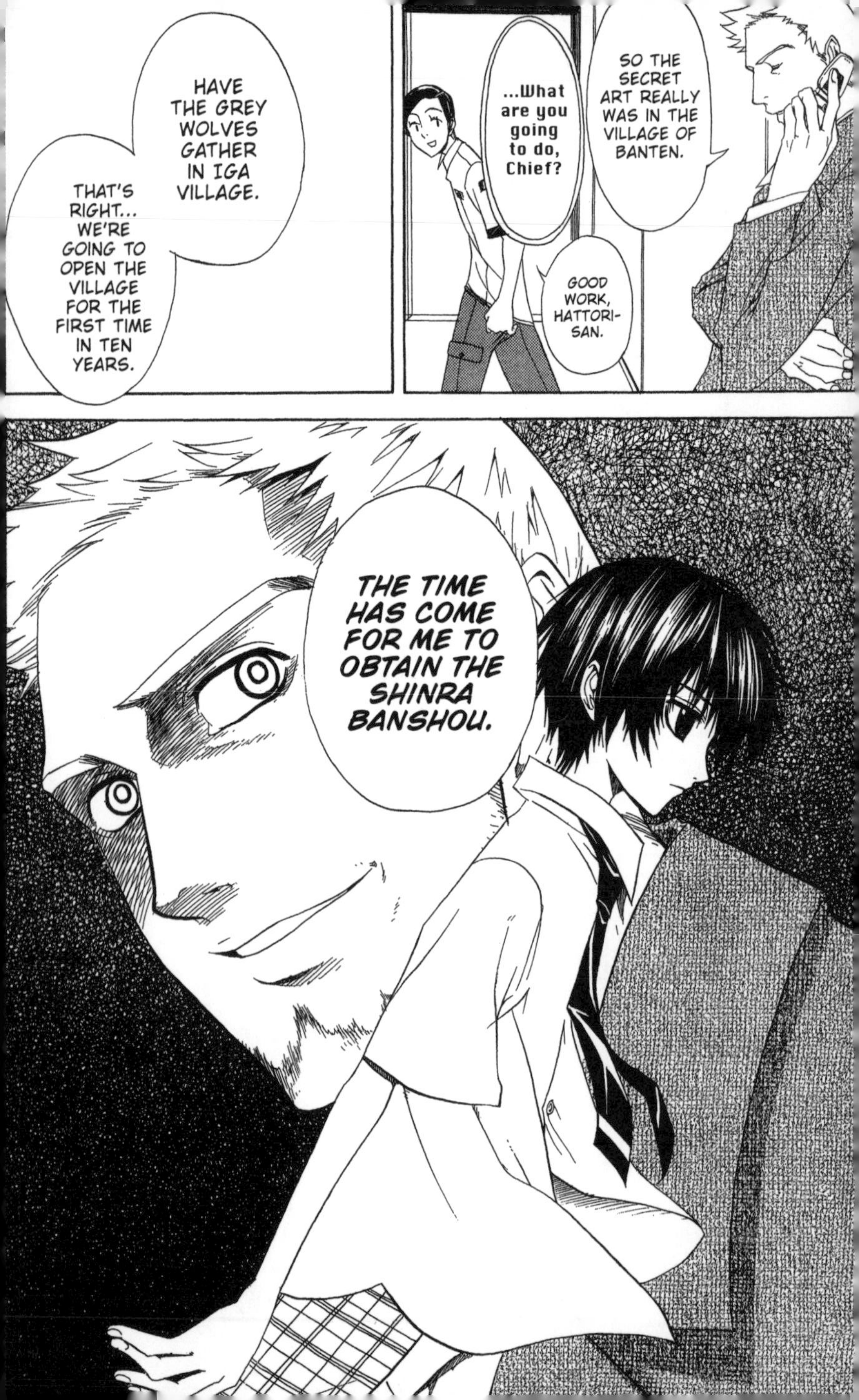
SO THE SECRET ART REALLY WAS IN THE VILLAGE OF BANTEN.
...What are you going to do, Chief?
GOOD WORK, HATTORI-SAN.
HAVE THE GREY WOLVES GATHER IN IGA VILLAGE.
THAT'S RIGHT... WE'RE GOING TO OPEN THE VILLAGE FOR THE FIRST TIME IN TEN YEARS.
THE TIME HAS COME FOR ME TO OBTAIN THE SHINRA BANSHOU.

CHAPTER 4: NONRECIPROCAL MEMORIES

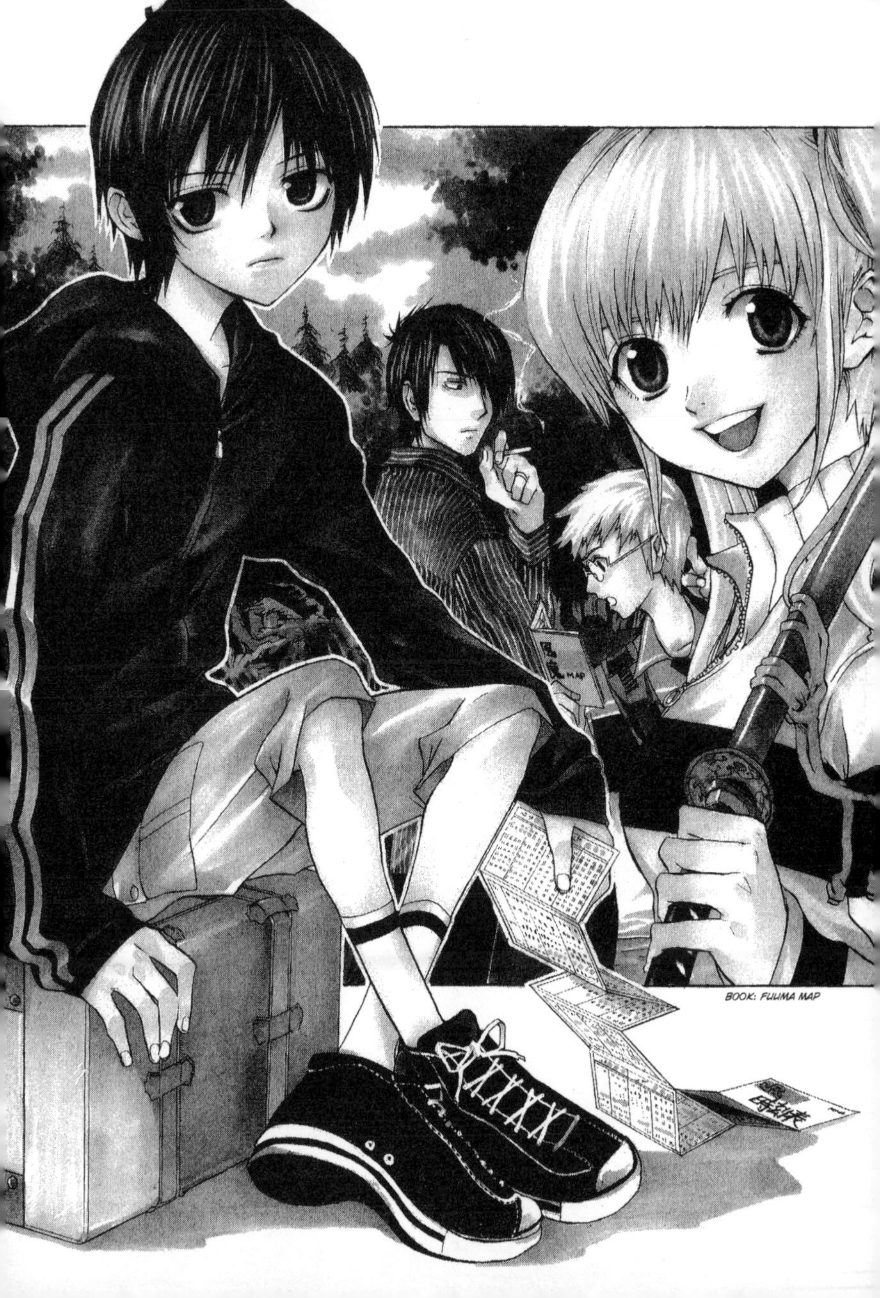
BOOK: FUUMA MAP

COME ON, HE CAN AT LEAST GO TO FUUMA VILLAGE!
I DON'T WANT TO RELY ON OUTSIDE NINJA IF I CAN HELP IT!
GO (RUMBLE)
GO
GO
GO
GO

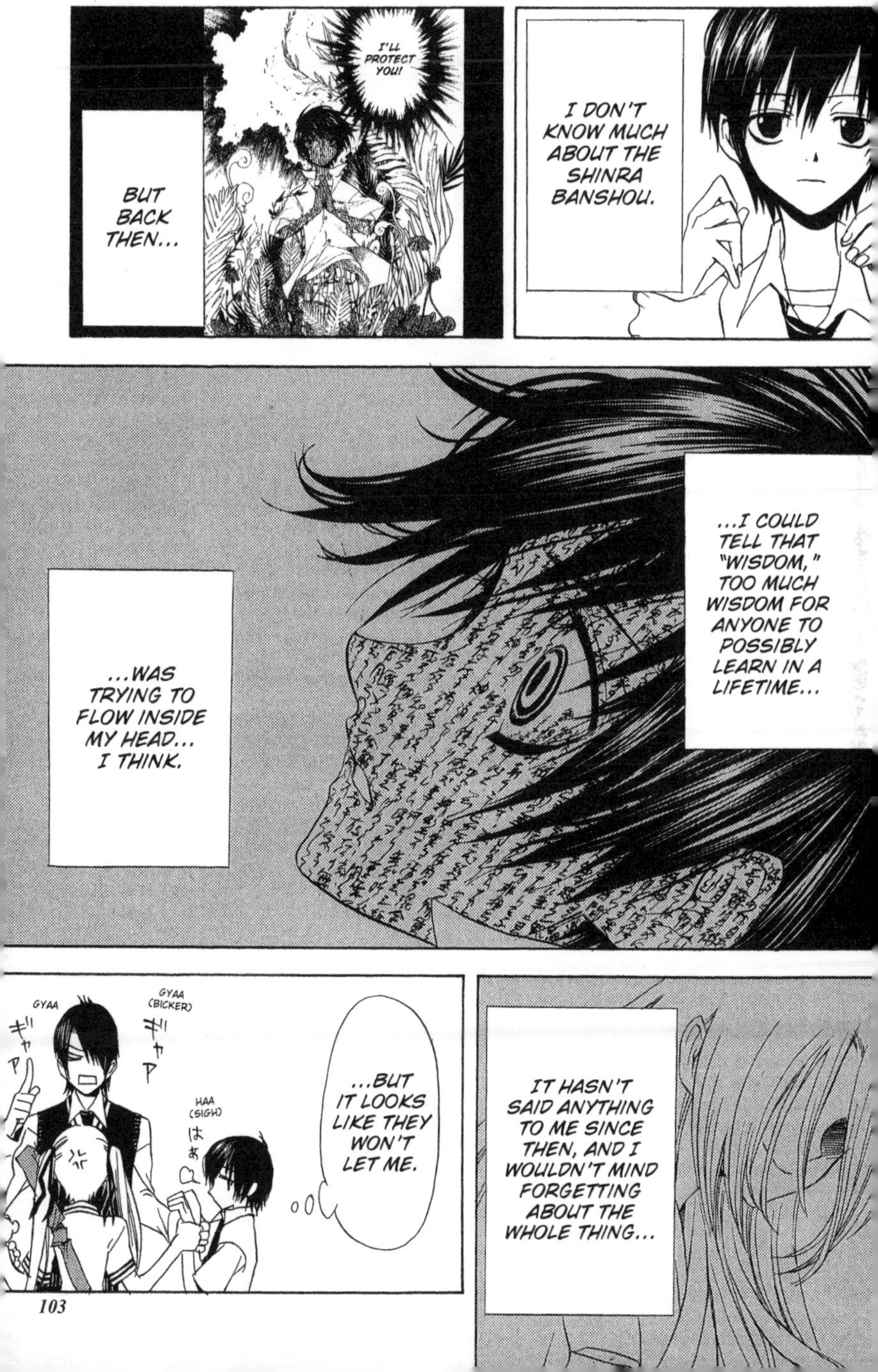
I DON'T KNOW MUCH ABOUT THE SHINRA BANSHOU.
I'LL PROTECT YOU!
BUT BACK THEN...
...I COULD TELL THAT "WISDOM," TOO MUCH WISDOM FOR ANYONE TO POSSIBLY LEARN IN A LIFETIME...
...WAS TRYING TO FLOW INSIDE MY HEAD... I THINK.
IT HASN'T SAID ANYTHING TO ME SINCE THEN, AND I WOULDN'T MIND FORGETTING ABOUT THE WHOLE THING...
...BUT IT LOOKS LIKE THEY WON'T LET ME.
GYAA (BICKER)
ギャア
HAA (SIGH)
はぁ
GYAA
ギャア

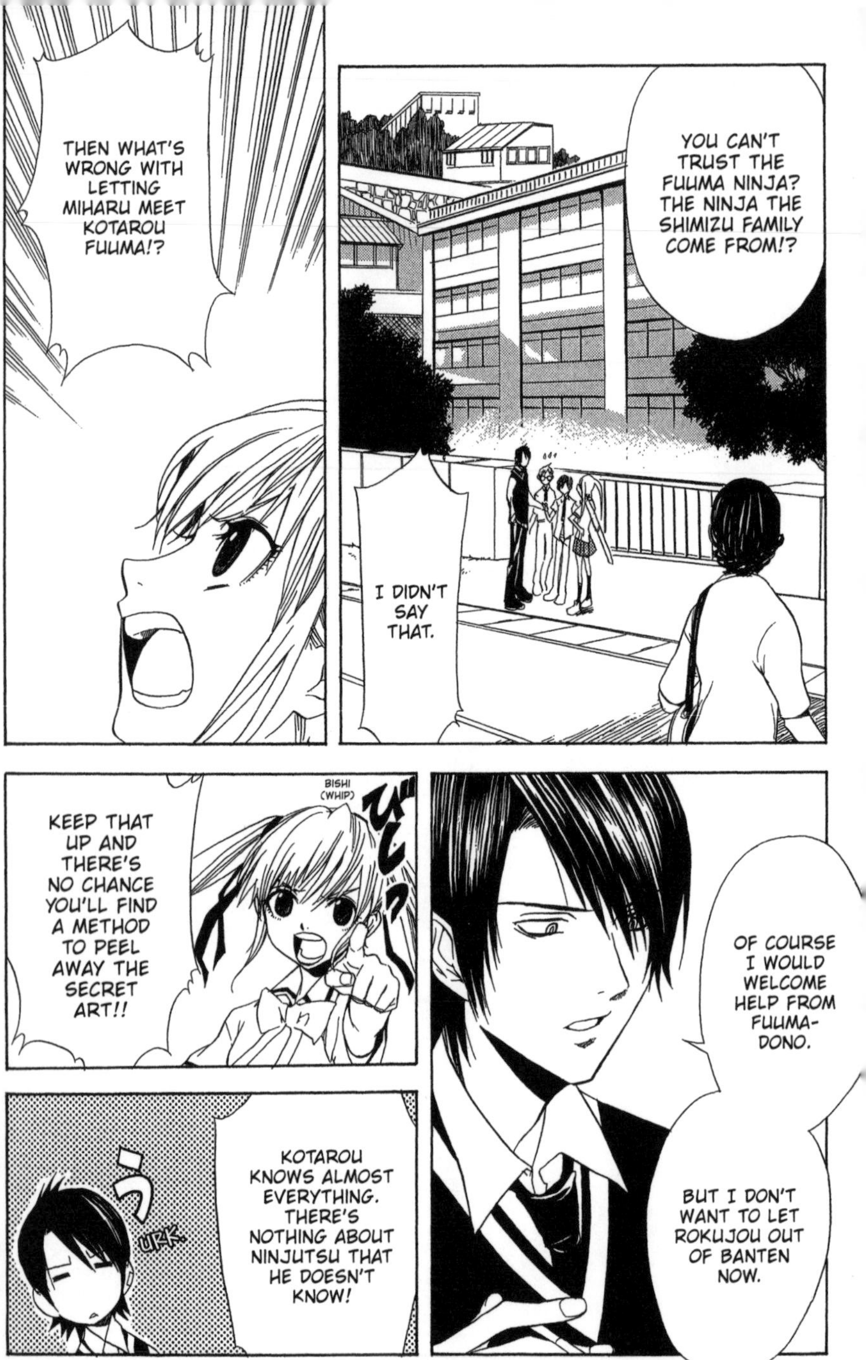
YOU CAN'T TRUST THE FUUMA NINJA? THE NINJA THE SHIMIZU FAMILY COME FROM!?
I DIDN'T SAY THAT.
THEN WHAT'S WRONG WITH LETTING MIHARU MEET KOTAROU FUUMA!?
OF COURSE I WOULD WELCOME HELP FROM FUUMA-DONO.
BUT I DON'T WANT TO LET ROKUJOU OUT OF BANTEN NOW.
BISHI (WHIP)
KEEP THAT UP AND THERE'S NO CHANCE YOU'LL FIND A METHOD TO PEEL AWAY THE SECRET ART!!
URK
KOTAROU KNOWS ALMOST EVERYTHING. THERE'S NOTHING ABOUT NINJUTSU THAT HE DOESN'T KNOW!

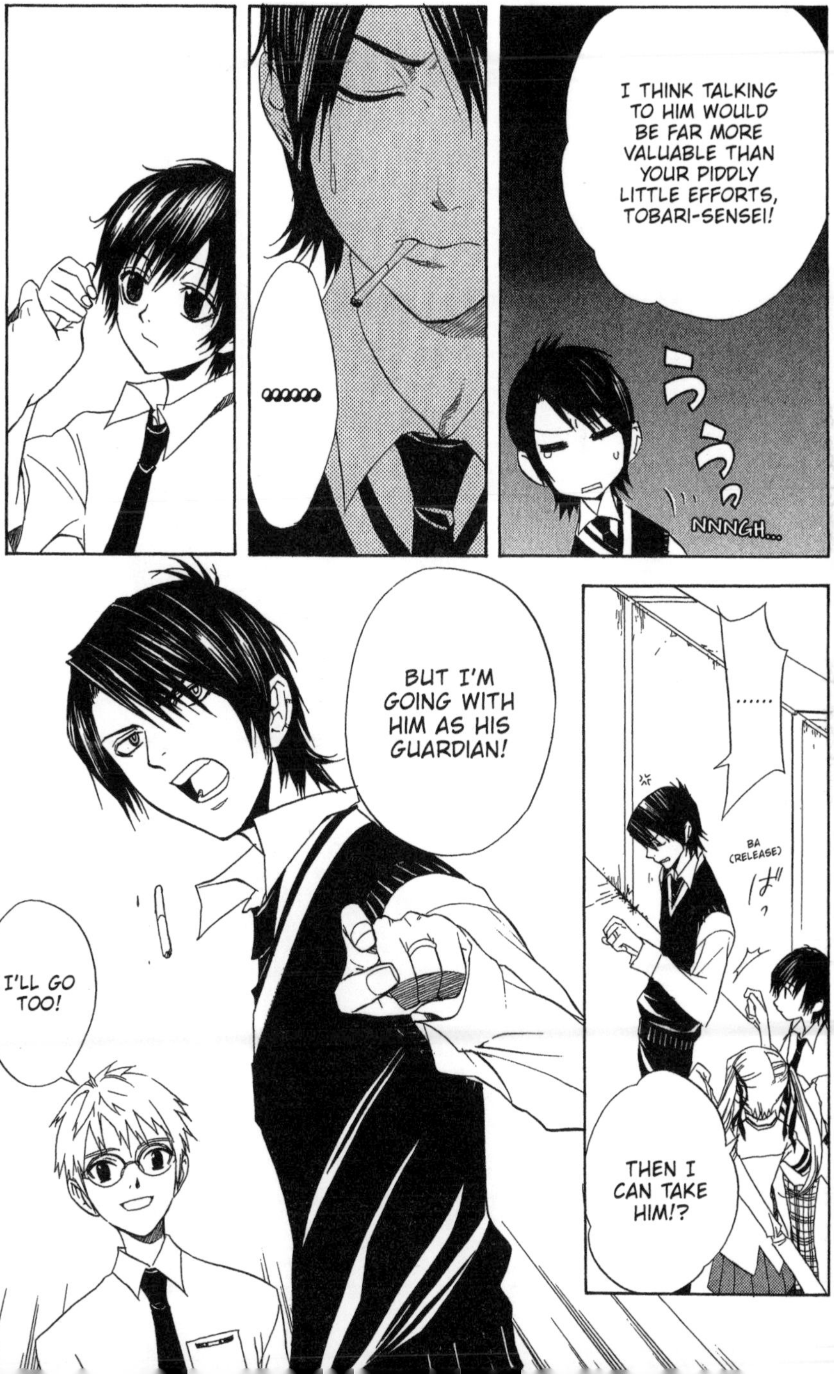

I THINK TALKING TO HIM WOULD BE FAR MORE VALUABLE THAN YOUR PIDDLY LITTLE EFFORTS, TOBARI-SENSEI!
NNNGH...
......
......
BA (RELEASE)
THEN I CAN TAKE HIM!?
BUT I'M GOING WITH HIM AS HIS GUARDIAN!
I'LL GO TOO!

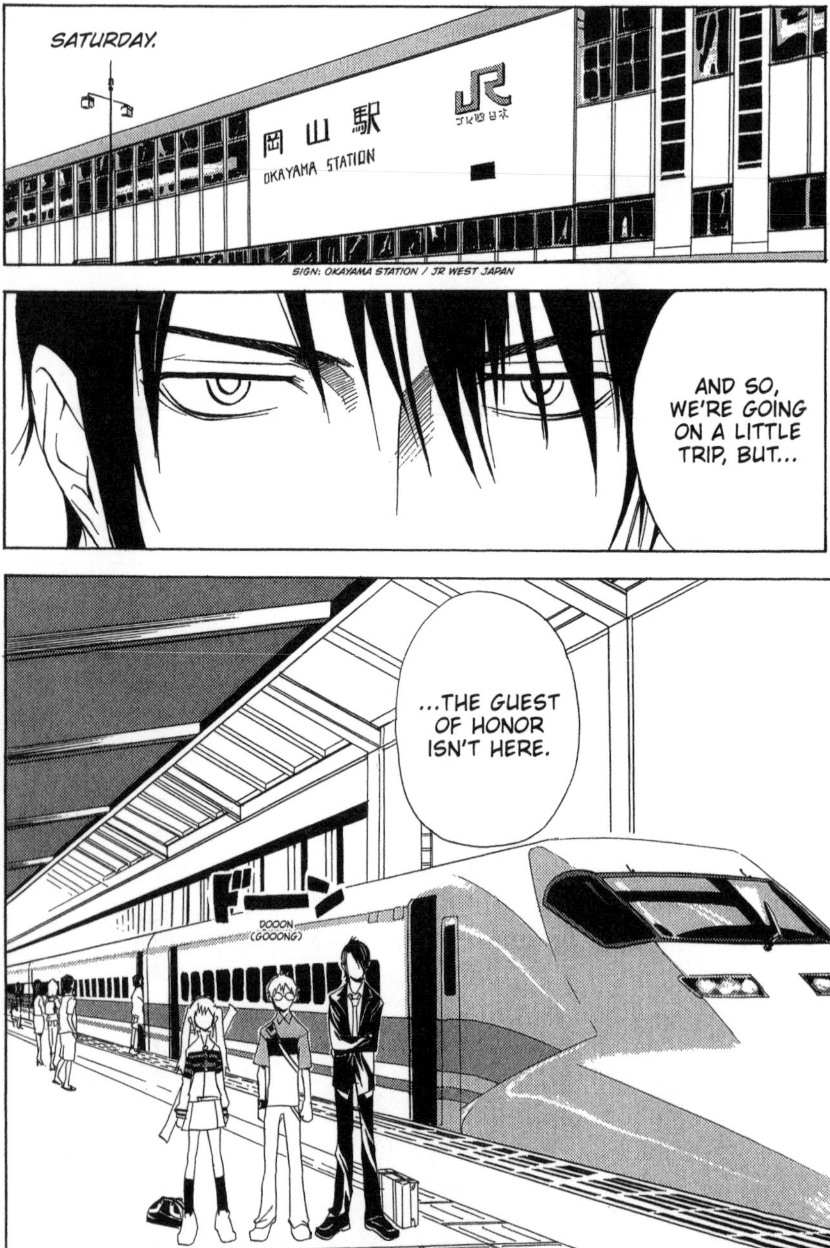
SATURDAY.
岡山駅
OKAYAMA STATION
JR
SIGN: OKAYAMA STATION / JR WEST JAPAN
AND SO, WE'RE GOING ON A LITTLE TRIP, BUT...
...THE GUEST OF HONOR ISN'T HERE.
ドーン
DOOON (GOOONG)

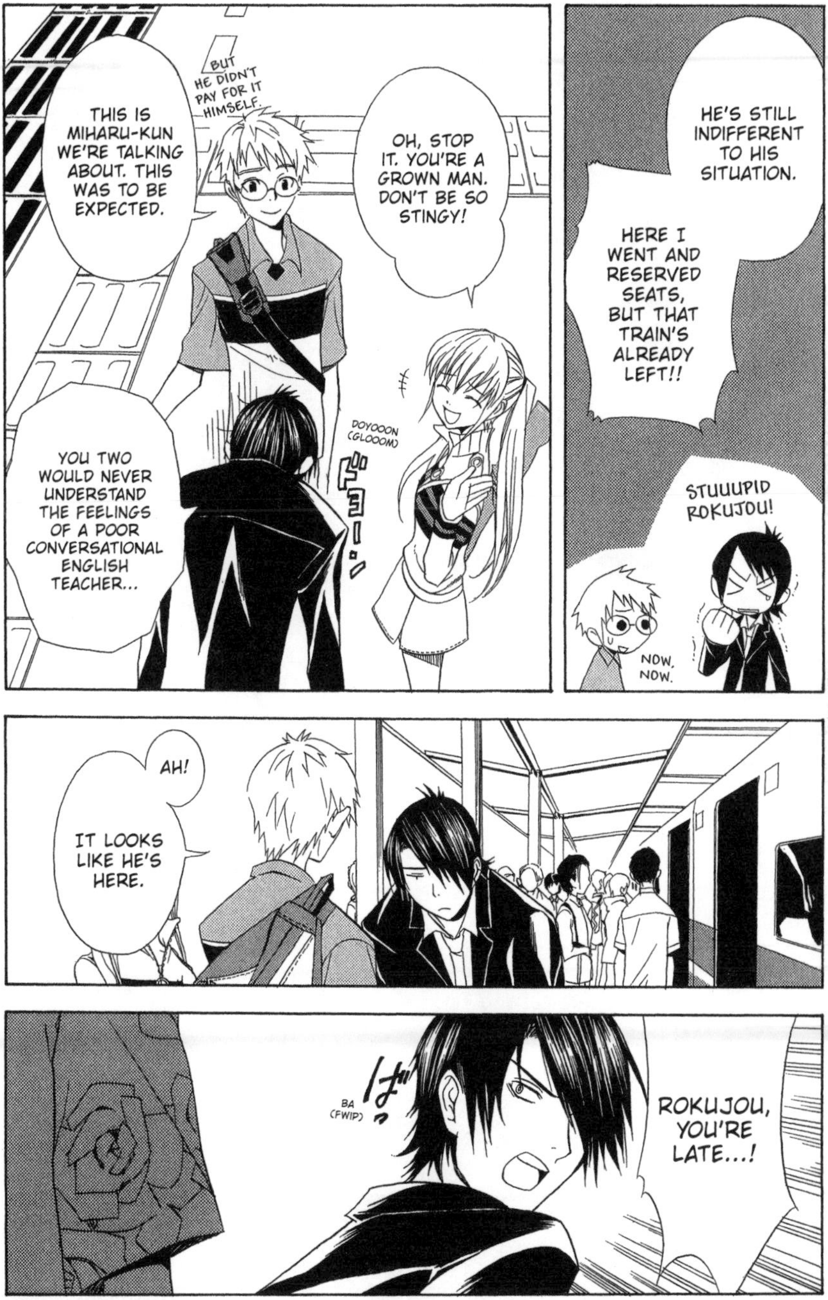
HE'S STILL INDIFFERENT TO HIS SITUATION.
HERE I WENT AND RESERVED SEATS, BUT THAT TRAIN'S ALREADY LEFT!!
STUUUPID ROKUJOU!
NOW, NOW.
OH, STOP IT. YOU'RE A GROWN MAN. DON'T BE SO STINGY!
BUT HE DIDN'T PAY FOR IT HIMSELF.
THIS IS MIHARU-KUN WE'RE TALKING ABOUT. THIS WAS TO BE EXPECTED.
DOYOOON (GLOOOM)
YOU TWO WOULD NEVER UNDERSTAND THE FEELINGS OF A POOR CONVERSATIONAL ENGLISH TEACHER...
AH!
IT LOOKS LIKE HE'S HERE.
ROKUJOU, YOU'RE LATE...!
BA (FWIP)

SHIRT: MUSCULAR PAIN / HAT: AGRICULTURAL COOPERATIVE

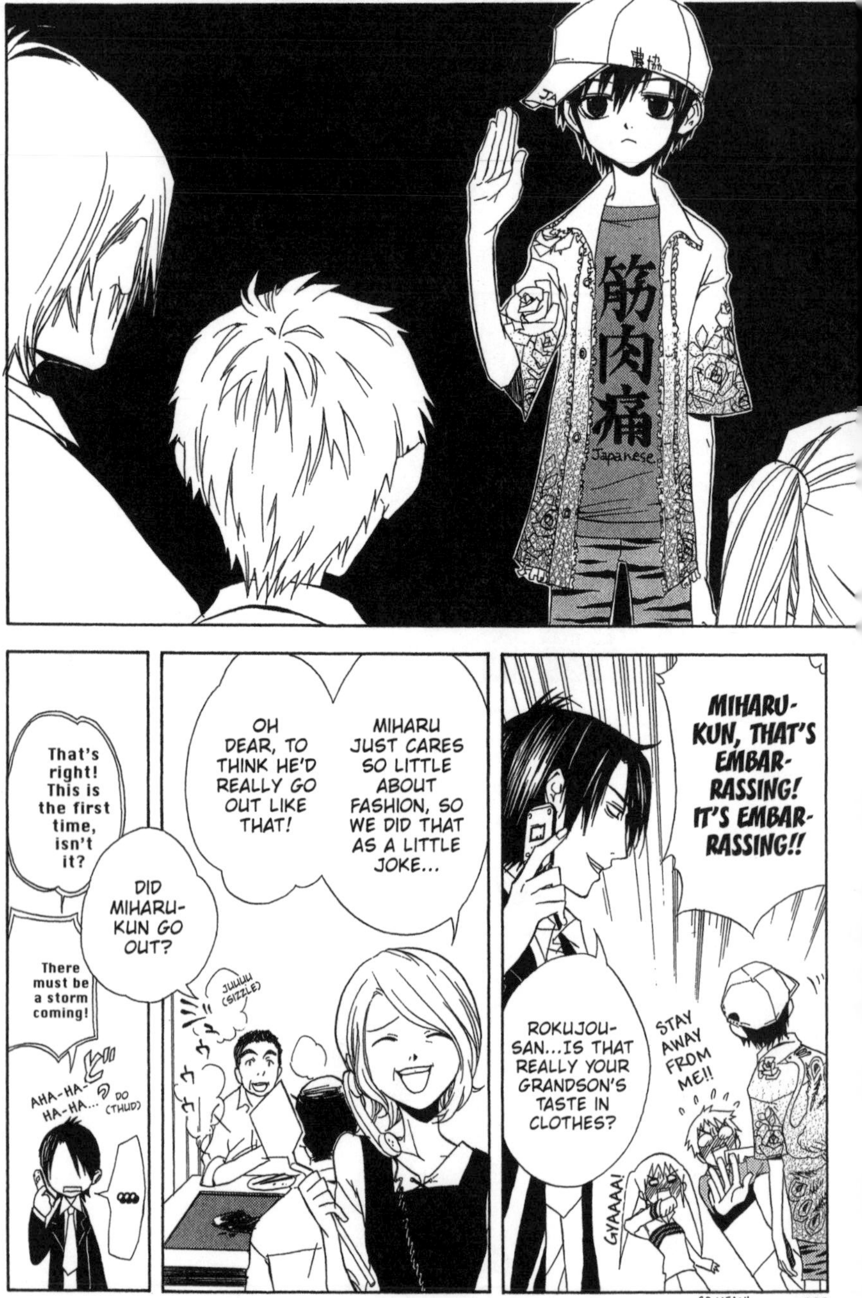
農協
筋肉痛
Japanese
MIHARU-KUN, THAT'S EMBARRASSING! IT'S EMBARRASSING!!
ROKUJOU-SAN...IS THAT REALLY YOUR GRANDSON'S TASTE IN CLOTHES?
STAY AWAY FROM ME!!
GYAAAA!
MIHARU JUST CARES SO LITTLE ABOUT FASHION, SO WE DID THAT AS A LITTLE JOKE...
OH DEAR, TO THINK HE'D REALLY GO OUT LIKE THAT!
DID MIHARU-KUN GO OUT?
JUUUU (SIZZLE)
That's right! This is the first time, isn't it?
There must be a storm coming!
AHA-HA-HA-HA...
DO (THUD)
...

SO MEAN!

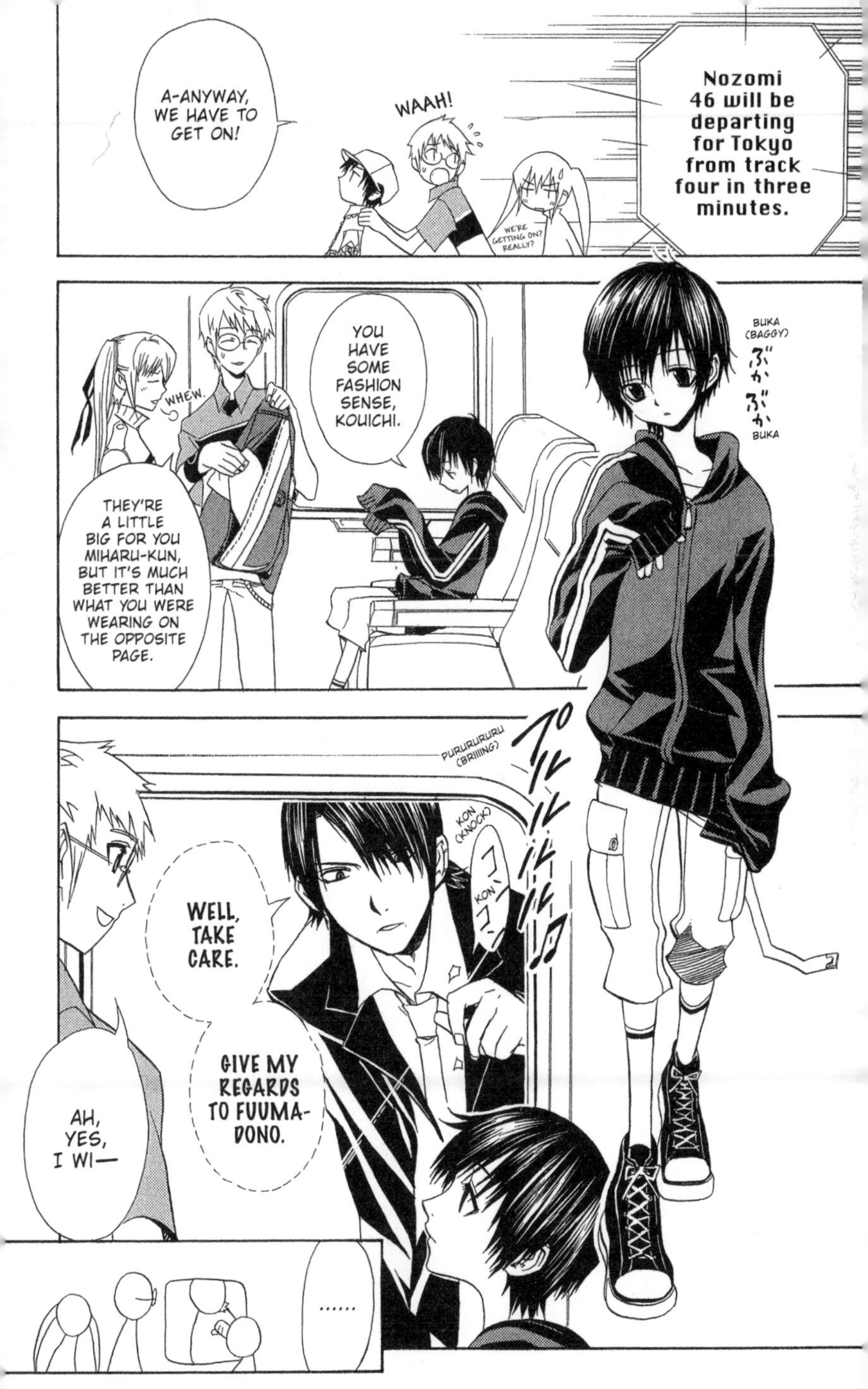
Nozomi 46 will be departing for Tokyo from track four in three minutes.
WAAH!
WE'RE GETTING ON? REALLY?
A-ANYWAY, WE HAVE TO GET ON!
BUKA (BAGGY)
ぶかぶか
BUKA
YOU HAVE SOME FASHION SENSE, KOUICHI.
WHEW.
THEY'RE A LITTLE BIG FOR YOU MIHARU-KUN, BUT IT'S MUCH BETTER THAN WHAT YOU WERE WEARING ON THE OPPOSITE PAGE.
PURURURURU (BRIIIING)
プルルルルル♪
KON (KNOCK)
コンコン
KON
WELL, TAKE CARE.
GIVE MY REGARDS TO FUUMA-DONO.
AH, YES, I WI—
......

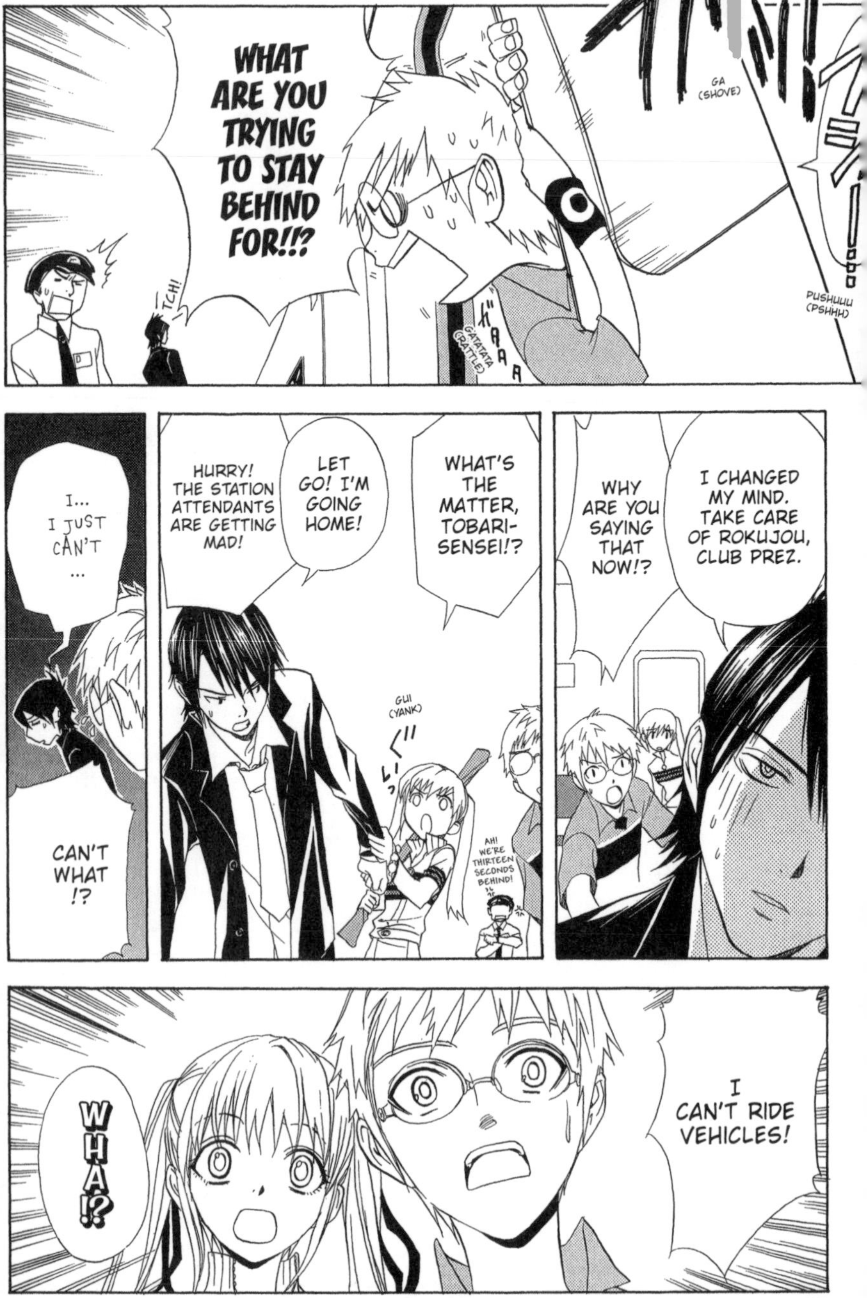
GA (SHOVE)
PUSHUUU (PSHHH)
WHAT ARE YOU TRYING TO STAY BEHIND FOR!!?
GATATATA (RATTLE)
TCH!
I CHANGED MY MIND. TAKE CARE OF ROKUJOU, CLUB PREZ.
WHY ARE YOU SAYING THAT NOW!?
WHAT'S THE MATTER, TOBARI-SENSEI!?
LET GO! I'M GOING HOME!
HURRY! THE STATION ATTENDANTS ARE GETTING MAD!
GUI (YANK)
AH! WE'RE THIRTEEN SECONDS BEHIND!
I... I JUST CAN'T ...
CAN'T WHAT!?
I CAN'T RIDE VEHICLES!
WHA!?

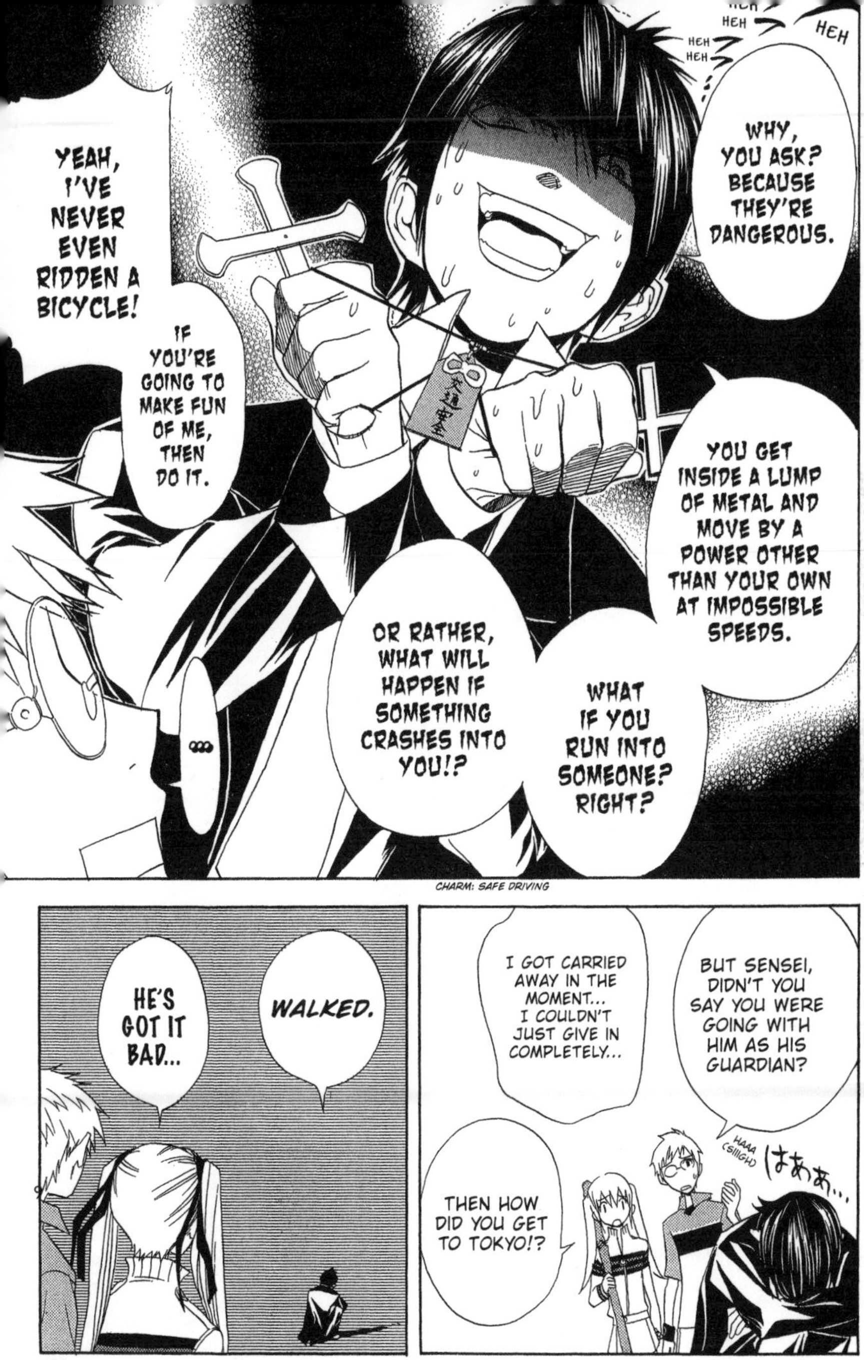
YEAH, I'VE NEVER EVEN RIDDEN A BICYCLE!
IF YOU'RE GOING TO MAKE FUN OF ME, THEN DO IT.
HEH HEH HEH HEH HEH
WHY, YOU ASK? BECAUSE THEY'RE DANGEROUS.
YOU GET INSIDE A LUMP OF METAL AND MOVE BY A POWER OTHER THAN YOUR OWN AT IMPOSSIBLE SPEEDS.
WHAT IF YOU RUN INTO SOMEONE? RIGHT?
OR RATHER, WHAT WILL HAPPEN IF SOMETHING CRASHES INTO YOU!?
...
BUT SENSEI, DIDN'T YOU SAY YOU WERE GOING WITH HIM AS HIS GUARDIAN?
I GOT CARRIED AWAY IN THE MOMENT... I COULDN'T JUST GIVE IN COMPLETELY...
HAAA (SIIIGH)
はあぁ…
THEN HOW DID YOU GET TO TOKYO!?
WALKED.
HE'S GOT IT BAD...

CHARM: SAFE DRIVING

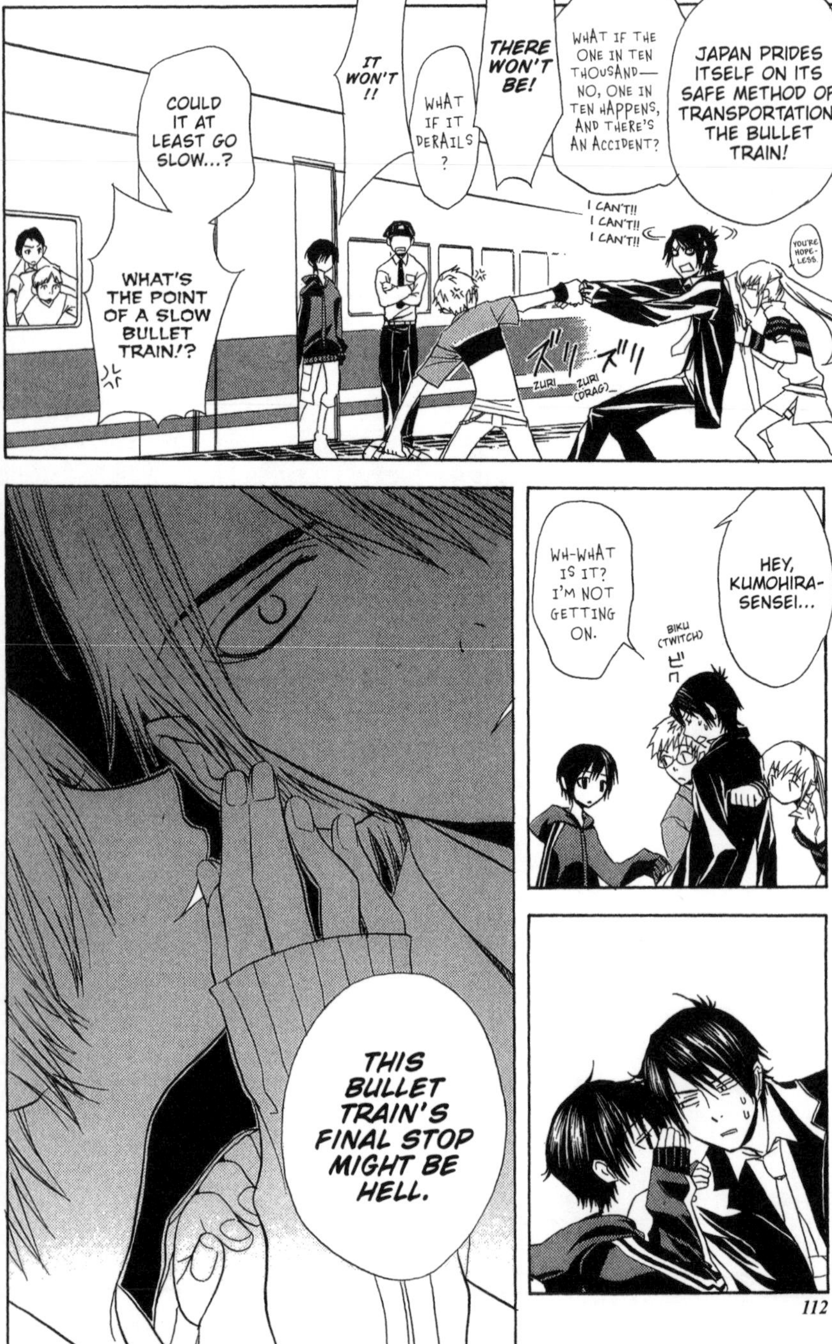
JAPAN PRIDES ITSELF ON ITS SAFE METHOD OF TRANSPORTATION, THE BULLET TRAIN!
WHAT IF THE ONE IN TEN THOUSAND—NO, ONE IN TEN HAPPENS, AND THERE'S AN ACCIDENT?
THERE WON'T BE!
WHAT IF IT DERAILS?
IT WON'T!!
COULD IT AT LEAST GO SLOW...?
YOU'RE HOPELESS.
I CAN'T!! I CAN'T!! I CAN'T!!
ZURI ZURI (DRAG)
WHAT'S THE POINT OF A SLOW BULLET TRAIN!?
HEY, KUMOHIRA-SENSEI...
BIKU (TWITCH)
WH-WHAT IS IT? I'M NOT GETTING ON.
THIS BULLET TRAIN'S FINAL STOP MIGHT BE HELL.

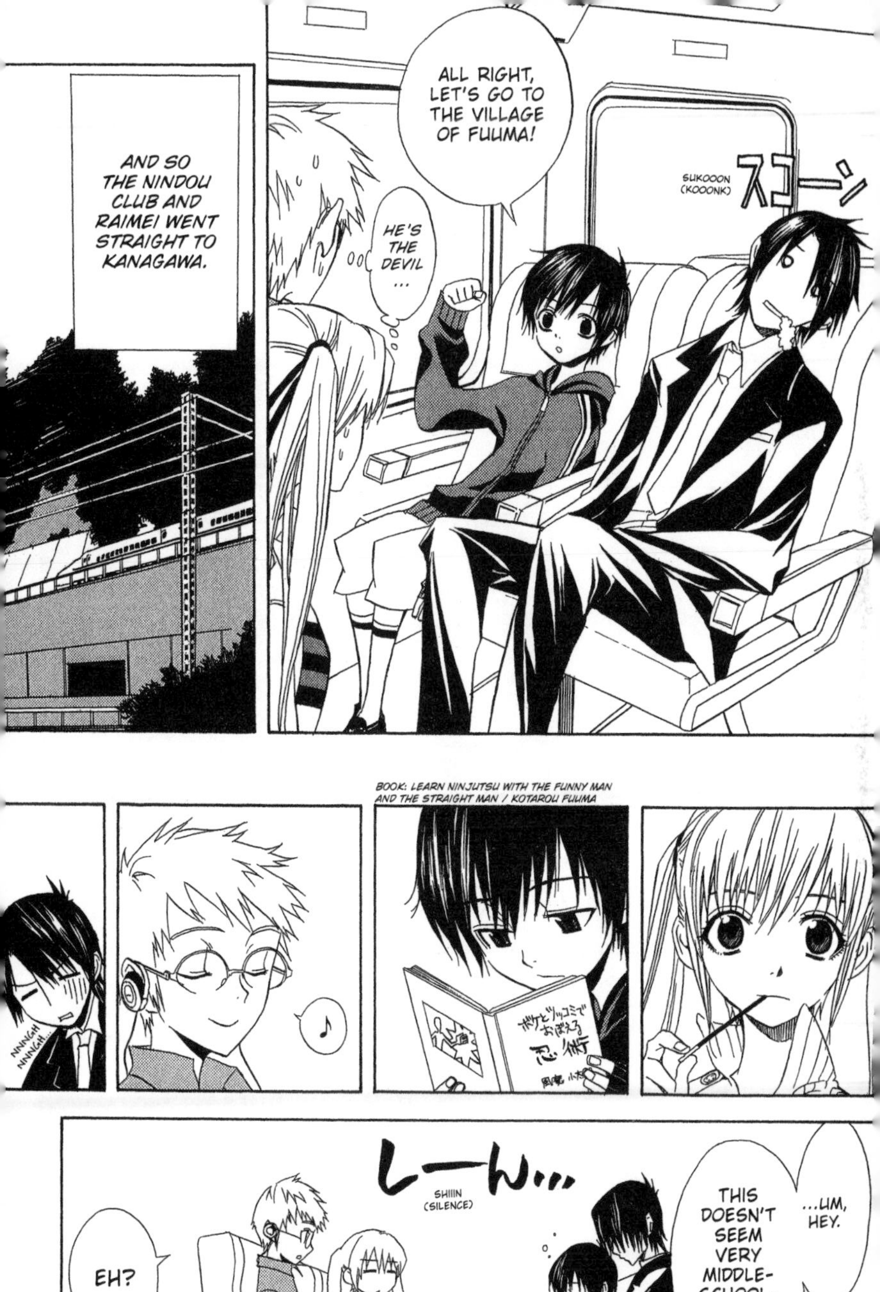
スコーン
SUKOOON (KOOONK)
ALL RIGHT, LET'S GO TO THE VILLAGE OF FUUMA!
HE'S THE DEVIL...
AND SO THE NINDOU CLUB AND RAIMEI WENT STRAIGHT TO KANAGAWA.
BOOK: LEARN NINJUTSU WITH THE FUNNY MAN AND THE STRAIGHT MAN / KOTAROU FUUMA
ボケとツッコミでおぼえる 忍術
♪
NNNGH NNNGH...
...UM, HEY.
THIS DOESN'T SEEM VERY MIDDLE-SCHOOL-LIKE.
しーん…
SHIIIN (SILENCE)
EH?

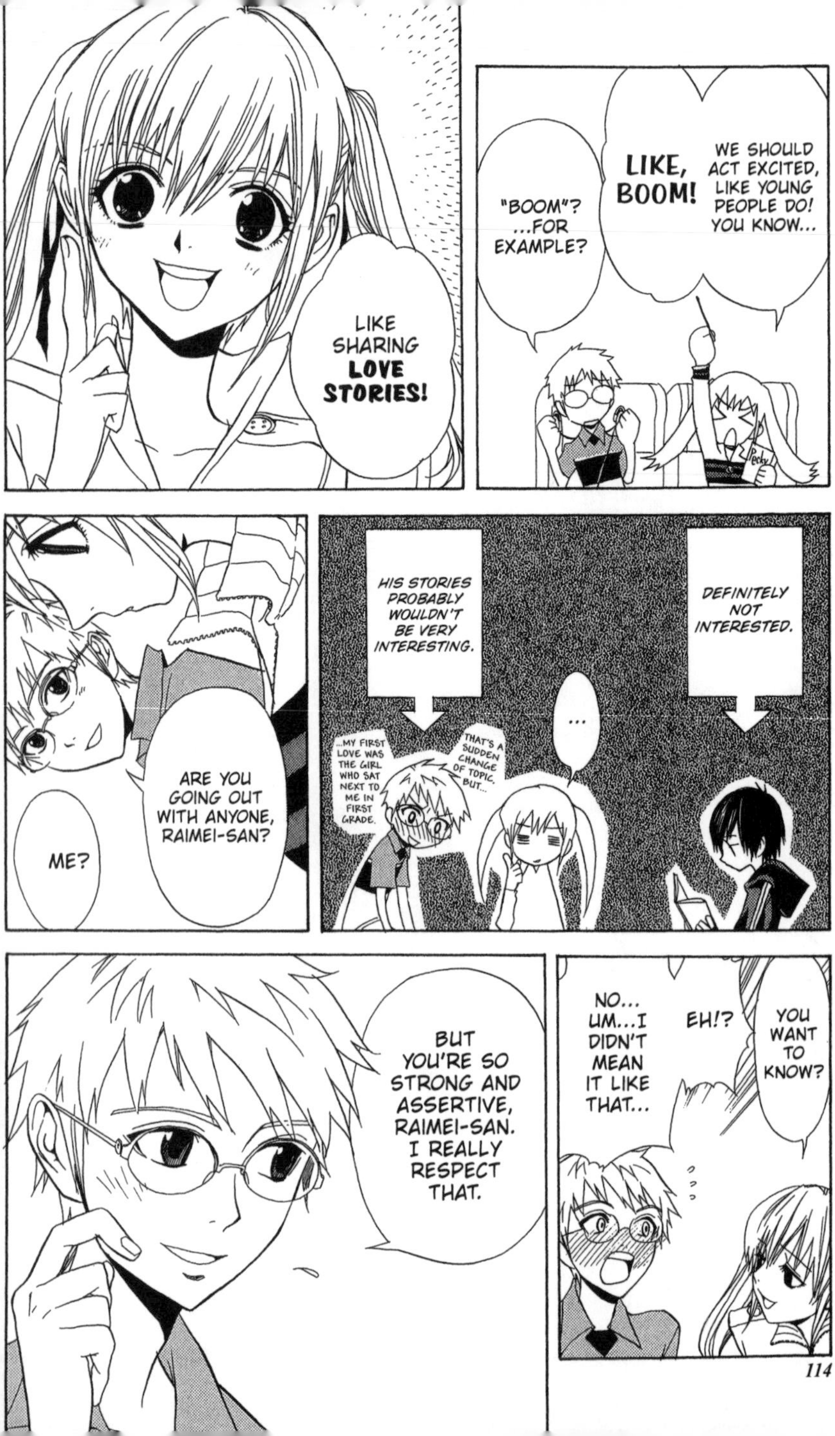
WE SHOULD ACT EXCITED, LIKE YOUNG PEOPLE DO! YOU KNOW...
LIKE, BOOM!
"BOOM"? ...FOR EXAMPLE?
LIKE SHARING LOVE STORIES!
DEFINITELY NOT INTERESTED.
HIS STORIES PROBABLY WOULDN'T BE VERY INTERESTING.
...
THAT'S A SUDDEN CHANGE OF TOPIC, BUT...
...MY FIRST LOVE WAS THE GIRL WHO SAT NEXT TO ME IN FIRST GRADE.
ARE YOU GOING OUT WITH ANYONE, RAIMEI-SAN?
ME?
YOU WANT TO KNOW?
EH!?
NO... UM...I DIDN'T MEAN IT LIKE THAT...
BUT YOU'RE SO STRONG AND ASSERTIVE, RAIMEI-SAN. I REALLY RESPECT THAT.

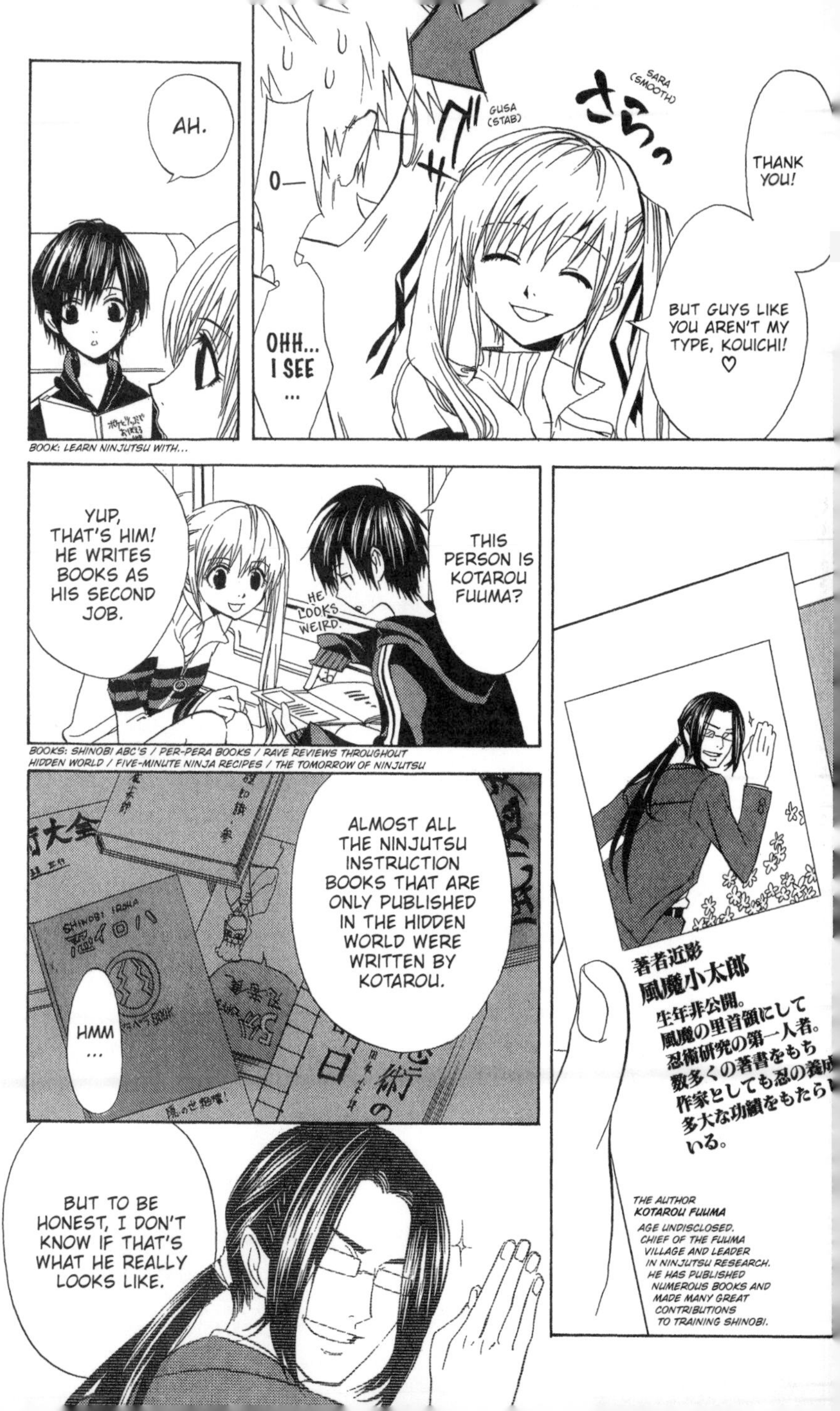
SARA (SMOOTH)
GUSA (STAB)
THANK YOU!
BUT GUYS LIKE YOU AREN'T MY TYPE, KOUICHI! ♡
O—
OHH... I SEE ...
AH.
BOOK: LEARN NINJUTSU WITH...
著者近影
風魔小太郎
生年非公開。
風魔の里首領にして
忍術研究の第一人者。
数多くの著書をもち
作家としても忍の養成
多大な功績をもたら
いる。
THE AUTHOR
KOTAROU FUUMA
AGE UNDISCLOSED. CHIEF OF THE FUUMA VILLAGE AND LEADER IN NINJUTSU RESEARCH. HE HAS PUBLISHED NUMEROUS BOOKS AND MADE MANY GREAT CONTRIBUTIONS TO TRAINING SHINOBI.
THIS PERSON IS KOTAROU FUUMA?
HE LOOKS WEIRD.
YUP, THAT'S HIM! HE WRITES BOOKS AS HIS SECOND JOB.
BOOKS: SHINOBI ABC'S / PER-PERA BOOKS / RAVE REVIEWS THROUGHOUT HIDDEN WORLD / FIVE-MINUTE NINJA RECIPES / THE TOMORROW OF NINJUTSU
ALMOST ALL THE NINJUTSU INSTRUCTION BOOKS THAT ARE ONLY PUBLISHED IN THE HIDDEN WORLD WERE WRITTEN BY KOTAROU.
HMM ...
BUT TO BE HONEST, I DON'T KNOW IF THAT'S WHAT HE REALLY LOOKS LIKE.

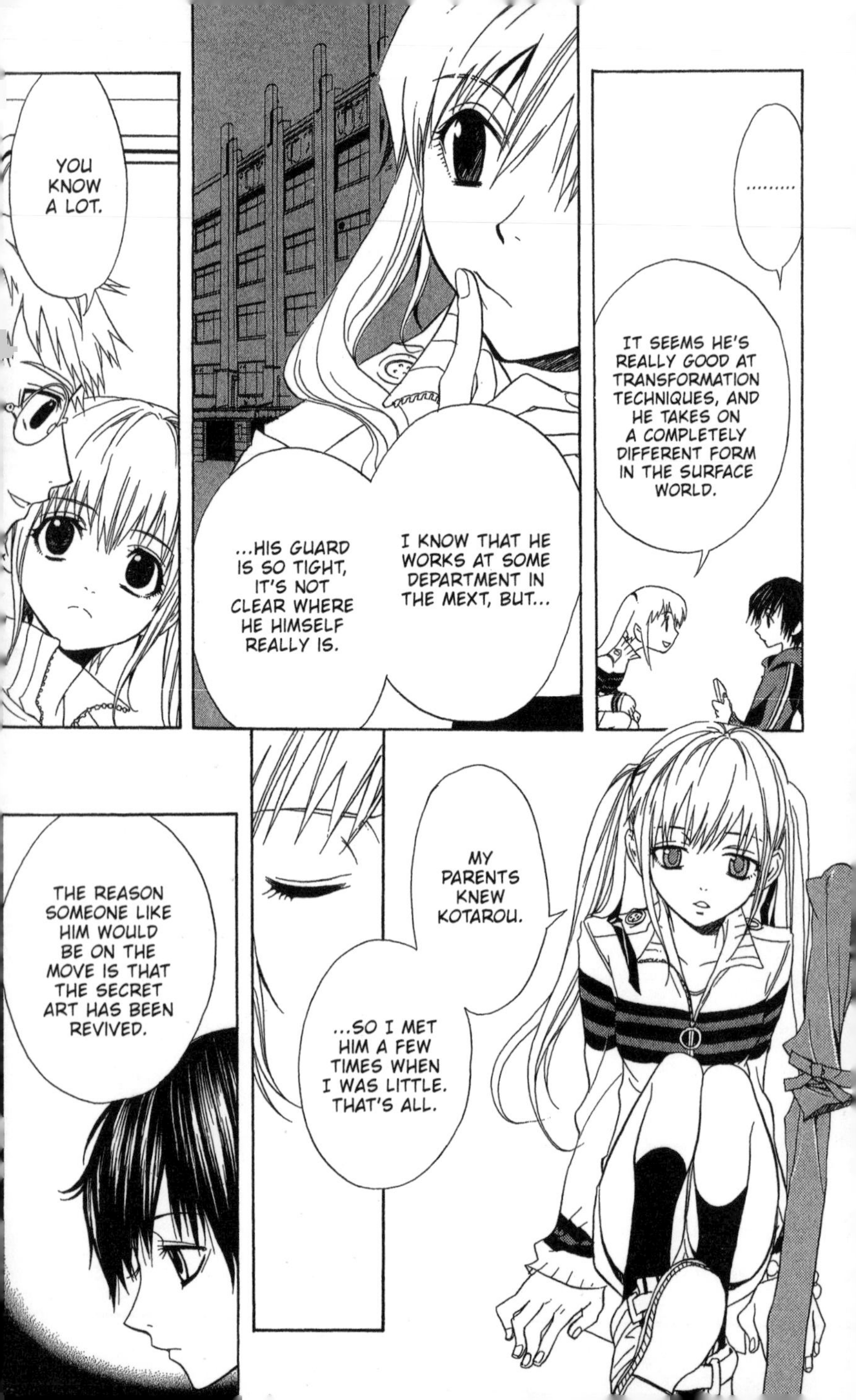
....
IT SEEMS HE'S REALLY GOOD AT TRANSFORMATION TECHNIQUES, AND HE TAKES ON A COMPLETELY DIFFERENT FORM IN THE SURFACE WORLD.
I KNOW THAT HE WORKS AT SOME DEPARTMENT IN THE MEXT, BUT...
...HIS GUARD IS SO TIGHT, IT'S NOT CLEAR WHERE HE HIMSELF REALLY IS.
YOU KNOW A LOT.
MY PARENTS KNEW KOTAROU.
...SO I MET HIM A FEW TIMES WHEN I WAS LITTLE. THAT'S ALL.
THE REASON SOMEONE LIKE HIM WOULD BE ON THE MOVE IS THAT THE SECRET ART HAS BEEN REVIVED.

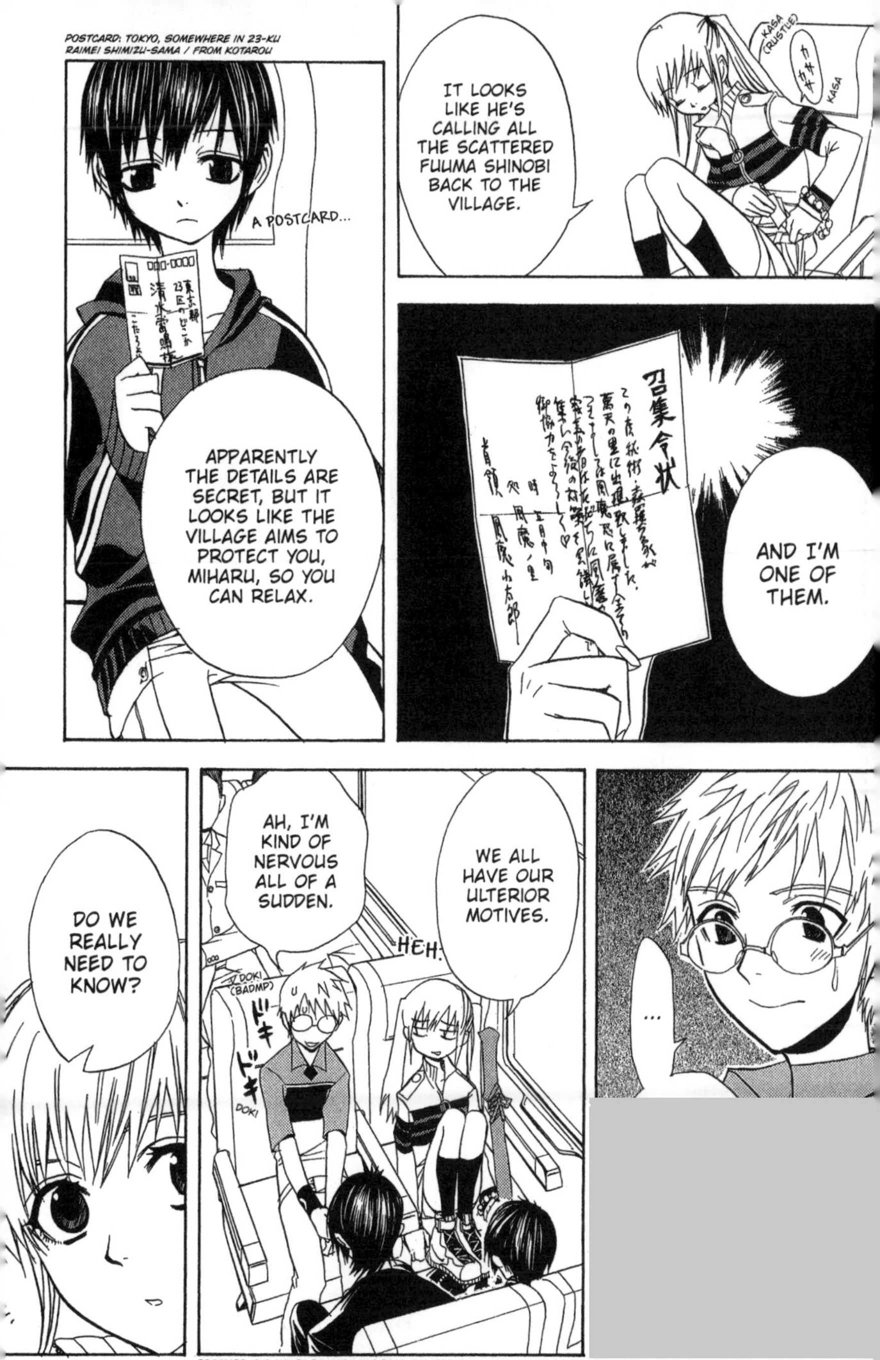
KASA (RUSTLE)
KASA
IT LOOKS LIKE HE'S CALLING ALL THE SCATTERED FUUMA SHINOBI BACK TO THE VILLAGE.
AND I'M ONE OF THEM.
A POSTCARD...
APPARENTLY THE DETAILS ARE SECRET, BUT IT LOOKS LIKE THE VILLAGE AIMS TO PROTECT YOU, MIHARU, SO YOU CAN RELAX.
...
WE ALL HAVE OUR ULTERIOR MOTIVES.
HEH.
AH, I'M KIND OF NERVOUS ALL OF A SUDDEN.
DOKI (BADMP)
DOKI
DO WE REALLY NEED TO KNOW?

POSTCARD: THE SHINRA BANSHOU HAS RECENTLY APPEARED IN THE VILLAGE OF BANTEN. THEREFORE, I WOULD LIKE ALL MEMBERS OF THE FUUMA CLAN TO CONVENE IN THE VILLAGE IMMEDIATELY TO DISCUSS OUR FUTURE COURSE OF ACTION. I LOOK FORWARD TO YOUR COOPERATION. / TIME: MID-MAY / PLACE: FUUMA VILLAGE / CHIEF: KOTAROU FUUMA

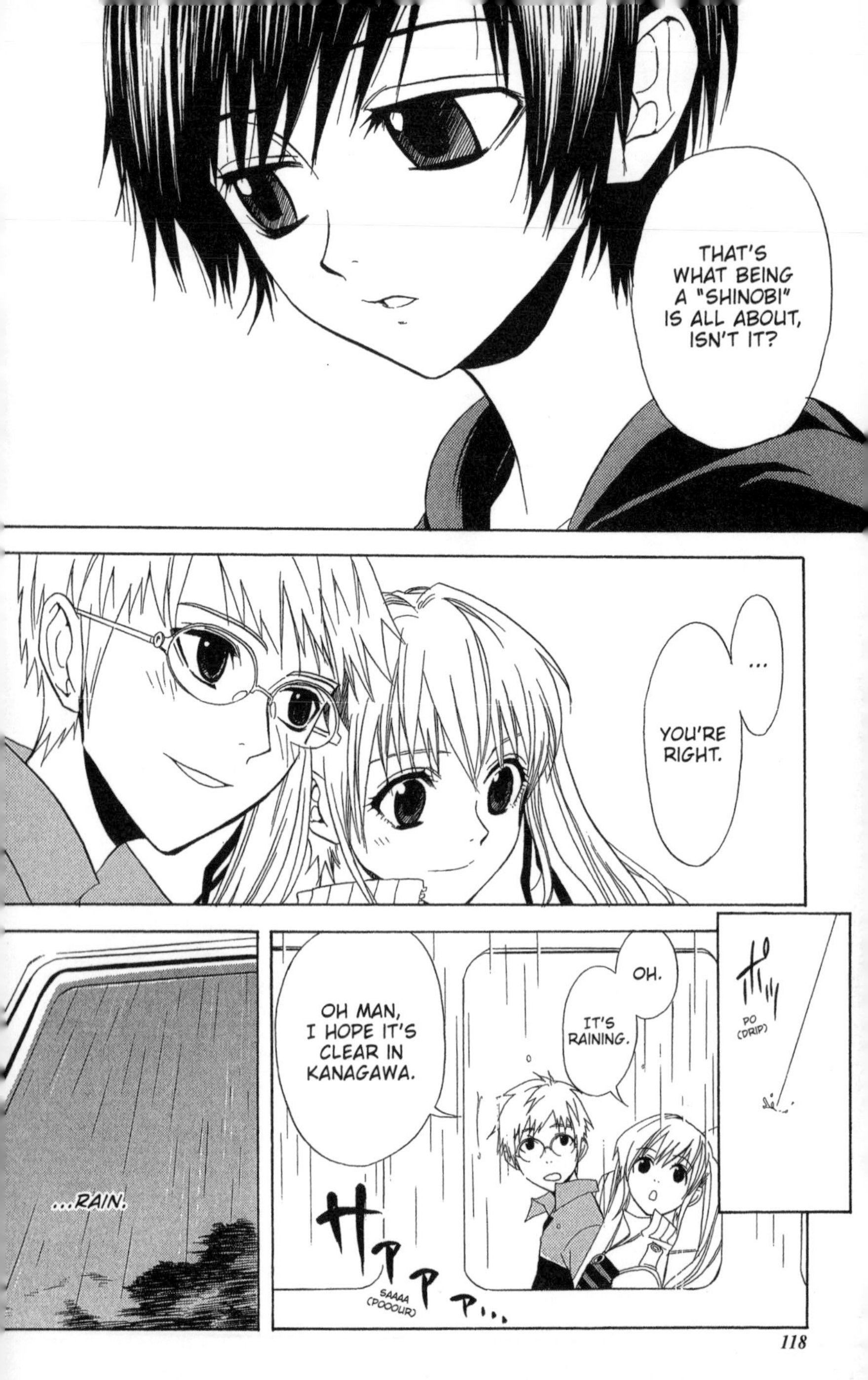
THAT'S WHAT BEING A "SHINOBI" IS ALL ABOUT, ISN'T IT?
...
YOU'RE RIGHT.
PO (DRIP)
OH.
IT'S RAINING.
OH MAN, I HOPE IT'S CLEAR IN KANAGAWA.
SAAAA (POOOUR)
...RAIN.

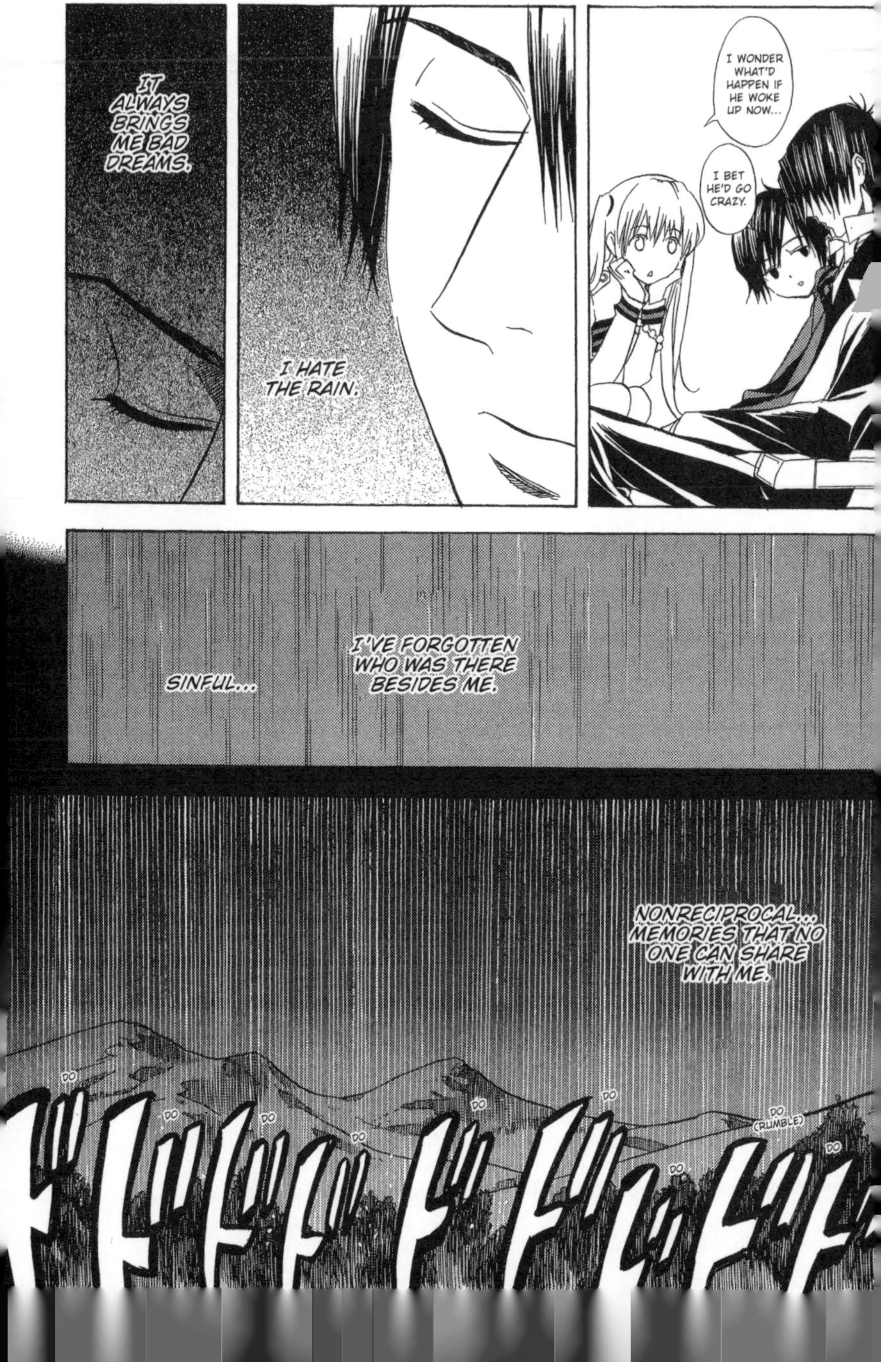
I WONDER WHAT'D HAPPEN IF HE WOKE UP NOW...
I BET HE'D GO CRAZY.
I HATE THE RAIN.
IT ALWAYS BRINGS ME BAD DREAMS.
I'VE FORGOTTEN WHO WAS THERE BESIDES ME.
SINFUL...
NONRECIPROCAL... MEMORIES THAT NO ONE CAN SHARE WITH ME.
DO
DO
DO (RUMBLE)
DO
DO
DO
DO
DO
DO

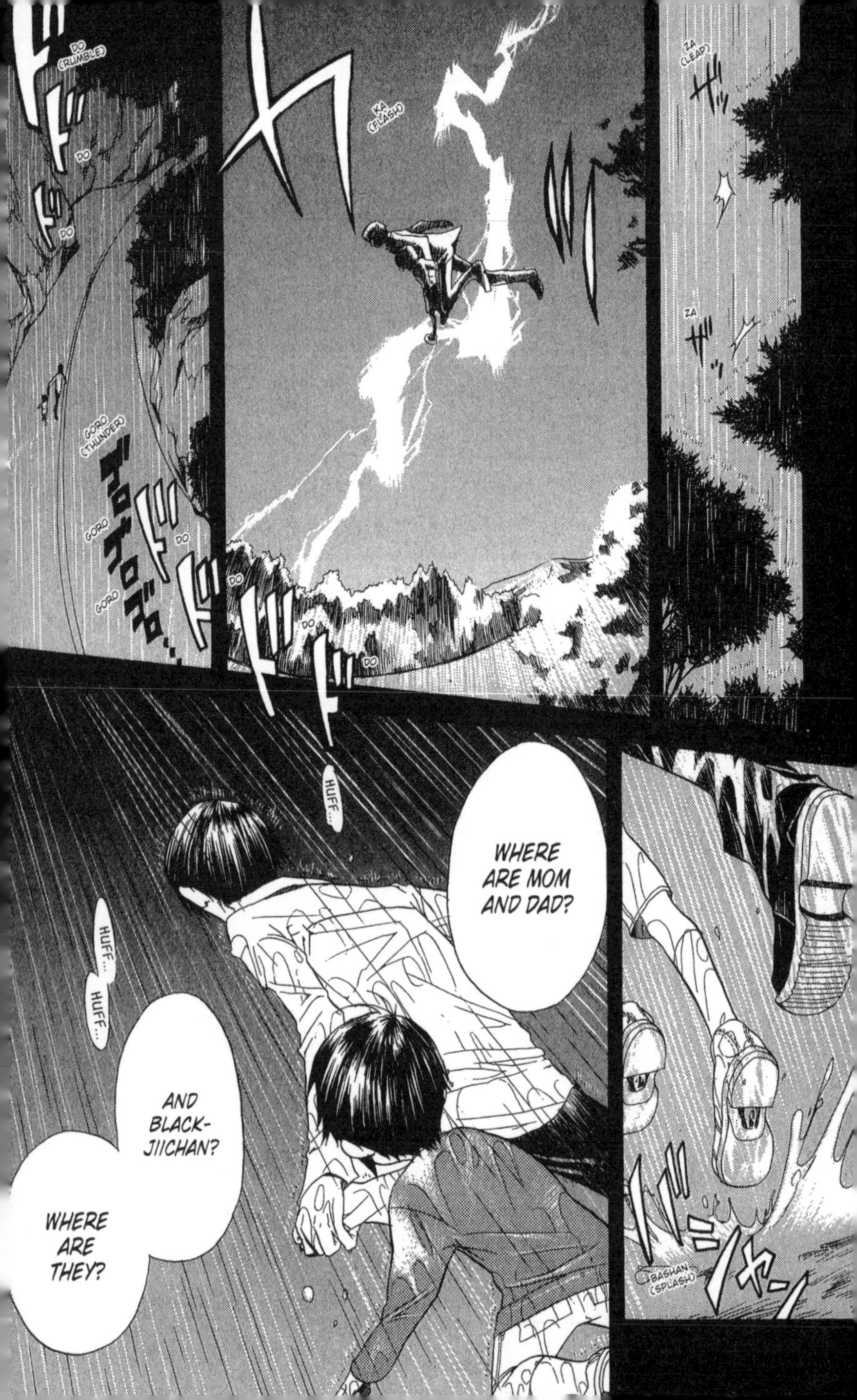
ZA (LEAP)
ZA
KA (FLASH)
DO (RUMBLE)
DO
DO
GORO (THUNDER)
GORO
GORO
DO
DO
DO
DO
BASHAN (SPLASH)
HUFF...
WHERE ARE MOM AND DAD?
HUFF... HUFF...
AND BLACK-JIICHAN?
WHERE ARE THEY?

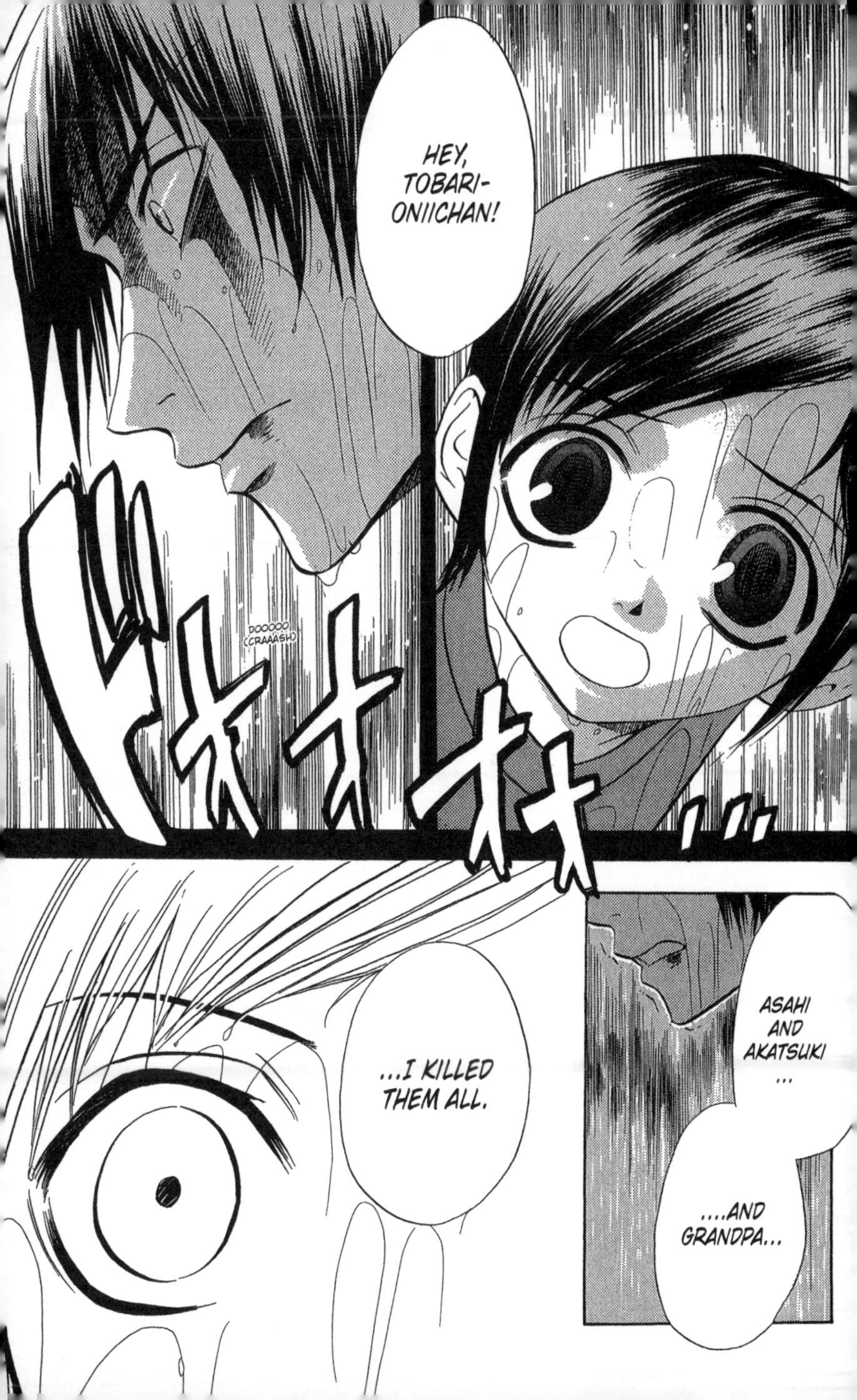
HEY, TOBARI-ONIICHAN!
DOOOOO (CRAAASH)
ASAHI AND AKATSUKI ...
....AND GRANDPA...
...I KILLED THEM ALL.

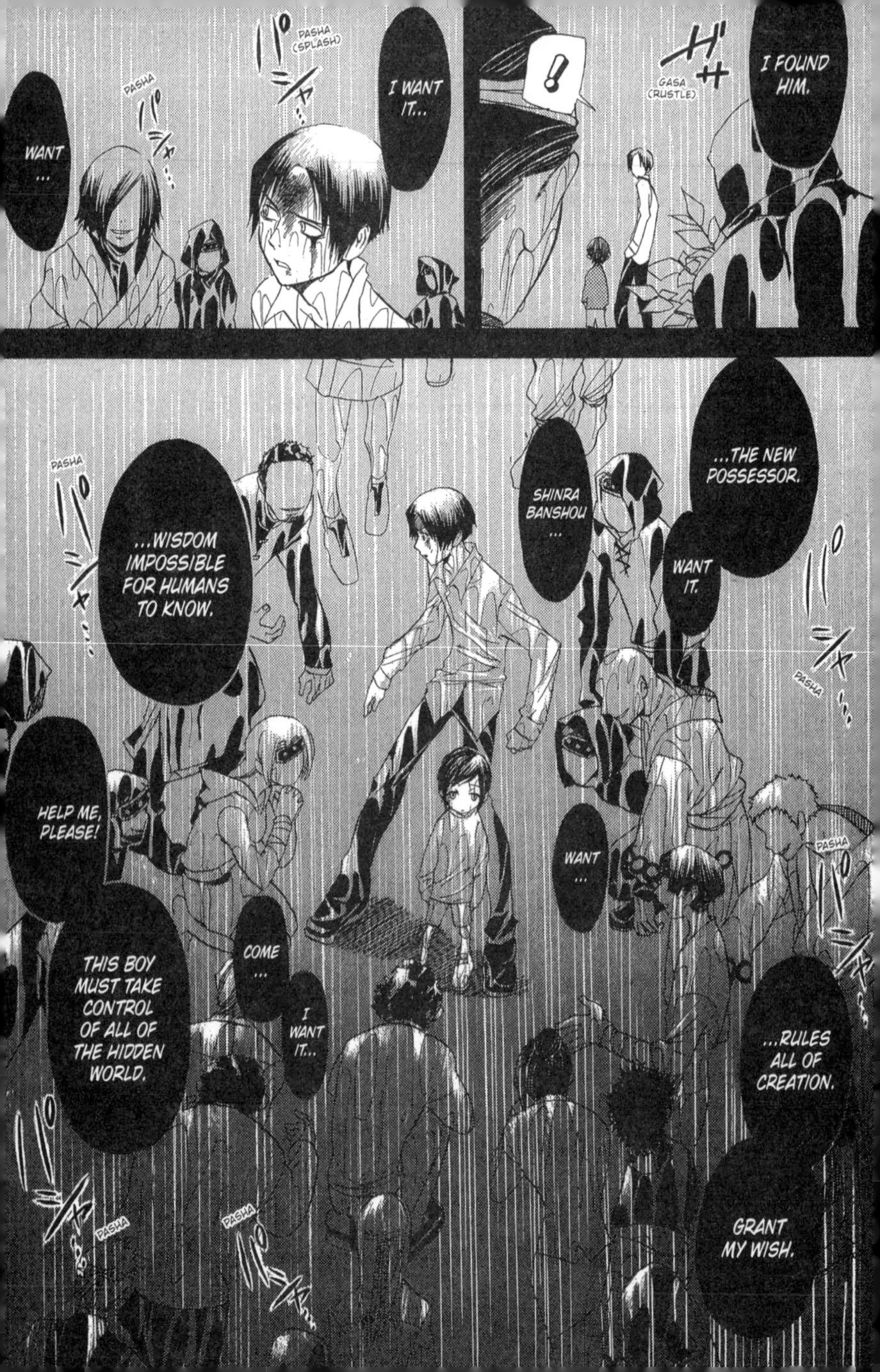
I FOUND HIM.
GASA (RUSTLE)
!
I WANT IT...
PASHA (SPLASH)
PASHA
WANT ...
...THE NEW POSSESSOR.
SHINRA BANSHOU ...
WANT IT.
PASHA
...WISDOM IMPOSSIBLE FOR HUMANS TO KNOW.
PASHA
PASHA
WANT ...
...RULES ALL OF CREATION.
GRANT MY WISH.
HELP ME, PLEASE!
COME ...
I WANT IT...
THIS BOY MUST TAKE CONTROL OF ALL OF THE HIDDEN WORLD.
PASHA
PASHA

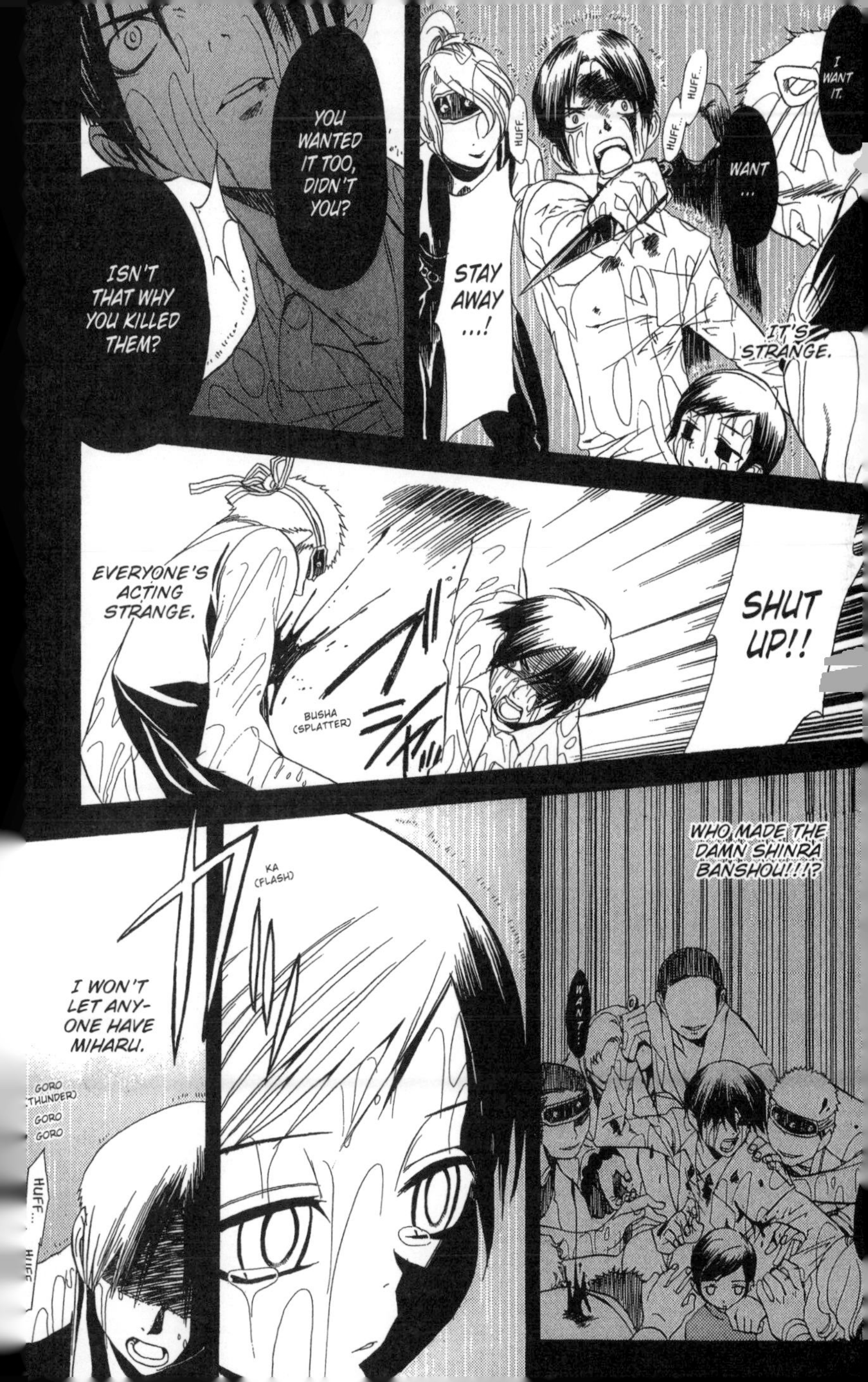
I WANT IT.
WANT ...
HUFF... HUFF...
HUFF...
STAY AWAY ...!
IT'S STRANGE.
YOU WANTED IT TOO, DIDN'T YOU?
ISN'T THAT WHY YOU KILLED THEM?
SHUT UP!!
EVERYONE'S ACTING STRANGE.
BUSHA (SPLATTER)
WHO MADE THE DAMN SHINRA BANSHOU!!!?
WANT...
KA (FLASH)
I WON'T LET ANY-ONE HAVE MIHARU.
GORO (THUNDER) GORO GORO
HUFF... HUFF

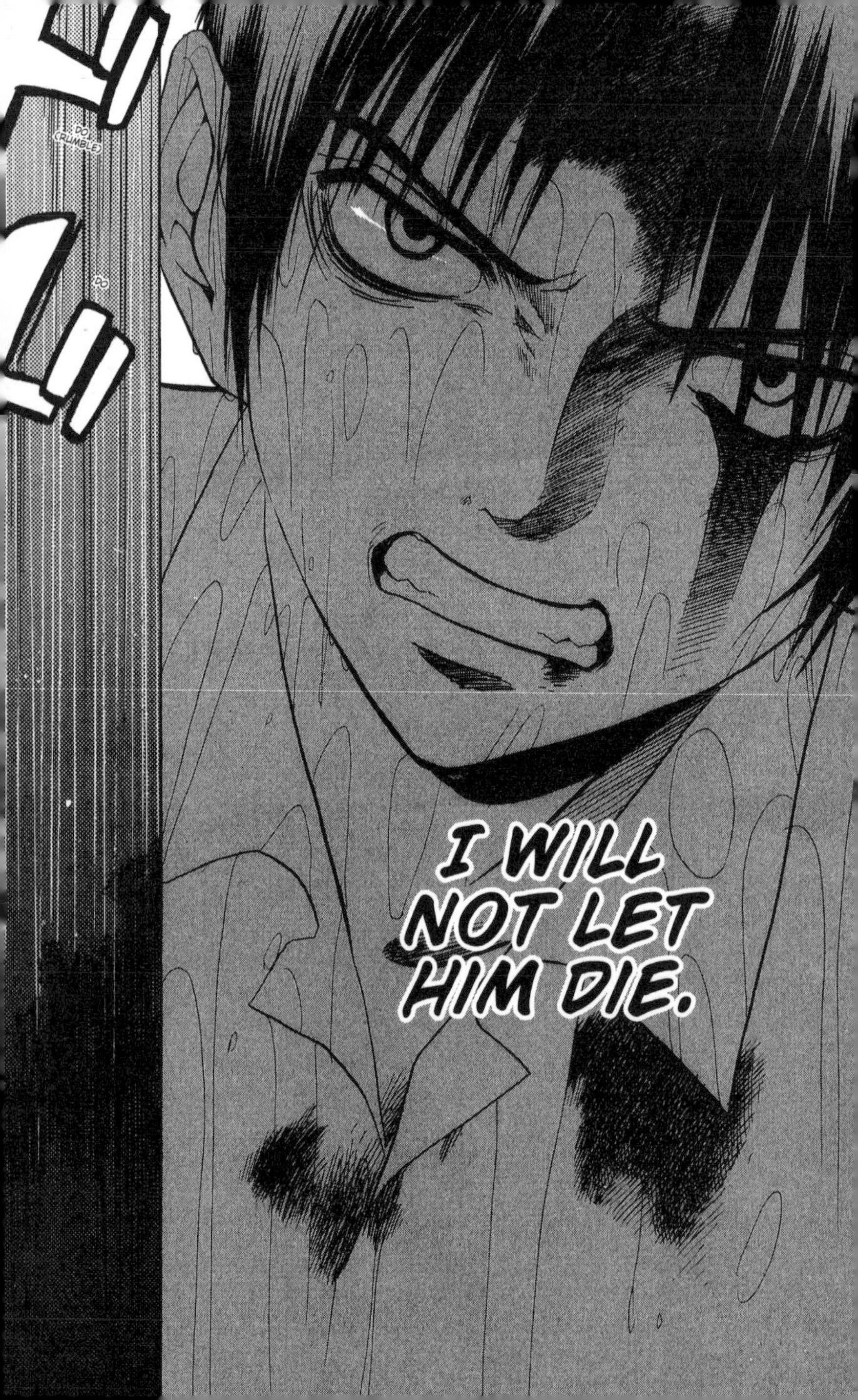
DO (RUMBLE)
DO
I WILL NOT LET HIM DIE.

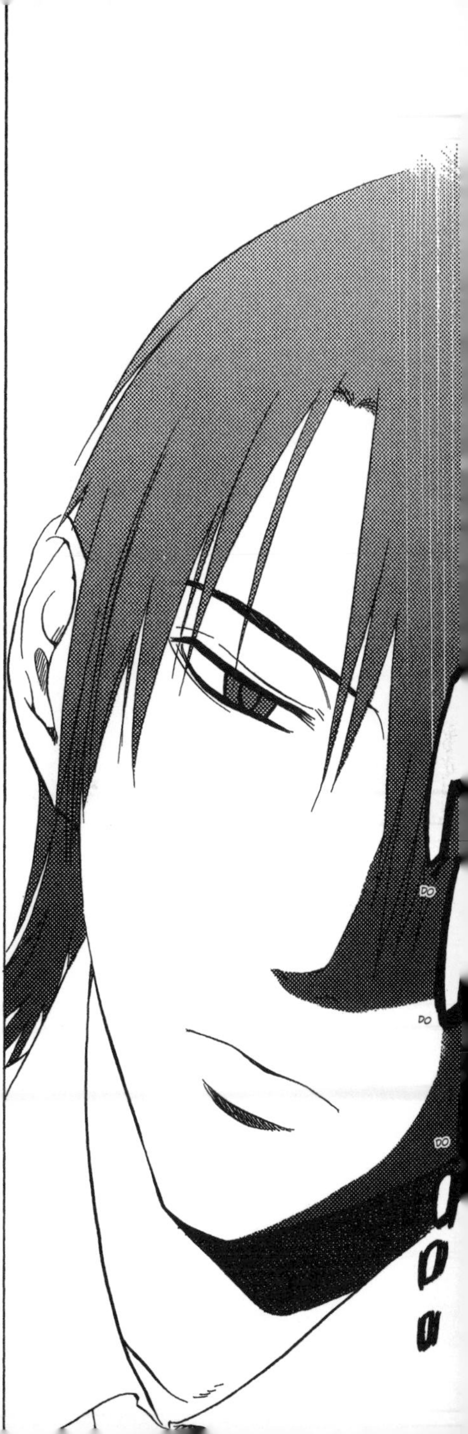

DO
DO
DO

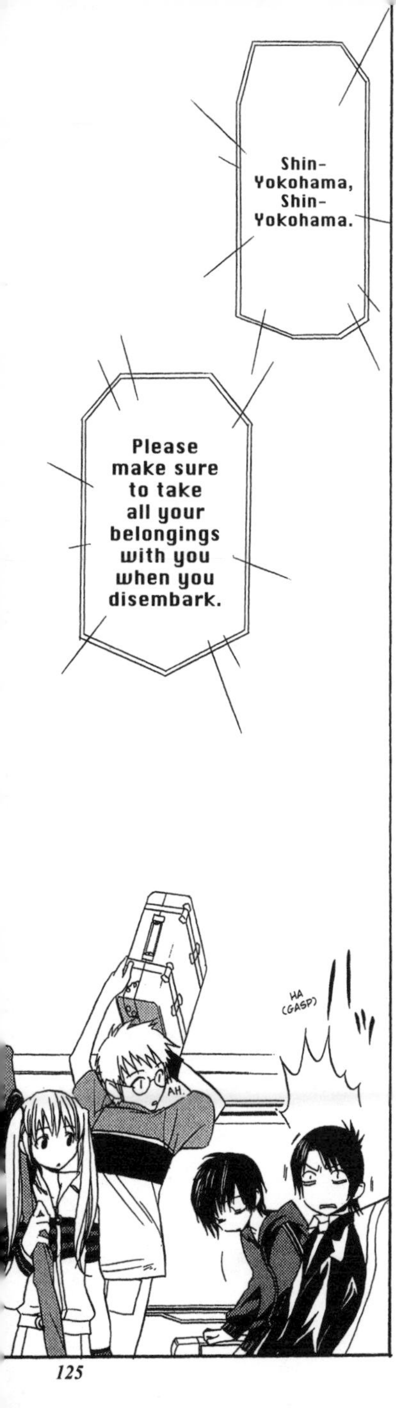

Shin-Yokohama, Shin-Yokohama.
Please make sure to take all your belongings with you when you disembark.
HA (GASP)
AH.

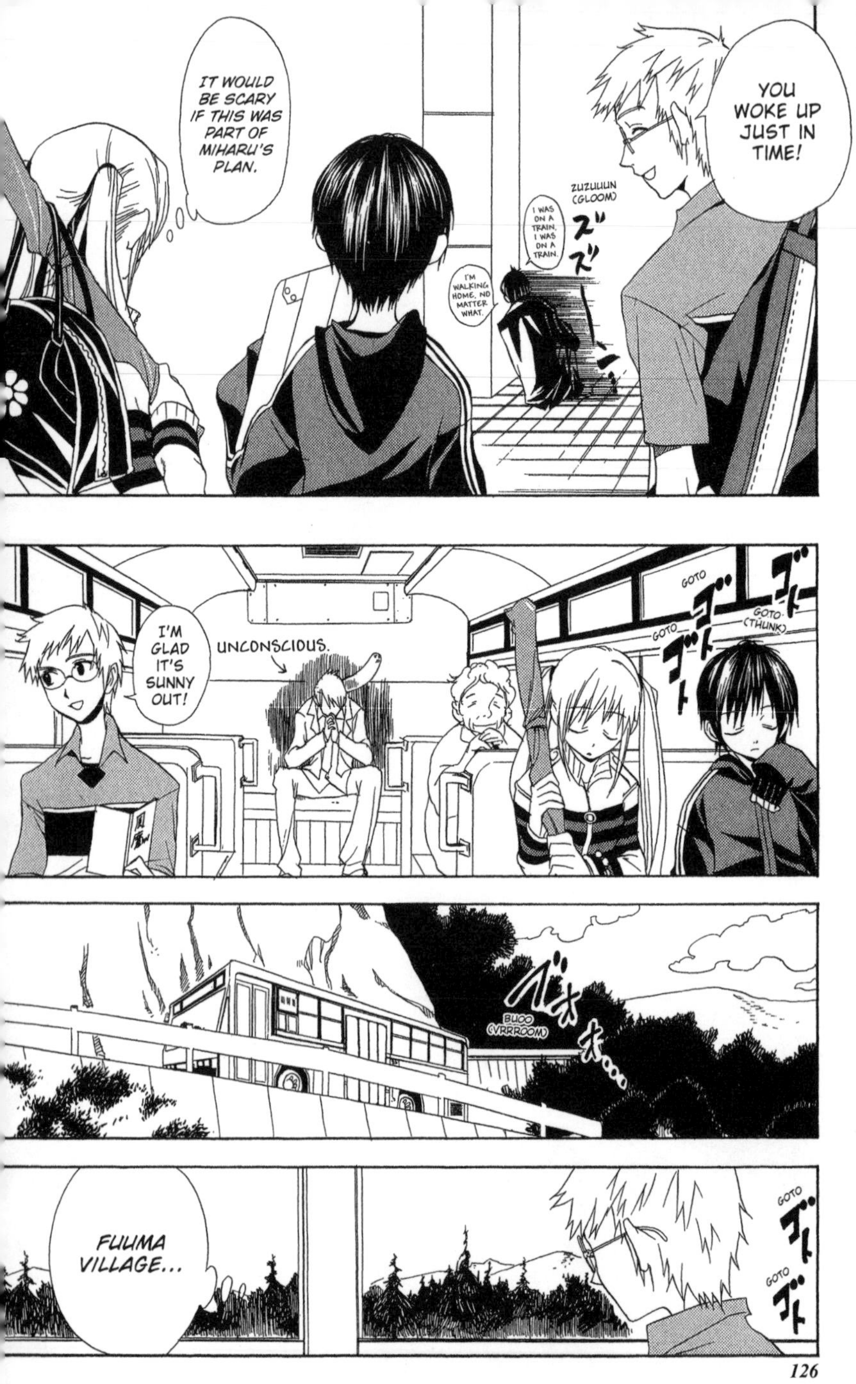
YOU WOKE UP JUST IN TIME!
ZUZUUUN (GLOOM)
I WAS ON A TRAIN, I WAS ON A TRAIN.
I'M WALKING HOME, NO MATTER WHAT.
IT WOULD BE SCARY IF THIS WAS PART OF MIHARU'S PLAN.
GOTO
GOTO (THUNK)
GOTO
UNCONSCIOUS.
I'M GLAD IT'S SUNNY OUT!
BUOO (VRRROOM)
GOTO
GOTO
FUUMA VILLAGE...

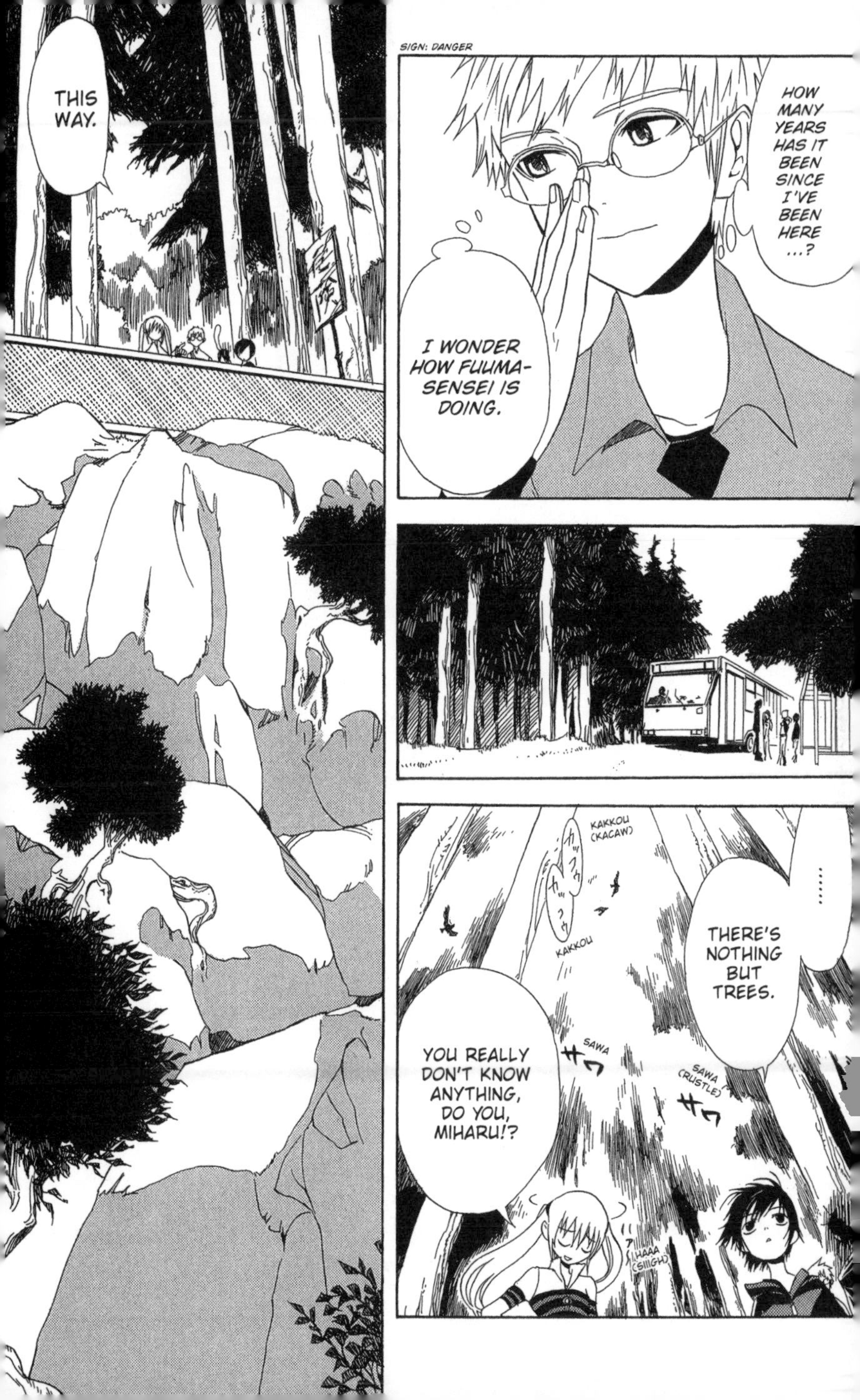
SIGN: DANGER
HOW MANY YEARS HAS IT BEEN SINCE I'VE BEEN HERE ...?
I WONDER HOW FUUMA-SENSEI IS DOING.
......
THERE'S NOTHING BUT TREES.
KAKKOU (KACAW)
KAKKOU
SAWA (RUSTLE)
SAWA
YOU REALLY DON'T KNOW ANYTHING, DO YOU, MIHARU!?
HAAA (SIIIGH)
THIS WAY.

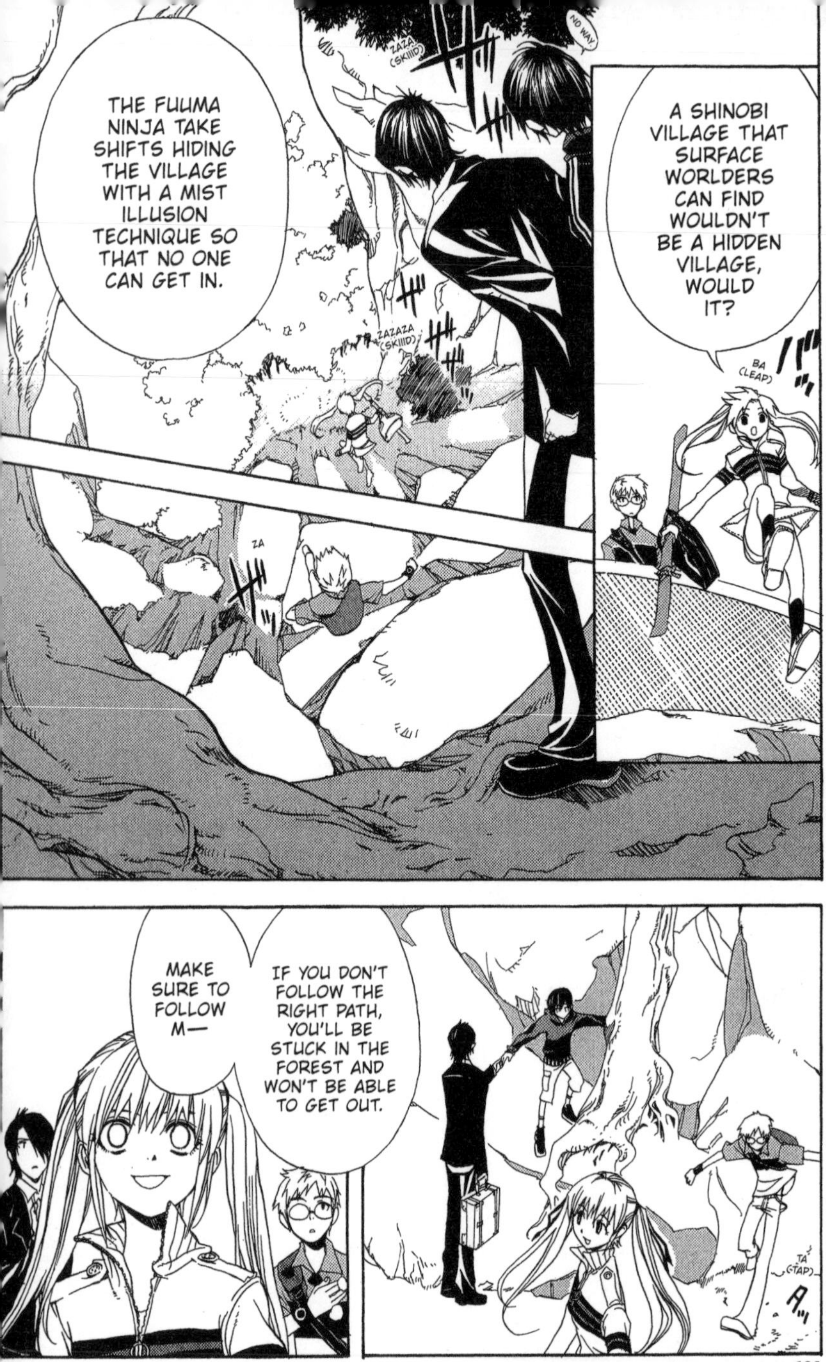
A SHINOBI VILLAGE THAT SURFACE WORLDERS CAN FIND WOULDN'T BE A HIDDEN VILLAGE, WOULD IT?
BA (LEAP)
NO WAY.
ZAZA (SKIIID)
THE FUUMA NINJA TAKE SHIFTS HIDING THE VILLAGE WITH A MIST ILLUSION TECHNIQUE SO THAT NO ONE CAN GET IN.
ZAZAZA (SKIIID)
ZA
IF YOU DON'T FOLLOW THE RIGHT PATH, YOU'LL BE STUCK IN THE FOREST AND WON'T BE ABLE TO GET OUT.
TA (TAP)
MAKE SURE TO FOLLOW M—

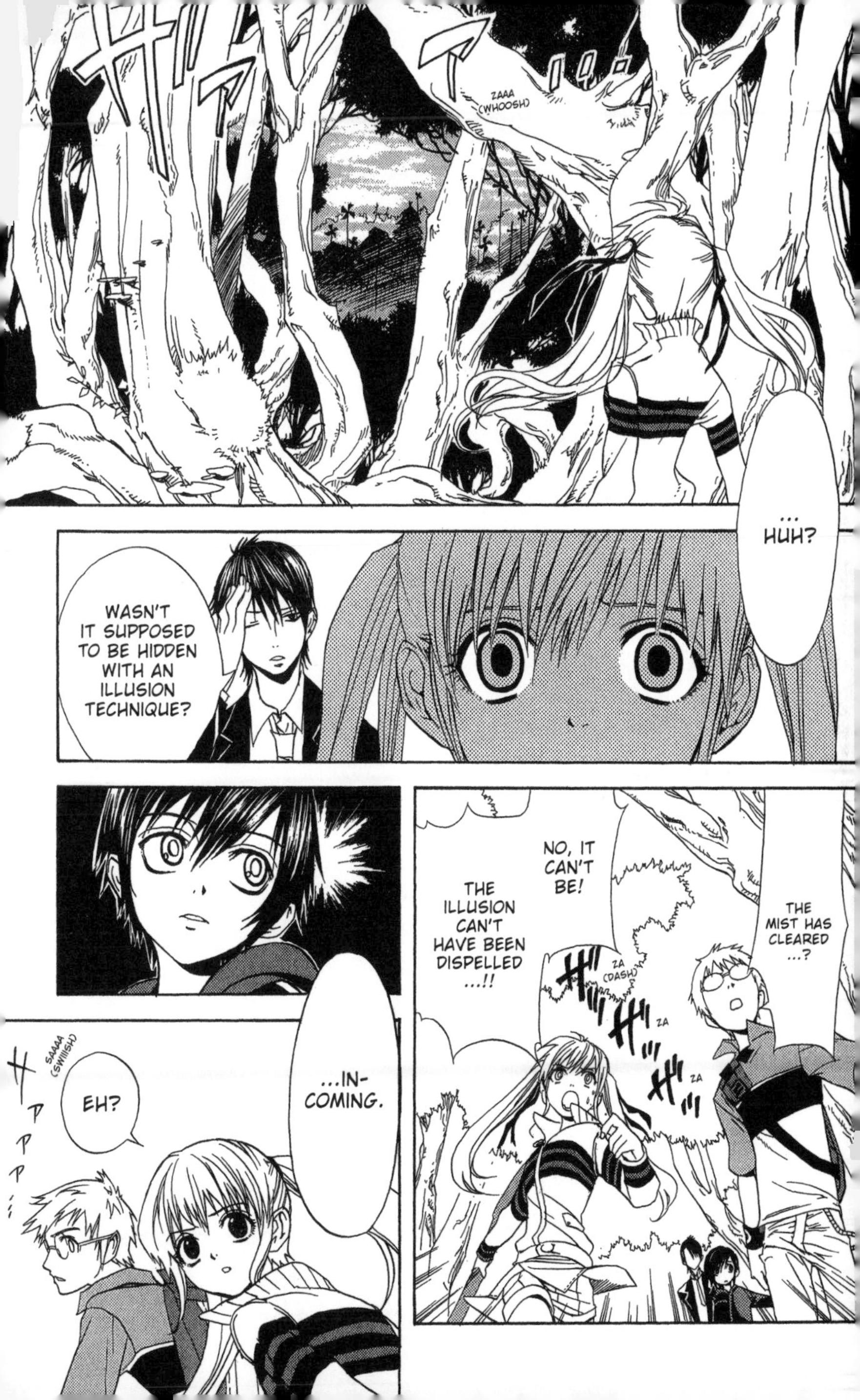
ZAAA (WHOOSH)
...HUH?
WASN'T IT SUPPOSED TO BE HIDDEN WITH AN ILLUSION TECHNIQUE?
THE MIST HAS CLEARED ...?
NO, IT CAN'T BE!
THE ILLUSION CAN'T HAVE BEEN DISPELLED ...!!
ZA (DASH)
ZA
ZA
...IN-COMING.
EH?
SAAAA (SWIIISH)

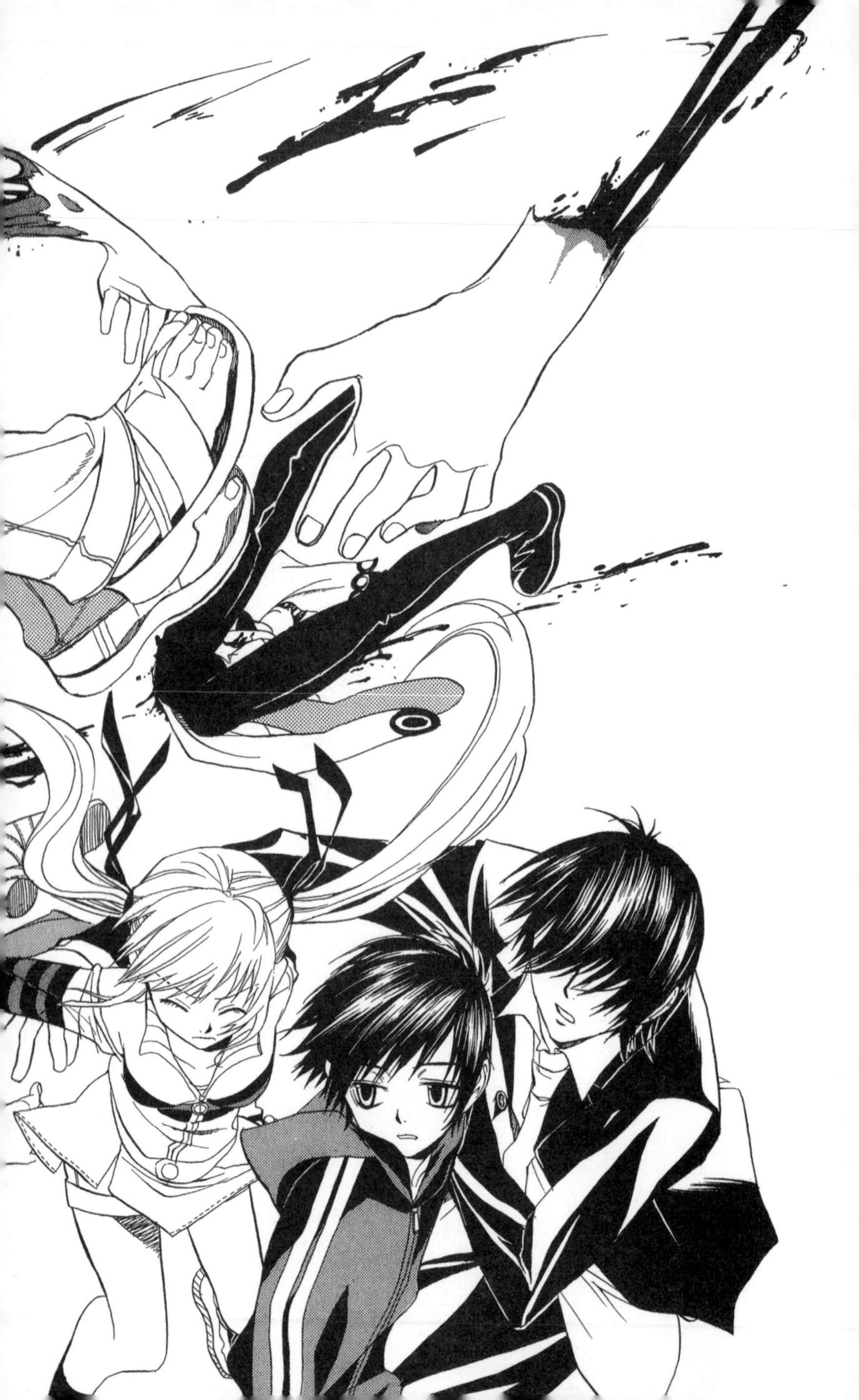

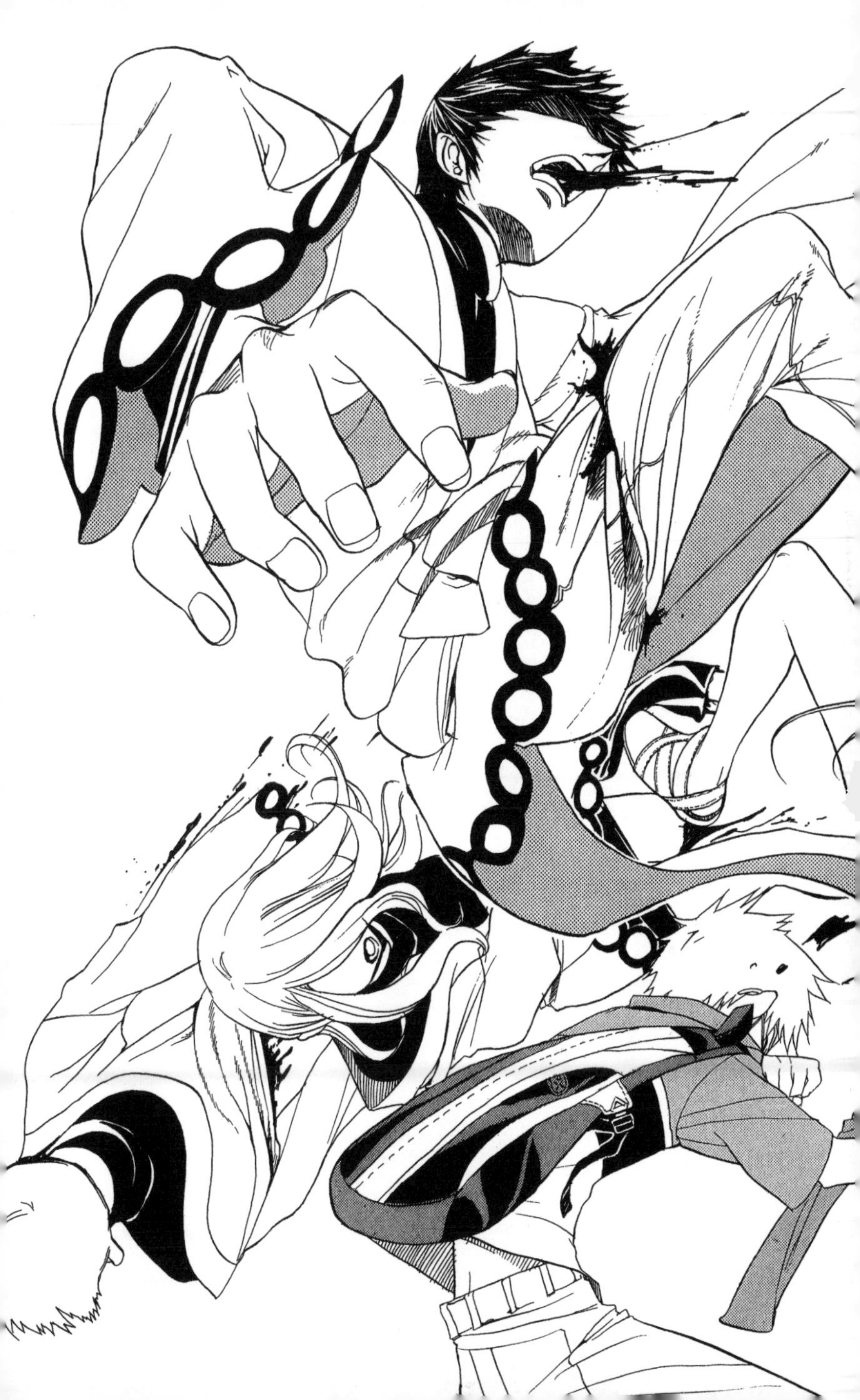

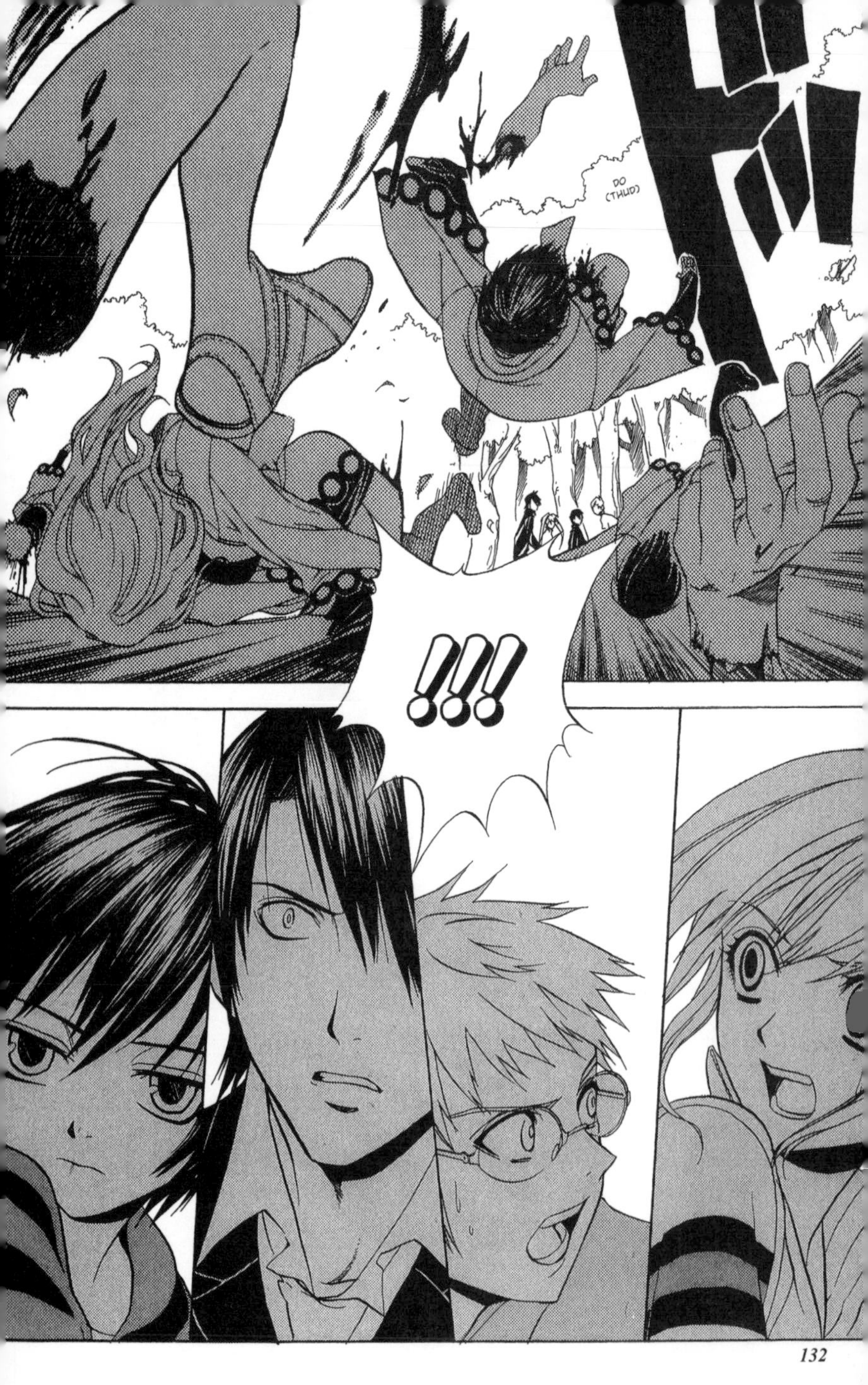
DO
(THUD)
!!!

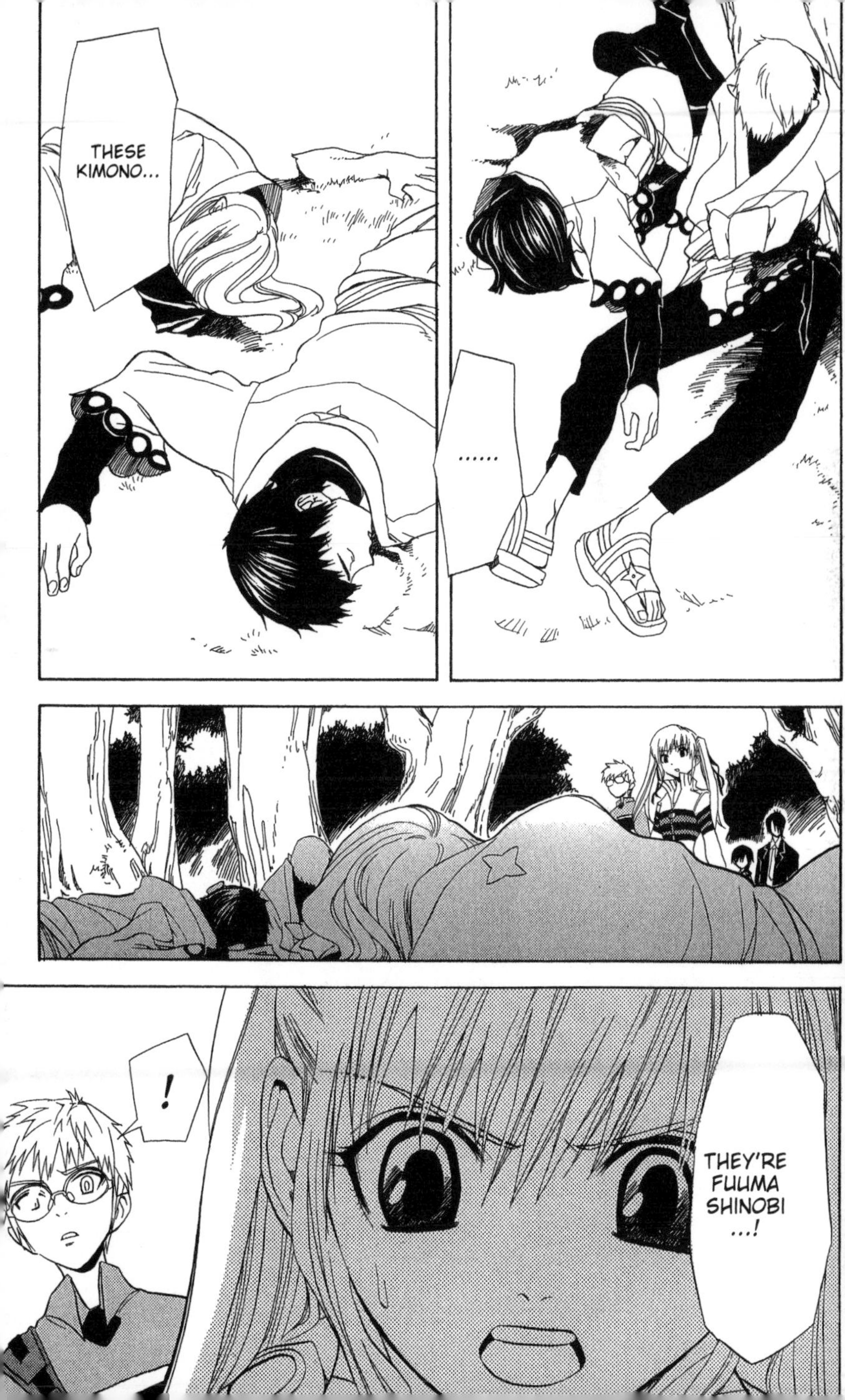
……
THESE KIMONO…
THEY'RE FUUMA SHINOBI …!
!

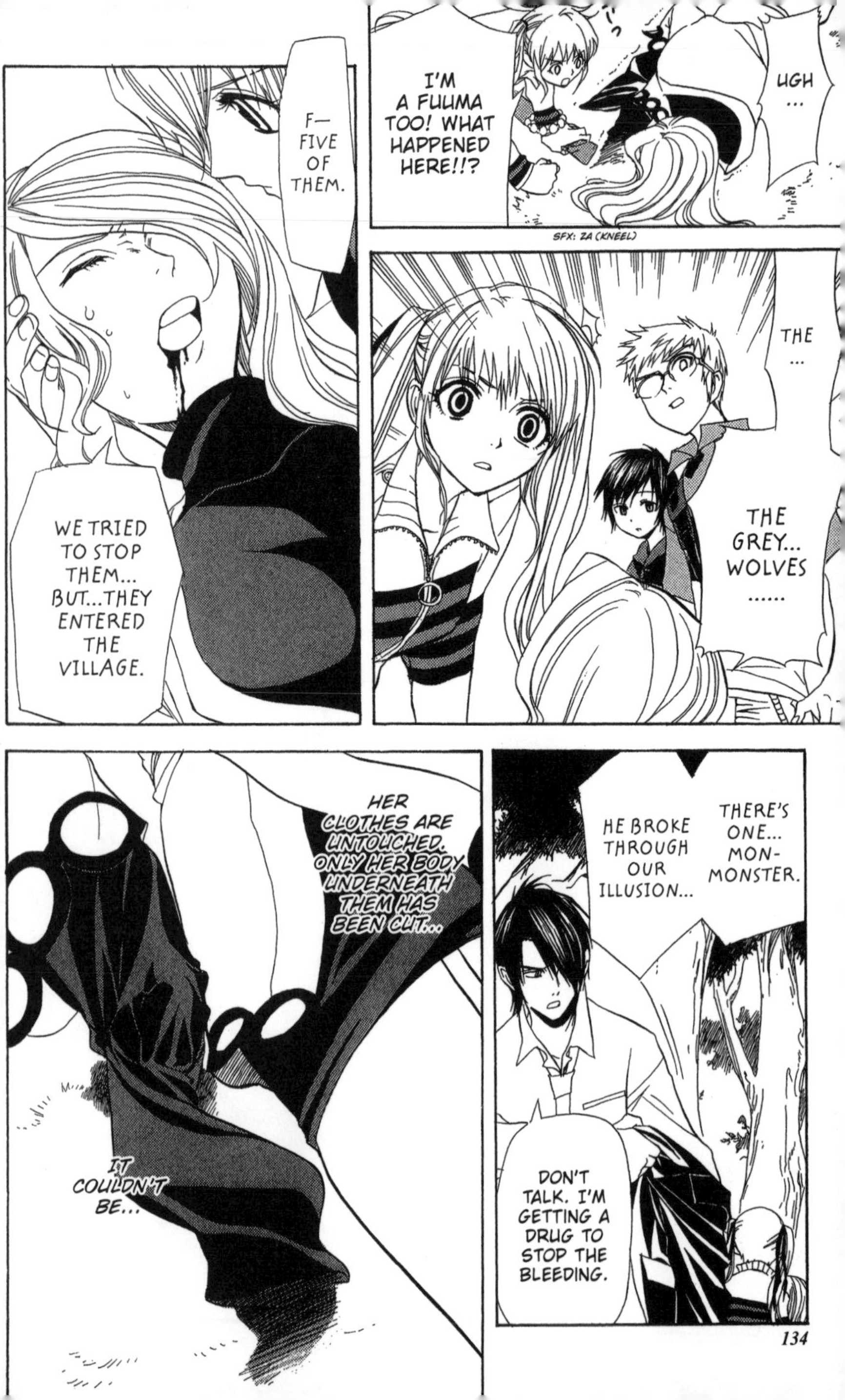
UGH ...
I'M A FUUMA TOO! WHAT HAPPENED HERE!!?
SFX: ZA (KNEEL)
THE ...
THE GREY... WOLVES ......
F— FIVE OF THEM.
WE TRIED TO STOP THEM... BUT...THEY ENTERED THE VILLAGE.
THERE'S ONE... MON- MONSTER.
HE BROKE THROUGH OUR ILLUSION...
DON'T TALK. I'M GETTING A DRUG TO STOP THE BLEEDING.
HER CLOTHES ARE UNTOUCHED. ONLY HER BODY UNDERNEATH THEM HAS BEEN CUT...
IT COULDN'T BE...

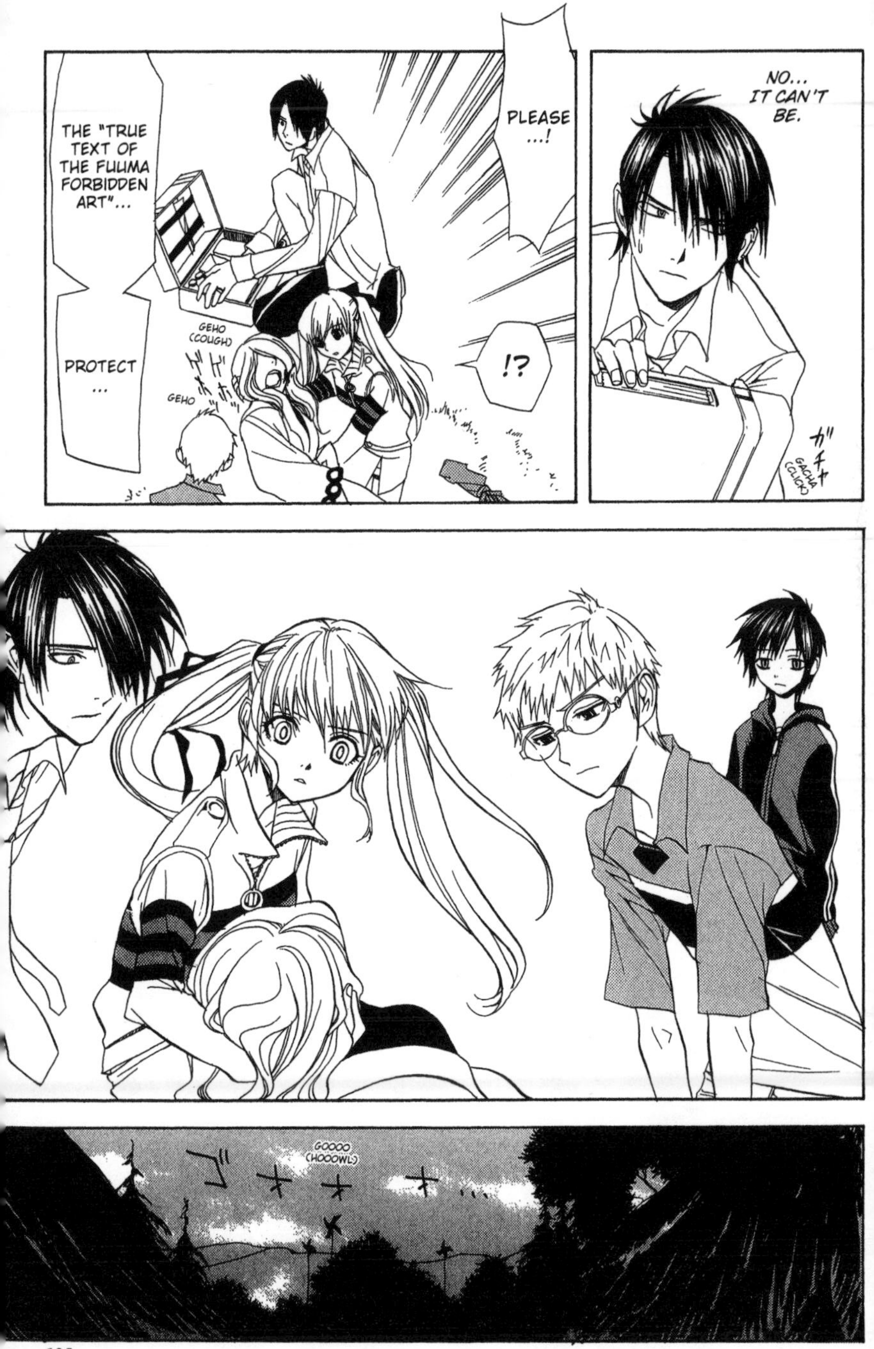
NO... IT CAN'T BE.
GACHA (CLICK)
PLEASE ...!
THE "TRUE TEXT OF THE FUUMA FORBIDDEN ART"...
!?
GEHO (COUGH)
GEHO
PROTECT ...
GOOOO (HOOOWL)

CHAPTER 5: ATTACK

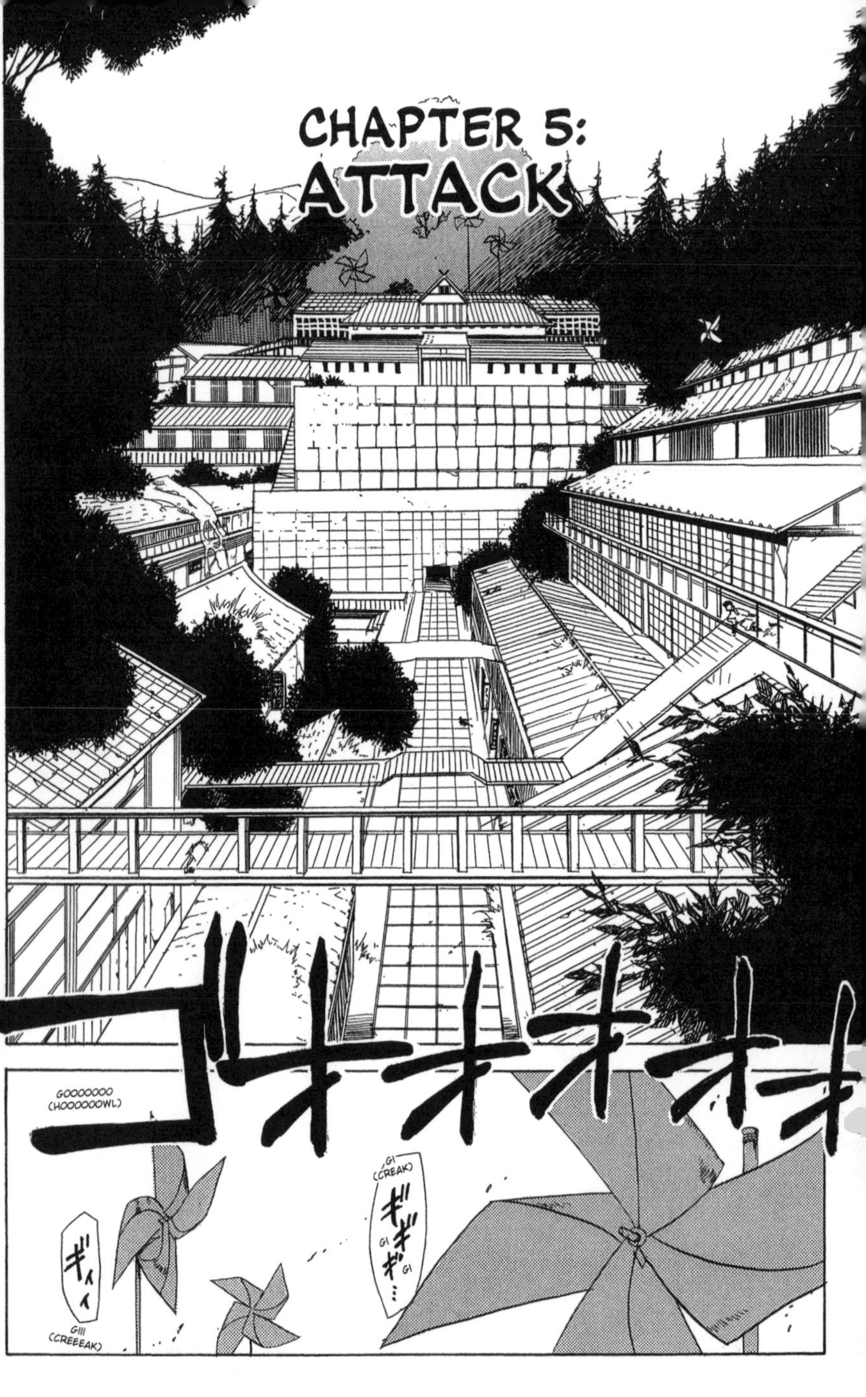
ゴオオオオ
GOOOOOOO (HOOOOOOWL)
ギギギ…
GI (CREAK) GI GI
ギィ
GIII (CREEEAK)

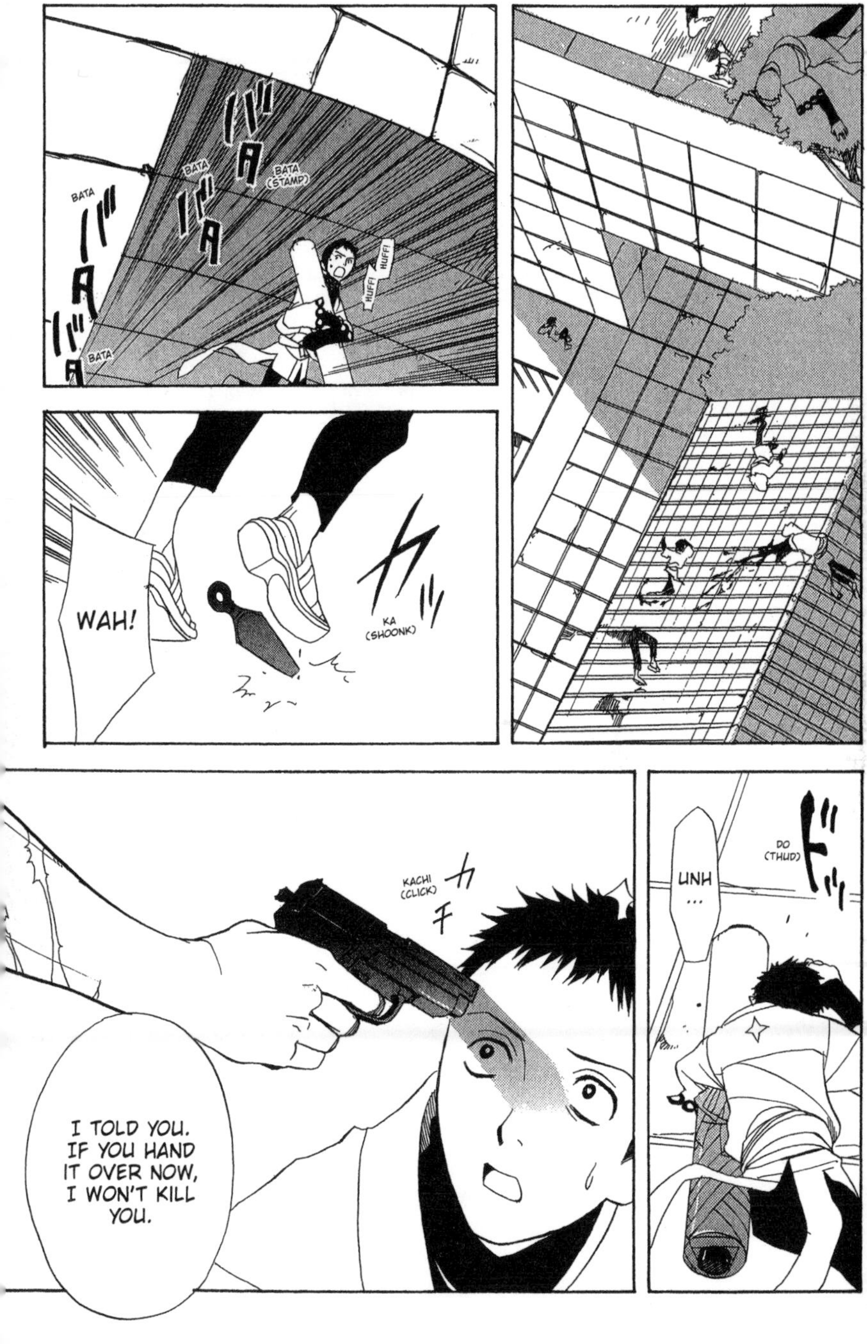
BATA (STAMP)
BATA
BATA
BATA
HUFF! HUFF!
WAH!
KA (SHOONK)
DO (THUD)
UNH...
KACHI (CLICK)
I TOLD YOU. IF YOU HAND IT OVER NOW, I WON'T KILL YOU.

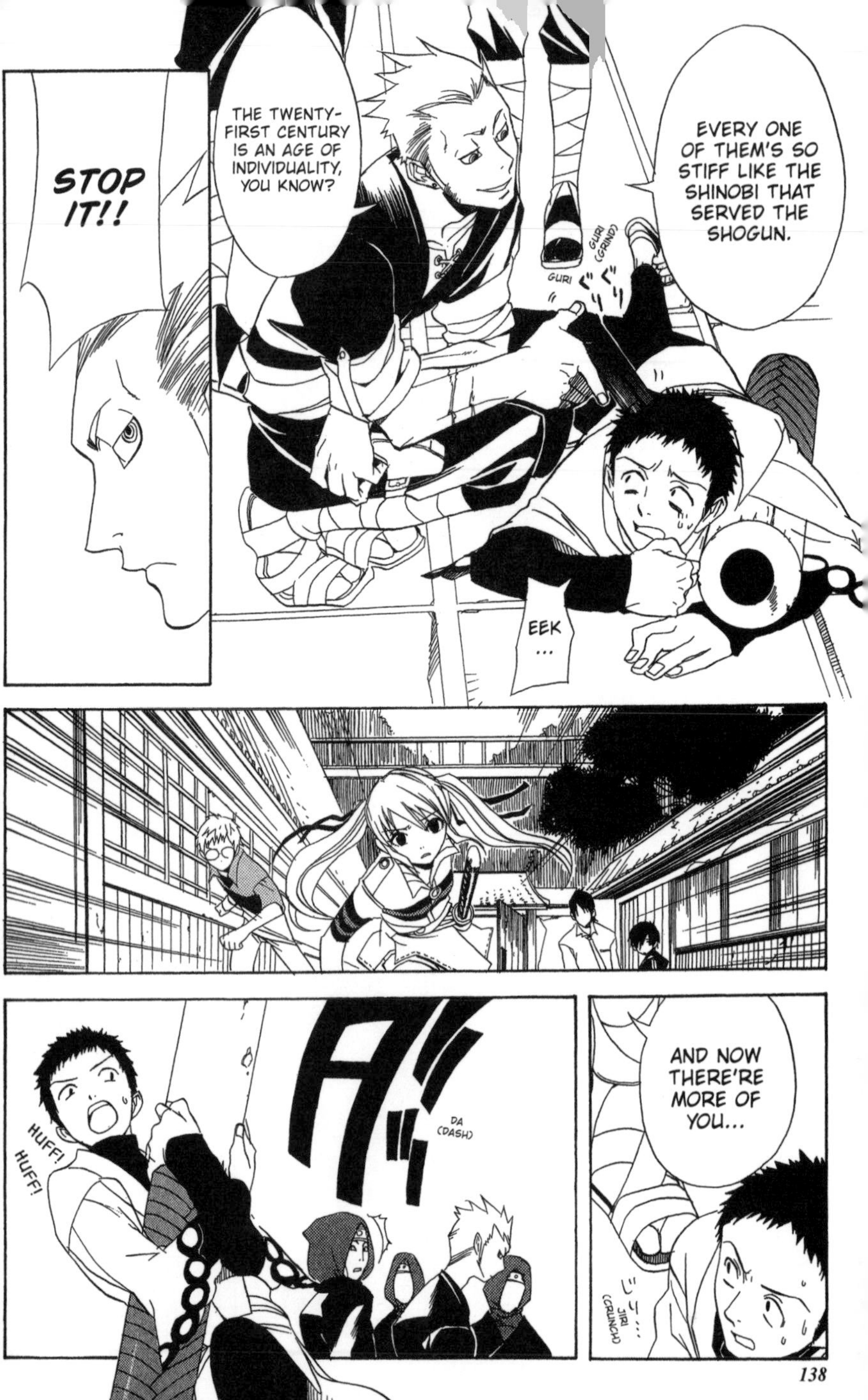
EVERY ONE OF THEM'S SO STIFF LIKE THE SHINOBI THAT SERVED THE SHOGUN.
THE TWENTY-FIRST CENTURY IS AN AGE OF INDIVIDUALITY, YOU KNOW?
GURI (GRIND)
GURI
EEK ...
STOP IT!!
AND NOW THERE'RE MORE OF YOU...
JIRI (CRUNCH)
DA (DASH)
HUFF! HUFF!

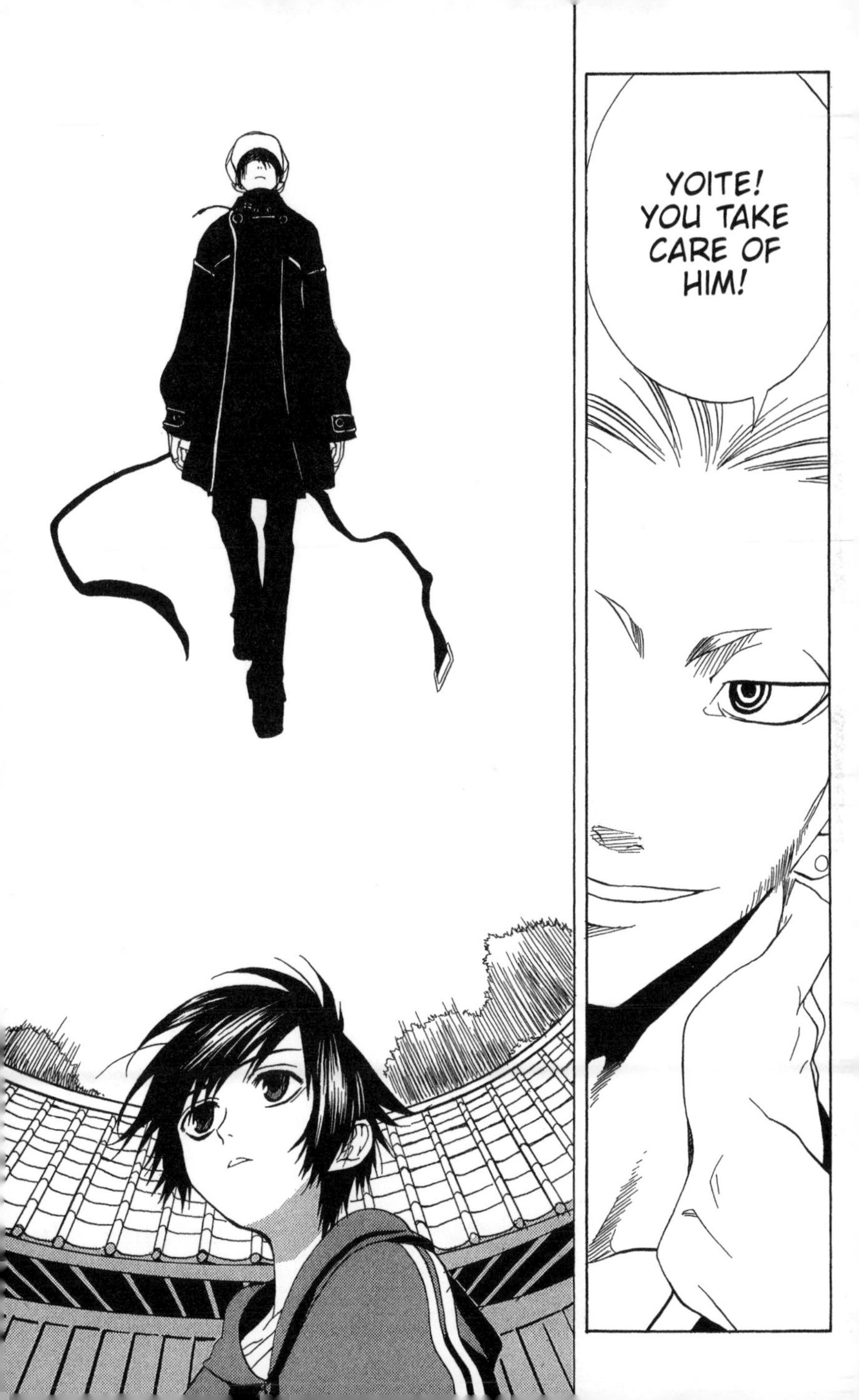
YOITE! YOU TAKE CARE OF HIM!

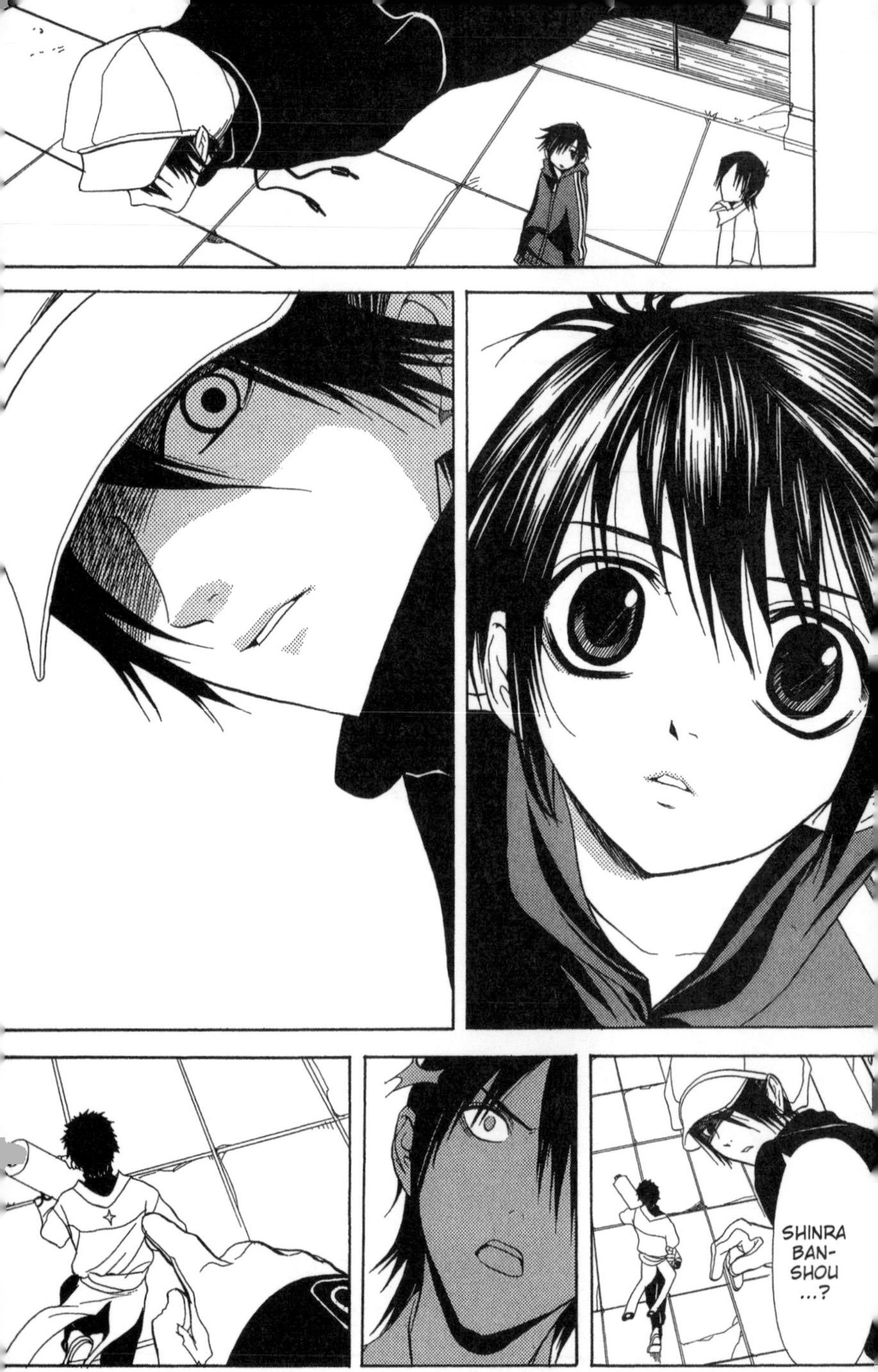
SHINRA BAN-SHOU ...?

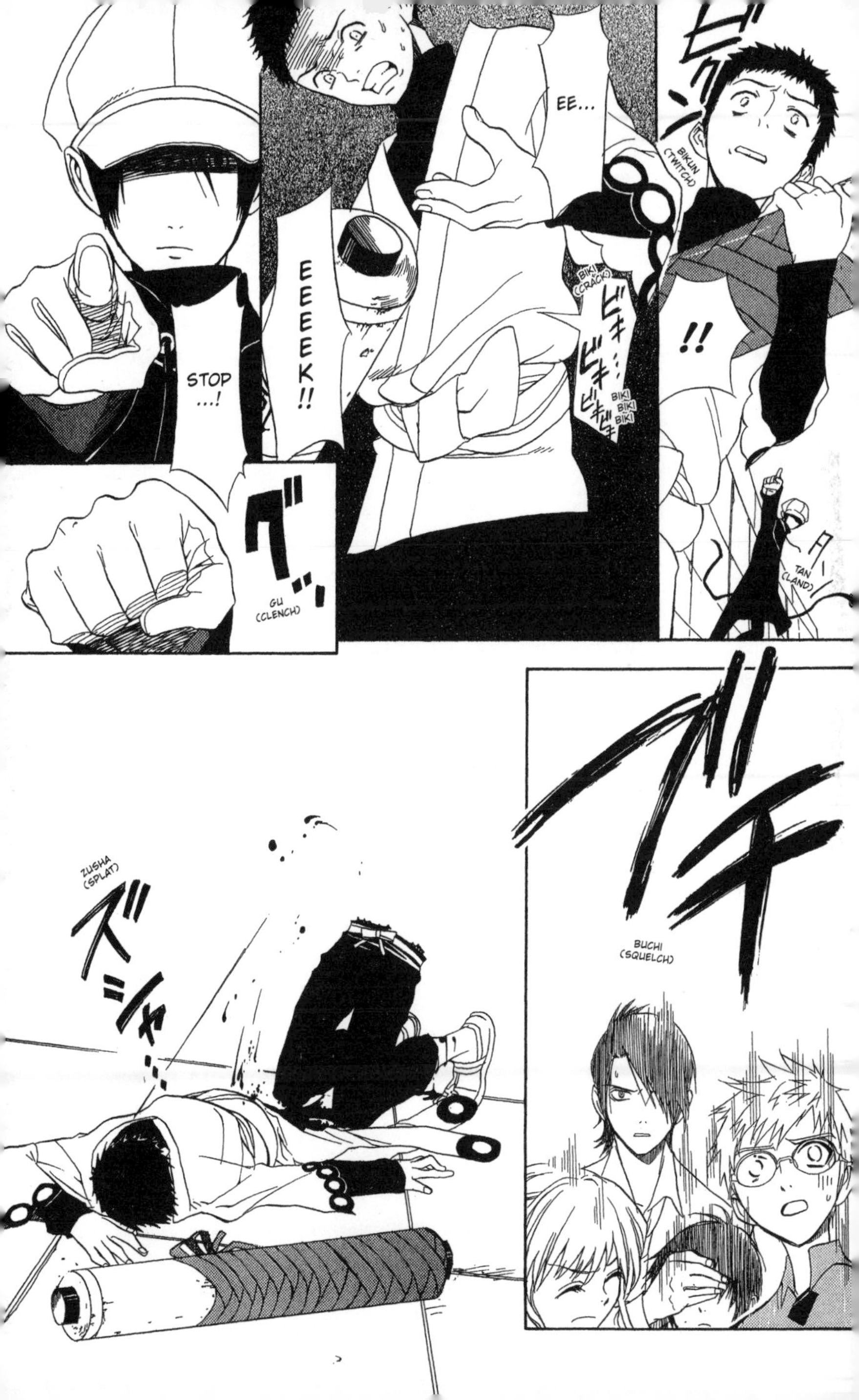

BIKUN (TWITCH)
!!
TAN (LAND)
EE...
BIKI (CRACK)
BIKI BIKI BIKI
EEEEEK!!
STOP ...!
GU (CLENCH)
BUCHI (SQUELCH)
ZUSHA (SPLAT)

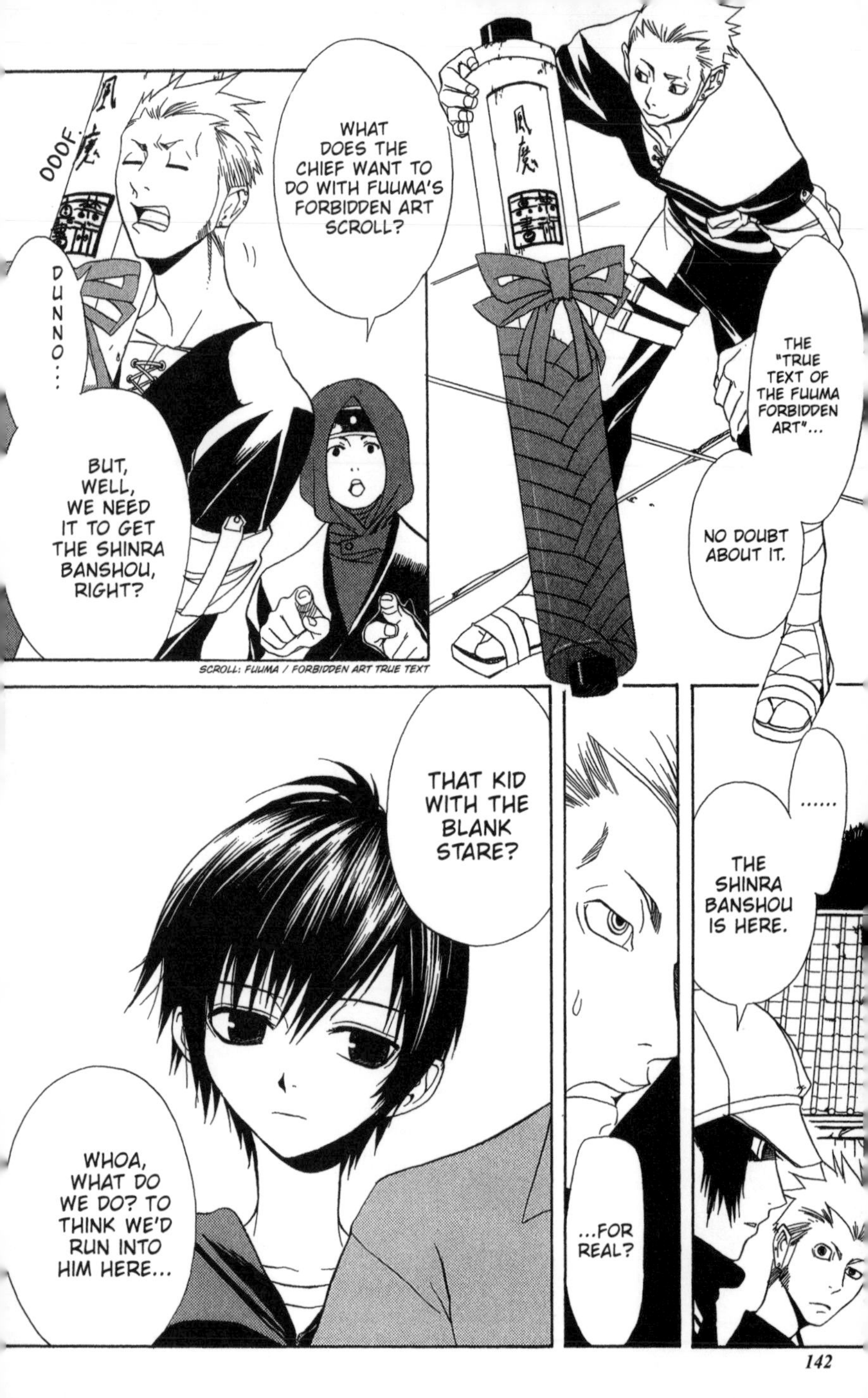
THE "TRUE TEXT OF THE FUUMA FORBIDDEN ART"...
NO DOUBT ABOUT IT.
WHAT DOES THE CHIEF WANT TO DO WITH FUUMA'S FORBIDDEN ART SCROLL?
OOOF.
DUNNO...
BUT, WELL, WE NEED IT TO GET THE SHINRA BANSHOU, RIGHT?
SCROLL: FUUMA / FORBIDDEN ART TRUE TEXT
......
THE SHINRA BANSHOU IS HERE.
...FOR REAL?
THAT KID WITH THE BLANK STARE?
WHOA, WHAT DO WE DO? TO THINK WE'D RUN INTO HIM HERE...

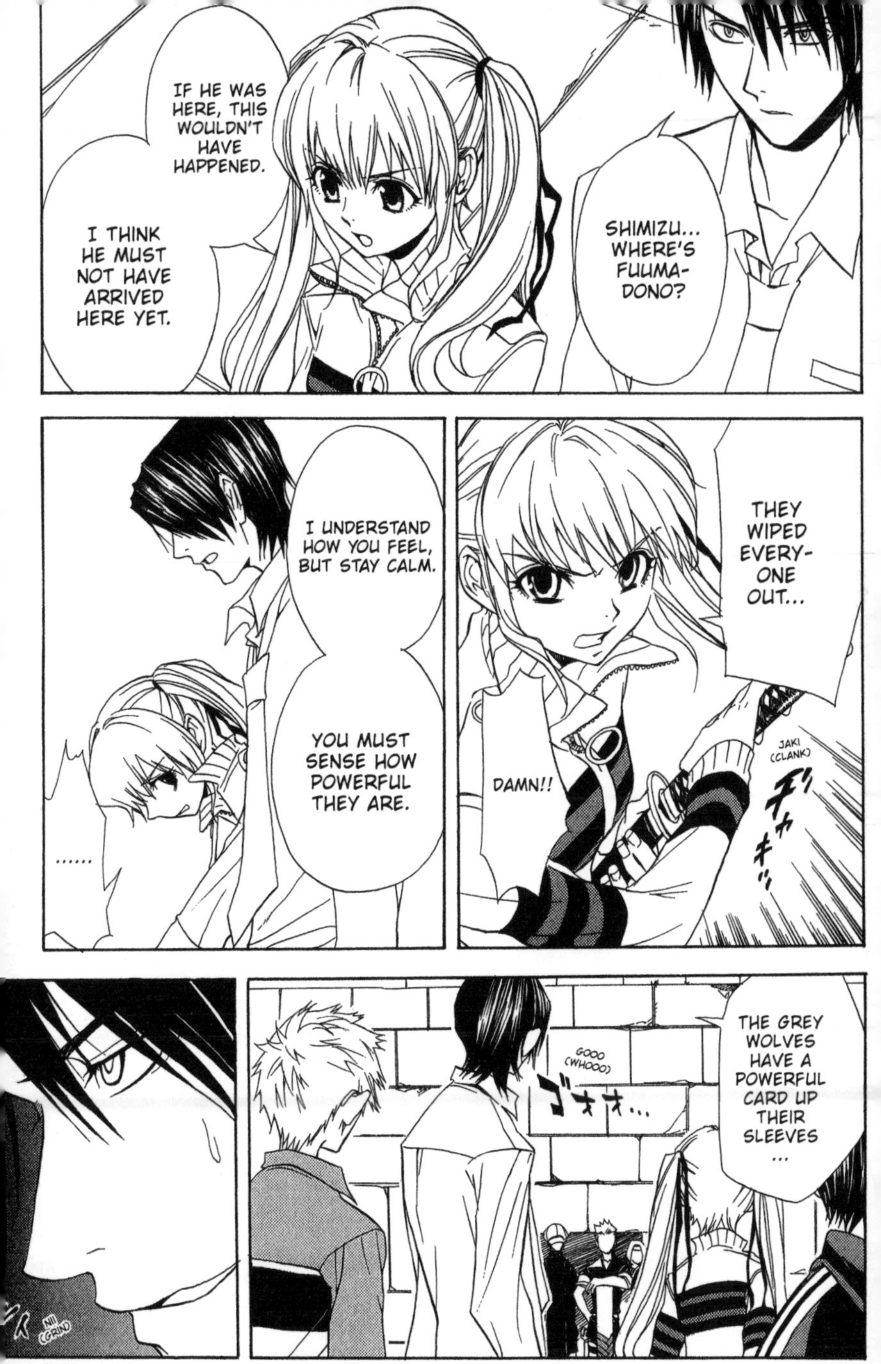
SHIMIZU... WHERE'S FUUMA-DONO?
I THINK HE MUST NOT HAVE ARRIVED HERE YET.
IF HE WAS HERE, THIS WOULDN'T HAVE HAPPENED.
THEY WIPED EVERY-ONE OUT...
JAKI (CLANK)
DAMN!!
I UNDERSTAND HOW YOU FEEL, BUT STAY CALM.
YOU MUST SENSE HOW POWERFUL THEY ARE.
......
THE GREY WOLVES HAVE A POWERFUL CARD UP THEIR SLEEVES ...
GOOO (WHOOO)
NII (GRIN)

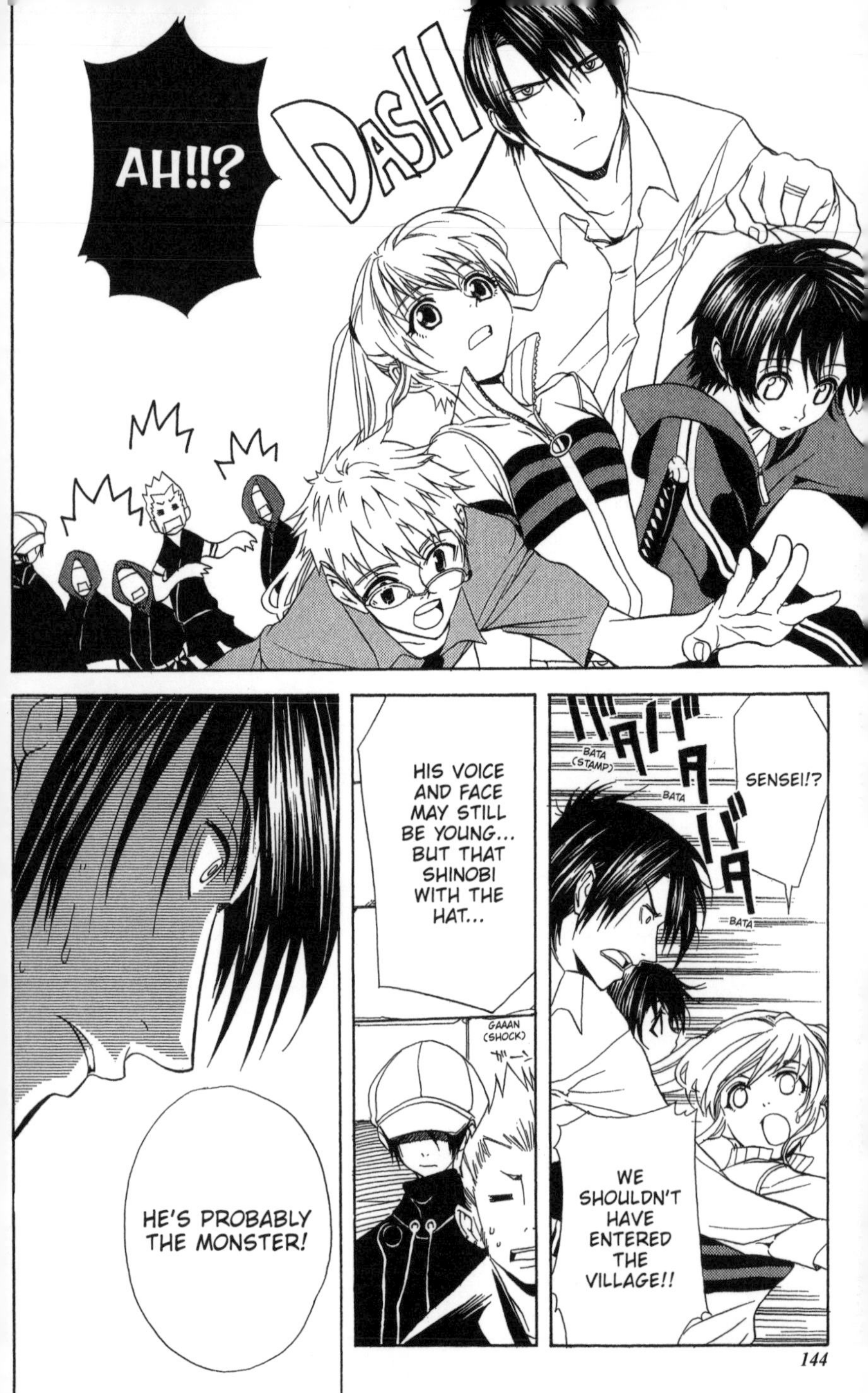
DASH
AH!!?
BATA (STAMP)
BATA
BATA
SENSEI!?
WE SHOULDN'T HAVE ENTERED THE VILLAGE!!
HIS VOICE AND FACE MAY STILL BE YOUNG... BUT THAT SHINOBI WITH THE HAT...
GAAAN (SHOCK)
HE'S PROBABLY THE MONSTER!

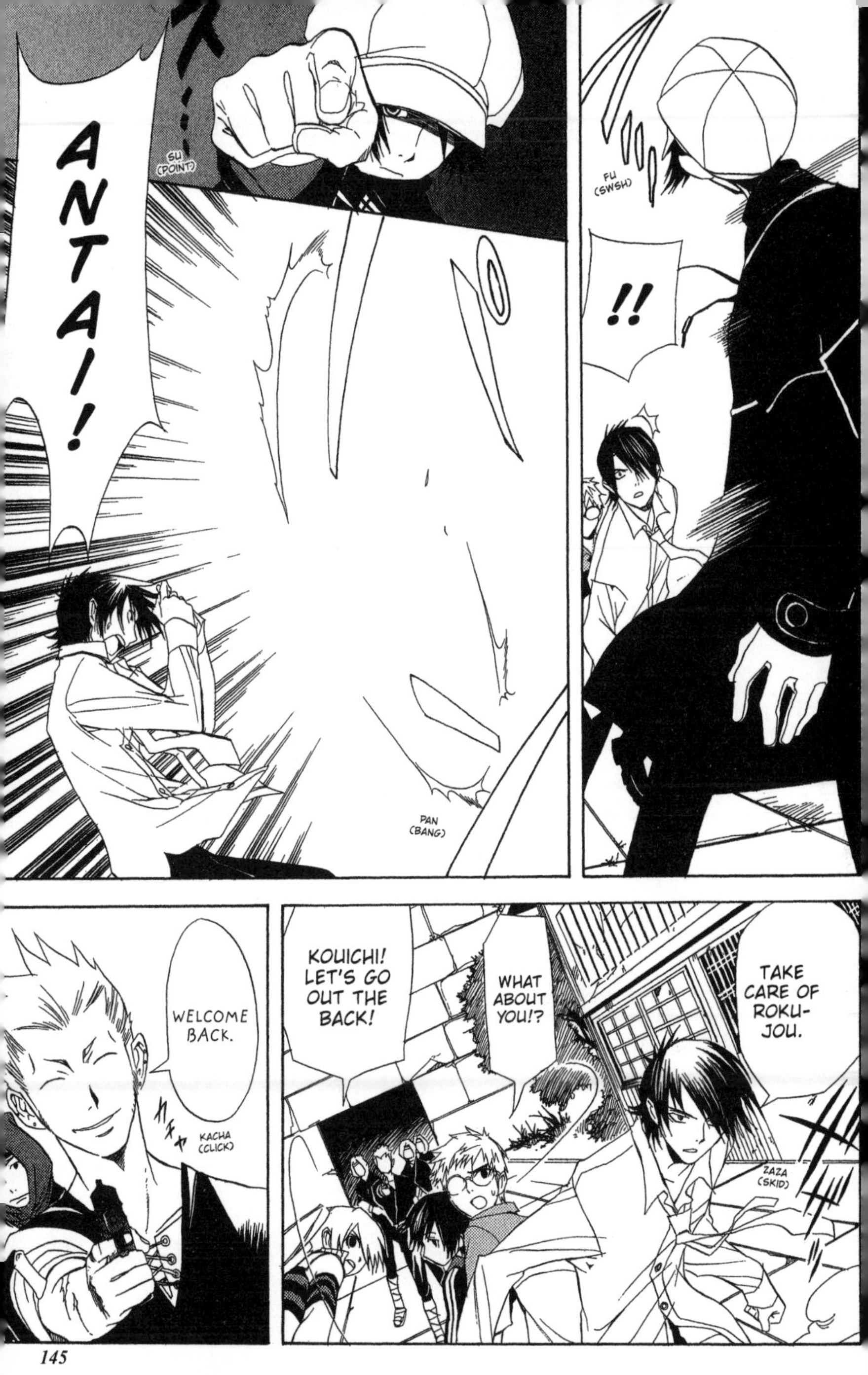
FU
(SWSH)
!!
SU
(POINT)
ANTA!!
PAN
(BANG)
TAKE CARE OF ROKU-JOU.
WHAT ABOUT YOU!?
KOUICHI! LET'S GO OUT THE BACK!
ZAZA
(SKID)
WELCOME BACK.
カチャ
KACHA
(CLICK)

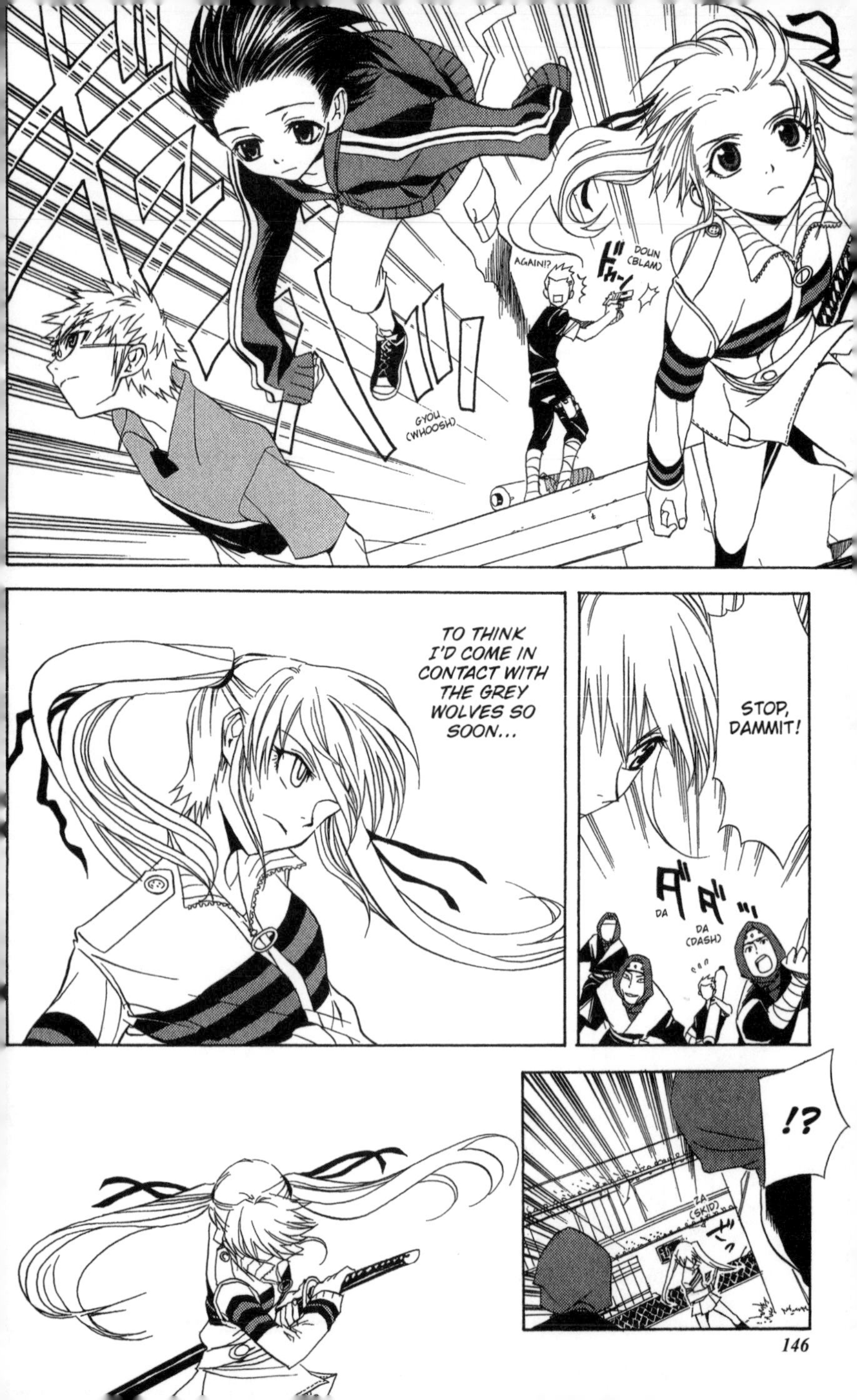
DOUN (BLAM)
AGAIN!?
GYOU (WHOOSH)
STOP, DAMMIT!
DA DA (DASH)
TO THINK I'D COME IN CONTACT WITH THE GREY WOLVES SO SOON...
!?
ZA (SKID)

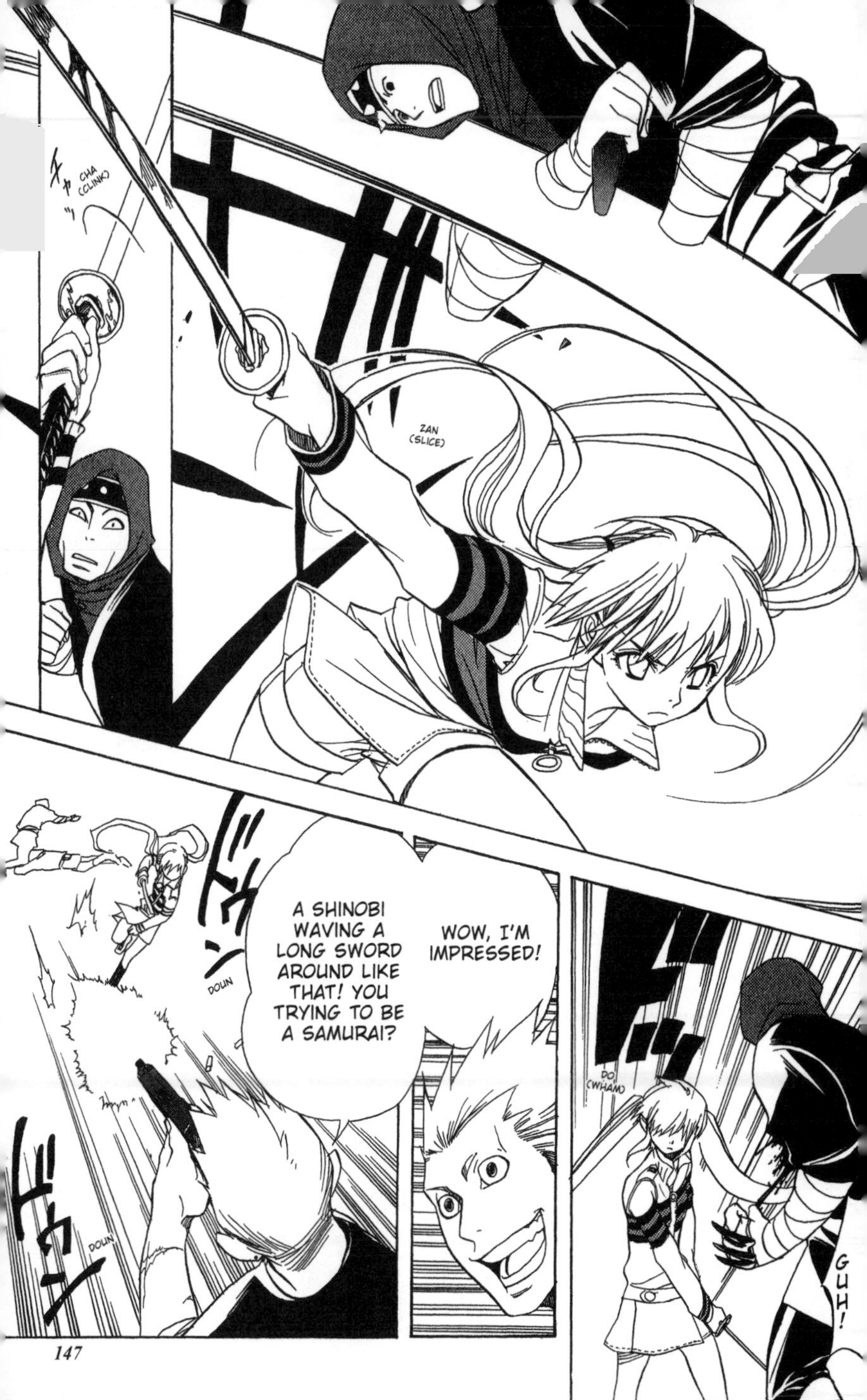
ZAN (SLICE)
CHA (CLINK)
DO (WHAM)
GUH!
WOW, I'M IMPRESSED!
A SHINOBI WAVING A LONG SWORD AROUND LIKE THAT! YOU TRYING TO BE A SAMURAI?
DOUN
DOUN

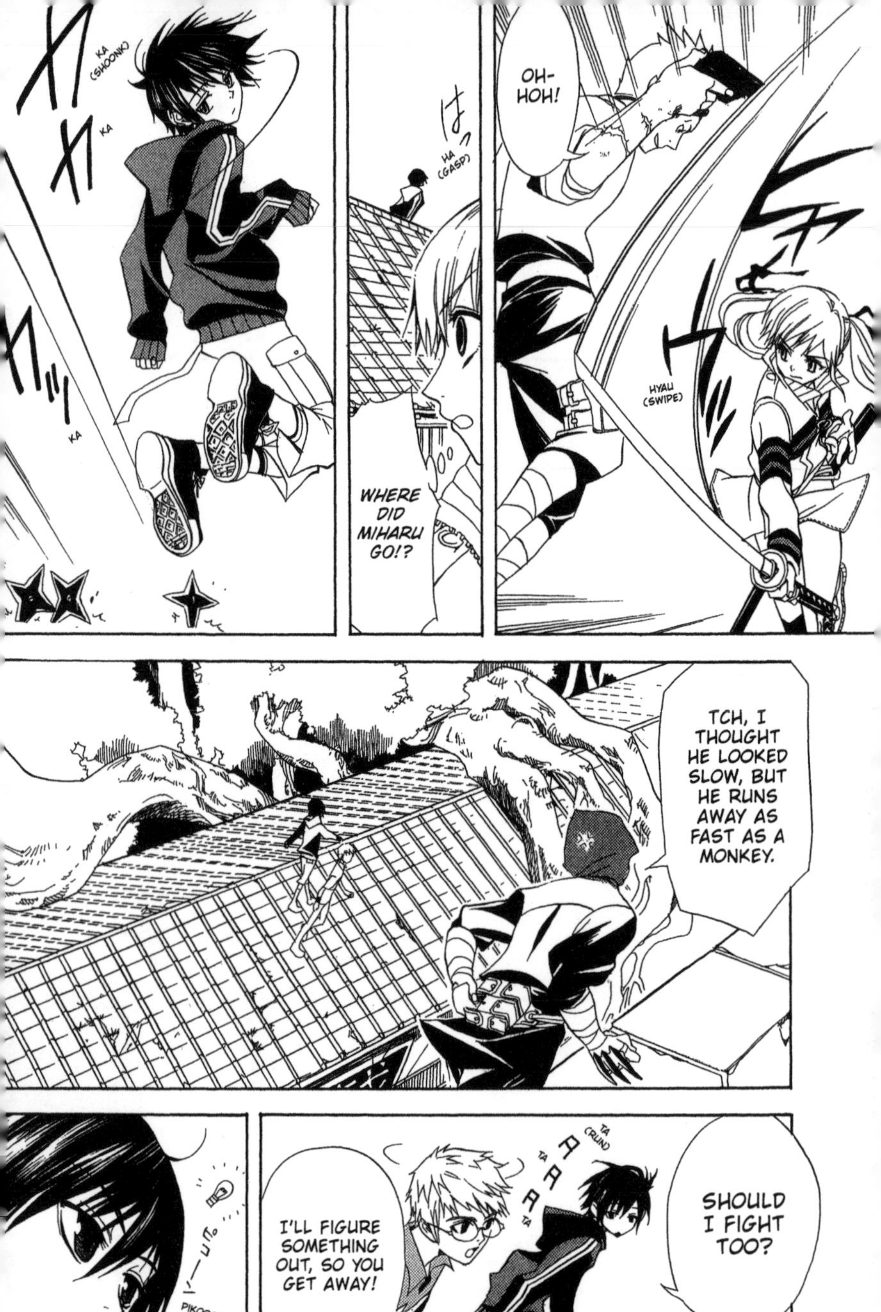
OH-HOH!
HYAU (SWIPE)
HA (GASP)
WHERE DID MIHARU GO!?
KA (SHOONK)
KA
KA
TCH, I THOUGHT HE LOOKED SLOW, BUT HE RUNS AWAY AS FAST AS A MONKEY.
SHOULD I FIGHT TOO?
TA (RUN)
TA
TA
I'LL FIGURE SOMETHING OUT, SO YOU GET AWAY!
PIKOOON (DIIING)

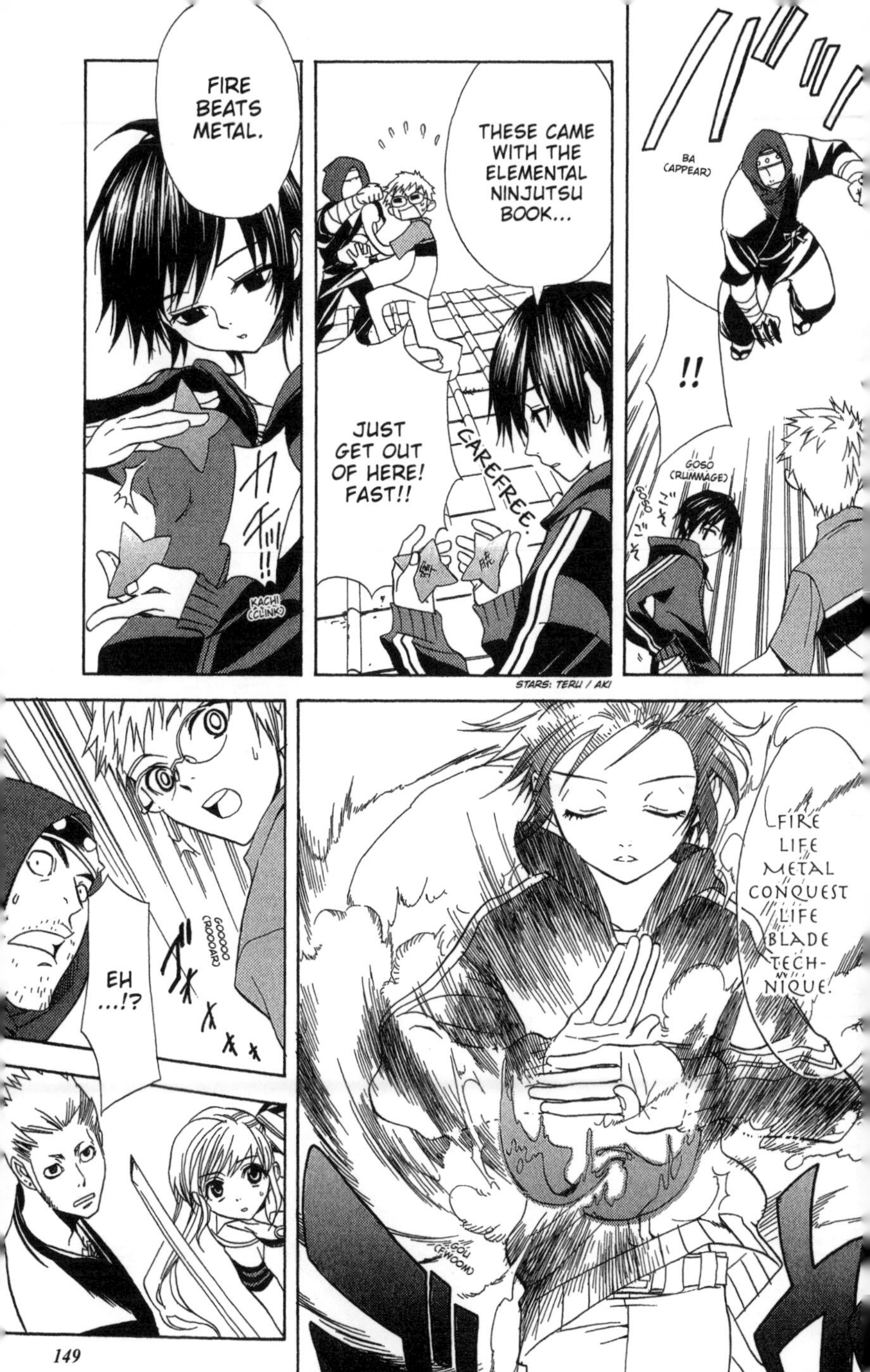
BA (APPEAR)
!!
GOSO (RUMMAGE)
GOSO
THESE CAME WITH THE ELEMENTAL NINJUTSU BOOK...
CAREFREE.
JUST GET OUT OF HERE! FAST!!
FIRE BEATS METAL.
KACHI (CLINK)
STARS: TERU / AKI
FIRE LIFE METAL CONQUEST LIFE BLADE TECH-NIQUE.
GOU (FWOOM)
GOOOOO (ROOOAR)
EH ...!?

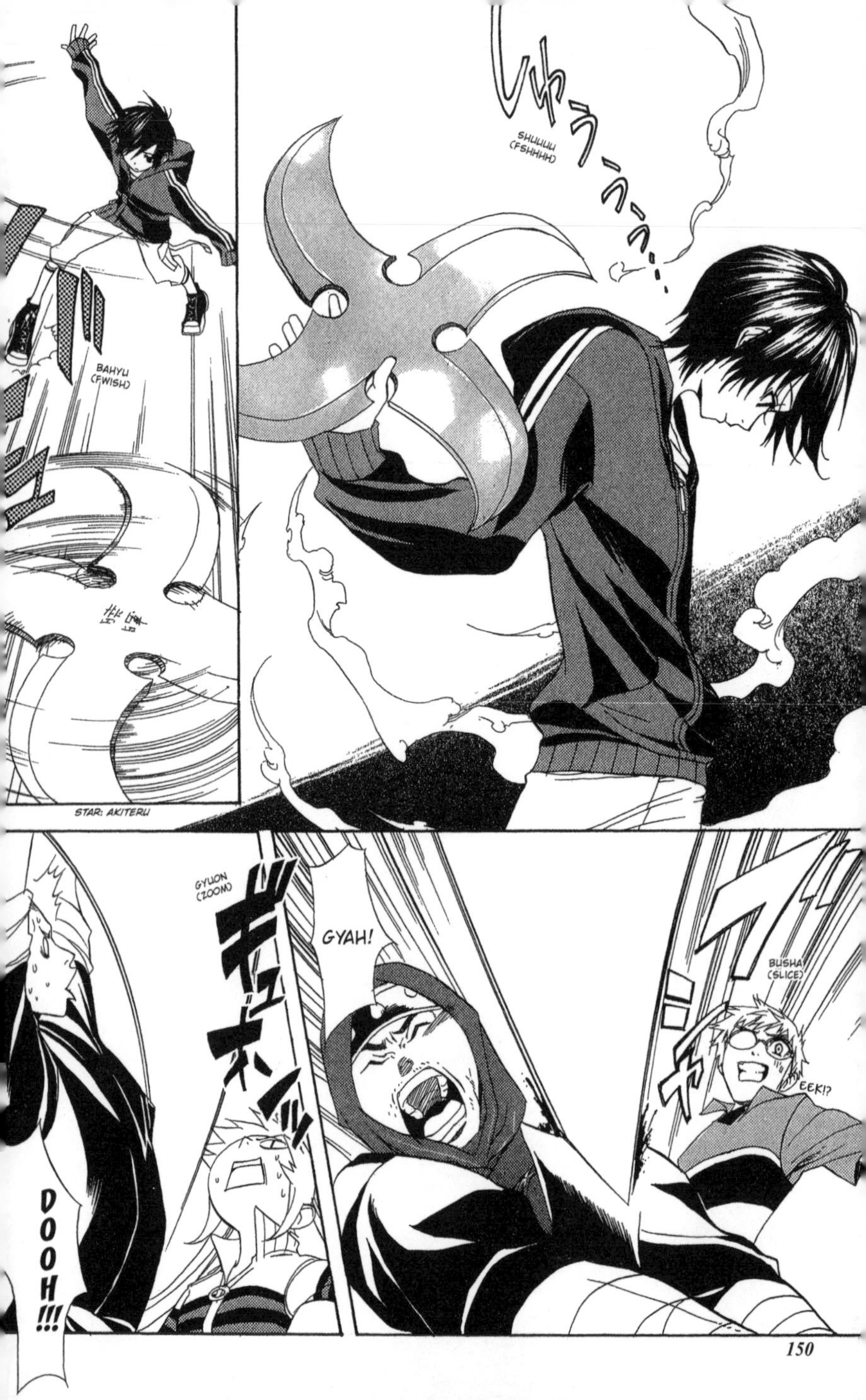
SHUUUU
(FSHHHH)
BAHYU
(FWISH)
STAR: AKITERU
BUSHA
(SLICE)
EEK!?
GYAH!
GYUON
(ZOOM)
DOOOH!!!

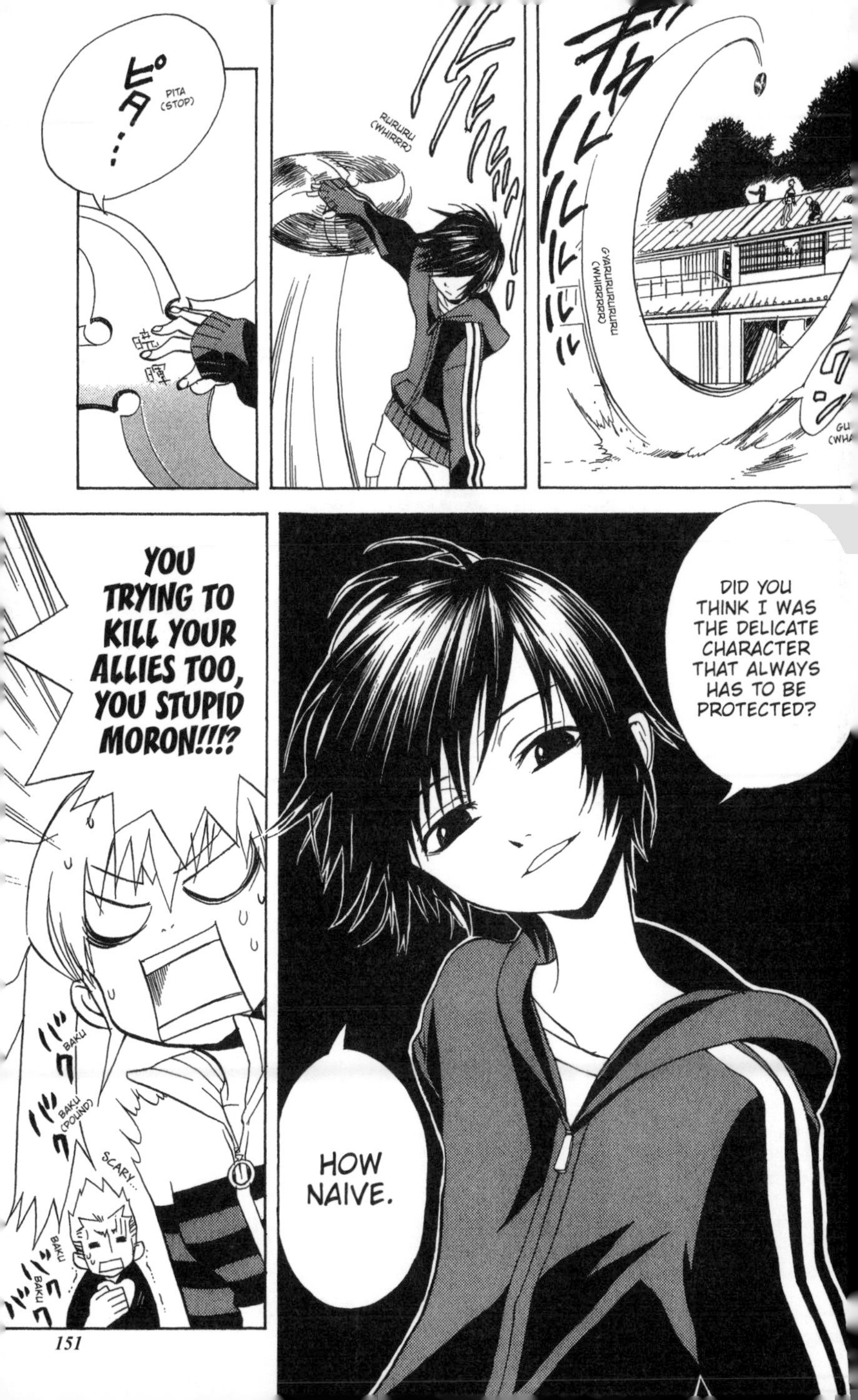
GYARURURURURU (WHIRRRR)
GU (WHA
RURURU (WHIRRR)
ピタ…
PITA (STOP)
DID YOU THINK I WAS THE DELICATE CHARACTER THAT ALWAYS HAS TO BE PROTECTED?
HOW NAIVE.
YOU TRYING TO KILL YOUR ALLIES TOO, YOU STUPID MORON!!!?
BAKU
BAKU (POUND)
SCARY...
BAKU
BAKU

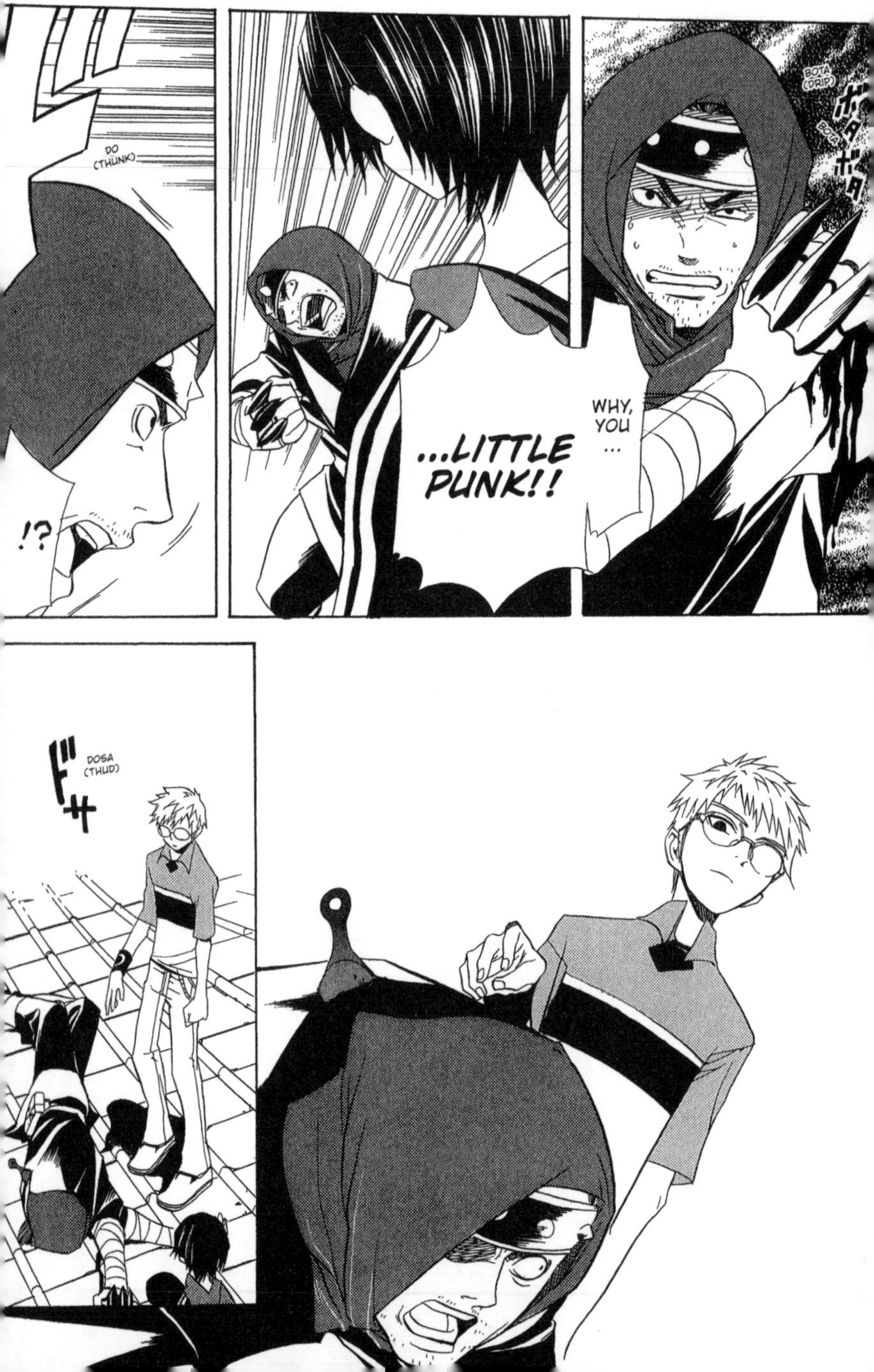

ボタボタ
BOTA (DRIP)
BOTA
WHY, YOU ...
...LITTLE PUNK!!
DO (THUNK)
!?
ドサ
DOSA (THUD)

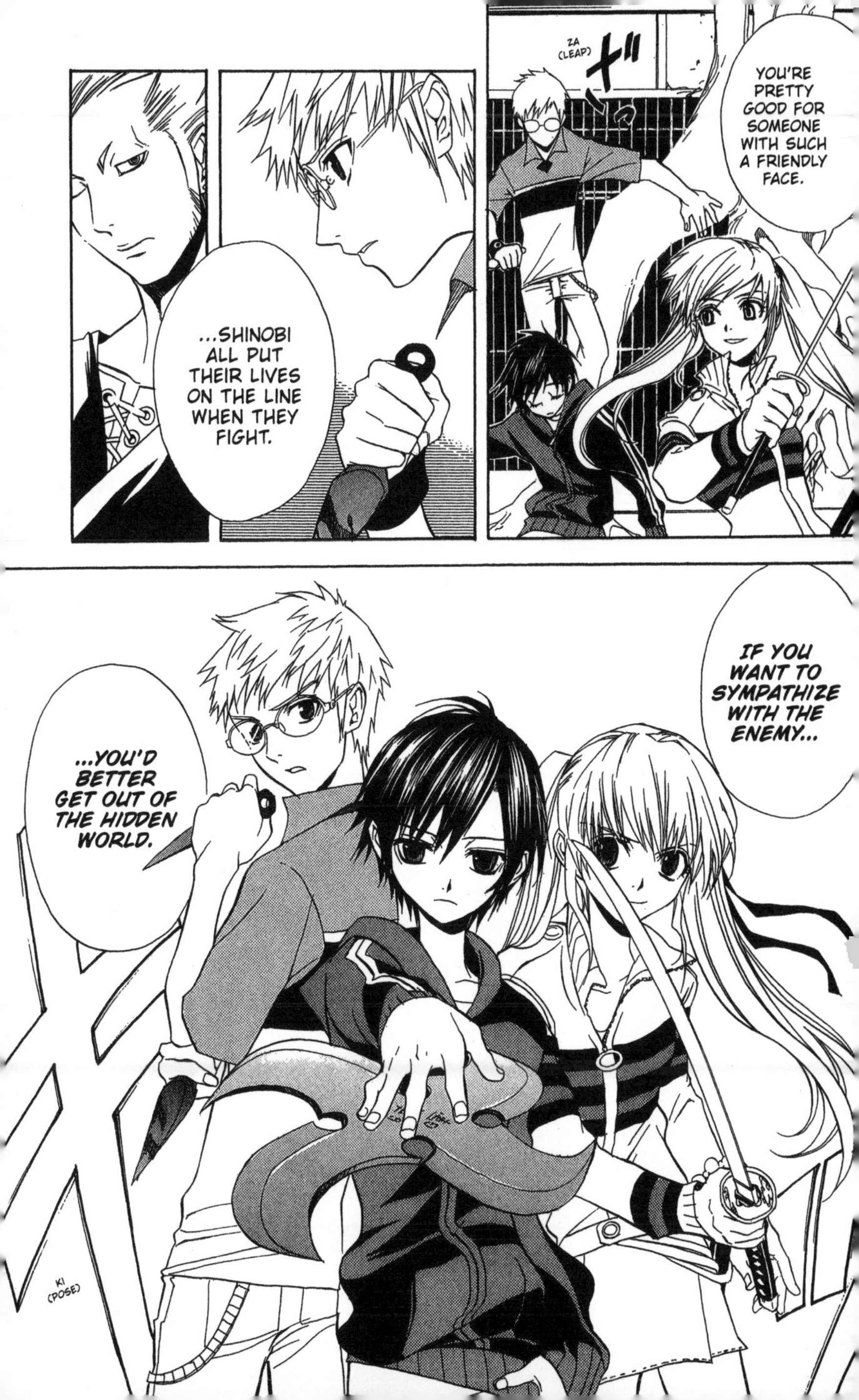
ZA (LEAP)
YOU'RE PRETTY GOOD FOR SOMEONE WITH SUCH A FRIENDLY FACE.
...SHINOBI ALL PUT THEIR LIVES ON THE LINE WHEN THEY FIGHT.
IF YOU WANT TO SYMPATHIZE WITH THE ENEMY...
...YOU'D BETTER GET OUT OF THE HIDDEN WORLD.
KI (POSE)

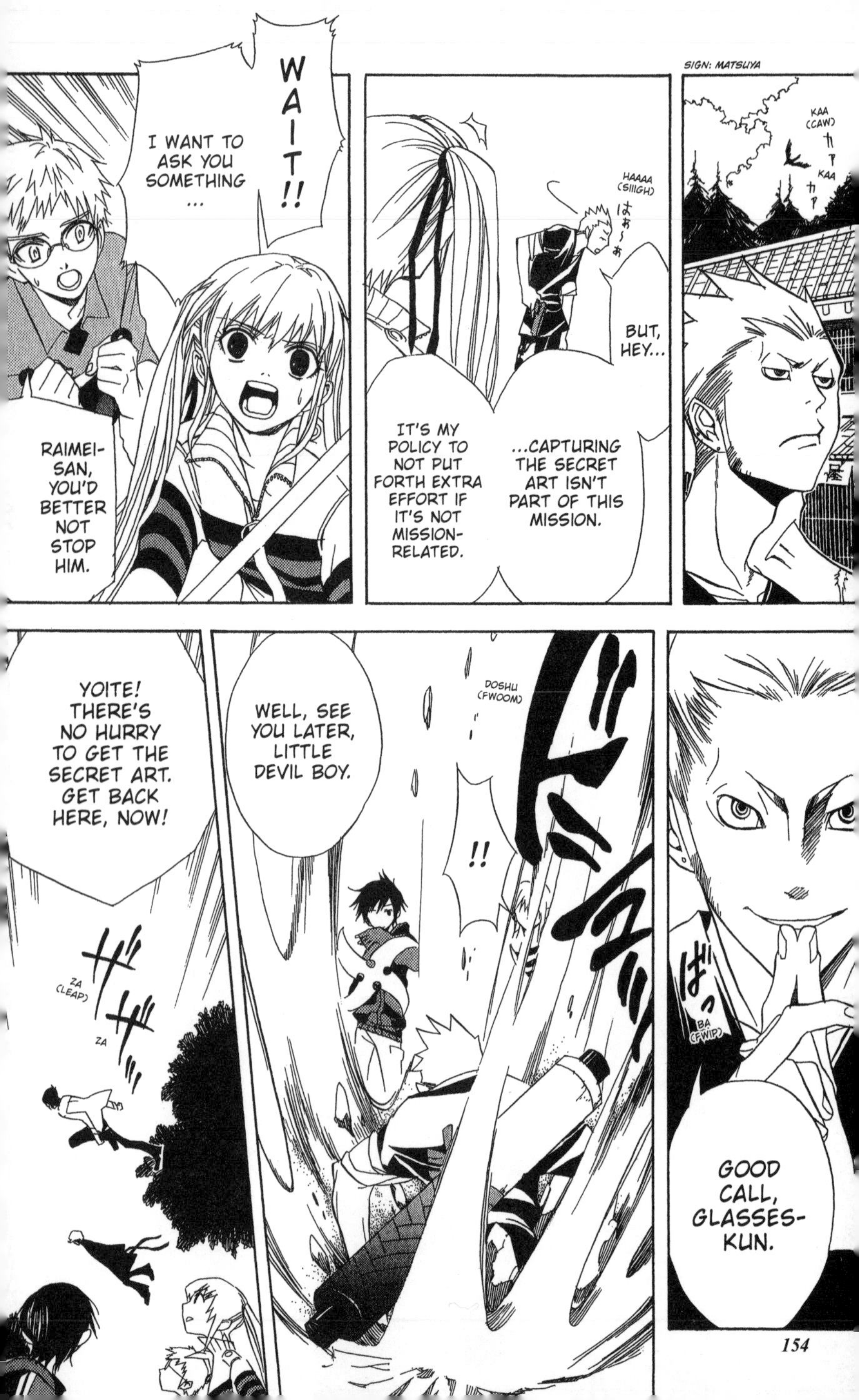
SIGN: MATSUYA
KAA (CAW) カア
KAA カア
HAAAA (SIIIGH) はあ〜あ
BUT, HEY...
...CAPTURING THE SECRET ART ISN'T PART OF THIS MISSION.
IT'S MY POLICY TO NOT PUT FORTH EXTRA EFFORT IF IT'S NOT MISSION-RELATED.
WAIT!!
I WANT TO ASK YOU SOMETHING ...
RAIMEI-SAN, YOU'D BETTER NOT STOP HIM.
BA (FWIP) ばっ
GOOD CALL, GLASSES-KUN.
DOSHU (FWOOM)
!!
WELL, SEE YOU LATER, LITTLE DEVIL BOY.
YOITE! THERE'S NO HURRY TO GET THE SECRET ART. GET BACK HERE, NOW!
ZA (LEAP)
ZA

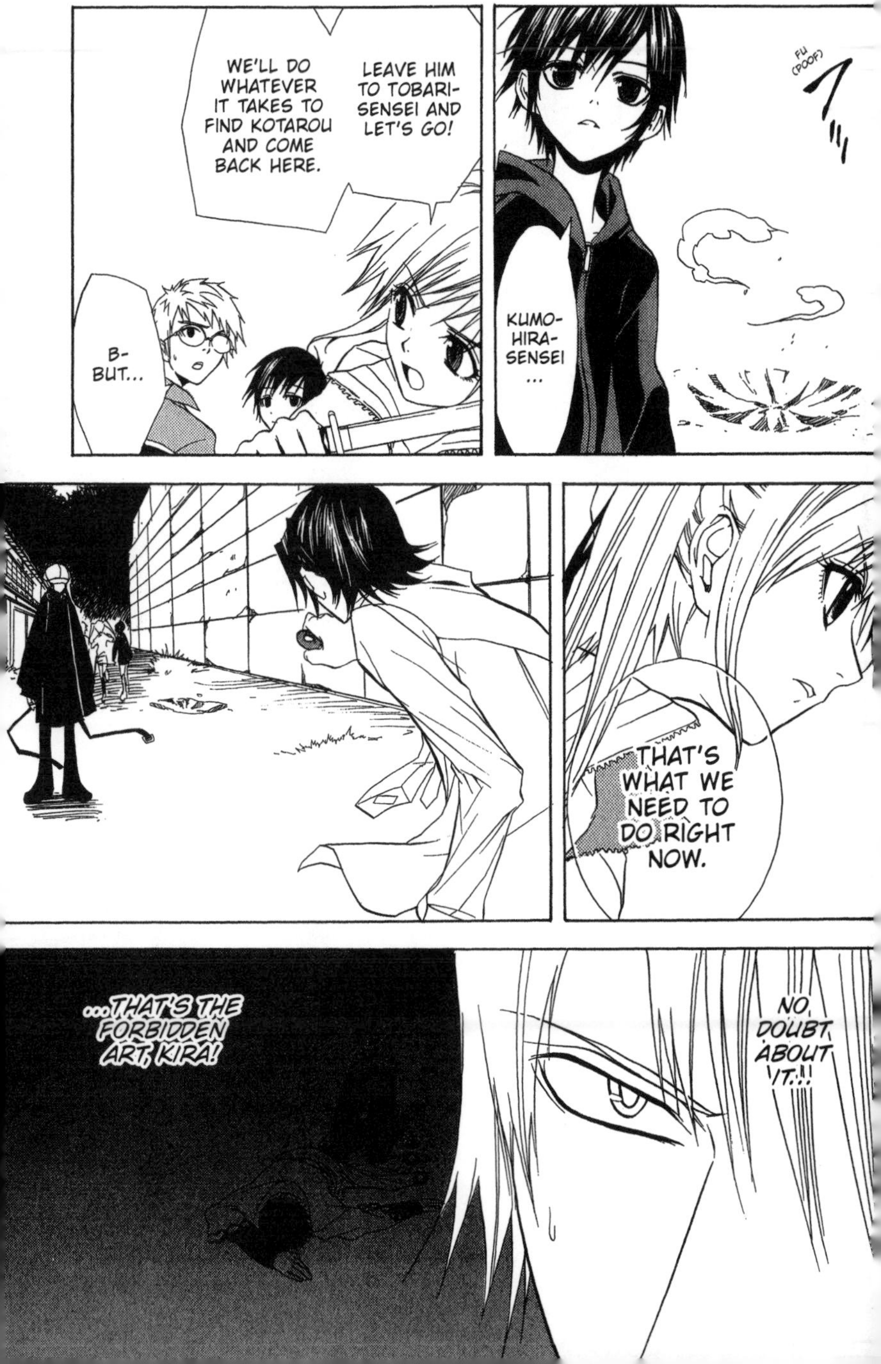
FU (POOF)
KUMO-HIRA-SENSEI...
LEAVE HIM TO TOBARI-SENSEI AND LET'S GO!
WE'LL DO WHATEVER IT TAKES TO FIND KOTAROU AND COME BACK HERE.
B-BUT...
THAT'S WHAT WE NEED TO DO RIGHT NOW.
NO DOUBT ABOUT IT...!
...THAT'S THE FORBIDDEN ART, KIRA!

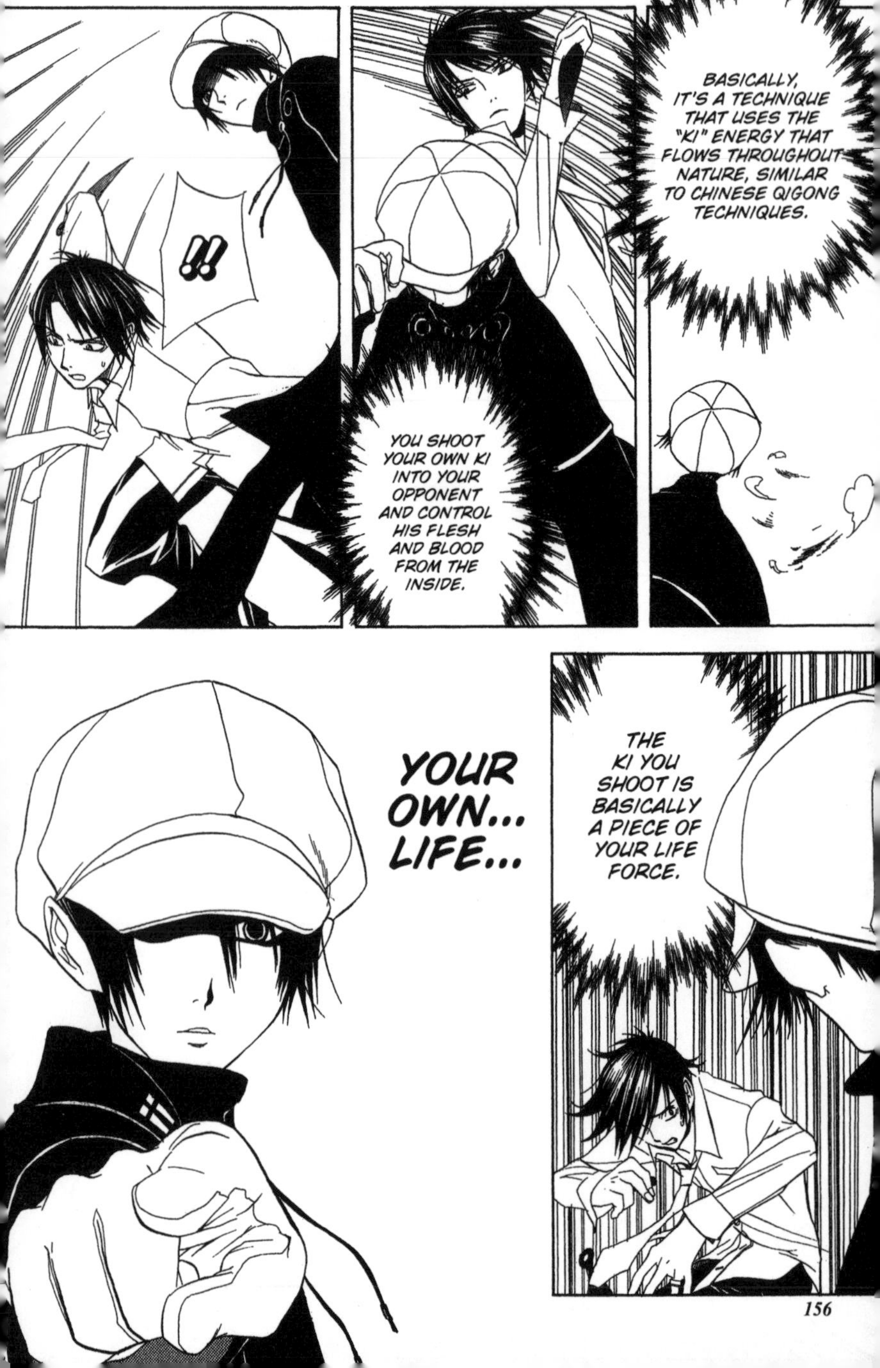
BASICALLY, IT'S A TECHNIQUE THAT USES THE "KI" ENERGY THAT FLOWS THROUGHOUT NATURE, SIMILAR TO CHINESE QIGONG TECHNIQUES.
YOU SHOOT YOUR OWN KI INTO YOUR OPPONENT AND CONTROL HIS FLESH AND BLOOD FROM THE INSIDE.
!!
THE KI YOU SHOOT IS BASICALLY A PIECE OF YOUR LIFE FORCE.
YOUR OWN... LIFE...

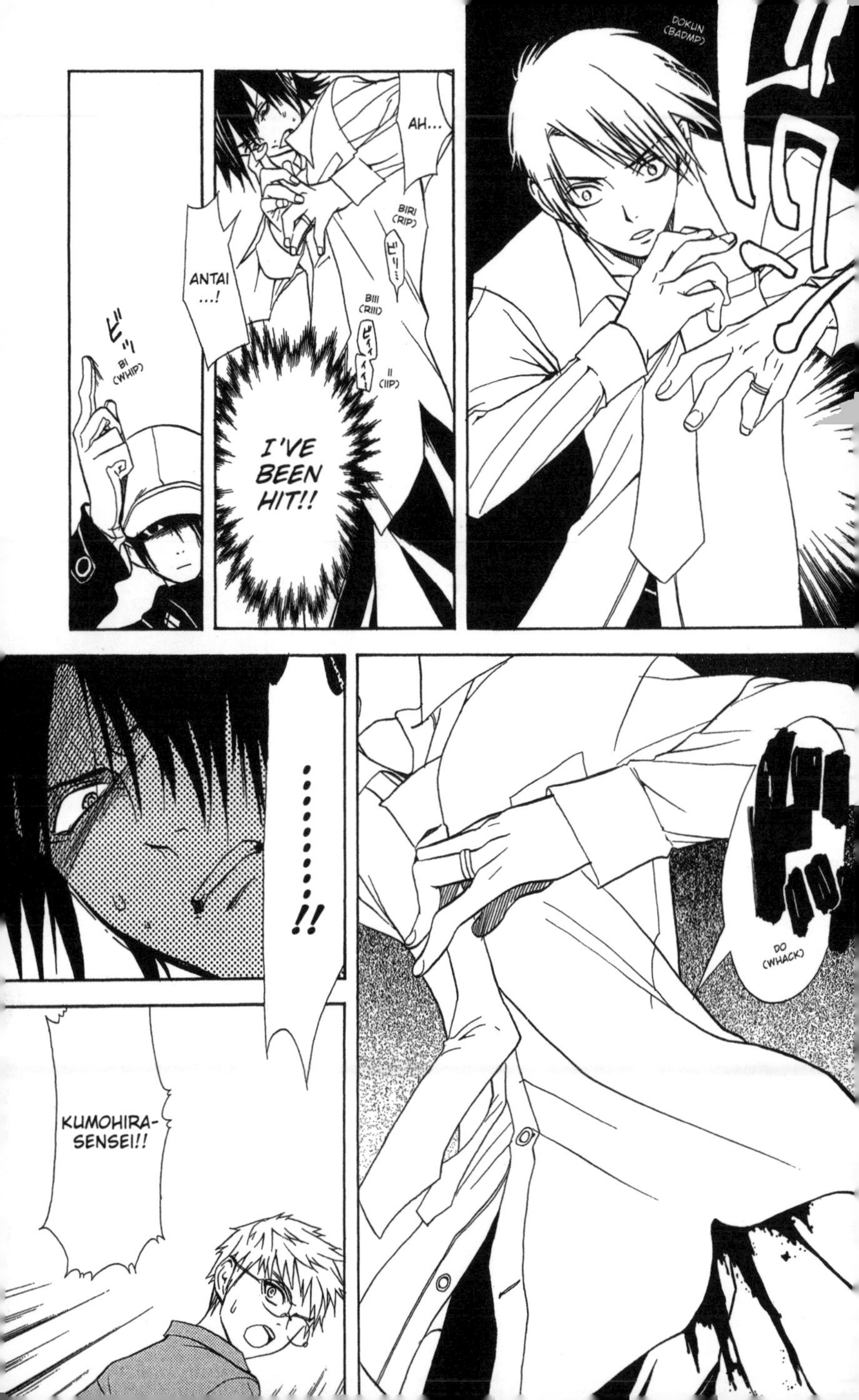
DOKUN (BADMP)
AH...
BIRI (RIP)
BIII (RIII)
II (IIP)
ANTAI ...!
I'VE BEEN HIT!!
BI (WHIP)
DO (WHACK)
..........!!
KUMOHIRA-SENSEI!!

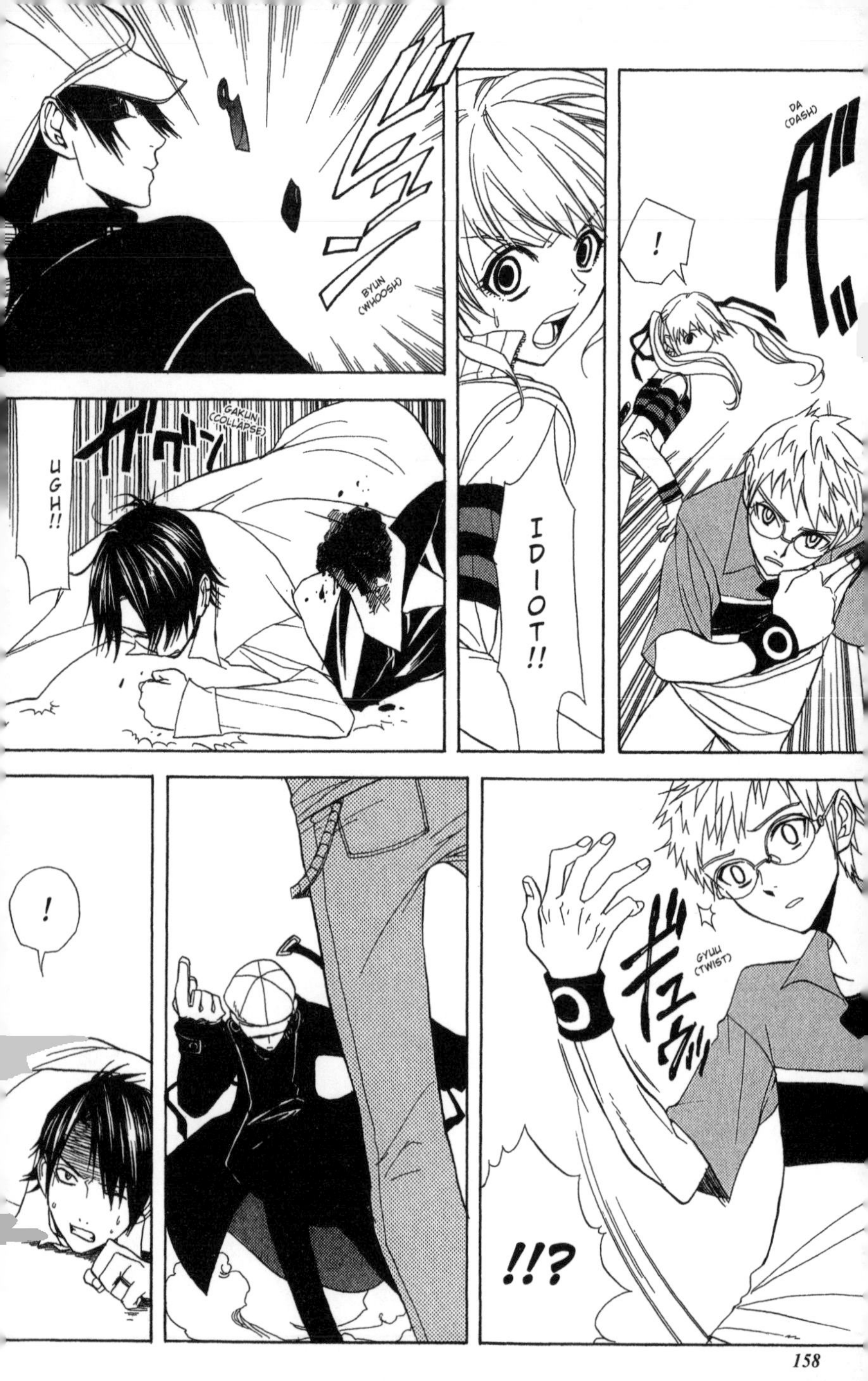
DA (DASH)
!
IDIOT!!
BYUN (WHOOSH)
GAKUN (COLLAPSE)
UGH!!
GYUU (TWIST)
!!?
!

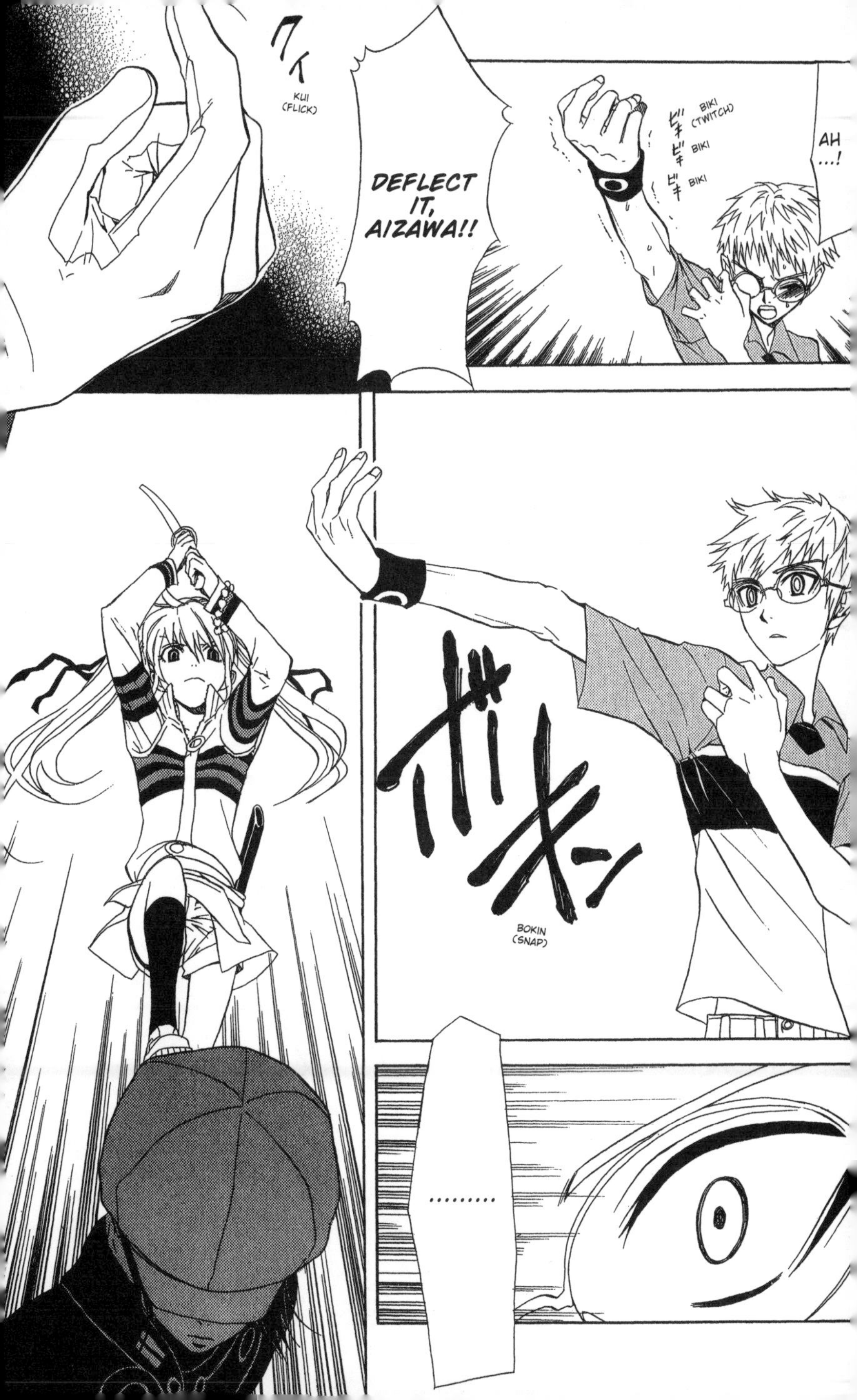

AH ...!
ビキ
BIKI (TWITCH)
ビキ
BIKI
ビキ
BIKI
DEFLECT IT, AIZAWA!!
クイ
KUI (FLICK)
ボキン
BOKIN (SNAP)
....

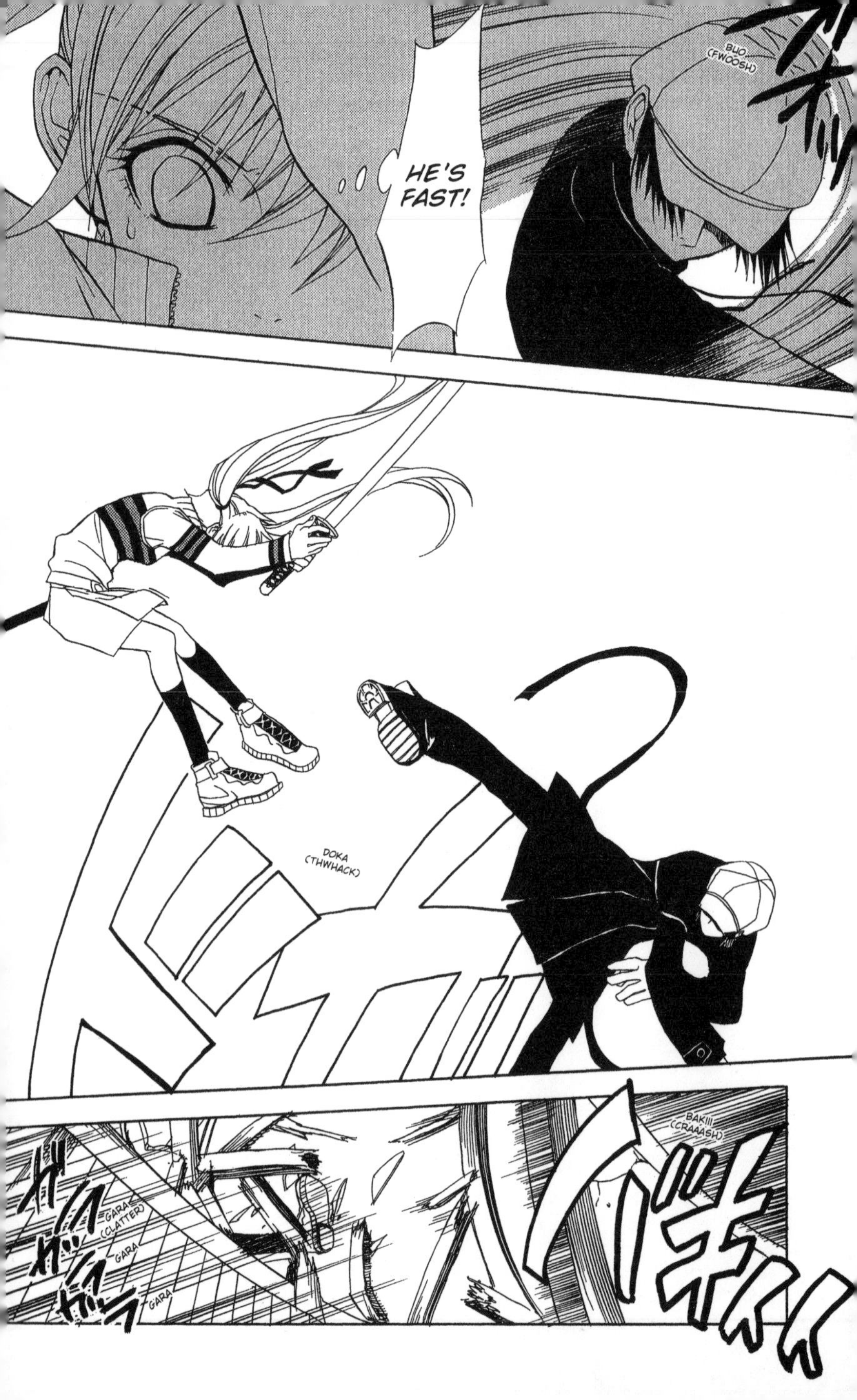
BUO (FWOOSH)
HE'S FAST!
DOKA (THWHACK)
BAKIII (CRAAASH)
GARA (CLATTER)
GARA
GARA

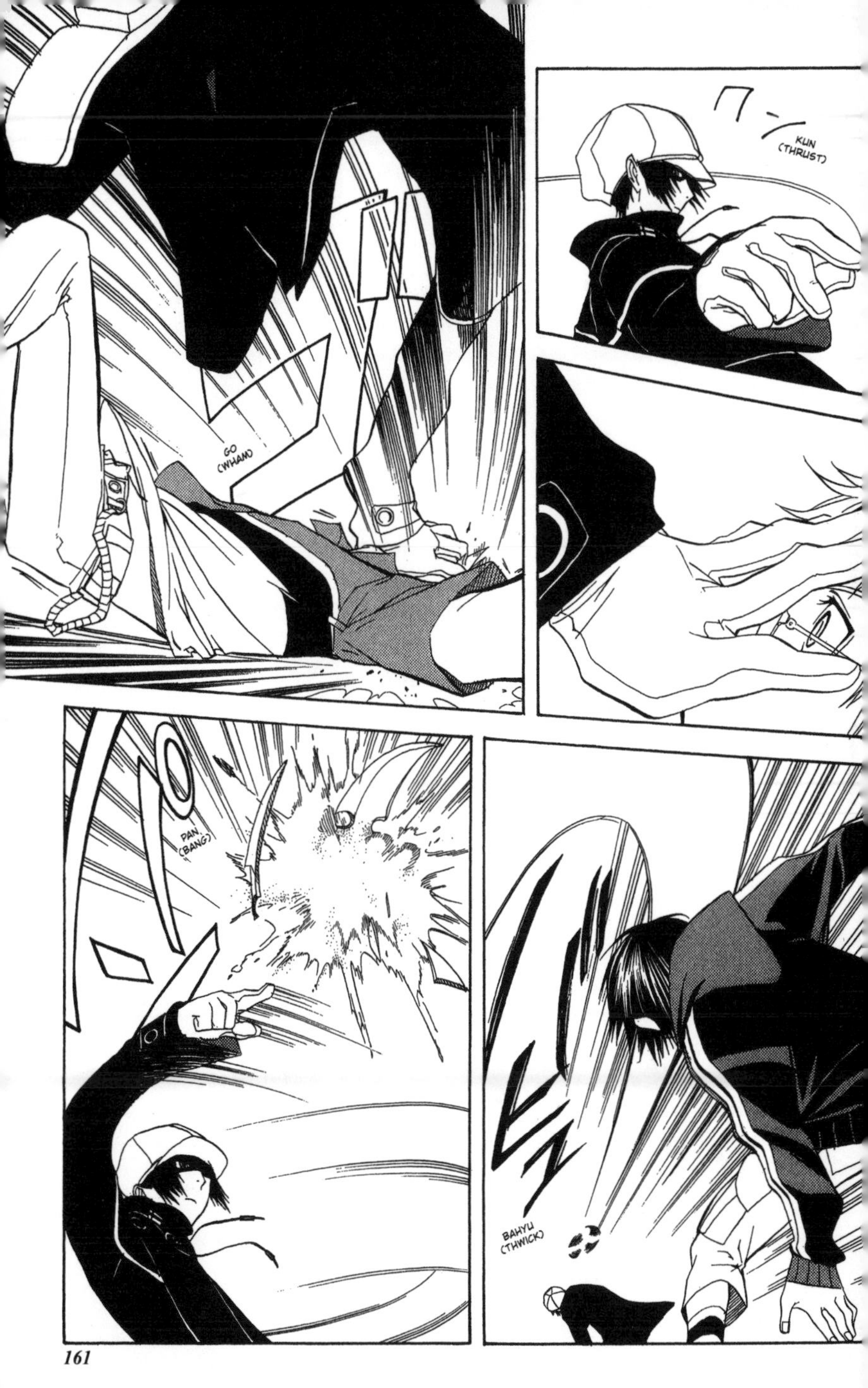
KUN
(THRUST)
GO
(WHAM)
BAHYU
(THWICK)
PAN
(BANG)

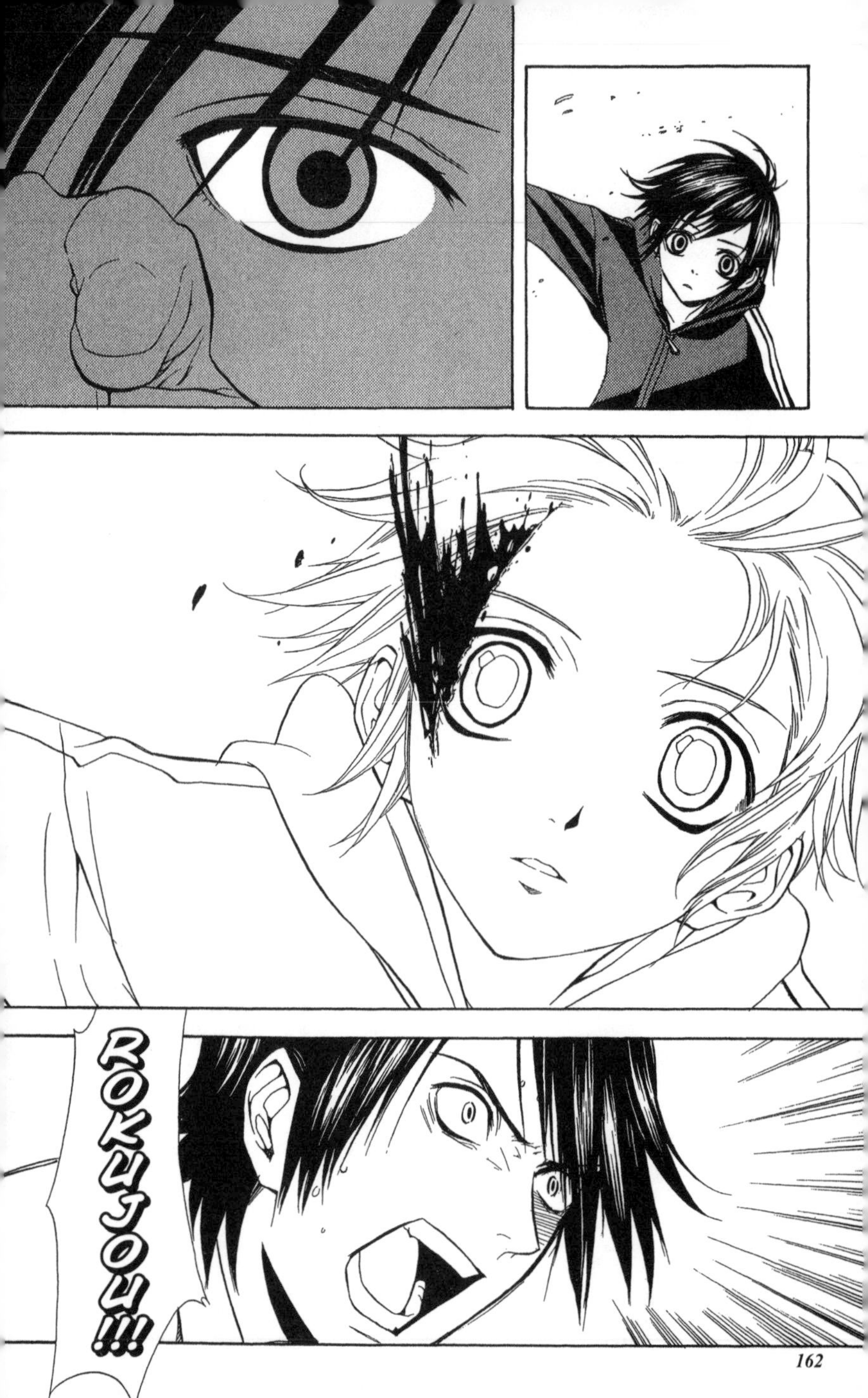
ROKUJOU!!!

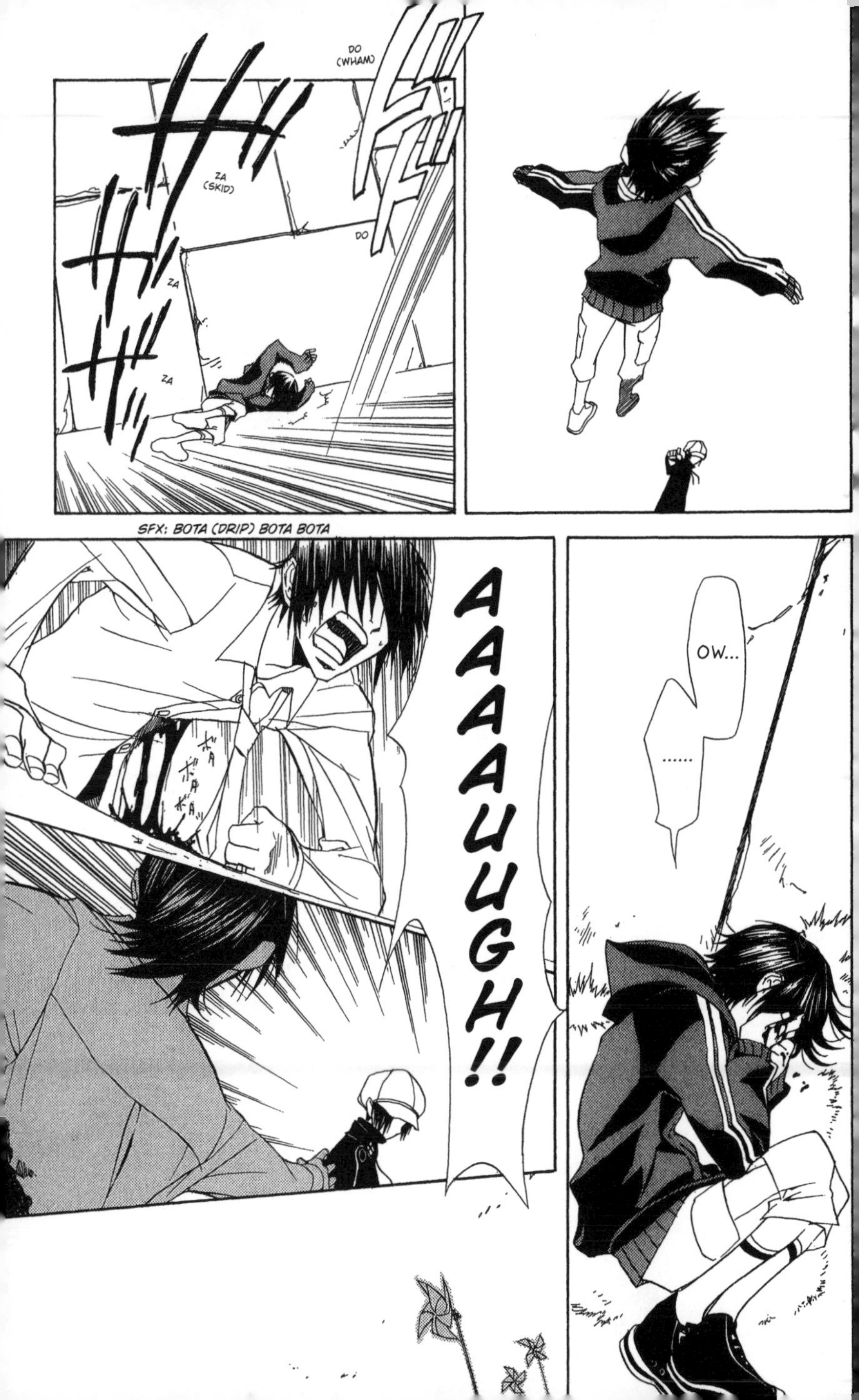
DO
(WHAM)
ZA
(SKID)
DO
ZA
ZA
SFX: BOTA (DRIP) BOTA BOTA
OW...
......
AAAAUUGH!!

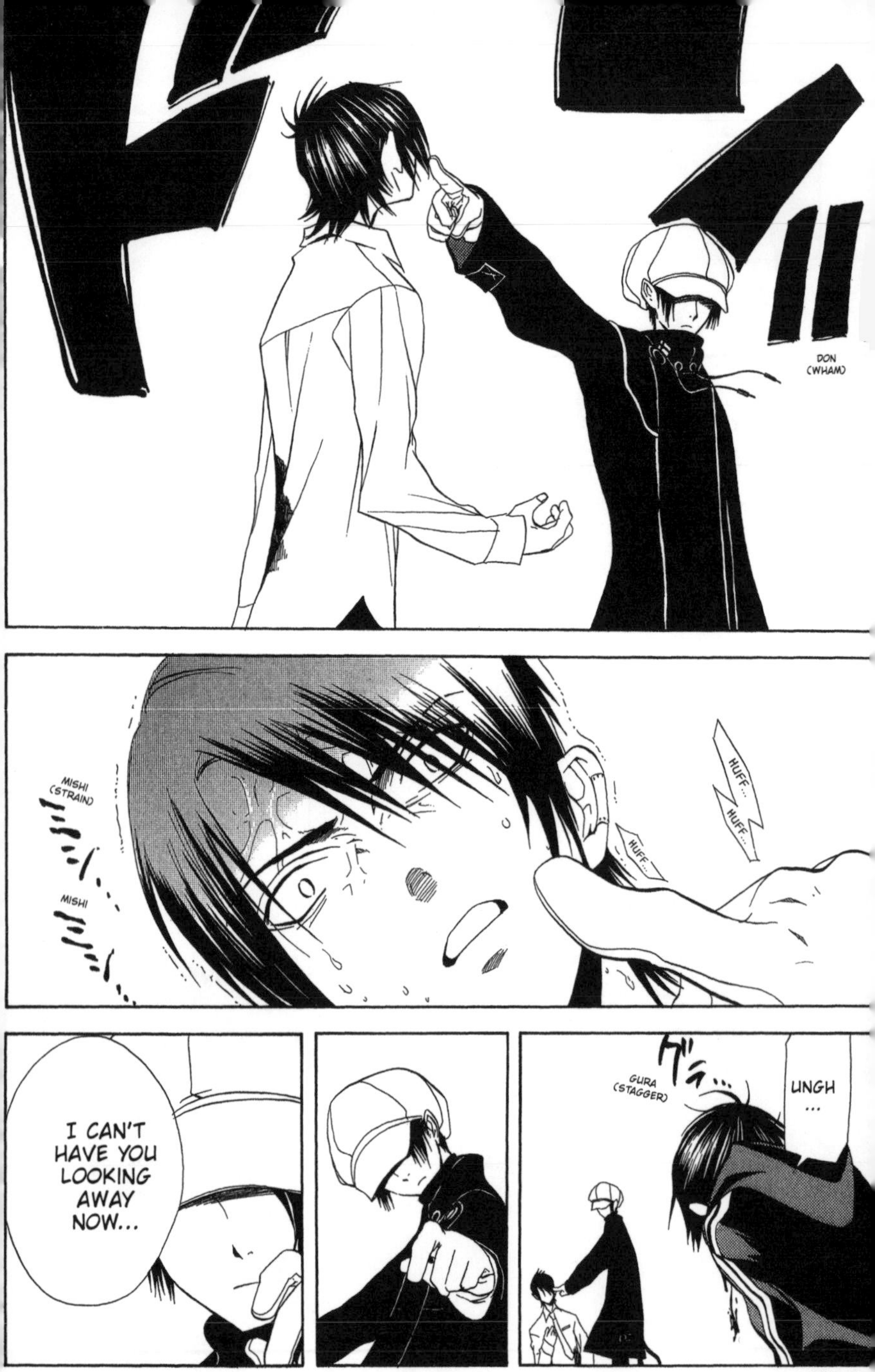
DON (WHAM)
HUFF... HUFF...
HUFF...
MISHI (STRAIN)
MISHI
UNGH...
GURA (STAGGER)
I CAN'T HAVE YOU LOOKING AWAY NOW...

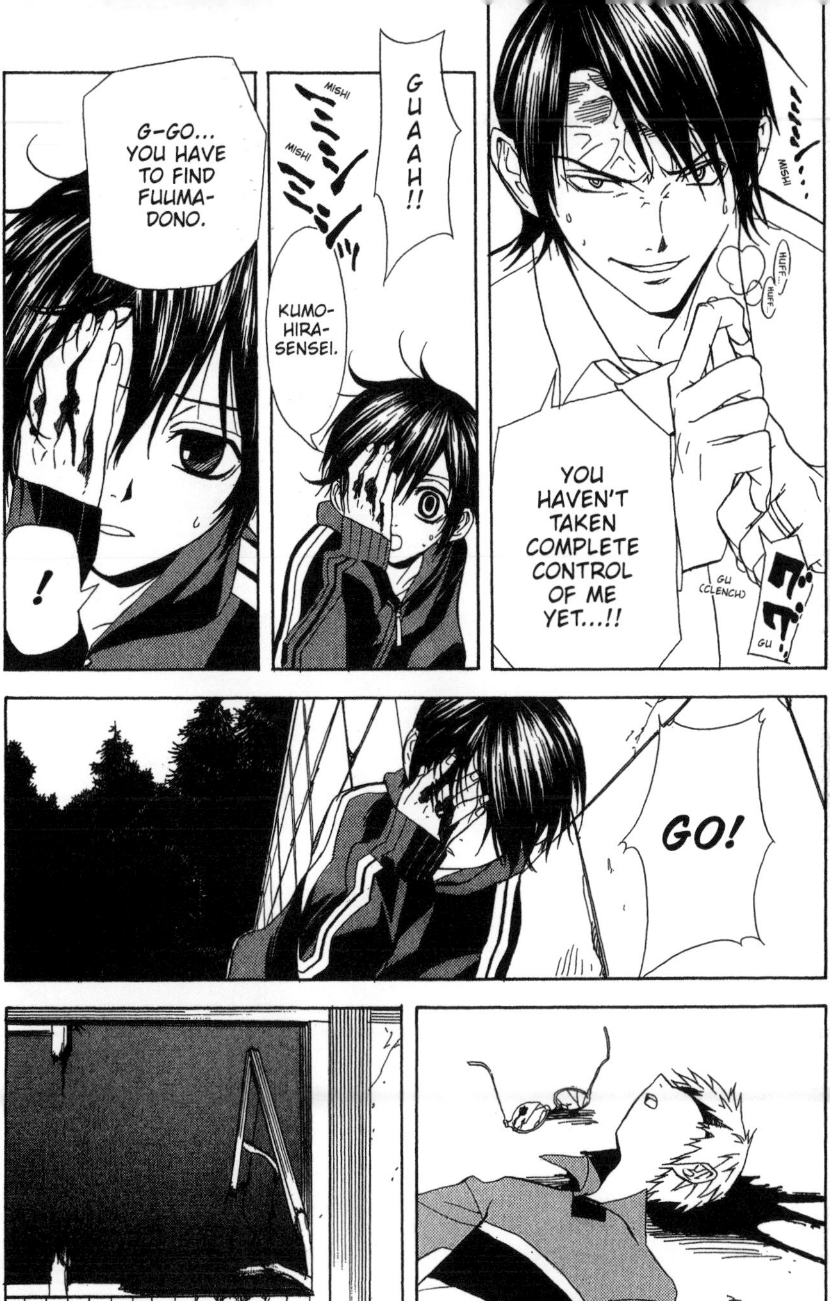
MISHI
HUFF... HUFF...
YOU HAVEN'T TAKEN COMPLETE CONTROL OF ME YET...!!
GU (CLENCH)
GU
GUAAAH!!
MISHI
MISHI
KUMO-HIRA-SENSEI.
G-GO... YOU HAVE TO FIND FUUMA-DONO.
!
GO!

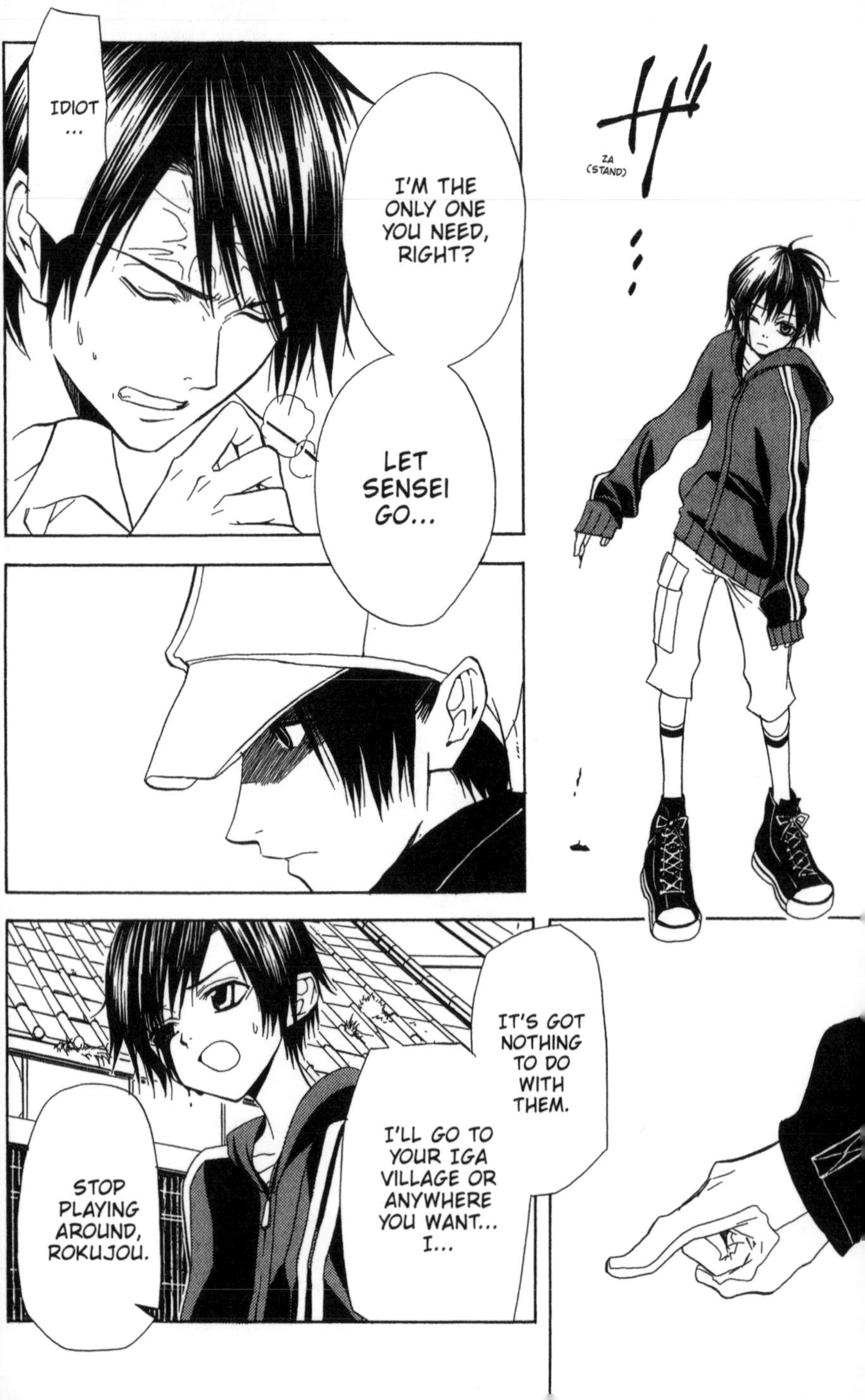
ZA (STAND)
...
I'M THE ONLY ONE YOU NEED, RIGHT?
LET SENSEI GO...
IDIOT ...
IT'S GOT NOTHING TO DO WITH THEM.
I'LL GO TO YOUR IGA VILLAGE OR ANYWHERE YOU WANT... I...
STOP PLAYING AROUND, ROKUJOU.

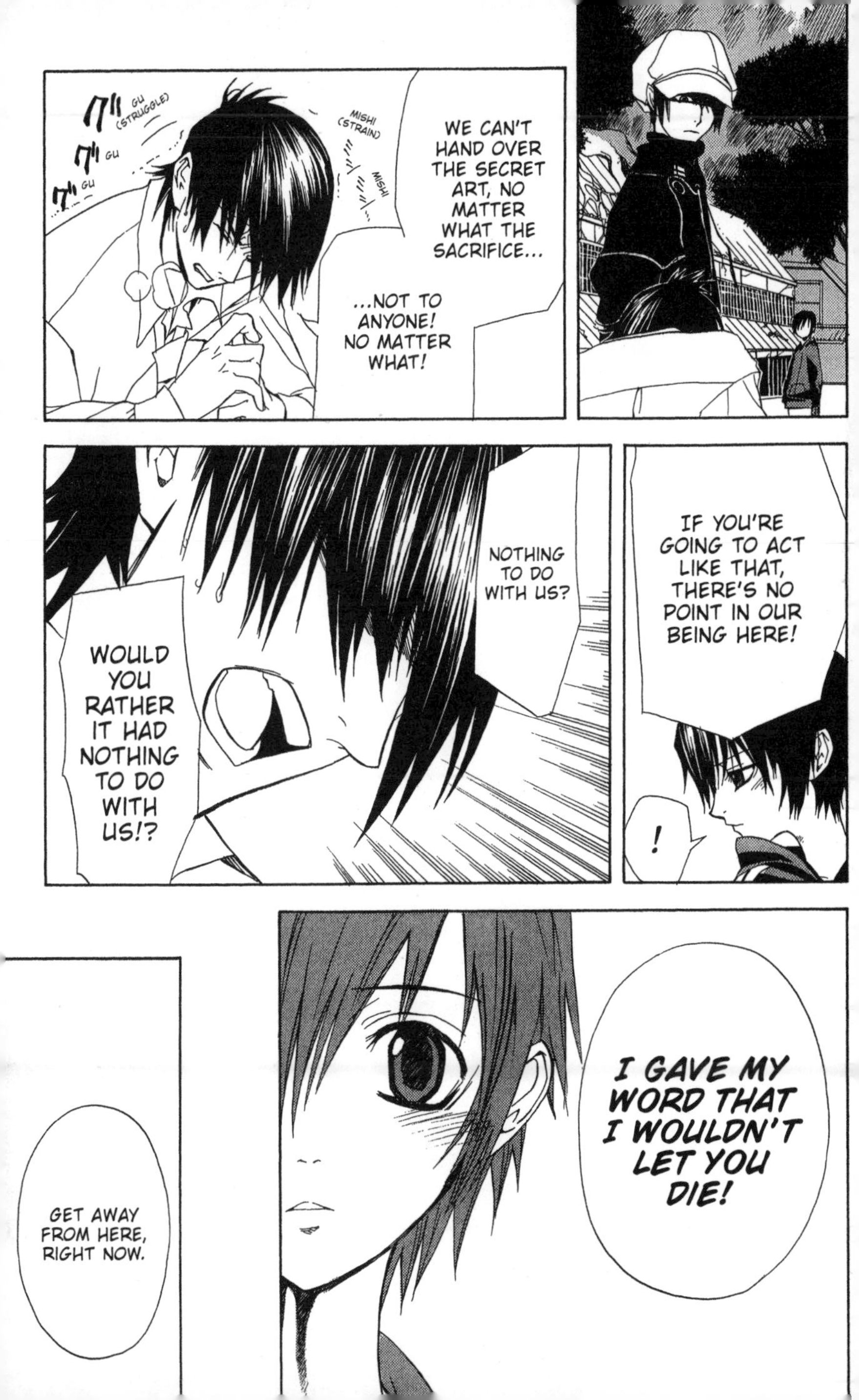

MISHI (STRAIN)
MISHI
WE CAN'T HAND OVER THE SECRET ART, NO MATTER WHAT THE SACRIFICE...
...NOT TO ANYONE! NO MATTER WHAT!
GU (STRUGGLE)
GU
GU
IF YOU'RE GOING TO ACT LIKE THAT, THERE'S NO POINT IN OUR BEING HERE!
!
NOTHING TO DO WITH US?
WOULD YOU RATHER IT HAD NOTHING TO DO WITH US!?
I GAVE MY WORD THAT I WOULDN'T LET YOU DIE!
GET AWAY FROM HERE, RIGHT NOW.

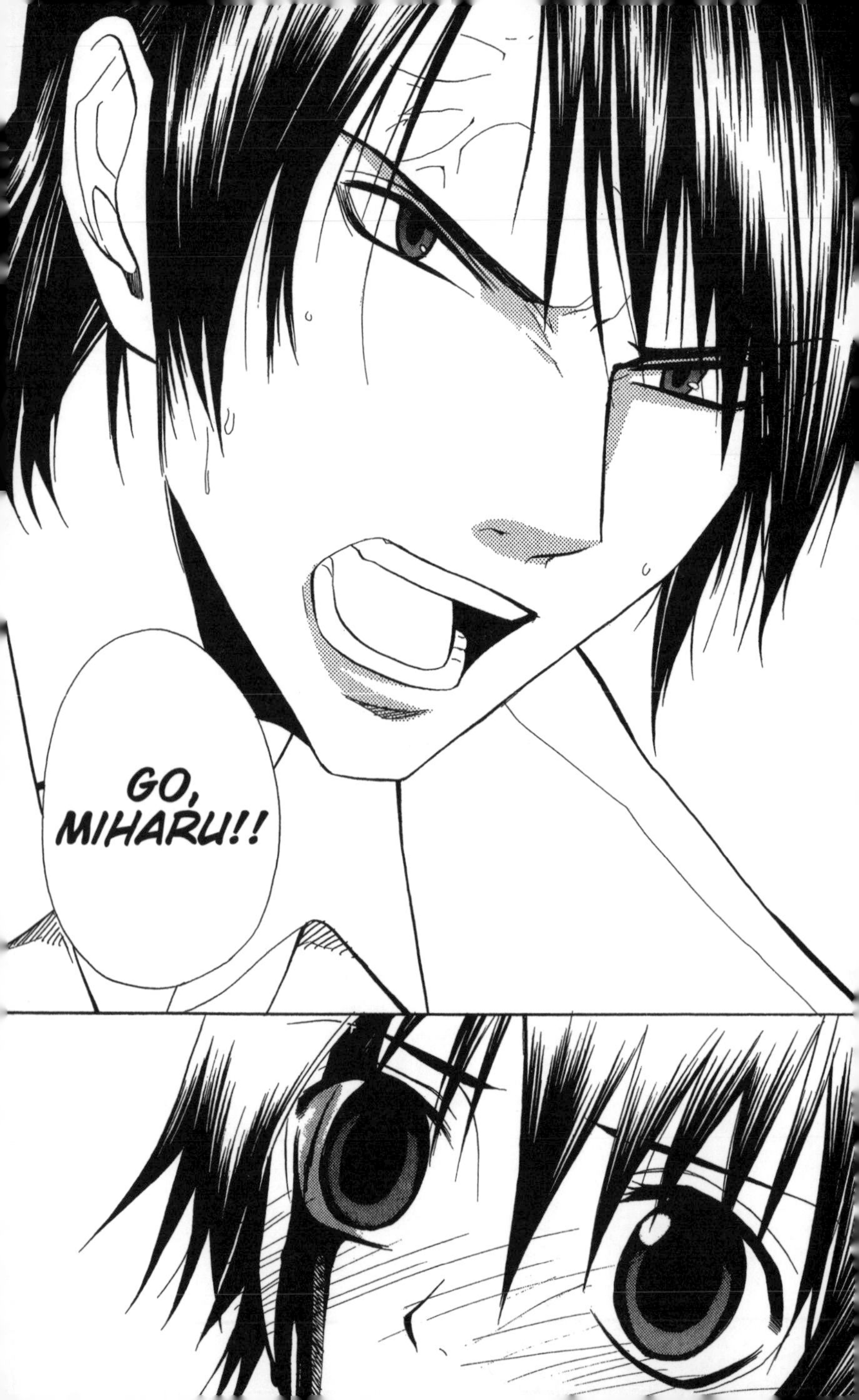
GO, MIHARU!!

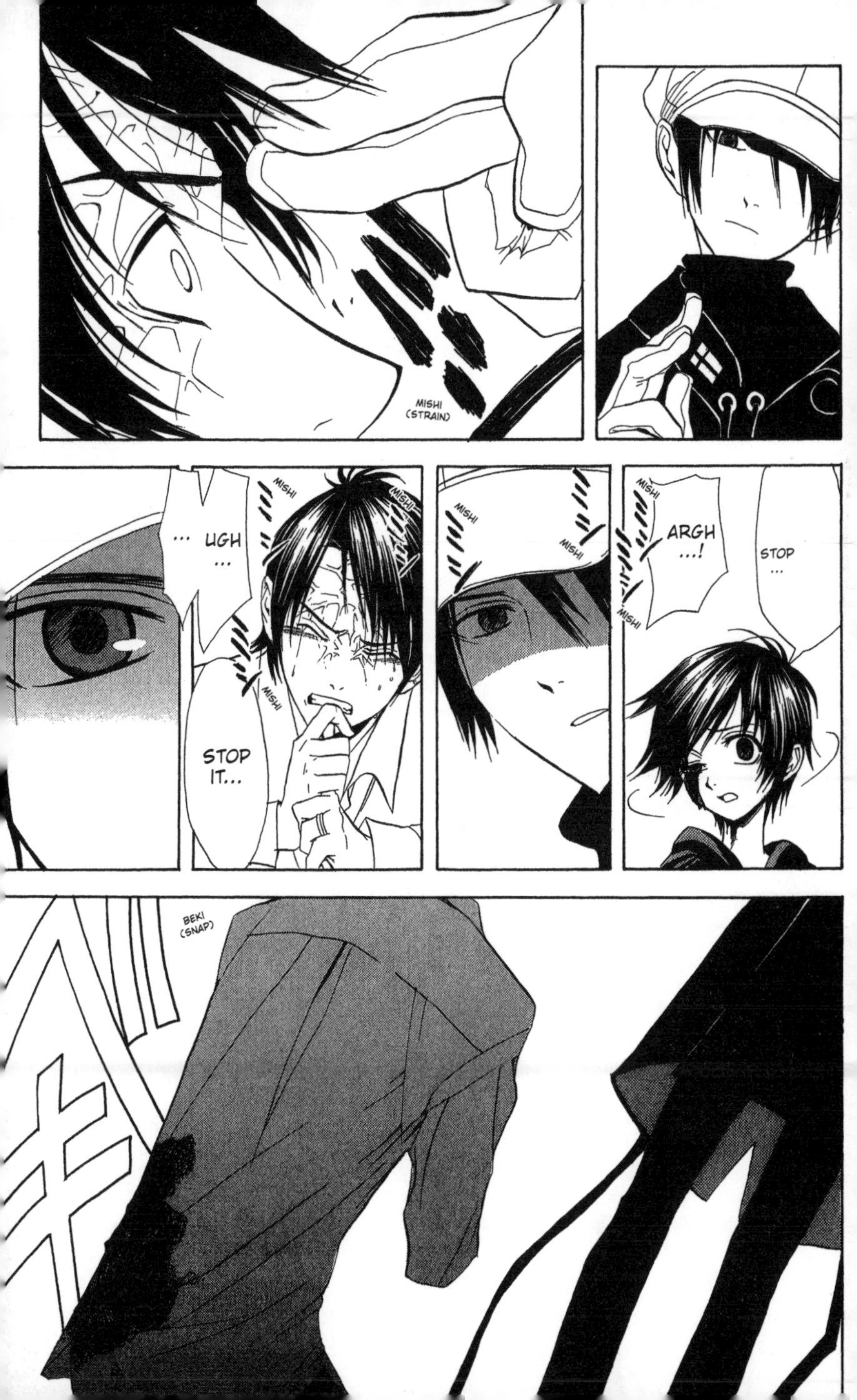
MISHI (STRAIN)
STOP ...
ARGH ...!
MISHI
MISHI
MISHI
MISHI
MISHI
... UGH ...
MISHI
STOP IT...
BEKI (SNAP)

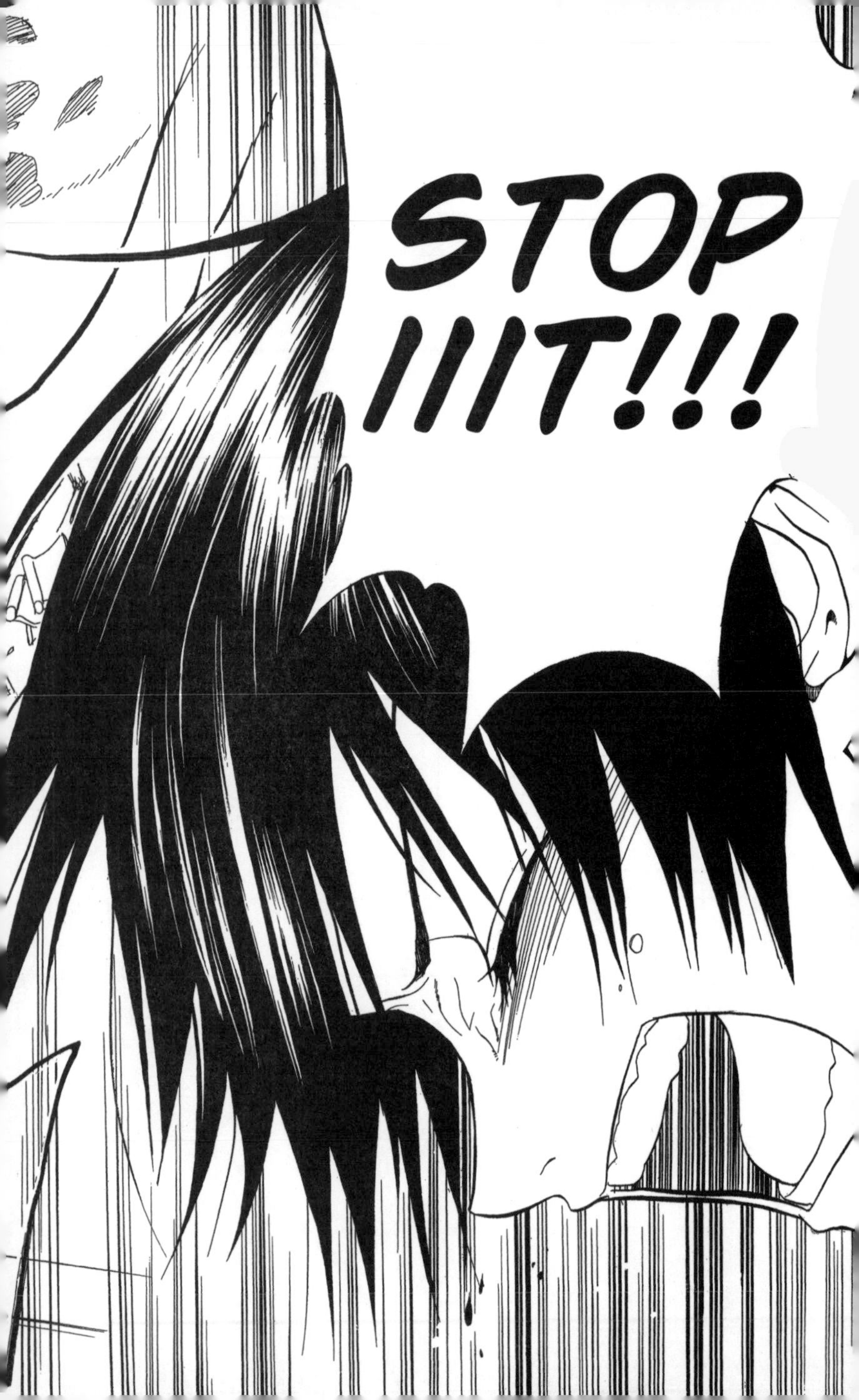
STOP IIIT!!!

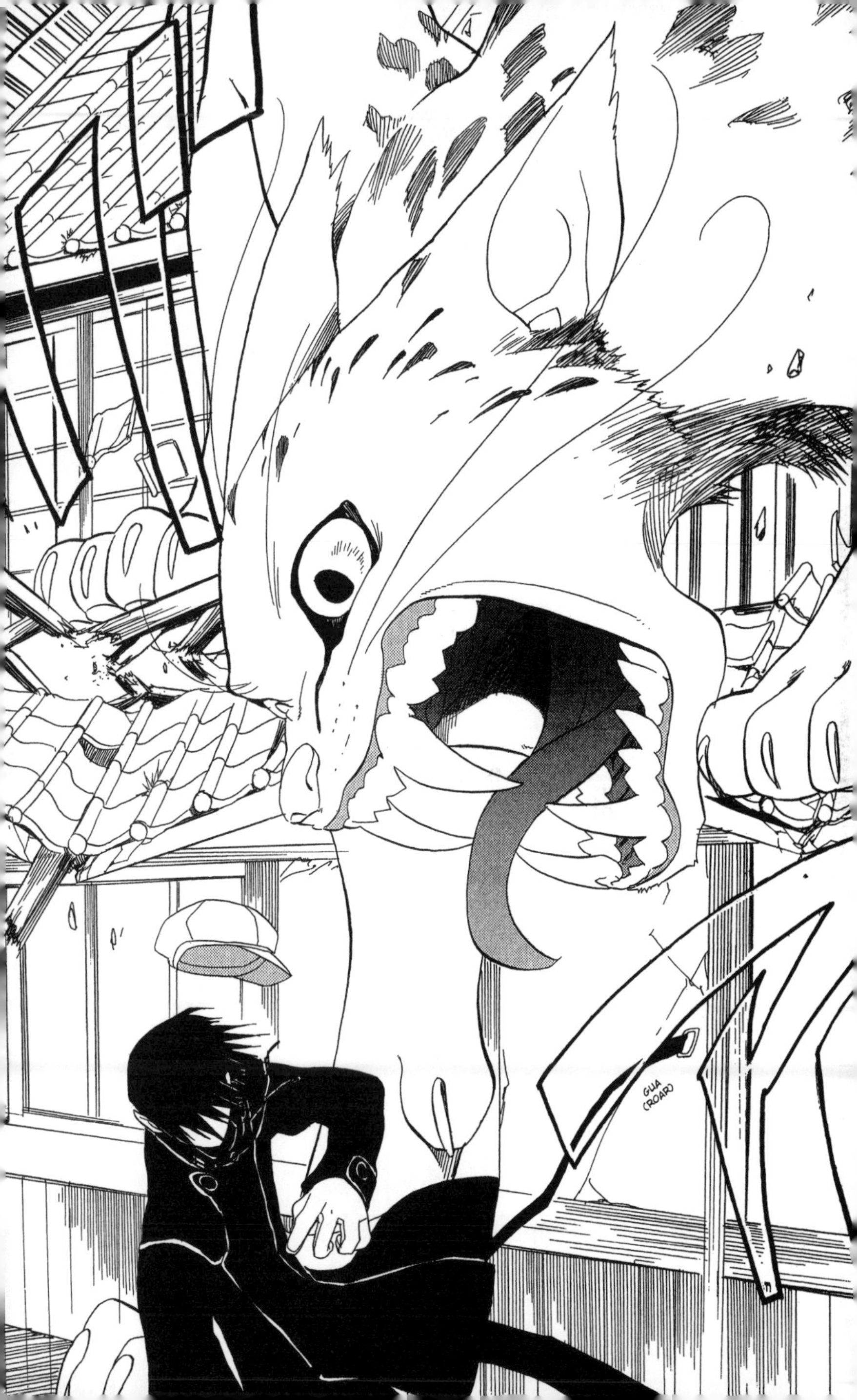
GUA
(ROAR)

ZAA
(SLIDE)

PASA
(FLOP)

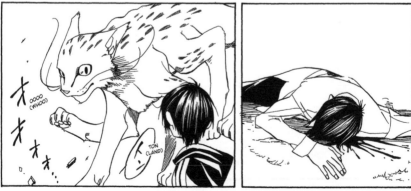

OOOO
(WHOO)

TON
(LAND)

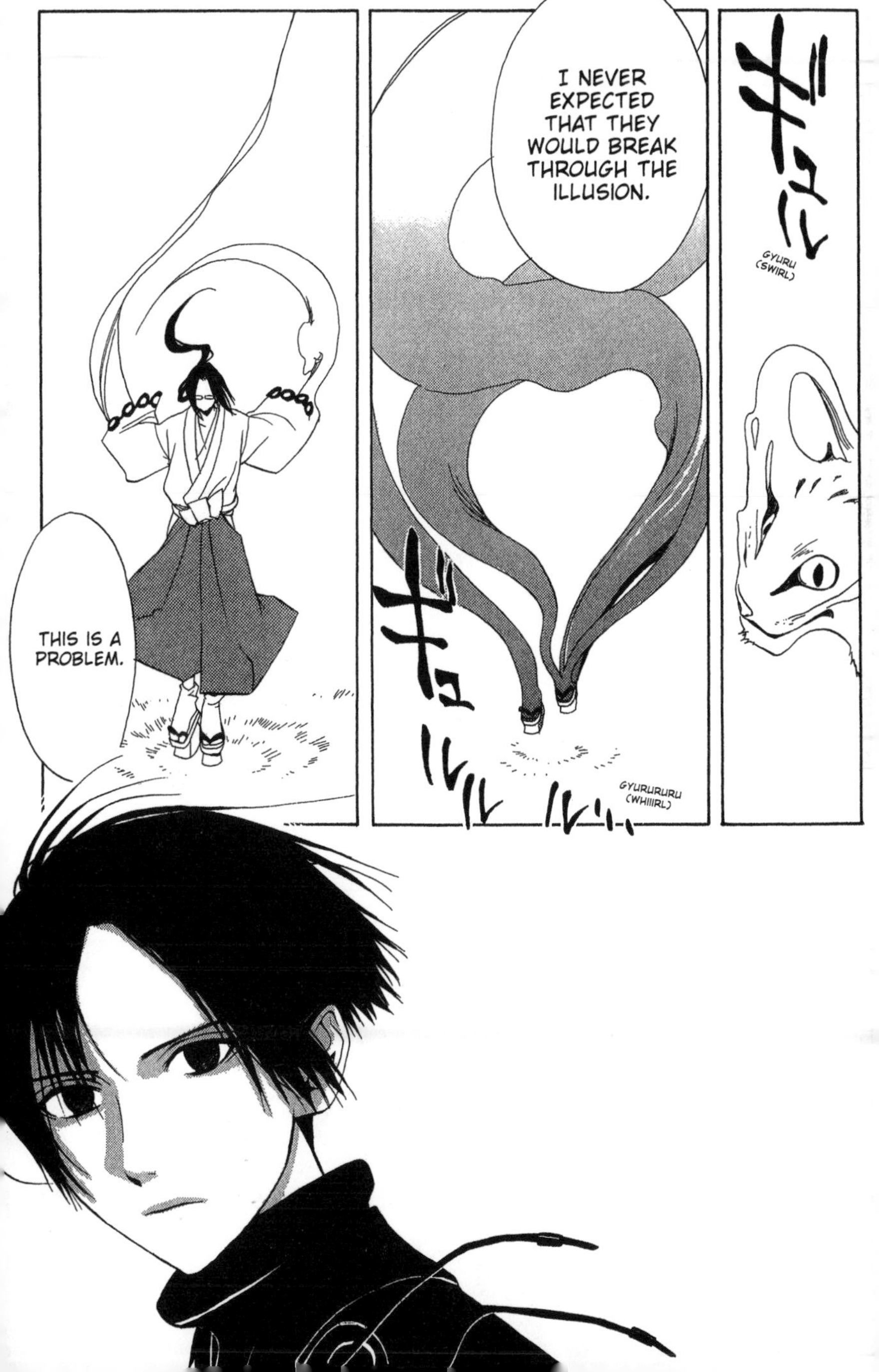
ギュル
GYURU (SWIRL)
I NEVER EXPECTED THAT THEY WOULD BREAK THROUGH THE ILLUSION.
ギュルルル…
GYURURURU (WHIIIRL)
THIS IS A PROBLEM.

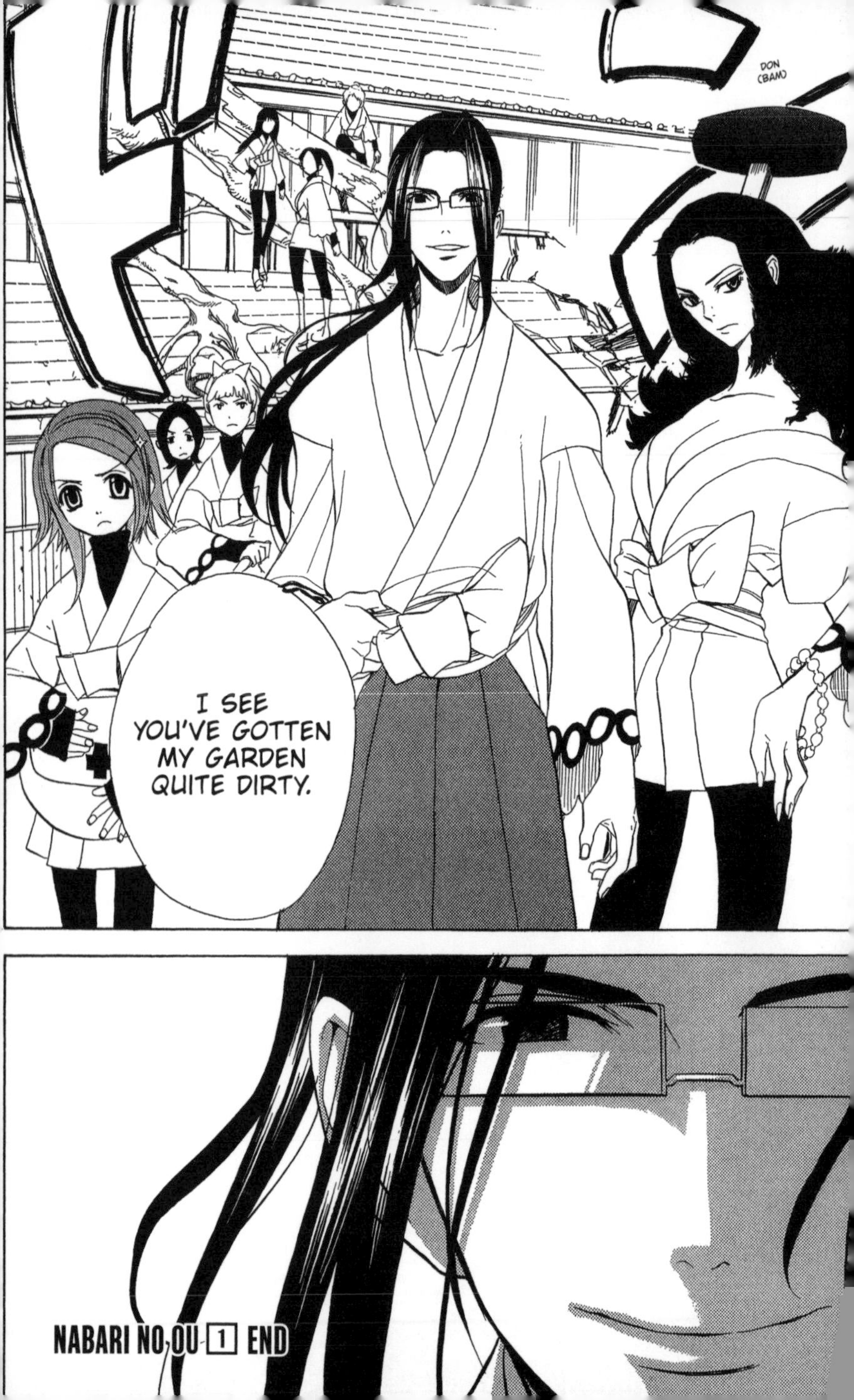
DON
(BAM)
I SEE YOU'VE GOTTEN MY GARDEN QUITE DIRTY.
NABARI NO OU 1 END

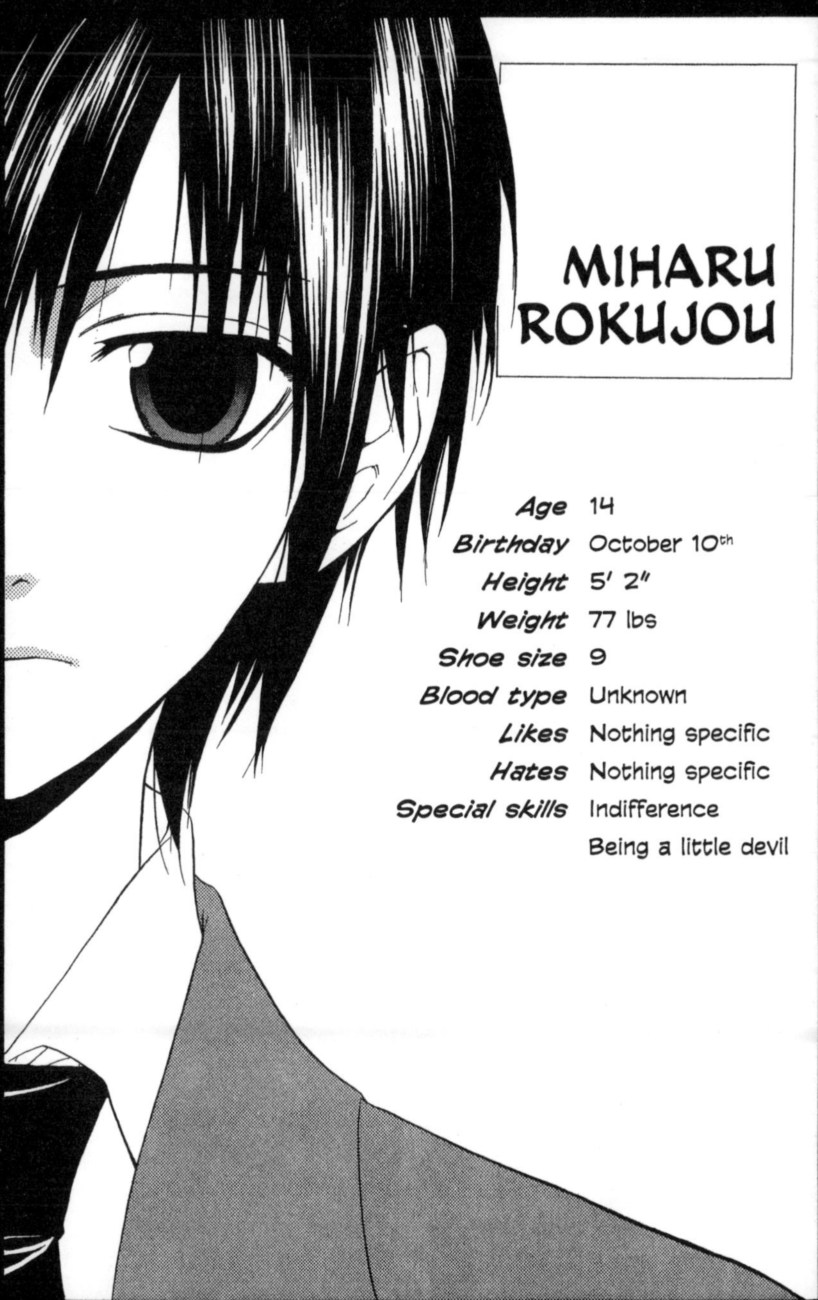

MIHARU ROKUJOU

Age	14
Birthday	October 10th
Height	5' 2"
Weight	77 lbs
Shoe size	9
Blood type	Unknown
Likes	Nothing specific
Hates	Nothing specific
Special skills	Indifference Being a little devil

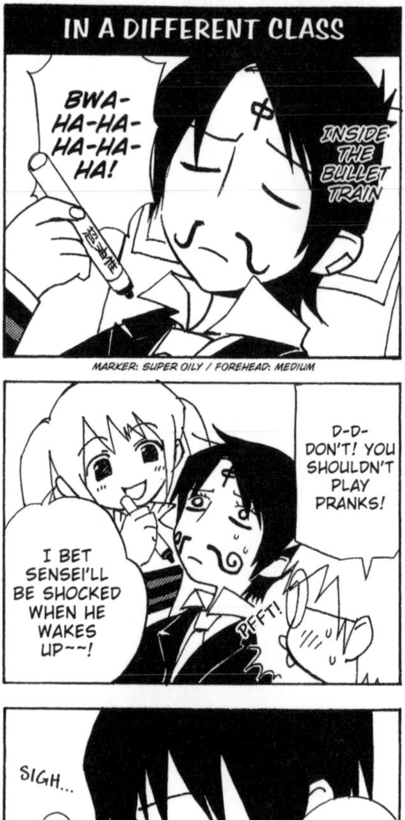
IN A DIFFERENT CLASS
INSIDE THE BULLET TRAIN
BWA-HA-HA-HA-HA!
MARKER: SUPER OILY / FOREHEAD: MEDIUM
D-D-DON'T! YOU SHOULDN'T PLAY PRANKS!
I BET SENSEI'LL BE SHOCKED WHEN HE WAKES UP~~!
PFFT!
SIGH...
THAT WOULDN'T SHOCK HIM...
I'LL TAKE EVERYTHING ON THAT CART, PLEASE.
PUT IT ALL ON HIS TAB.
THAT'LL BE ¥1,000!
HE REALLY IS A DEVIL!!

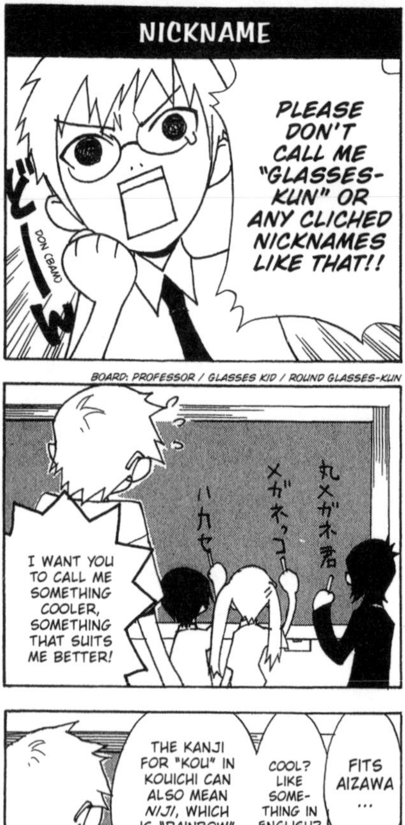
NICKNAME
PLEASE DON'T CALL ME "GLASSES-KUN" OR ANY CLICHED NICKNAMES LIKE THAT!!
DON (BAM)
BOARD: PROFESSOR / GLASSES KID / ROUND GLASSES-KUN
丸メガネ君
メガネっコ
ハカセ
I WANT YOU TO CALL ME SOMETHING COOLER, SOMETHING THAT SUITS ME BETTER!
FITS AIZAWA...
COOL? LIKE SOMETHING IN ENGLISH?
THE KANJI FOR "KOU" IN KOUICHI CAN ALSO MEAN NIJI, WHICH IS "RAINBOW" IN ENGLISH...
YES, THAT'S IT!
BOARD: NEW NAME / RAINBOW GLASSES-KUN
命名
レインボーメガネ君
CAN WE AT LEAST GET AWAY FROM THE "GLASSES" PART?

Special Thanks

My friends
My family
My editor
My awesome assistant, Omi-sama

and

You!

Well, see you in the next volume!

Web site (in Japanese): http://karasuba.main.jp

TRANSLATION NOTES

page 5, *Shinobi*
Another word for "ninja," from the verb *shinobu*, "to conceal oneself)." The characters in "ninja" can also be pronounced *shinobu mono*, meaning "one who conceals himself."

Shinra Banshou
Meaning "all things in creation," *Shinra Banshou* is a fitting name for a hidden art that would allow someone to control all things in creation.

page 7, *Nindou*
Just as *kendo* is "the way of the sword" and *bushido* is "the way of the warrior," *nindou* is the way of the ninja.

page 12, *Bansenshukai*
A collection of things a ninja needs to know. Its name means "Sea of Myriad Rivers Merging."

page 13, *Okonomiyaki*
Loosely translated to "fried the way you like it," *okonomiyaki* is kind of like a pizza and kind of like a pancake, made with all kinds of ingredients.

page 21, *Katsubushi*
Katsubushi, or *katsuobushi*, are small pieces of sliced fish, used as an ingredient in okonomiyaki.

page 74, *MEXT*
MEXT is the acronym for Japan's Ministry of Education, Culture, Sports, Science, and Technology. As the name implies, they promote and improve education, culture, sports, science, and technology in Japan.

page 88, *Rakkumi*
A brand of soy milk that comes in various flavors, sold by Yakult.

page 108, *"There must be a storm coming!"*
In Japan, when someone does something out of character, it is said, often jokingly, that there must be a drastic change in the weather on the horizon.

page 109, *Nozomi*
Nozomi is the name of a kind of bullet train—the fastest running on its line.

page 120, *-jiichan*
A cute, childish way of addressing one's grandfather.

page 121, *Oniichan*
A cute, childish form of address for one's elder brother or for someone who is like an elder brother to the speaker. Children often employ this to address young men who are older than themselves, related or otherwise.

page 156, *Ki*
Ki is the Japanese equivalent of the more commonly known Chinese *chi* energy.

PREVIEW

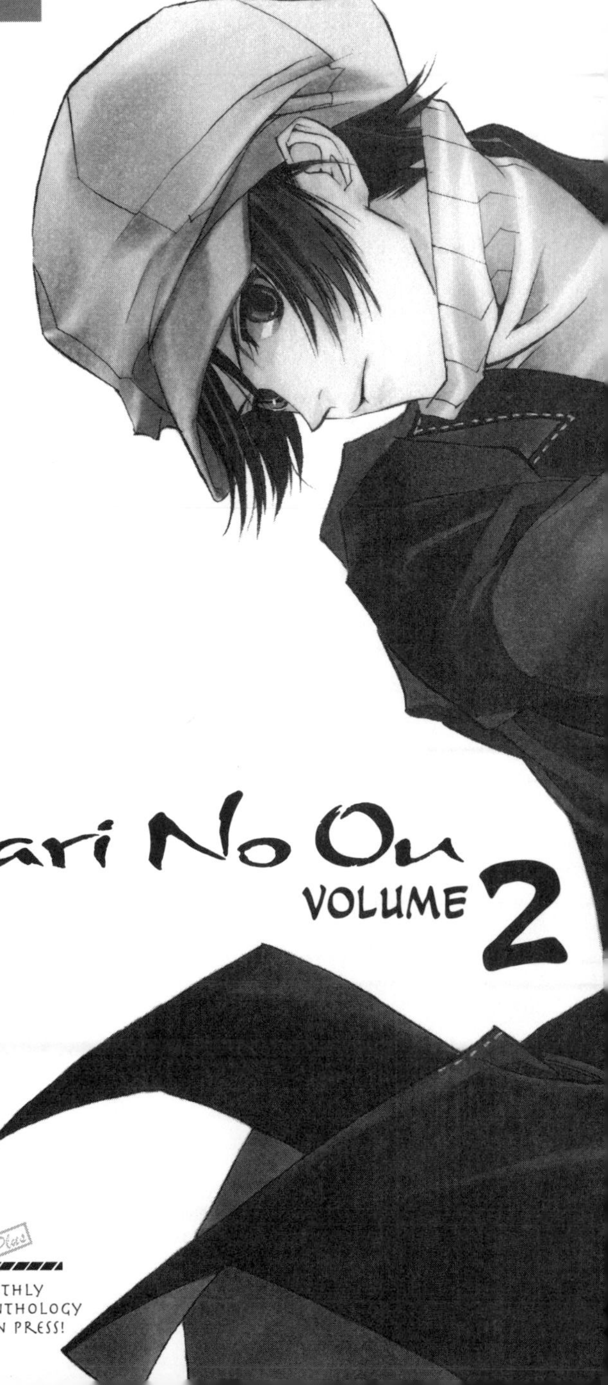

Nabari No Ou VOLUME 2

FOR MORE
NABARI NO OU,
CHECK OUT

YEN+ Plus

A MONTHLY
MANGA ANTHOLOGY
FROM YEN PRESS!

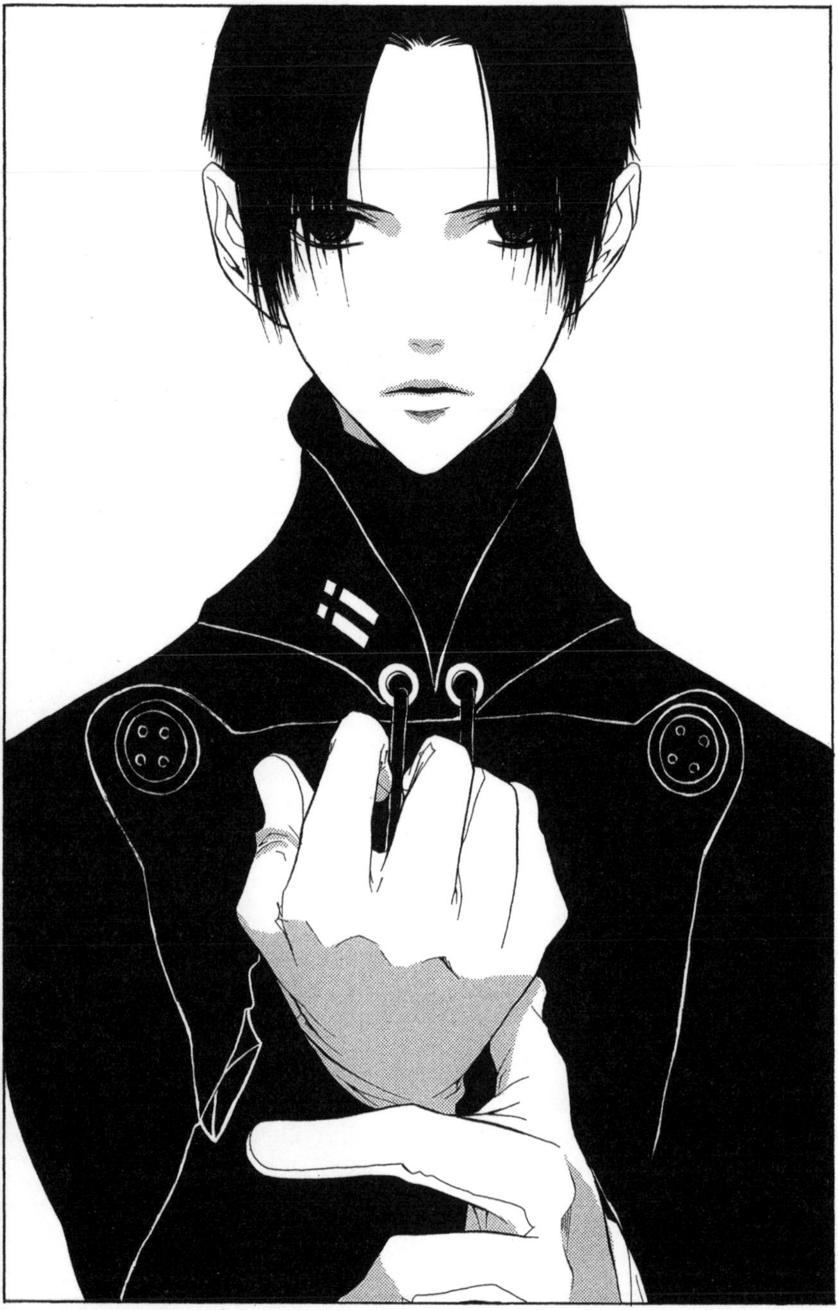

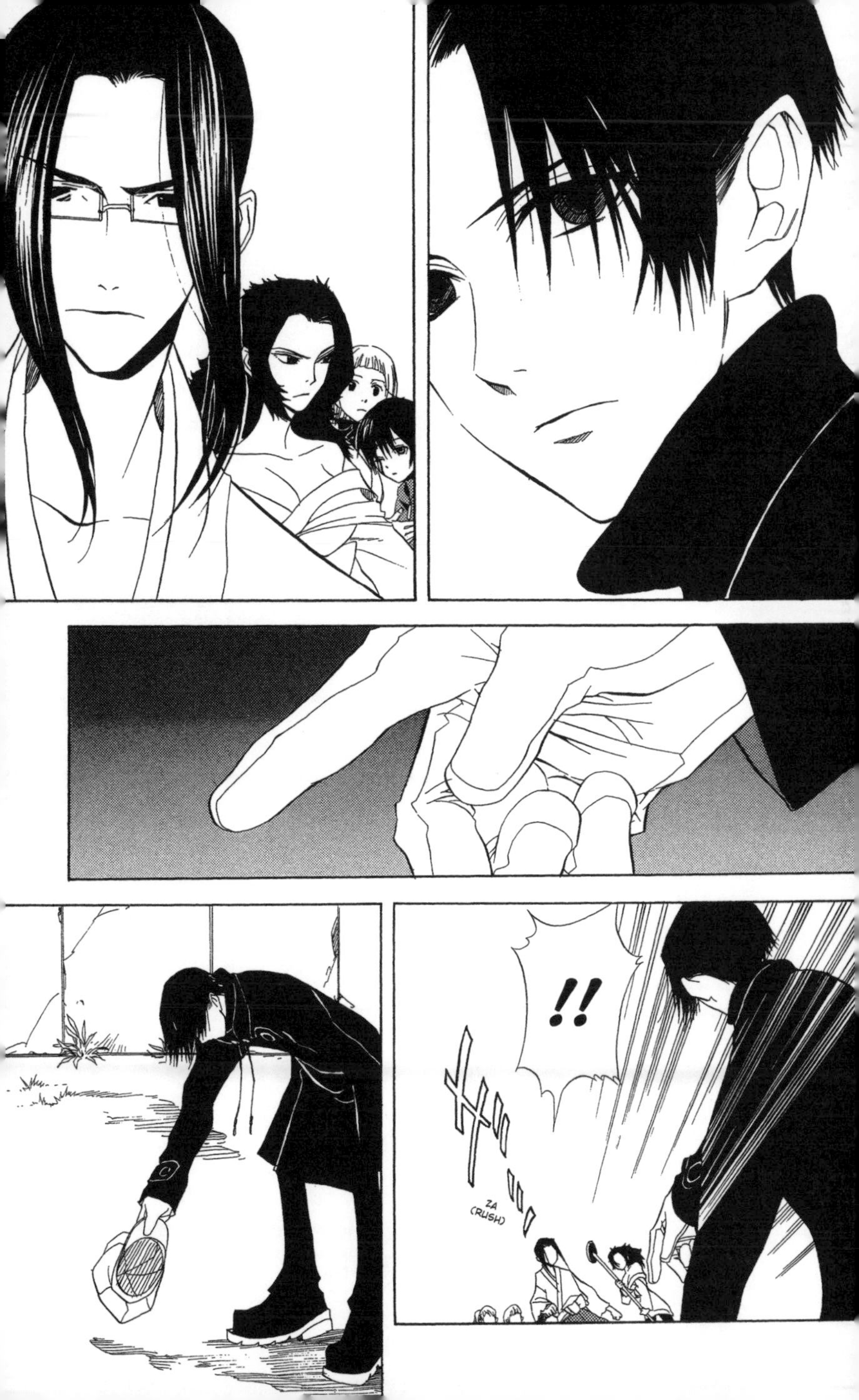
!!
ZA
(RUSH)

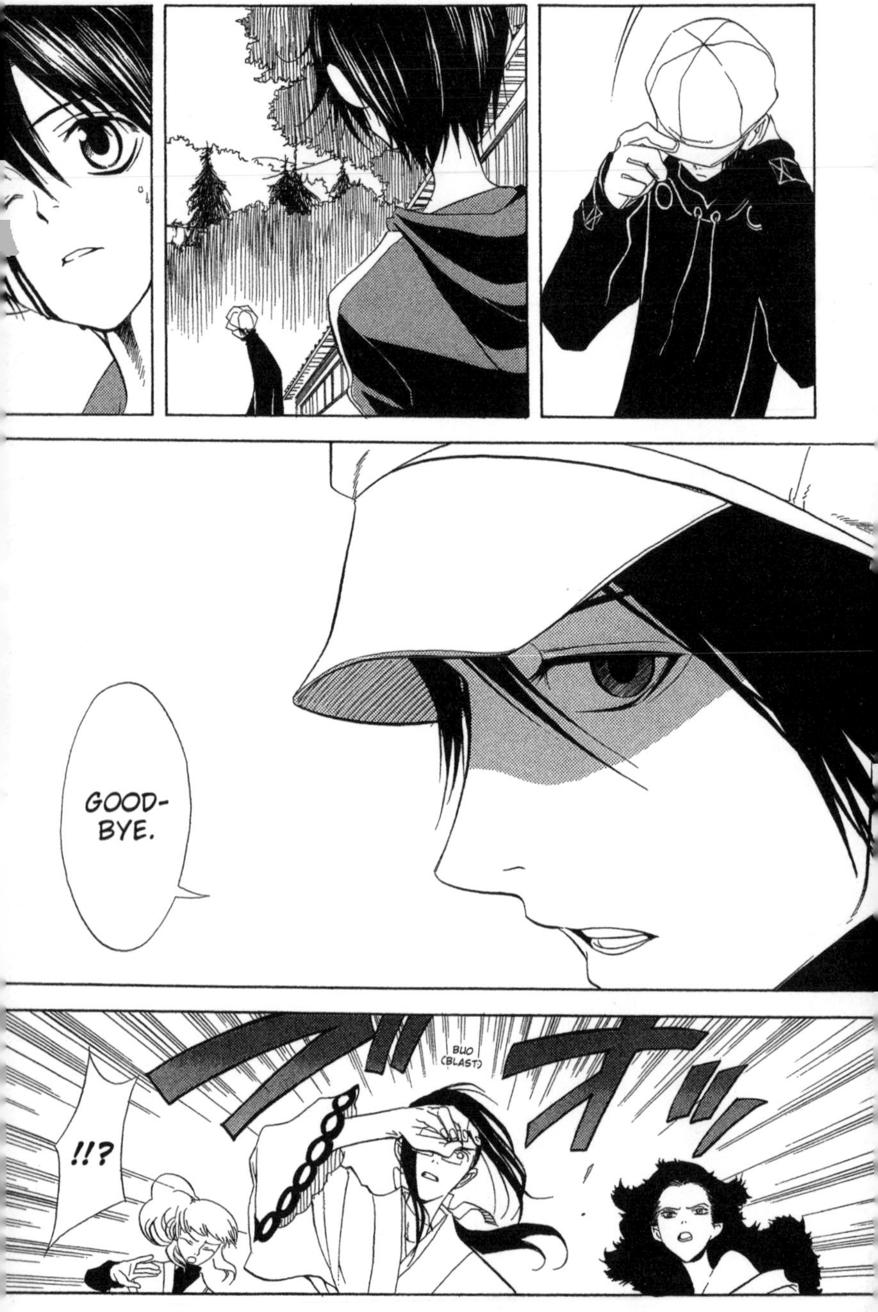
GOOD-BYE.
BUO (BLAST)
!!?

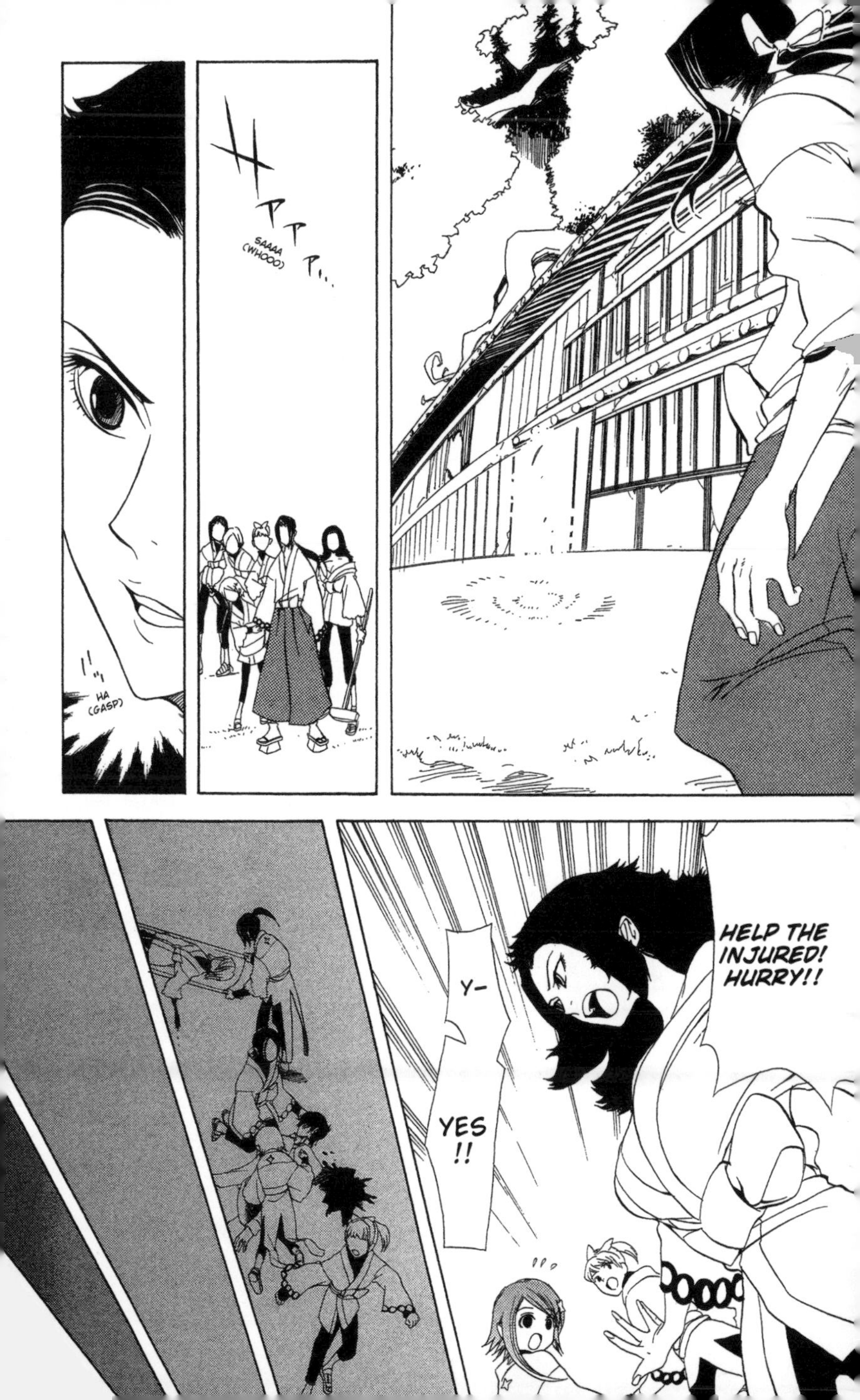
SAAAA (WHOOO)
HA (GASP)
HELP THE INJURED! HURRY!!
Y-
YES!!

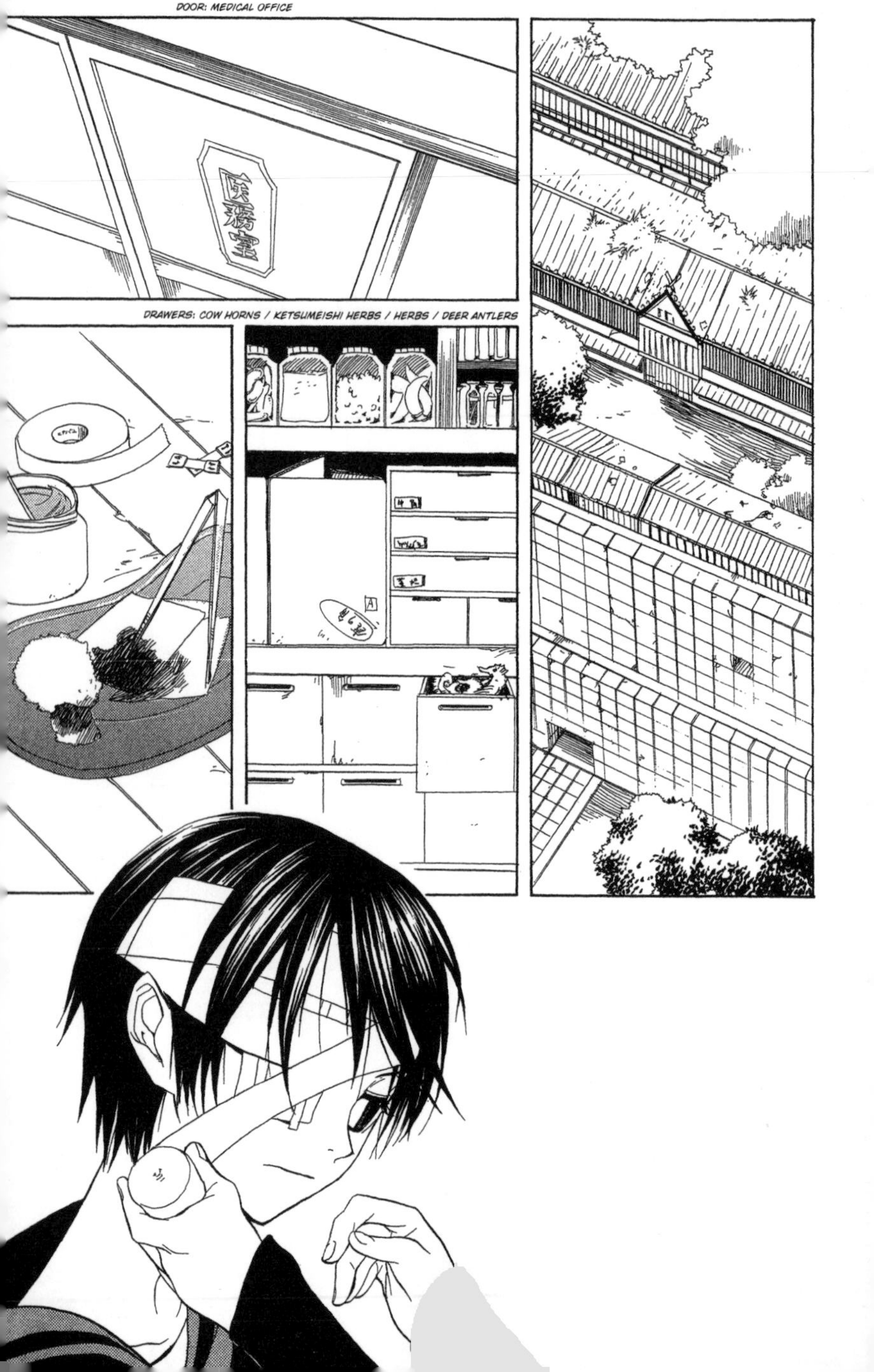
DOOR: MEDICAL OFFICE
医務室
DRAWERS: COW HORNS / KETSUMEISHI HERBS / HERBS / DEER ANTLERS

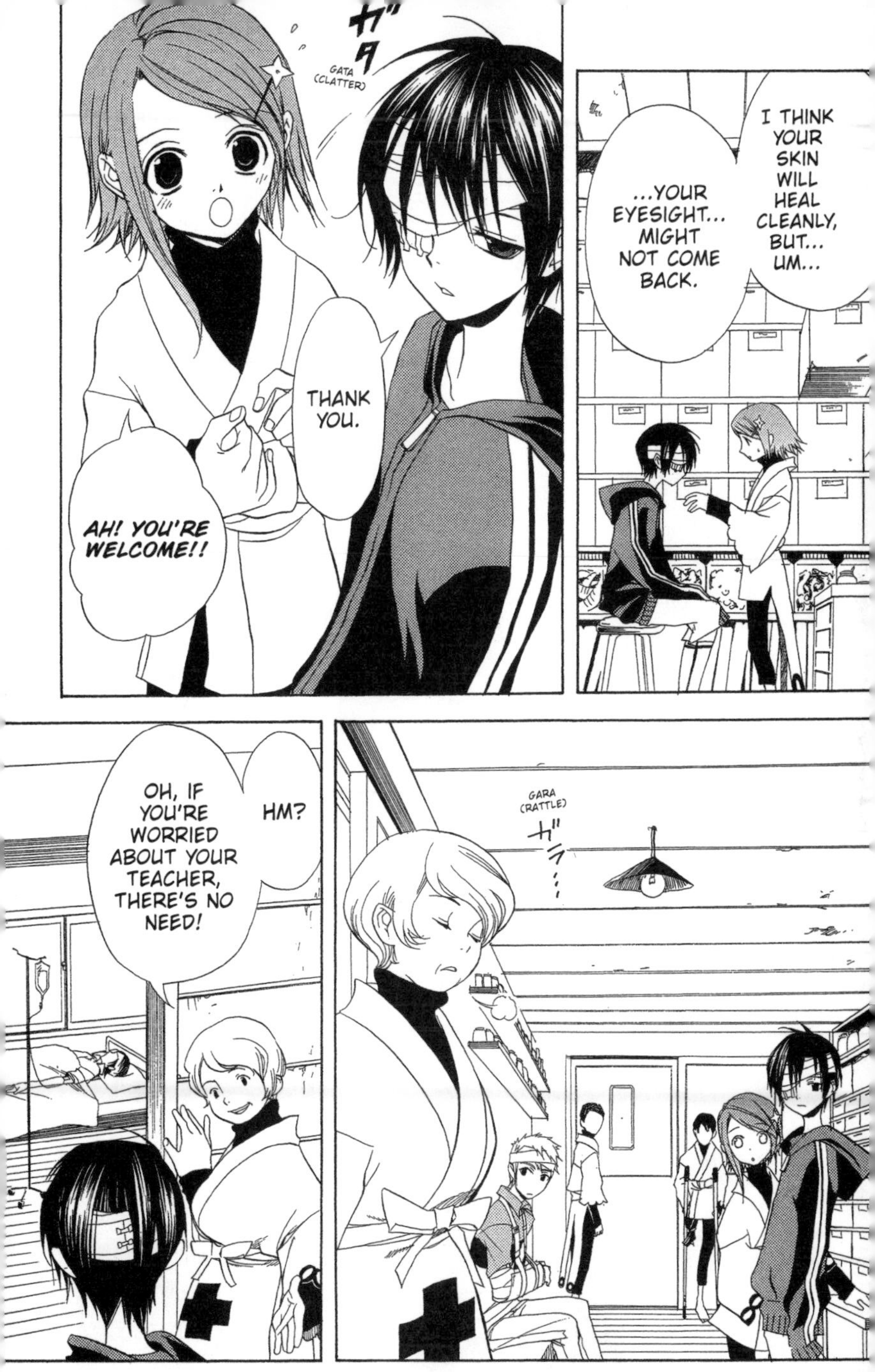
I THINK YOUR SKIN WILL HEAL CLEANLY, BUT... UM...
...YOUR EYESIGHT... MIGHT NOT COME BACK.
GATA (CLATTER)
THANK YOU.
AH! YOU'RE WELCOME!!
GARA (RATTLE)
HM?
OH, IF YOU'RE WORRIED ABOUT YOUR TEACHER, THERE'S NO NEED!

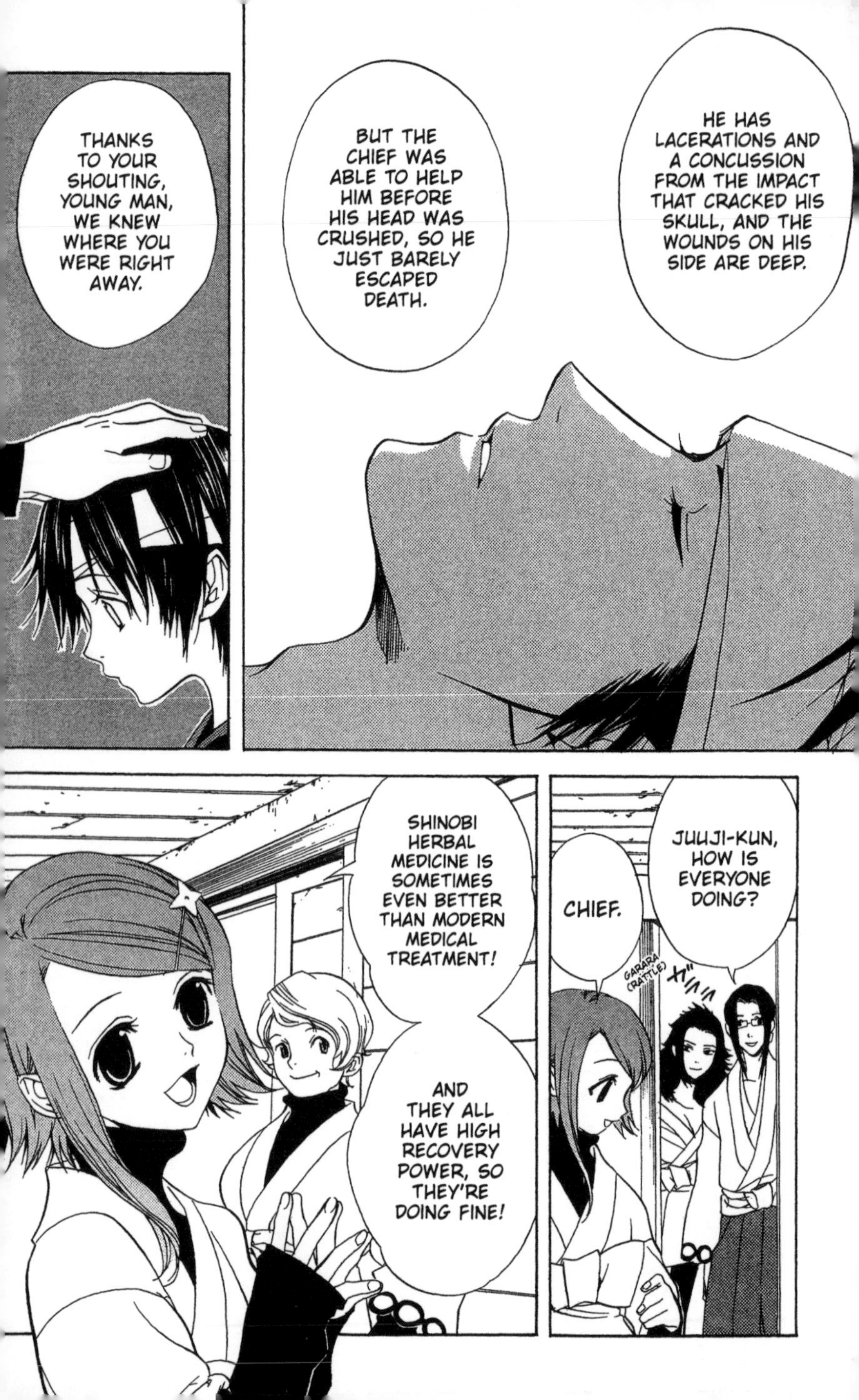
HE HAS LACERATIONS AND A CONCUSSION FROM THE IMPACT THAT CRACKED HIS SKULL, AND THE WOUNDS ON HIS SIDE ARE DEEP.
BUT THE CHIEF WAS ABLE TO HELP HIM BEFORE HIS HEAD WAS CRUSHED, SO HE JUST BARELY ESCAPED DEATH.
THANKS TO YOUR SHOUTING, YOUNG MAN, WE KNEW WHERE YOU WERE RIGHT AWAY.
JUUJI-KUN, HOW IS EVERYONE DOING?
GARARA (RATTLE)
CHIEF.
SHINOBI HERBAL MEDICINE IS SOMETIMES EVEN BETTER THAN MODERN MEDICAL TREATMENT!
AND THEY ALL HAVE HIGH RECOVERY POWER, SO THEY'RE DOING FINE!

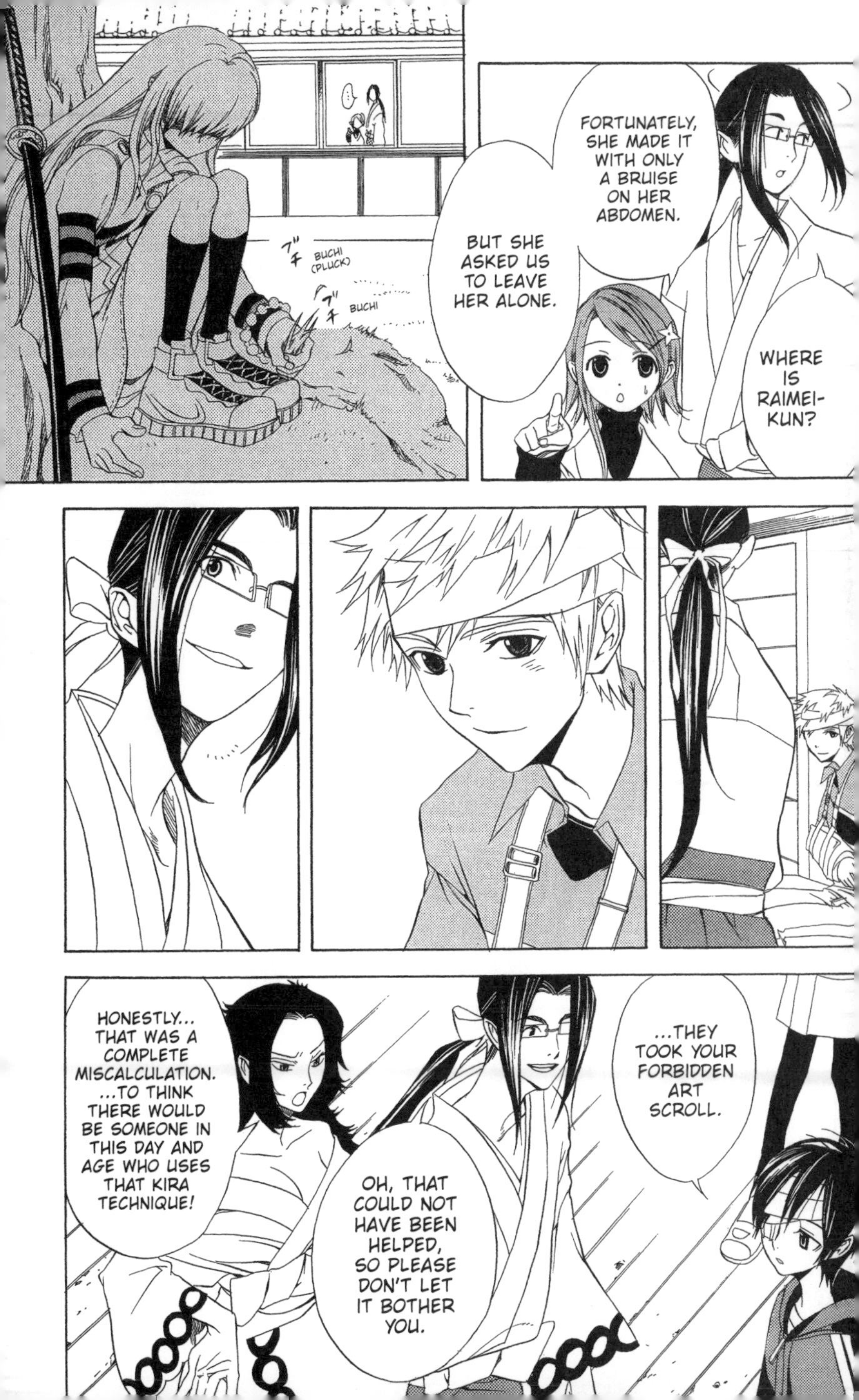
WHERE IS RAIMEI-KUN?
FORTUNATELY, SHE MADE IT WITH ONLY A BRUISE ON HER ABDOMEN.
BUT SHE ASKED US TO LEAVE HER ALONE.
…
ブチ BUCHI (PLUCK)
ブチ BUCHI
...THEY TOOK YOUR FORBIDDEN ART SCROLL.
HONESTLY... THAT WAS A COMPLETE MISCALCULATION. ...TO THINK THERE WOULD BE SOMEONE IN THIS DAY AND AGE WHO USES THAT KIRA TECHNIQUE!
OH, THAT COULD NOT HAVE BEEN HELPED, SO PLEASE DON'T LET IT BOTHER YOU.

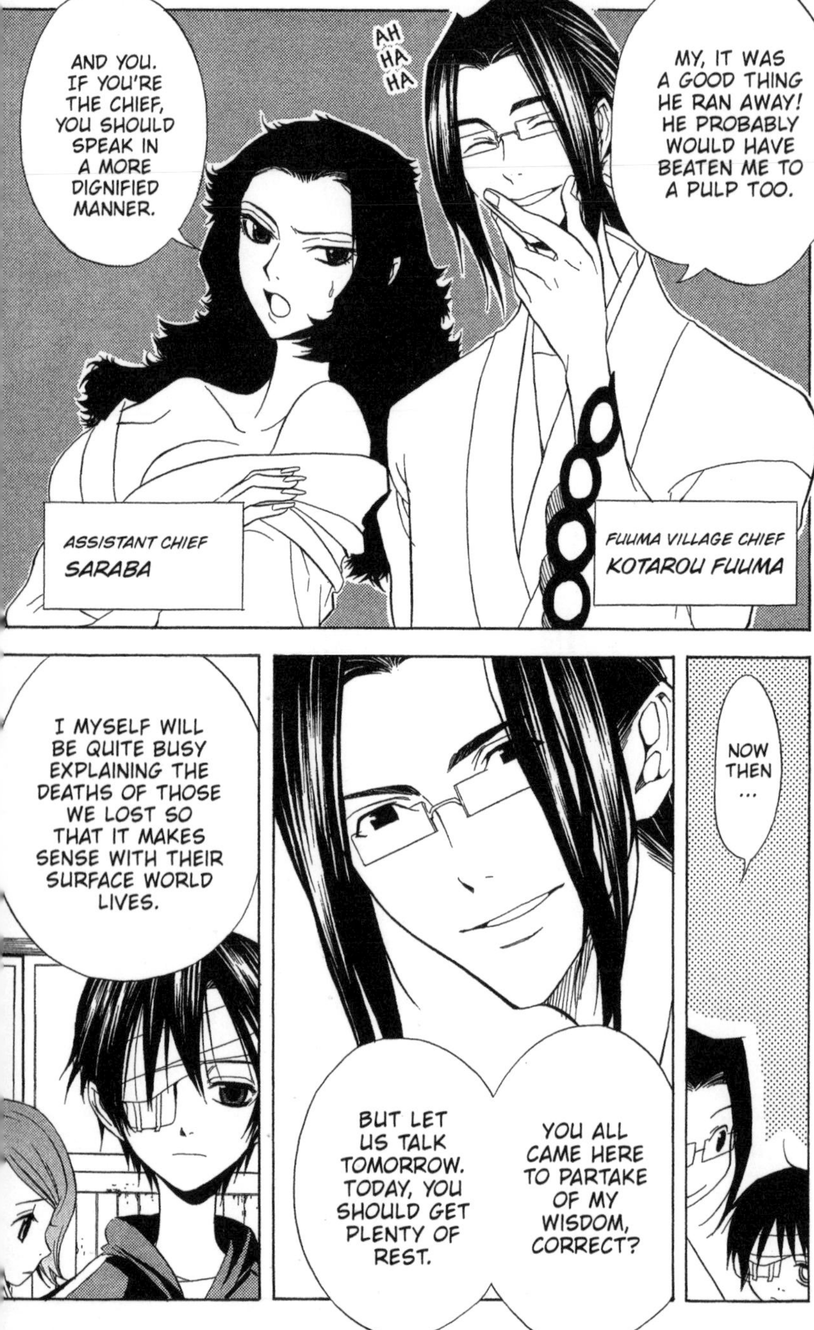
MY, IT WAS A GOOD THING HE RAN AWAY! HE PROBABLY WOULD HAVE BEATEN ME TO A PULP TOO.
AH HA HA
AND YOU. IF YOU'RE THE CHIEF, YOU SHOULD SPEAK IN A MORE DIGNIFIED MANNER.
FUUMA VILLAGE CHIEF KOTAROU FUUMA
ASSISTANT CHIEF SARABA
NOW THEN ...
YOU ALL CAME HERE TO PARTAKE OF MY WISDOM, CORRECT?
BUT LET US TALK TOMORROW. TODAY, YOU SHOULD GET PLENTY OF REST.
I MYSELF WILL BE QUITE BUSY EXPLAINING THE DEATHS OF THOSE WE LOST SO THAT IT MAKES SENSE WITH THEIR SURFACE WORLD LIVES.

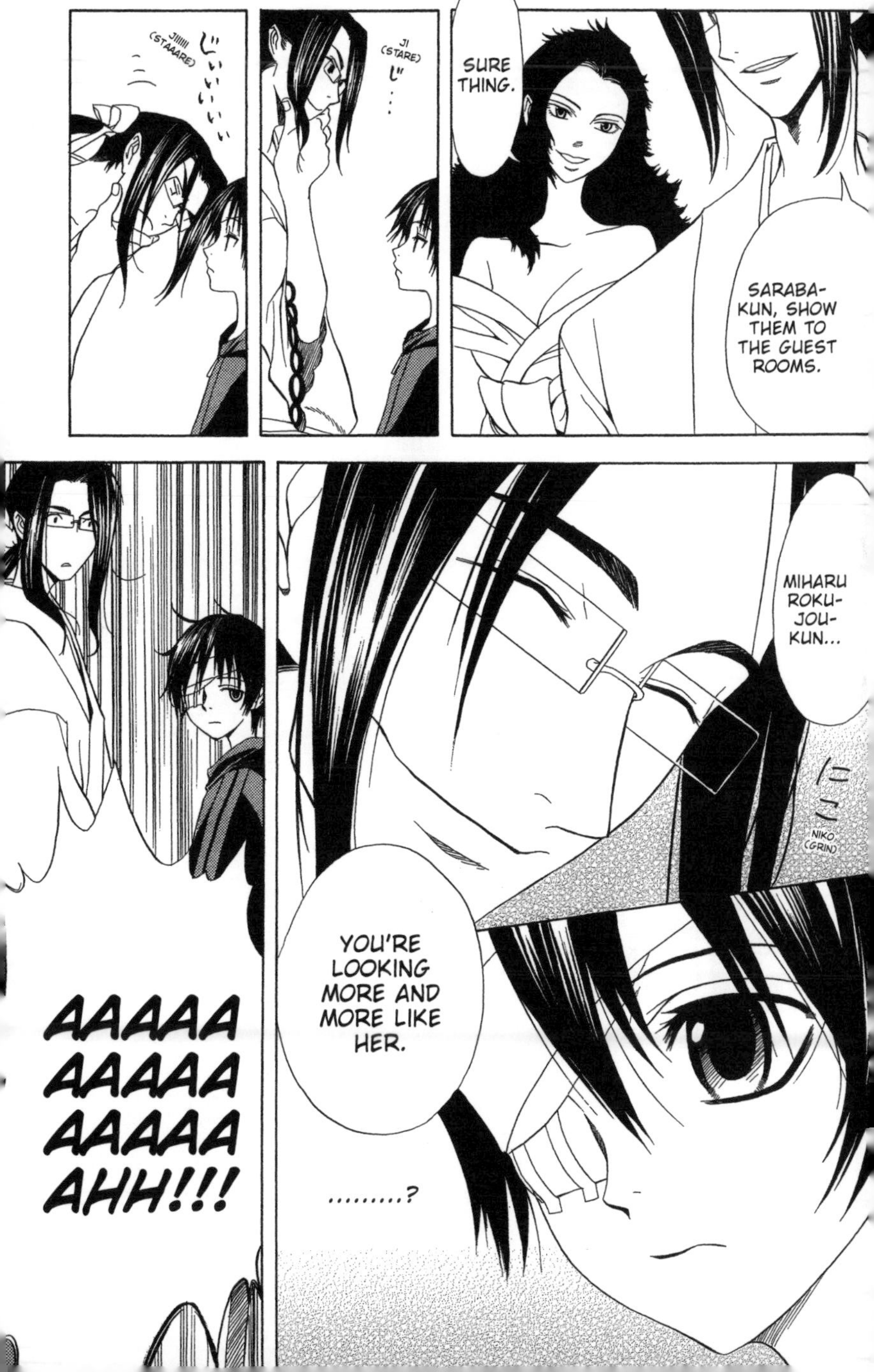
SARABA-KUN, SHOW THEM TO THE GUEST ROOMS.
SURE THING.
じ・・・
JI (STARE)
じぃぃぃぃぃ
JIIIIII (STAAARE)
MIHARU ROKU-JOU-KUN...
にこ
NIKO (GRIN)
YOU'RE LOOKING MORE AND MORE LIKE HER.
.........?
AAAAAAAAAAAAAAAAHH!!!

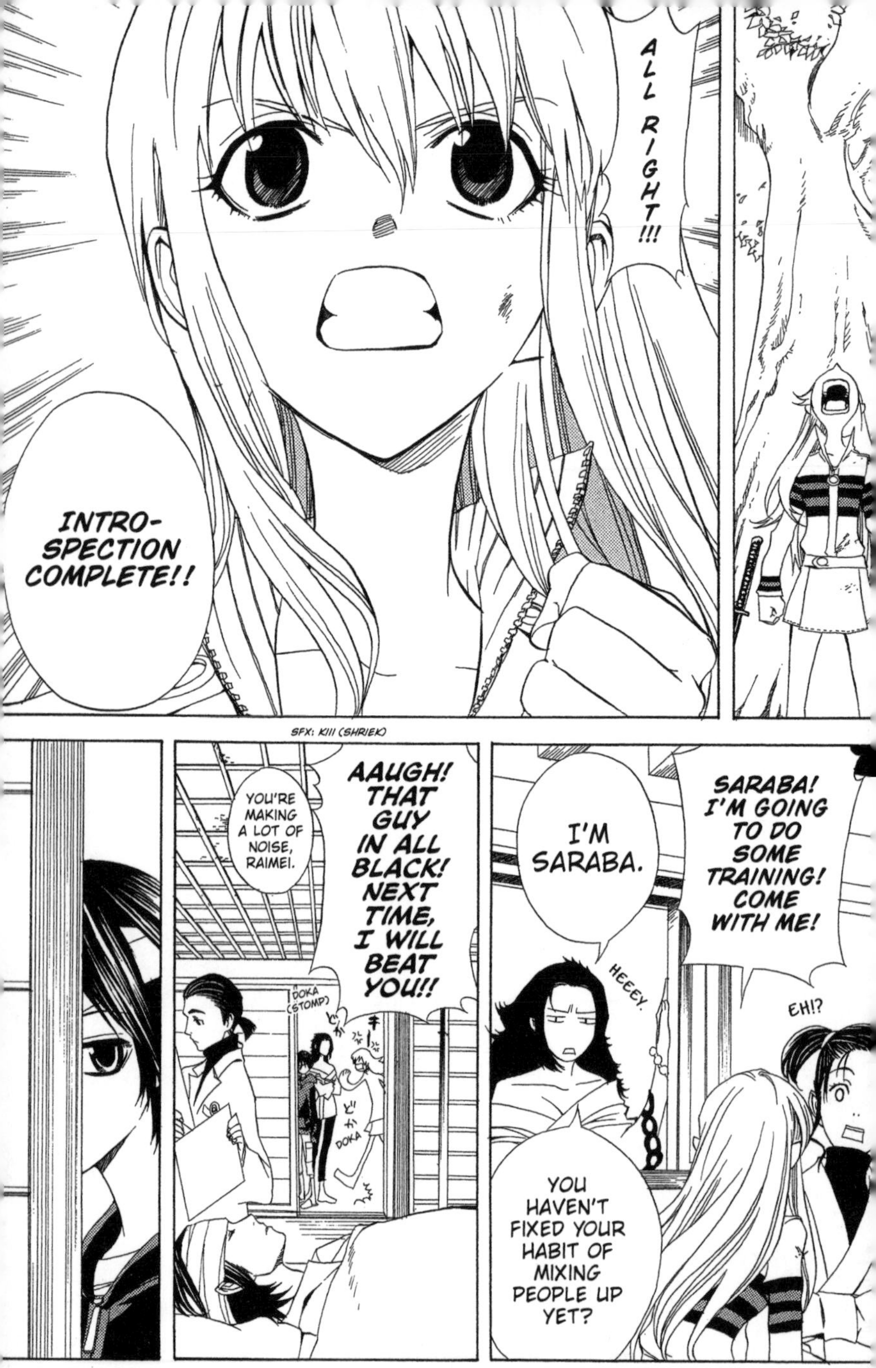
ALL RIGHT!!!
INTRO-SPECTION COMPLETE!!
SFX: KIII (SHRIEK)
SARABA! I'M GOING TO DO SOME TRAINING! COME WITH ME!
I'M SARABA.
HEEEY.
EH!?
YOU HAVEN'T FIXED YOUR HABIT OF MIXING PEOPLE UP YET?
AAUGH! THAT GUY IN ALL BLACK! NEXT TIME, I WILL BEAT YOU!!
YOU'RE MAKING A LOT OF NOISE, RAIMEI.
DOKA (STOMP)
DOKA

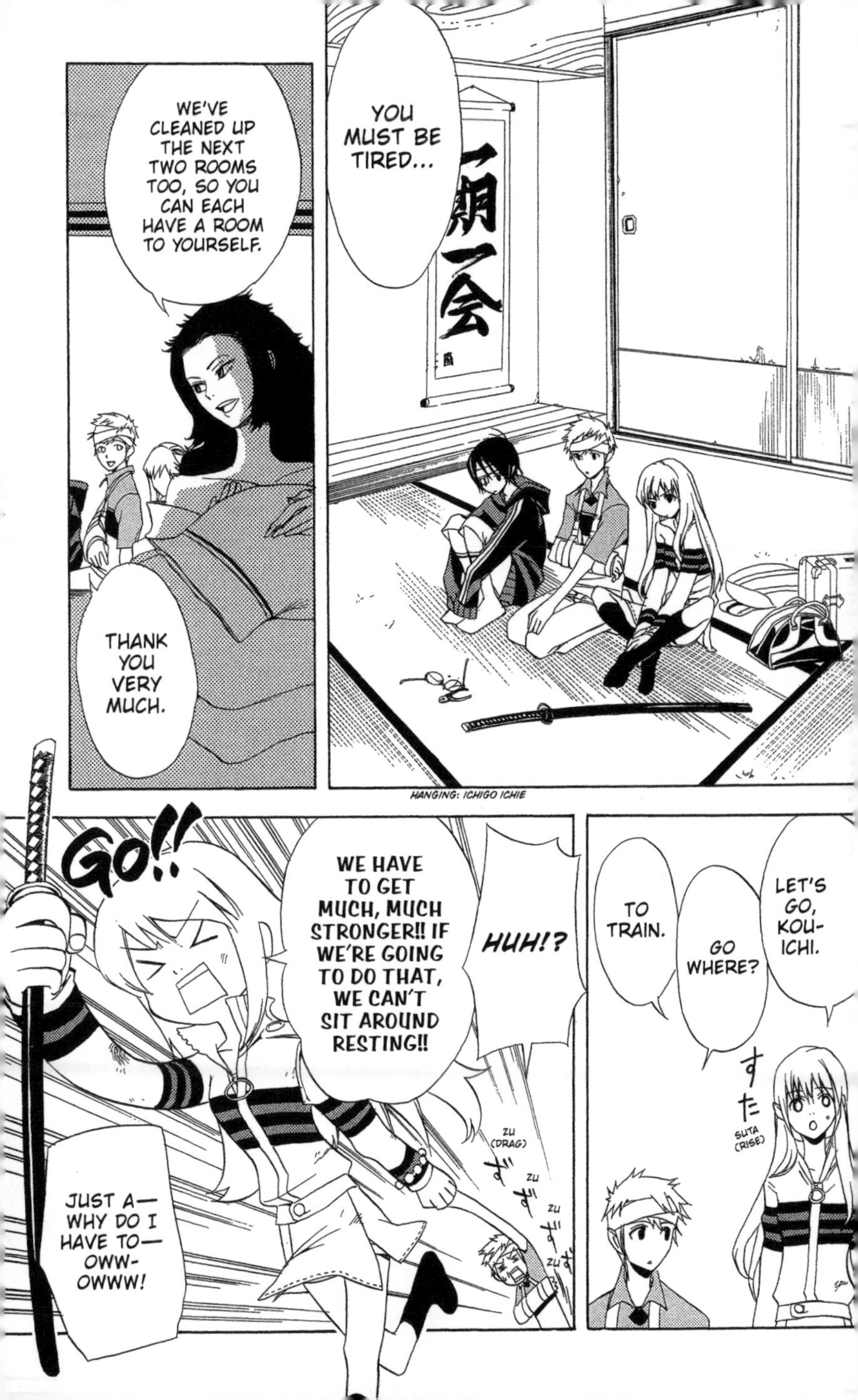
YOU MUST BE TIRED...
WE'VE CLEANED UP THE NEXT TWO ROOMS TOO, SO YOU CAN EACH HAVE A ROOM TO YOURSELF.
THANK YOU VERY MUCH.
HANGING: ICHIGO ICHIE
LET'S GO, KOU-ICHI.
GO WHERE?
TO TRAIN.
すた
SUTA (RISE)
HUH!?
WE HAVE TO GET MUCH, MUCH STRONGER!! IF WE'RE GOING TO DO THAT, WE CAN'T SIT AROUND RESTING!!
GO!!
ZU (DRAG)
ZU
ZU
ZU
JUST A— WHY DO I HAVE TO— OWW-OWWW!

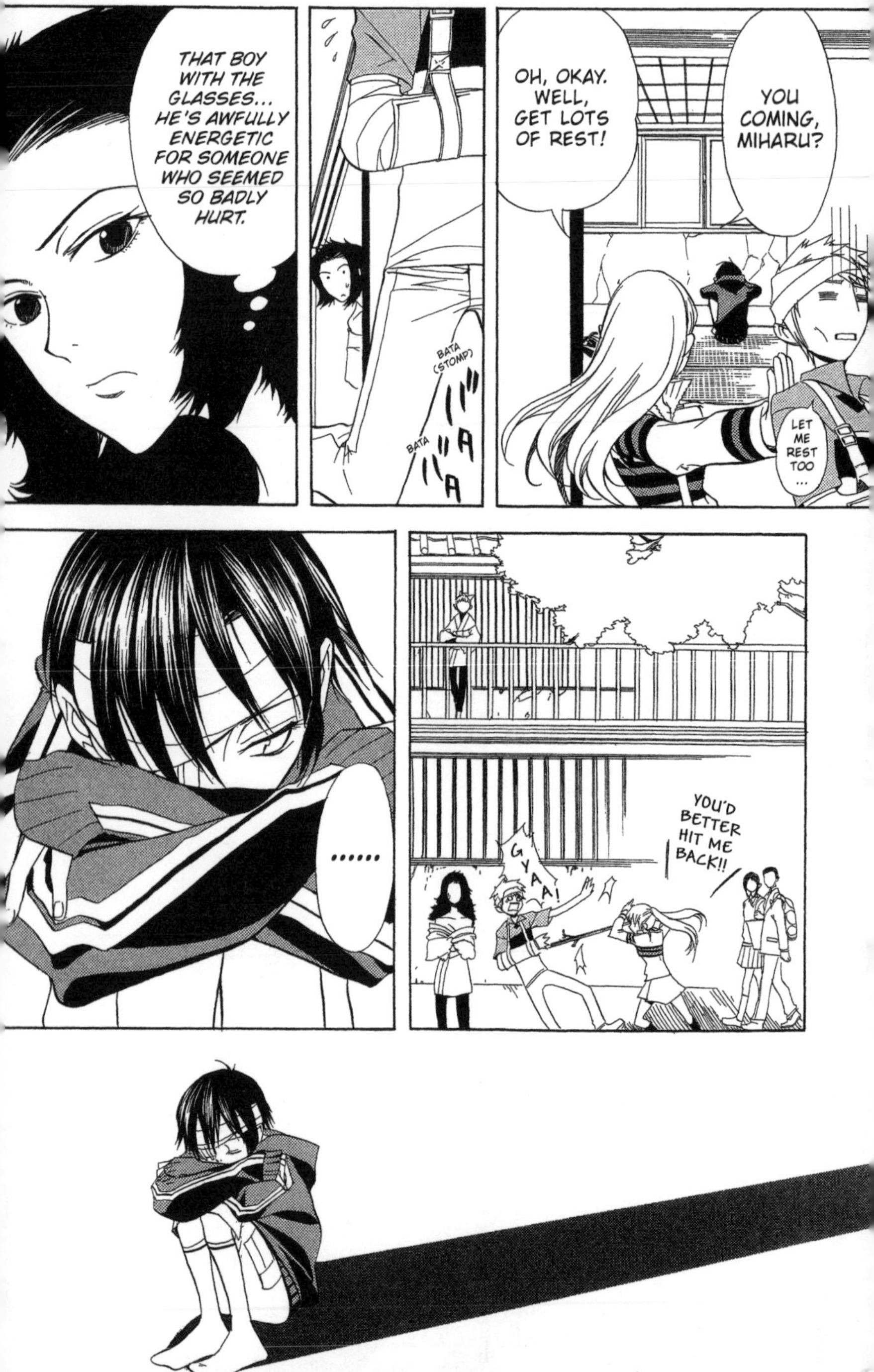
YOU COMING, MIHARU?
OH, OKAY. WELL, GET LOTS OF REST!
LET ME REST TOO...
BATA (STOMP)
BATA
THAT BOY WITH THE GLASSES... HE'S AWFULLY ENERGETIC FOR SOMEONE WHO SEEMED SO BADLY HURT.
YOU'D BETTER HIT ME BACK!!
GYAA!
......

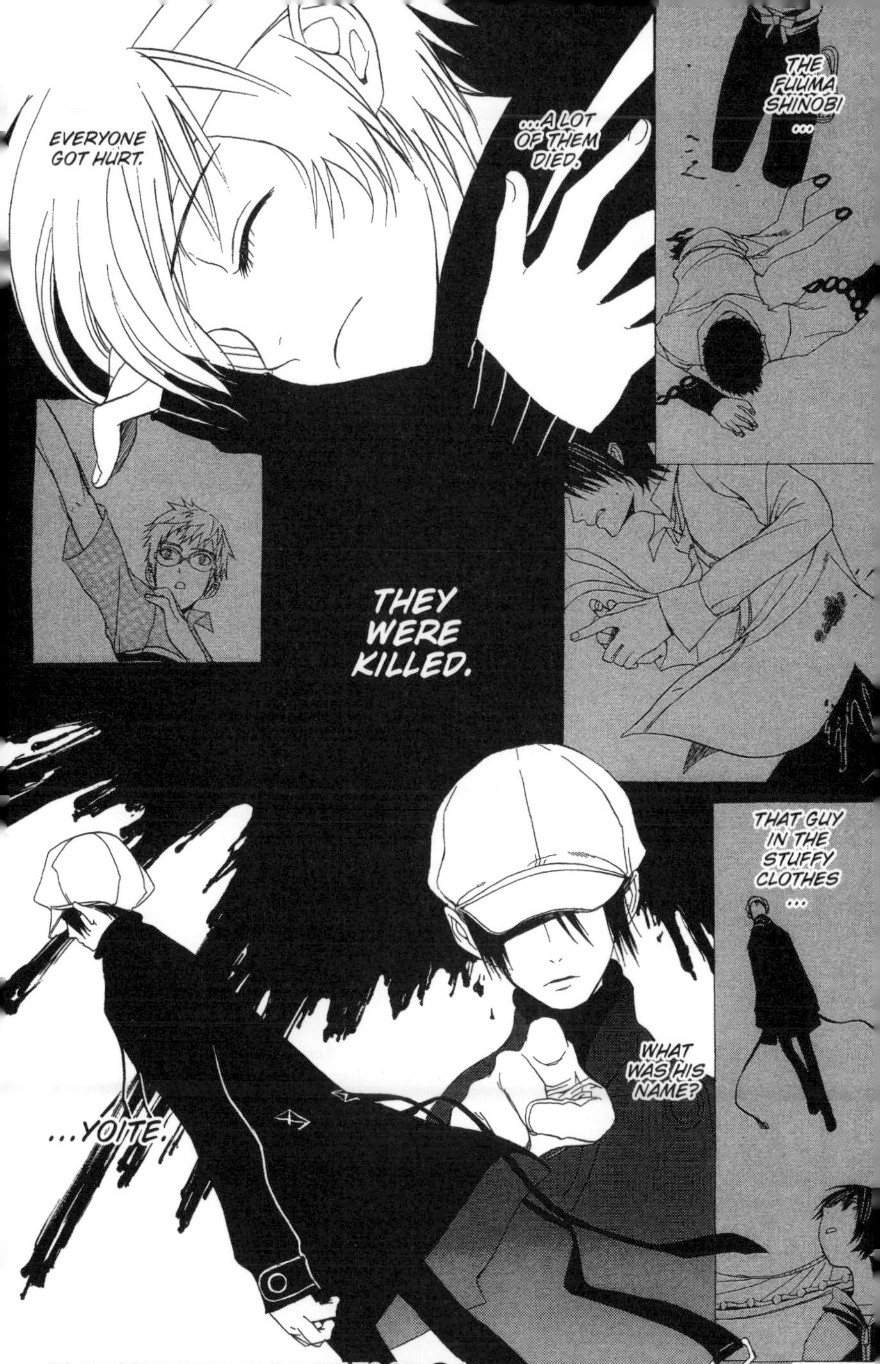
THE FUUMA SHINOBI ...
...A LOT OF THEM DIED.
EVERYONE GOT HURT.
THEY WERE KILLED.
THAT GUY IN THE STUFFY CLOTHES ...
WHAT WAS HIS NAME?
...YOITE.

TO BE CONTINUED IN NABARI NO OU ❷!

NABARI NO OU ❶

YUHKI KAMATANI

Translation: Alethea Nibley and Athena Nibley

Lettering: Alexis Eckerman

NABARI NO OU Vol. 1 © 2004 Yuhki Kamatani / SQUARE ENIX. All rights reserved. First published in Japan in 2004 by SQUARE ENIX CO., LTD. English translation rights arranged with SQUARE ENIX CO., LTD. and Hachette Book Group through Tuttle-Mori Agency, Inc.

Translation © 2009 by SQUARE ENIX CO., LTD.

The characters and events in this book are fictitious. Any similarity to real persons, living or dead, is coincidental and not intended by the author.

Yen Press
Hachette Book Group
237 Park Avenue, New York, NY 10017

Visit our Web sites at www.HachetteBookGroup.com and www.YenPress.com.

Yen Press is an imprint of Hachette Book Group, Inc. The Yen Press name and logo are trademarks of Hachette Book Group, Inc.

First Yen Press Edition: May 2009

ISBN-13: 978-0-7595-3003-4

10 9 8 7 6 5 4 3

BVG

Printed in the United States of America